RENAISSANCE
AND
REFORMATION

RENAISSANCE
AND
REFORMATION

EDITOR

JAMES A. PATRICK
Chancellor, College of Saint Thomas More

ADVISERS

CHRISTOPHER FLETCHER
Queen Mary, University of London
Department of History

NATALIA NOWAKOWSKA
Oxford University
History Faculty

NORMAN TANNER, SJ
Pontificia Università Gregoriana
Faculty of Theology

RENAISSANCE
— AND —
REFORMATION

Editor
James A. Patrick

Chancellor, College of Saint Thomas More

4

Michelangelo – Portugal

Marshall Cavendish
Reference
New York

Marshall Cavendish
99 White Plains Road
Tarrytown, New York 10591-9001

www.marshallcavendish.us

MARSHALL CAVENDISH
EDITOR: Thomas McCarthy
EDITORIAL DIRECTOR: Paul Bernabeo
PRODUCTION MANAGER: Michael Esposito

WHITE-THOMSON PUBLISHING
EDITORS: Steven Maddocks, Alison Cooper, and
   Clare Hibbert
DESIGN: Derek Lee and Ross George
CARTOGRAPHER: Peter Bull Design
PICTURE RESEARCH: Amy Sparks
INDEXER: Cynthia Crippen, AEIOU, Inc.

Library of Congress Cataloging-in-Publication Data
Renaissance and Reformation / editor, James A. Patrick.
     p. cm.
   Includes bibliographical references.
   Contents: 1. Agincourt, Battle of-Dams and drainage -- 2. Descartes, René-
Households -- 3. Humanism and learning-Medicis, the -- 4. Michelangelo-
Portugal -- 5. Preaching-Wren, Christopher -- 6. Index.
   ISBN-13: 978-0-7614-7650-4 (set: alk. paper)
   ISBN-10: 0-7614-7650-4 (set: alk. paper)
   1. Renaissance--Encyclopedias. 2. Reformation--Encyclopedias. I. Patrick,
James, 1933-

CB359.R455 2007
940.2'1--dc22

                                                                        2006042600

ISBN-13: 978-0-7614-7650-4   (set)
ISBN-10: 0-7614-7650-4   (set)
ISBN-13: 978-0-7614-7654-2   (vol. 4)
ISBN-10: 0-7614-7654-7   (vol. 4)

Printed in Malaysia

10 09 08 07 06 5 4 3 2 1

ILLUSTRATION CREDITS
See page 1152.

COVER: Titian, *Emperor Charles V at Mühlberg* (detail), 1548 (Art Archive/Museo
   del Prado, Madrid/Dagli Orti).
TITLE PAGE: Michelangelo's *Pièta,* 1498–1499 (Art Archive/Galleria
   dell'Accademia, Florence/Dagli Orti).

Contents

Michelangelo

THE WORKS OF THE CELEBRATED
FLORENTINE ARTIST MICHELANGELO
BUONARROTI (1475–1564), AN OUT-
STANDING SCULPTOR, PAINTER, ARCHI-
TECT, AND POET, INCLUDE THE FAMED
STATUE OF DAVID AND THE FRESCOED
CEILING OF THE SISTINE CHAPEL.

Michelangelo di Lodovico Buonarroti Simoni was born in 1475 in the Tuscan village of Caprese, where his father, Lodovico, was magistrate. Soon after, the family moved to Florence. Michelangelo's mother died when he was six years old.

Early Artistic Career
The thirteen-year-old Michelangelo was apprenticed to Domenico Ghirlandaio (1449–1494), the leading painter in Florence. Ghirlandaio admired Flemish painting and included Flemish-influenced landscapes and distant views in the frescoes (paintings on wet plaster) he produced for the Church of Santa Maria Novella. Michelangelo, who did not share his master's taste, argued that Flemish artists "paint landscapes, with many figures, without symmetry or proportion or skilful selection."

The Florentine ruler Lorenzo de' Medici (1449–1492), also known as Lorenzo the Magnificent, took an interest in Michelangelo and introduced him to the family's collection of classical sculpture, which was supervised by the sculptor Bertoldo di Giovanni (1420–1491). One of Lorenzo's literary friends, the Italian poet Politian, suggested the subject of Michelangelo's first surviving (but unfinished) sculpture, the *Battle of Lapiths and Centaurs* (c. 1491–1492). Working not in bronze—Bertoldo's medium—but in the much more difficult medium of marble, Michelangelo demonstrated his command of the male form and his ability to link figures together convincingly. Michelangelo's other surviving sculpture from this period, the *Madonna of the Stairs* (c. 1490), also remained unfinished. It emulated the style of the early Renaissance sculptor Donatello (1386–1466).

Contact with Lorenzo de' Medici's circle prompted Michelangelo to take up poetry. During his lifetime he wrote over a hundred and fifty sonnets (and the same number of unfinished fragments) on the traditional themes of love, beauty, and death.

Move to Rome
In 1494 Italy's long period of peace was broken when King Charles VIII of France pursued his claims on the kingdom of Naples. Charles invaded Florentine territory, and in the ensuing crisis the ruling Medicis were driven out of the city, and Florence became a republic for a few years. Michelangelo had already left to visit Venice and Bologna, where he carved three figures for the Church of San Domenico Maggiore. Michelangelo returned to Florence in 1495 but in the following year was in Rome, where he tried to reclaim his sculpture *Sleeping Cupid* (1496), which had been artificially aged and was being sold as an antique.

Soon after his arrival in Rome, Michelangelo was introduced to one of the city's leading patrons, Cardinal Raffaello Riario (1461–1521). The cardinal commissioned a life-size marble of Bacchus, the ancient Greek god of wine, for the courtyard of his palace, which already contained classical statues. Michelangelo adopted not one but three major viewpoints for the *Bacchus* (1496–1497). The artist gently mocks his subject by depicting him swaying drunkenly: the

▼ *The Birth of the Virgin is one of the frescoes that Domenico Ghirlandaio painted in the Church of Santa Maria Novella in Florence, when Michelangelo was one of his apprentices. The scene—a richly decorated contemporary Florentine room—contrasts with the simple settings used by Michelangelo in his frescoes in the Sistine Chapel.*

THE *PIETÀ*

The contract for Michelangelo's *Pietà* included the promise that it would be "the most beautiful marble work presently in Rome." The *Pietà* (an Italian word that means "pity") was a scene commonly depicted in Christian paintings and sculpture during the Renaissance; typically, the piteous figure of the Virgin Mary cradles the dead body of Jesus Christ in her lap.

In Michelangelo's life-size *Pietà*, the Virgin's high forehead, long nose, and downcast eyes are based on ideals of female beauty found earlier in the century, most notably in Donatello's sculptures of the Virgin. Michelangelo demonstrates his virtuosity in the deep undercutting of Mary's drapery—found commonly in bronze sculpture but not in marble—and in the detailed musculature of the dead Christ. As a representation of perfect beauty, the dead Christ more than matches the finest examples of the male nude in classical statuary.

god's staggering gait is realized with incomparable mastery. *Bacchus* was one of two statues that established Michelangelo's reputation: the other was the *Pietà* (1498–1499), commissioned to mark the burial site of its patron, the French cardinal Jean de Bilhères-Lagrulas, in the Roman Church of Santa Petronilla. Santa Petronilla was destroyed soon after the sculpture was placed there, and the *Pietà* was moved to the Basilica of Saint Peter.

▼ *A marble ribbon that runs across Michelangelo's* Pietà *reads Michaelangelus Buonarotus Florentin Faciebat ("Michelangelo Buonarroti the Florentine made this").*

The original block of marble for the *David* belonged to Florence Cathedral and had been intended for a statue to be placed high up on the outside of the cathedral. In 1550 an Italian painter and art historian provided a vivid account of the problems that Michelangelo faced:

The block was nine braccia [literally, "arms"—a unit of measurement equal to two feet (60 cm)] of the most beautiful marble, but one Simone da Fiesole had unfortunately started a large figure in it. And the work had been done so badly, that he made a hole between the legs; and it was altogether bungled and ruined, so that it had been given up for dead. Michelangelo decided to ask for it, and he was granted it as a thing of no use. So Michelangelo made a wax model and portrayed in it, as a device for the palace, a young David with a sling in his hand: as he had defended his people and governed them with justice, so might whoever governed the city defend it bravely and rule it justly. Because the marble had been spoiled it was not in some place sufficient to satisfy Michelangelo's wishes. He therefore let some of the old marks of Maestro Simone's chisel remain on the outside of the marble. It was indeed a miracle on Michelangelo's part to resurrect a thing considered dead in a work which has surpassed all other statues, modern and ancient, Greek and Roman.

Giorgio Vasari, *Lives of the Most Eminent Painters, Sculptors, and Architects*

▼ The David (1501–1504) was carved from a block of marble that had been acquired by Florence Cathedral in 1466 and subsequently abandoned. It had been intended as part of a scheme for giant figures high on one of the cathedral's buttresses.

Working for the Florentine Republic

Michelangelo returned to Florence in 1501. Major commissions came from Pietro Soderini, leader of the new Florentine republic. Late in 1501 Soderini granted Michelangelo a huge but narrow block of marble. Michelangelo used it to carve a statue of the young David, which was placed outside the doorway of Palazzo della Signoria (the seat of the republican government) in 1504. David rests his weight on his right foot, raises the sling with his left hand, and turns to look south (the direction of the republic's major threat, the Medicis in Rome). David's intense gaze captures the moment of concentration before the physical effort of his battle with Goliath and adds to the overall impression of tension and control.

While working on *David*, Michelangelo also contributed four rather indifferent statues to the Piccolomini altar in Siena Cathedral (1503). He was commissioned to produce a set of the Twelve Apostles for Florence Cathedral but never even completed the first of these, a statue of Saint Matthew. Two unfinished marble medallions depicting the Virgin and Child with the infant John the Baptist also date from this period, as does the marble *Madonna* intended for Bruges. Paintings from this time include the highly polished *Doni Tondo* (1504)—celebrating the marriage of its patron, Angelo Doni, to Maddalena Strozzi—and the unfinished *Entombment*.

The mastery of *David* ensured further commissions. In 1503 Leonardo da Vinci (1452–1519), the most famous Florentine artist, had begun work on a huge fresco titled the *Battle of Anghiari* inside the great council chamber of the Palazzo della Signoria. A year later Michelangelo prepared a cartoon (a design for a fresco) of another republican victory, this time over the Pisans, the *Battle of Cascina*. Copies of the central part depict an alert leader rousing the Florentine soldiers as they bathe in the Arno River. The cartoon was cut up by eager artists and collectors, but its reputation can be appreciated in the light of Michelangelo's surviving *Study of a Bather*. Seated on the edge of the river, the bather turns as he hears the call to arms. The pose is more complex than any classical prototype, and the figure is realized with a new command of surface musculature.

Rome and Julius II

In March 1505 Michelangelo was called back to Rome by Pope Julius II (1443–1513). Julius's admiration of classical Rome was evident in his choice of papal name—taken from the undefeated Roman general Julius Caesar—and in his commissions to Michelangelo for his tomb and for the ceiling of the Sistine Chapel. The tomb was planned for a new choir (the area behind the altar) of Saint Peter's, but the papal architect, Donato Bramante (c. 1444–1514), persuaded the pope to rebuild the whole church.

liberal arts cultivated by Pope Julius II but now returned to captivity by his death. There were to be further statues at the next level; a bier (stand) for the statue of the pope was to be supported by two angels, one laughing and one crying.

After Julius's death, the plan for the tomb was greatly simplified, and Michelangelo began preparing some of the statues, the *Rebellious Slave,* the *Dying Slave,* and the *Moses,* the great Old Testament figure chosen as Julius's role model. In 1545, when the tomb was being installed in the Church of San Pietro in Vincoli ("Saint Peter in chains"), in Rome, Michelangelo carved the *Leah* (in the Bible, she is the mother of the founders of six of Israel's twelve tribes) and, with assistants, a *Virgin and Child, Prophet, Sibyl* (classical prophetess), and *Image of Julius II.* He did not include the *Victory* and *Four Slaves,* which he had produced in the 1520s.

▲ *Michelangelo worked on the tomb of Pope Julius II between 1513 and 1547. He developed the pose of the Moses, shown here in the center, from Donatello's Saint John the Evangelist (1415) but added a new classical grandeur and pathos.*

The change in plan put off work on the tomb, and Michelangelo was commissioned to work on other projects. He returned to the tomb in 1513, and parts of it were finally set up in 1545.

The initial scheme was for a rectangular tomb, whose niches were to be decorated with terms (square pillars topped with busts) and life-size statues of slaves, intended to embody the

The Sistine Ceiling

When Julius's plans for his tomb were sidelined, he commissioned Michelangelo to fresco the ceiling of the Sistine Chapel, built by his uncle, Pope Sixtus IV (1414–1484). Michelangelo erected high scaffolding that protected the earlier wall frescoes. The first half of the ceiling, down to the *Creation of Eve,* was completed in two and a half years (between May 1508 and September 1510), the second in under two (between August

---

THE PROGRAM OF THE SISTINE CEILING

In the fifteenth century the Sistine Chapel ceiling had been painted to look like a starry sky. Michelangelo was commissioned to replace the sky with the Twelve Apostles, but he came up with a much more ambitious plan: a Creation cycle based on the book of Genesis. This cycle added a third era (the time before the Law) to the two already featured on the walls—the Old Testament time when God gave the Law was represented in the Moses cycle, while the New Testament time when Grace replaced the Law was represented in the fresco of the life of Christ.

Like the wall frescoes, the Old Testament cycle progresses from the altar wall to the entrance. In sequence the narrative scenes depict the division of light from darkness, the creation of the sun and moon, the creation of marine life, the creation of Adam, the creation of Eve, the Fall and Expulsion, Noah's sacrifice, the Flood, and the drunkenness of Noah.

Around the narrative scenes Michelangelo painted a frame that runs the 130-foot (40 m) length of the chapel and includes thrones for the twelve prophets and sibyls. The thrones are supported by pairs of cherubs, or putti, and topped by smaller blocks that provide seats for *ignudi* (nude youths). Between the *ignudi* are medallions, painted to resemble bronze, that were inspired by illustrations in the Malermi Bible (1490) and chosen as *exempla* (examples) of the transmission of divine authority. The whole painted frame is set over lunettes (semicircular panels) where Michelangelo included Christ's ancestors, who were also depicted in the spandrels (triangular spaces above the windows).

1511 and October 1512). During the break in the work, the scaffolding was moved and Michelangelo could see the completed first section. After viewing it, he worked with a new sense of scale. All the figures in the second half, from the *Creation of Adam* down to the altar end, are larger, and the narrative frescoes are unified through the zigzag motion of God the Father across the ceiling. The earliest commentary on the ceiling—by the bishop and historian Paolo Giovio, writing between 1527 and 1540—struggles to express the impact of the second half. Giovio noted, "among the most important figures is one in the center of the vault of an old man flying [God the Father]. He is drawn with such calculation that from wherever in the chapel you view him he seems by some optical illusion to move and change his gesture."

Florence and the Medici

Julius II was succeeded by Leo X (Giovanni de' Medici; 1475–1521), who withdrew most of the funding for Julius's tomb. Michelangelo was commissioned instead to produce a marble facade for San Lorenzo, the Medici family church in Florence. This project was abandoned in 1519 following the deaths of Lorenzo de' Medici (1492–1519) and his uncle Giuliano, duke of Nemours (1479–1516). Michelangelo was appointed to design two new buildings: the Medici Chapel, where the two tombs would be placed, and the Laurentian Library, which would house the Medicis' precious collection of books and manuscripts.

The Laurentian Library, named in honor of Lorenzo, was built in the cloisters of San Lorenzo over existing monastic buildings. The gray pilasters (rectangular columns embedded in a wall) that line the reading room follow the principles of Doric architecture—each fluted column is topped by an ovolo (a round molding) and then an abacus (a square molding). Constrained by the need for regular windows to let in light, the design of the reading room contrasts with the inventiveness of the vestibule. Double columns are set into the wall, in a free adaptation of a classical mausoleum on the Appian Way outside Rome. Inverted window frames were introduced between the columns, apparently supported by decorative scrolls. The most admired feature of the vestibule, the triple staircase, was completed later from suggestions sent by Michelangelo from Rome. The wider central section was for the ruler; the narrow side staircases were for his retinue.

The Medici Chapel

The Medici Chapel, also known as the New Sacristy (the sacristy is the room in a church, usually near the altar, where the priest prepares for Mass), was intended as a companion to the Old Sacristy, designed by the Florentine architect Filippo Brunelleschi (1377–1446) for the tomb of the Medici founder, Cosimo il Vecchio (1389–1464).

Michelangelo established an architectural framework of giant pilasters based on the Corinthian style—each one was topped by a capital decorated with carved acanthus leaves (the acanthus plant is a Mediterranean herb). Between the giant pilasters are smaller pilasters of *pietra serena,* a gray sandstone, which frame marble doorways under blank windows.

 ▶ *In his tomb for Giuliano de' Medici, Michelangelo shows Giuliano as a seated Roman soldier rather than a reclining effigy. The other striking feature of the tomb is its inclusion of the figures* Night *(on the right) and* Day *(on the left), which signify the triumph of time over even the most powerful rulers.*

The statues of Lorenzo and Giuliano, known as the "captains" because they wear classical armor, sit in rich marble niches. They are accompanied by reclining statues—Lorenzo by representations of dusk and dawn and Giuliano, of night and day. River gods were planned for the tombs' bases. The entrance wall also remained unfinished, although Michelangelo began the *Virgin and Child* for the central niche.

Rome: A Glorious Old Age

Between 1532 and 1536 Michelangelo was working in both Florence and Rome, but in 1536 he settled in Rome, where he spent the remaining thirty years of his life. In addition to his public commissions, he produced work for private patrons, including a group of highly finished drawings of classical mythological subjects for his young friend Tommaso de' Cavalieri (1509/1510–1587) and a similar devotional set for Vittoria Colonna, the marchioness of Pescara (1492–1547). A distinguished poet who dedicated a collection of sonnets to Michelangelo, Vittoria Colonna was also a reform-minded Christian, and Michelangelo was sympathetic to the ideas for reform expressed by her circle of friends.

In 1534 Alessandro Farnese (1468–1549) was elected pope and took the name Paul III. He commissioned three frescoes from Michelangelo: the *Last Judgment* (1536–1541) for the altar wall of the Sistine Chapel and the *Conversion of Saint Paul* and *Crucifixion of Saint Peter* for his new Pauline Chapel in the Vatican, the latter two being Michelangelo's last paintings.

▲ The Last Judgment (1536–1541). The choice of theme is unusual for an altar wall: it reminds the members of the congregation of their fate throughout Mass. The prominent siting, in the pope's private chapel, combined with Michelangelo's austere style, prompted concern about the nudity. After Michelangelo's death, the figures in the fresco were given modest loincloths.

THE *LAST JUDGMENT*

Christ towers at the center of the *Last Judgment*, flanked on his right by the much smaller Virgin and John the Baptist and on his left by Saint Peter, who holds the keys to the gates of heaven. At Christ's feet Saint Lawrence leans on the griddle on which he burned to death, while Saint Bartholomew holds his butcher's knife and his own flayed skin, which is decorated with a self-portrait of the artist. These two saints complete the aureole, or halo, of the saved around Christ.

Above Christ, the lunettes (semicircular panels) are filled with angels carrying the cross and other instruments of Christ's Passion (his suffering and death). Beneath Christ the figures on his right side are resurrected and their souls are saved, but those on his left are falling down to hell, where Charon—the ancient Greek boatman who ferried dead souls to the underworld—bullies them onto his boat. The power of the figures in the fresco is undeniable, but they lack the easy grace of the figures Michelangelo painted on the Sistine Chapel ceiling. The change reflects both the influence of Michelangelo's friend Vittoria Colonna and his own heightened spirituality and concern for inner grace rather than outward beauty.

Late Architecture

The field of architecture dominated the last decades of Michelangelo's life. In 1536 he became involved with the restorations on top of Capitoline Hill, the center of Rome's municipal government. He designed a base for the ancient monument of the Roman emperor Marcus Aurelius on horseback. He also transformed the Senate by installing new steps that changed the orientation of the building away from the Roman forum and the past and toward Saint Peter's and the Christian present.

From 1546 Michelangelo led the rebuilding of Saint Peter's, which Bramante had begun forty years earlier. Bramante had planned a centralized, domed church with four short arms, each with its own smaller dome. The plan was based on a Greek cross. Bramante left relatively few drawings, and subsequent architects had complicated his plans. When Michelangelo took over, key parts of the building had been completed: the piers that support the drum (and hence the central dome), but not the drum itself, and the inner walls of each of the four arms. Michelangelo retained the piers, raised the inner drum, and converted the walls from interior to exterior ones; the resulting reduction in size of Saint Peter's brought a new unity to the interior spaces. Bramante's dome had been based on that of the Pantheon, the great classical temple rebuilt in Rome by the emperor Hadrian in 128 CE. Michelangelo died before his dome was completed; its design was inspired by Brunelleschi's dome for Florence's cathedral (1436).

Death and Legacy

Michelangelo was recognized as the premier sculptor, painter, and architect of his day, and his drawings became collector's items during his lifetime. The Sistine ceiling inspired younger artists in Rome and Florence to produce works where elegance and invention in the details were more significant than the overall story or theme. Historians coined the term *mannerism* (from the Italian *maniera,* meaning "style") for art of the period from 1520 to 1600. The Italian painter Caravaggio (1571–1610), the naturalism of whose style was a reaction against mannerism, is Michelangelo's true successor.

In this poem, written around 1554, Michelangelo appears to reject art in preparation for death:

At last my life's course, in its frail barque
Has crossed the stormy seas to reach that port
Where all arrive and give a due account
For every deed done ill or piously.
No painting and no sculpture can now soothe
The soul which turns to divine love.

Sonnet 285

FURTHER READING

De Vecchi, Pierluigi, ed. *Michelangelo: The Vatican Frescoes.* New York, 1996.

Hughes, Anthony. *Michelangelo.* London, 1997.

Pietrangeli, Carlo, ed. *The Sistine Chapel: A Glorious Restoration.* New York, 1994.

Wallace, William E. *Michelangelo at San Lorenzo: The Genius as Entrepeneur.* New York, 1994.

Richard Cocke

SEE ALSO

- Architecture • Bramante, Donato
- Brunelleschi, Filippo • Florence • Medicis, The
- Painting and Sculpture • Palladio, Andrea
- Reformation • Rome

▲ The *cordonata (double staircase)* that Michelangelo designed for Rome's Senate can be seen in the background of this imaginative eighteenth-century painting of Capitoline Hill by Canaletto (1697–1768).

Milton, John

WITH HIS EPIC POEM *PARADISE LOST,* THE ENGLISH POET JOHN MILTON (1608–1674) CREATED A CHALLENGING VISION OF THE SUBLIME, WHILE IN HIS POLITICAL PROSE HE PRESENTED REVOLUTIONARY IDEAS ON GOVERNMENT AND THE CHURCH.

John Milton was born in 1608, the first surviving child of John and Sara Milton. His father worked as a scrivener (a writer of legal documents) and maintained a prosperous business that provided Milton with the education and leisure in later life to develop his intellectual and poetic capabilities. Milton's father was also a composer and musician: being exposed to music during boyhood instilled in Milton an appreciation of rhythm that proved valuable when he later came to write metrical verse. Milton's brother, Christopher, whose writings are the source of much biographical material about John, was born in 1615.

Early Education

Milton was originally taught at home. His father hired private tutors, including a Scottish Presbyterian clergyman, Thomas Young, who later became master of Jesus College, Cambridge. Milton received early instruction in Latin and Greek as well as French, Italian, Spanish, Hebrew, and—possibly—Aramaic and Syriac. Around 1620 Milton was enrolled in Saint Paul's Cathedral School. Probably founded in 1103, the school had been revitalized in 1509 by the dean of Saint Paul's Cathedral, John Colet. The Dutch humanist and scholar Desiderius Erasmus (c. 1466–1536) helped Colet to plan the curriculum, contributed textbooks, and even recruited staff. A century later, when Milton enrolled, the standard of education set by Colet continued. Milton was taught by some of the foremost scholars in England. At school he became friends with Charles Diodati, later renowned as a physician and scholar, and the friendship continued until Diodati's death in 1638.

▶ In this earliest-known portrait of John Milton, by Cornelis Janssen, the young boy wears the typical dress of a child from the prosperous professional class in Jacobean London.

1608
Milton is born on December 9 in Bread Street, London.

1627
Lends his future father-in-law, Richard Powell, five hundred pounds.

1632
Milton's sonnet "On Shakespeare" prefaces the second folio of Shakespeare's works.

1637
A Maske is published anonymously with the help of Henry Lawes, who wrote the music.

1640
Milton repossesses Richard Powell's lands in Wheatley, Oxfordshire.

1642
Marries Mary Powell, whose family sides with the royalists.

1643
The Doctrine and Discipline of Divorce is published.

1649
Milton becomes secretary for foreign languages in Oliver Cromwell's government at a yearly salary of 288 pounds. Moves into lodgings in Scotland Yard.

1652
Becomes totally blind, most probably because of glaucoma.

1654
Publishes his second *Defensio.*

1655
The government grants Milton a pension of 150 pounds a year.

1667
Paradise Lost is published in ten books by the printer Samuel Simmons.

1674
The second edition of *Paradise Lost* is published in twelve books. Milton dies on November 9.

▲ *Painted around 1629, when Milton was a student at Cambridge University, this anonymous portrait, known as the Onslow Portrait, shows Milton as a serious yet confident young man.*

Cambridge Years

Milton arrived at Cambridge in 1625 and was admitted to Christ's College. His tutor was William Chappell, who was later to become provost of Trinity College, Dublin. Milton quickly became dissatisfied with the quality of teaching at the university. His relationships at Cambridge were often hostile, though he did continue his warm friendship with his former tutor Thomas Young and with Charles Diodati, both of whom were at Cambridge when Milton arrived. Within a year of entering the university, Milton began writing a series of Latin elegies (meditative and often sorrowful lyrics written in pairs of dactylic lines known as elegiac couplets) for important religious figures, including Nicholas Felton, bishop of Ely. He also wrote Latin poems critical of Catholicism to mark the twentieth anniversary of the Gunpowder Plot—the Catholic conspiracy of 1605 to blow up Parliament and assassinate King James I. In the

first of these poems Milton portrays Satan, a figure he would later develop for *Paradise Lost.*

In March 1626 Milton was suspended from college after a serious conflict with his tutor, Chappell. The nature of this conflict is unclear, though it was probably some form of insubordination or religious disagreement. Milton was readmitted by Easter 1627 and assigned a new tutor, Nathaniel Tovey. While his relationship with Tovey was much more satisfactory, Milton continued to be critical of the university curriculum, which he believed led to ignorance rather than enlightenment.

Milton was awarded his bachelor's degree in March 1629. He remained at Cambridge to study for his master's degree. The verse he wrote during the next two years already demonstrates poetic maturity and power. Important works of the period include "On the Morning of Christ's Nativity" (1629), "Epitaph on the Marchioness of Winchester," and "On Shakespeare" (1630), his first published poem. The twin poems "L'Allegro" and "Il Penseroso" were probably written during his last year at Cambridge. On July 3, 1632, Milton received his master's degree, and his university life ended.

Rural Retreat

Milton returned to his family, who had moved six miles west of London to Hammersmith, then a rural village. The intention of sending Milton to Cambridge had been to train him as a minister, but by 1632 Milton appears to have decided against the church as a career. Instead he used this period in his life for further study and the composition of poetry. The famous sonnet known as "How soon hath Time" was written in this period. It reveals that Milton, while enjoying his freedom to pursue scholarly and creative endeavors, was increasingly aware that he was growing older without the outward show of success that others of his age possessed. Perhaps this anxiety led him to take advantage of his connections and enter public life.

In 1634 Milton received a commission to write a masque for John Egerton, earl of Bridgewater, in celebration of Egerton's appointment as lord president of the Council of Wales. Known as *A Maske,* or *Comus,* the play was performed at Ludlow Castle on September 29, 1634. It celebrated Egerton's Calvinist beliefs and presented him as a defender against the depravity of the Royalists and the policies of Archbishop William Laud that appeared to reintroduce Catholic elements to Protestant worship. The villain of the piece, Comus, embodies deception and sexual depravity and is another early embodiment of many of the qualities given later to Satan in *Paradise Lost.*

By 1636 Milton's father had retired, and the family moved again, this time farther west, to Horton, near Windsor. Here Milton began collecting his ideas and observations in a manuscript; now at Cambridge and known as the Trinity Manuscript, this work is invaluable as it gives an insight into Milton's creative practice during this time of retirement, when little published work appeared.

▼ *In this illustration of a scene from Milton's Comus, the enchanter Comus lures a virtuous young woman to his palace, urges her to drink from a magic glass, and traps her in an enchanted chair. In exploring the theme of decadence, Milton was indirectly criticizing Charles I's court .*

"HOW SOON HATH TIME"

How soon hath Time, the subtle thief of youth,
Stolen on his wing my three and twentieth year!
My hasting days fly on with full career,
But my late spring no bud or blossom shew'th.
Perhaps my semblance might deceive the truth,
That I to manhood am arrived so near,
And inward ripeness doth much less appear,
That some more timely-happy spirits endu'th.
Yet be it less or more, or soon or slow,
It shall be still in strictest measure even
To that same lot, however mean or high,
Toward which Time leads me, and the will of Heaven;
All is, if I have grace to use it so,
As ever in my great Taskmaster's eye.

Milton uses the complex form of the Petrarchan (or Italian) sonnet to give voice to his personal anxieties, both spiritual and psychological. The imagery in this poem is powerful and emotive. He initially personifies Time as a thief who is stealing his youth, while later imagining this same Time as a messenger of the will of Heaven. The sestet (the last six lines of the poem) seeks to counter the anxieties raised in the octave (the first eight lines) through the Calvinistic doctrine of divine predestination (the idea that God, because of his foreknowledge, guides those destined for salvation). The sonnet, itself a "predestined," strictly measured poetic form, becomes the avenue by which Milton comes to terms with his own predestined life.

The next year Milton's mother, Sara, died. Apparently Milton did not write an elegy for his mother, but he did write one, "Lycidas" (1637), for John King, a fellow student at Cambridge who drowned off the coast of Anglesey, in northwestern Wales, on August 10, 1637. "Lycidas" became one of Milton's most famous poems. Using the death of King, in the fullness of youth and promise, Milton explores the vocation of the poet and his own anxieties about his poetic and spiritual future. The poem's appeal lies in the way it transcends Milton's personal circumstances to provide a powerful exploration of human potential and mortality.

European Travels

In April or May 1638, Milton set off for Europe, wishing to complement his five years of personal study with firsthand experience of the cultures he had read about. During his travels Milton's education in languages enabled him to converse with important men of the period. His itinerary took him quickly through France, a country where he evidently found little to admire. His brief experience of the absolutism of King Louis XIII (reigned 1610–1643) and Cardinal Richelieu

may have influenced Milton's later republican political ideology. From Paris he traveled south to Nice, visited Genoa and Pisa, and arrived in Florence in June 1638, where he stayed for nearly five months. Milton formed friendships with several Florentine scholars, including the poet Antonio Malatesti and Vincenzo Galilei, the son of the great astronomer Galileo (Vincenzo later introduced Milton to his esteemed father).

In October 1638 Milton traveled to Siena and on to Rome. Here Milton again met several scholars. He was introduced to Cardinal Francesco Barberini, who arranged for Milton to visit the Vatican library with its ancient manuscripts and impressive collection of books. In March 1639 Milton returned to his friends in Florence, "that city, which I have always admired above all others because of the elegance, not just of its tongue, but also of its wit." He continued his travels north, through Bologna, Ferrara, and Venice. He also traveled to Geneva, where he met with the theologian Giovanni Diodati, the uncle of Milton's childhood friend Charles Diodati, who had died the previous August. In Geneva, a Protestant republic, Milton's experiences added fuel to his later republican beliefs. By July 1639

▼ *The highlight of Milton's European tour (1638–1639) was the dazzling Tuscan city of Florence, the subject of this colored copperplate engraving made about eighty years after Milton's visit.*

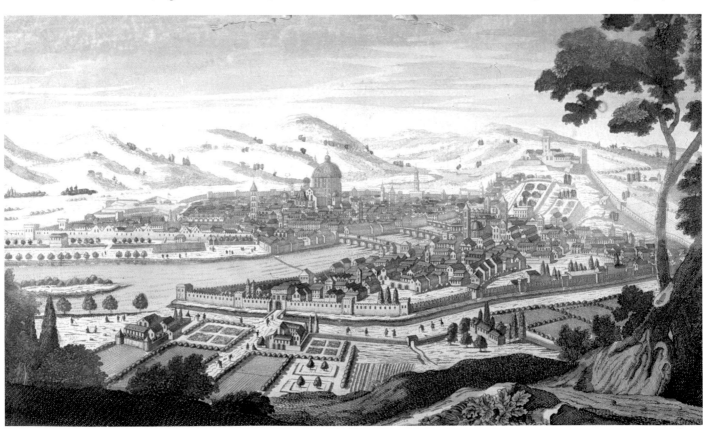

On his travels Milton met the Florentine scholar and writer Carlo Dati (1619–1676). Dati expressed his admiration of Milton in a "tribute of admiration, reverence, and love," which he wrote in Latin. In 1645 Milton included Dati's letter with other commendations in his *Poems*:

To a man whose gifts of mind and body move the senses to admiration, ... one in whose memory the whole world is lodged, in whose intellect is wisdom, in whose will is a passion for glory, in whose mouth is eloquence.

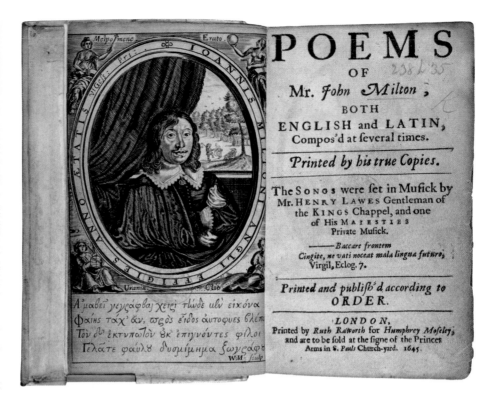

Milton was back in England, called back by news of the imminent civil war. He probably wrote his greatest Latin poem, "Epitaphium Damonis" (Epitaph for Damon), for Charles Diodati at this time.

Civil War Years

The years 1639 to 1642 mark Milton's emergence into public life. Upon returning to England, Milton settled in London and divided his time between teaching and writing essays on issues of the day, especially relating to church government and the political situation. His writing on religious matters reflected his belief that Scripture, not custom, should dictate the forms of religious worship and church government. Increasingly his essays argued for religious toleration and independent congregations rather than a unified church under government control.

Milton's poetry during this time consists mainly of sonnets, including sonnet 8, "When the Assault was intended to the City," possibly written in the expectation that Charles I's armies would take London after the Battle of Edgehill (October 23, 1642), the first major armed conflict of the English civil wars. Earlier that year, in June 1642, Milton paid a visit to Richard Powell in Oxfordshire to collect an interest payment on a loan Milton had made to him in 1627. After only a month, Milton returned to London accompanied by his new wife, Powell's eldest daughter, the seventeen-year-old Mary.

Within a few weeks Mary returned home for a visit that was intended to be short but eventually lasted three years. It was protracted partly by the outbreak of the civil wars but possibly also by Mary's dawning realization of what life with the thirty-three-year-old scholar would entail. Mary returned in 1645, only after the collapse of the royalist cause, which her family supported, and after hearing the rumor that Milton was planning to arrange a divorce and marry someone else.

One important consequence of Milton's marital troubles was a series of pamphlets in which he argued for the right to divorce and asserted that the primary end of marriage was fellowship of mind and spirit. The best-known of these pamphlets, *The Doctrine and Discipline of Divorce,* was published in 1643. Milton's writing on divorce ignited controversy, and many joined the call for greater censorship. These calls resulted in the Licensing Order of June 16, 1643, which required all publications to be submitted to government scrutiny. Milton, in his most admired polemical work, *Areopagitica: A Speech for the Liberty of Unlicensed Printing* (1644), criticized governmental prior restraint on publishing and asserted that such interference damaged the free circulation of ideas, which was needed to ensure a just government.

▲ *From an engraving by William Marshall, the portrait on the frontispiece of Milton's* Poems *(1645) bears a Greek inscription that attests to Milton's learning. The pastoral scene behind the poet's left shoulder alludes to the pastoral nature of many of Milton's poems.*

► Milton was a staunch supporter of the Commonwealth government (1649–1660) and its leader Oliver Cromwell, the subject of this oil portrait by Peter Lely (1618–1680). Milton's "Tenure of Kings and Magistrates" (1649) justified the trial and execution of Charles I. Milton also wrote prose tracts defending the actions of the Commonwealth to other nations.

Amid the continuing controversy arising from Milton's writings on divorce, Milton published his *Poems* (1645), a collection of sonnets, other poems, and translations that included "Lycidas" and *A Maske*. Anne, Milton's first daughter with Mary, was born in July 1646. This birth was followed by the death of Milton's father in 1647. A second daughter, Mary, was born the next year. Milton's scholarly projects during this period included researching for a history of Britain. He also continued writing sonnets and occasional poetry.

Milton and the Commonwealth

The trial of King Charles I elicited another essay from Milton, "The Tenure of Kings and Magistrates" (1649). In it Milton argued that for a government to maintain liberty, both the ruler and the ruled needed qualities such as reason, justice, fortitude, commitment to the common good, and dedication to liberty. He derided those who used political conflict to further their own agendas. Milton asserted that men should rule through law and reason. Should this principle be ignored, men had the right and the responsibility to redress their wrongs. In this way Milton gave tacit approval for the trial and execution of Charles I.

In March 1649 the Commonwealth appointed Milton as secretary for foreign languages. His duties required him to translate international correspondence into Latin and letters from foreign governments into English. The government also looked to Milton to respond to pro-Royalist propaganda, especially the increasingly popular tract *Eikon Basilike* (Image of the King). Milton did so with his *Eikonoklastes* (Image Breaker). At the request of the government, Milton also wrote the first of his two *Defensiones,* as they are called. "Pro Populo Anglicano Defensio" (In Defense of the English People; 1650) explained the decision to execute Charles I and was intended to reassure other European nations.

By this time Milton was going blind; he lost his sight completely in 1652. He had other troubles, too. In 1651 a son, John, was born, but the following year his wife, Mary, died after giving birth to a daughter, Deborah. Six weeks later John died. The blind Milton was left to care for his daughters alone. Later in the year he and his children were evicted from their Whitehall home. The family moved to a house near Saint James's Park, where Milton was to remain until the Restoration. However, the government continued to employ Milton despite his blindness and provided him with secretaries.

In addition to his official work, Milton continued to compose poetry. His sonnets from this time express not only private emotions but also more public responses to contemporary events. Sonnet 18, "On the Late Massacre in Piedmont," was written following the massacre of 1,700 French Protestants in Vaudois in April 1655. Milton also wrote sonnet 16, "To the Lord General Cromwell," and the celebrated poem on his own blindness, sonnet 19.

On November 12, 1656, Milton married Katherine Woodcock, who gave birth to a daughter, Katherine, a year later. Both mother and infant died within months of the birth.

Probably in response to this loss, Milton wrote his sonnet 23, "Methought I saw my late espoused Saint." At about this time he also began working on *Paradise Lost* while continuing to write political and religious essays.

▲ In this unfinished sketch, the eighteenth-century artist William Hogarth depicts a scene from Milton's epic poem Paradise Lost (1665). Hogarth's portrayal of the encounter between Satan and a sinner is in keeping with the highly developed and often sensual imagery that Milton used in Paradise Lost.

PARADISE LOST

In *Paradise Lost,* Milton considers the nature of God; he expresses the belief that God's omniscience (the quality of being all-knowing) derives from his eternal dwelling in the present, not from predestination. Milton strives to persuade the reader that while the Fall was always possible, it was not a preordained certainty. Adam and Eve are presented as beings who, though fallible, also retain the ability to choose their destiny. God is justified in giving Adam and Eve challenges, since it is only by meeting such challenges that a richer life may be attained. Indeed, the poem is fundamentally concerned with knowledge and choices—not only for the characters but also for the reader, who must navigate through the ambiguities of the text.

This element of ambiguity is clearest in Milton's presentation of the character of Satan. As early as *A Maske,* Milton revealed an interest in the nature of temptation and the motivations that prompt the tempter. In *Paradise Lost,* Satan remains intriguing because his true nature is never revealed. Milton's Satan is a multilayered character driven by conflicting desires and ambitions; his many powerful soliloquies, rather than clarify his character, add further depths and complexities to it.

In this epic poem Milton rejects a purely mechanistic view of the universe and instead puts forward a universe that is constructed of spirit and matter. The poem couples the poignant loss of human innocence with the promise of consolation through spiritual redemption. This consolation is in keeping with much of Milton's writing. He offers the companionship of loved ones, learning, patience, and religious faith as the means through which the spirit is redeemed. At the end of the poem, Adam and Eve transcend their faults by undertaking the journey of the enlightened and moving toward spiritual integrity. The final lines promise a patient acceptance of their struggles in a world now littered with snares that may entrap and humiliate the body but cannot destroy the spirit.

Return to Private Life

By February 1660 the Commonwealth was nearing collapse. In Milton's last pamphlet before the Restoration, *Brief Notes upon a Late Sermon,* he made one final attempt to influence his countrymen. He argued that if they were to again take on the yoke of a monarch, they should at least choose that monarch. Instead, in May 1660, Charles II was proclaimed king (he reigned until his death in 1685) . The republic whose principles Milton had labored to support had collapsed. He went into hiding, fearing the worst from those he had consistently opposed in the most public fashion. A proclamation issued on August 13 ordered the burning of Milton's *Eikonoklastes* and *Defensiones.* Milton was imprisoned for several months but escaped the death sentence following the intervention of his former assistant, the younger poet Andrew Marvell (1621–1678), who was, despite his republican leanings, a favorite of Charles II. On December 15, 1660, Milton was released from custody after paying a heavy fine.

Milton's financial position was precarious, so he was forced to take a small house on Jewin Street, Westminster. Yet despite his change in fortune, he retained many loyal friends and had a nearly completed manuscript of *Paradise Lost.*

In 1663, when he was fifty-four, Milton remarried, his choice being the twenty-four-year-old Elizabeth Minshull, a woman described as possessing good humor and an agreeable personality. This marriage soured Milton's problematic relationship with his daughters, who feared that their already meager expectations of an inheritance had been dashed. Despite this domestic discord, Milton was able to settle into a comfortable routine of study and writing (through dictation to a secretary). The famous London plague of 1665/1666 forced the family to move to a cottage at Chalfont in Buckinghamshire in July 1665. Upon their return to London, they witnessed the Great Fire, which destroyed Milton's father's house on Bread Street. During this turbulent period Milton completed *Paradise Lost* (1665), which was published in 1667. The poem was positively received. John Hobart, a Presbyterian minister, proclaimed Milton the equal of the great poets of antiquity.

In the meantime Milton was busy composing two other long poems, *Paradise Regained* and *Samson Agonistes,* both published in 1671. *Paradise Regained* portrays Jesus's confrontation with Satan the tempter in the desert. Jesus is depicted as a hero who steadfastly resists the lure of a licentious society and rejects the false idola-

▶ *By the nineteenth century Milton's life had become mythologized, and this oil painting by Hungarian-born Mihaly Munkacsy (1844–1900) depicts one of the most enduring myths. The blind Milton did dictate his great poem* Paradise Lost *but to one of his male secretaries, not to his daughters.*

try of a degenerate church. Samson, the hero of *Samson Agonistes,* wins back his lost physical strength by striving for spiritual strength. The robustness and passion of Milton's heroes set these poems apart from the more formulaic work of most of Milton's contemporaries. The poems, like much else of Milton's work, celebrate the individual who chooses a painfully earned liberty over an easy but soul-destroying enslavement.

In 1671 Milton published his *History of Britain* and other essays on a variety of topics. In July 1674 the second edition of *Paradise Lost,* now expanded from ten to twelve books, was published. Shortly after the appearance of this edition, Milton dictated his will to his brother, Christopher. In it the resentments of his first marriage reappear. He leaves the one-thousand-pound dowry that he never received from his father-in-law, Richard Powell, to his "unkind children from her [Mary Powell]." To his third wife, Elizabeth Minshull, he left everything else. Milton died of gout in the night of November 9, 1674, and was buried beside his father at Saint Giles Cripplegate, the London church where Oliver Cromwell had married.

Milton's political ideas found fertile ground a century later, in the work of the Americans Benjamin Franklin, Thomas Jefferson, and John Adams, who drafted America's Declaration of Independence (1776). In France some of the arguments from Milton's "Pro Populo Anglicano Defensio" were used to justify the executions of political figures in the French Revolution (1789–1799). Above all, *Paradise Lost* ensured Milton a place among the most renowned of British writers. Readers of successive generations have found in it a fascinating depiction of humanity that continues to inform their own understanding of life's meaning. Milton's vast body of work communicates the struggles of a man who survived the conflicts of his time, along with crushing personal blows, without compromising his integrity or surrendering his spirit.

In 1688 the poet laureate John Dryden (1631–1700) wrote a tribute to Milton in which he favorably compared the English poet to the great poets of ancient Greece and Rome, Homer and Virgil:

Three poets, in three distant ages born,
Greece, Italy, and England did adorn.
The first in loftiness of thought surpassed,
The next in majesty, in both the last:
The force of Nature could no farther go;
To make a third, she joined the former two.

"Epigram on Milton"

▲ *This anonymous engraving of the poet, made several years after his death, was printed in the eighteenth century with John Dryden's* Epigram *beneath.*

FURTHER READING

Levi, Peter. *The Public and Private Life of John Milton.* New York, 1997.

Lewalski, Barbara Kiefer. *The Life of John Milton: A Critical Biography.* Malden, MA, 2000.

Parker, William Riley. *Milton: A Biography.* 2nd ed. New York, 1996.

Wolfe, Don M., ed. *Complete Prose Works of John Milton.* New Haven, CT, 1953–1982.

Jessica L. Malay

SEE ALSO

- Calvinism • Church of England
- English Civil Wars • Florence • Hobbes, Thomas
- Iconoclasm • Literature • London • Reformation
- Stuarts, The

Missionaries

CHRISTIAN MISSIONARIES WERE THE VANGUARD OF EUROPEAN CIVILIZATION AND RELIGION DURING THE AGE OF EXPLORATION.

The Christianization of Europe, begun by the Twelve Apostles in the mid-first century CE and largely completed by 1100, was accomplished by missionaries, many of whom died a martyr's death. Sometimes conversions were effected by the sword. The Frankish king Charlemagne (742–814) repeatedly conquered the Saxons and had them baptized. Seven centuries later, the

Spanish used coercion to drive native peoples of the Americas into Christianized agricultural communities. Sometimes peoples were expected to conform to the convention that the religion of the king was the religion of the tribe. However, it was broadly characteristic of Christianity that it was propagated successfully only when preaching, persuasion, and the sacraments gained willing converts.

Age of Exploration

When the Renaissance began, Europe was solidly Christian, and the only missionary efforts were undertaken by Franciscans in North Africa. The Age of Exploration, led by great explorers such as Christopher Columbus, John Cabot, Ferdinand Magellan, and Hernando de Soto, called forth a new wave of missionary activity.

Explorers and their governments claimed that a main reason for their voyages was to extend Christendom by converting the native peoples of the newly discovered lands. Of course, they had other motives for voyages of discovery—the drive for wealth, usually in the form of silver and gold; a genuine scientific interest in discovering new sea routes, notably the famous Northwest Passage; and an interest in forestalling their European competitors in the rush for American possessions.

Portugal and Spain were the great colonial powers of the sixteenth and seventeenth centuries. In 1493 Pope Alexander VI decreed that all new lands discovered west of an imaginary line to the west of the Azores, a group of islands in the Atlantic—the line was later placed near the Cape Verde Islands, off the west coast of Africa—should belong to Spain, while all new lands discovered east of that line should belong to Portugal. The pope also stated that the conversion of the inhabitants would be the first

◀ *An early-sixteenth-century portrait of Pope Alexander VI by an anonymous German artist. The pope was accepted as the arbiter of colonial boundaries in the New World because European monarchs believed that sovereignty was, in part, granted by God through the church. This belief did not prevent kings from putting pressure on Alexander and his successors in order to protect their overseas interests.*

In 1493, the year that Christopher Columbus returned from his first voyage, Pope Alexander VI wrote to the Spanish monarchs, Ferdinand and Isabella:

Alexander, bishop, servant of the servants of God, to the illustrious sovereigns, our very dear son in Christ, Ferdinand, and our very dear daughter in Christ, Isabella.... We have indeed learned that you have intended to seek out certain islands and mainlands ... to the end that you might bring to the worship of our Redeemer and the profession of the Catholic Faith their residents ... [you] chose our beloved son Christopher Columbus to make diligent quest for these remote and unknown mainlands and islands through the sea.... By the authority of Almighty God conferred on us in Blessed Peter and the vicarship of Jesus Christ, which we hold on earth ... [we] give grant and assign to you ... all the islands and mainlands found and to be found ... toward the west and the south, by drawing and establishing a line from the Arctic pole, namely the north, to the Antarctic pole, namely the south ... the said line to be distant one hundred leagues toward the west and south from any of the islands known as the Azores.

Inter Caetera

purpose of exploration and settlement. This division of the world was formalized in the Treaty of Tordesillas (1494). Portuguese and Spanish missionaries came from the great religious orders and included Franciscans, Jesuits, Dominicans, and Recollects, who had all taken vows of poverty, chastity, and obedience. The Jesuits had also taken a fourth vow, to serve the pope.

When explorers landed on new territory, their first act was to claim it for their king by planting a flag. Their second act was to claim it for their religion by celebrating a mass led by the expedition chaplain. The second patent granted to the Spanish explorer Juan Ponce de León included a document that recited the history of the world since Adam and Eve, acknowledged that the Indies had been given to Spain by Pope Alexander VI, and demanded that the native peoples be obedient to the pope and the king of Spain and allow the Catholic faith to be preached to them. Those who did not accept these conditions would have their property seized and might be taken as slaves.

Missionaries to New Spain

The great admiral Christopher Columbus, a Genoese in the service of the Spanish crown, reached the Caribbean island of San Salvador in

October 1492. Soon after, Spain claimed the area it called New Spain, including all of present-day Mexico, Florida, southern Georgia, the lower part of South Carolina, Texas, New Mexico, southern Colorado, Arizona, and California.

Within a year the Franciscans arrived in Santo Domingo, the Spanish colony on the island of Hispaniola (divided in the present day between Haiti and the Dominican Republic). In 1505 the Franciscan province of Santa Cruz was founded on Hispaniola. By this time there were about three thousand converts to Christianity. By 1513 Franciscan missionaries had reached Panama and Cuba, and by 1522, Mexico City, from which the kingdom of the Aztecs would be evangelized.

▼ *In this engraving from Filippo Marini's* Historia et relatione de Tunchino e del Giappone *(1665), a Jesuit father preaches in Japan. The sunburst containing the letters* IHS *(the first three letters of Jesus's name in Greek) is the emblem of the Jesuits. Its place beside the papal crown indicates that the Jesuits are in the service of the pope.*

A *Tunkino* B *Cocincina* C *Cambogia* D *Siam* E *Lao* F *Macassar* G *Cantaom* H *Giappone*

▶ In this anonymous seventeenth-century Mexican painting, a bishop prays for a wounded American Indian. The Catholic Church regards this healing as the first miracle granted through the intercession of Our Lady of Guadalupe.

The Franciscans' initial success was made possible by the Spanish officer Hernán Cortés, who defeated the Aztecs in November 1519. The Aztec emperor, Montezuma, had half believed that Cortés was the god Quetzalcoatl and allowed himself to be taken prisoner. The Franciscan missions made great headway in New Spain. By 1600 there were two hundred Franciscan centers ministering to a thousand native communities.

In 1591 two Jesuit missionaries, Gonzalo de Tapia and Martín Pérez, set out for Sinaloa on the west coast of Mexico, and from that center Sonora and the north were evangelized. The line of missions had been pushed northward to Santa Fe by 1610, and the mission San Francisco de los Tejas was established on the Trinity River in 1691 in what would become Texas. An essential part of missionary strategy was the conversion of the nomadic tribes to a settled life. Cattle herding and agriculture on a scale unknown to the indigenous peoples were introduced so that they could be encouraged or even forced to settle around the established mission churches.

Crucial to the successful conversion of Mexican Indians was the belief that the Virgin Mary had appeared to a peasant boy, Juan Diego, near Mexico City in 1531. Mary was said to have impressed her image on the boy's *tilma* (coat), a miracle that grew into the tradition of Our Lady of Guadalupe, protector of the Americas. Despite the success of the missionaries in planting Christianity, elements of African and American Indian religions persisted.

Innocents or Savages?

Throughout the sixteenth century the attempt to evangelize native peoples was complicated by the existence of two contradictory views. In Spain and Portugal, American Indians were seen as unspoiled peoples with souls, who should be converted by persuasion. The first native inhabitants that Columbus encountered, the friendly Arawak people, measured up to the view held by authorities in Spain (their gentleness led to their destruction, first by the warlike Caribs and then by the Spanish, despite the protests of Bartolomé de Las Casas and other missionaries). In continental Central and South America the colonizers found the people to be neither better nor worse than their European conquerors—given intermittently to friendliness and duplicity. The Aztecs and Tlaxcalans of Mexico, for example, were as warlike as any European nation and as adept at tyrannizing their neighbors.

The authorities in distant Spain legislated against enslavement, but it persisted and grew, partly because of the demand for labor in the mines and partly because slavery was already common among many native tribes as the usual fate of captured enemies. The destruction of the native population was greater in the first generation of Spanish colonization than later, when royal and church authority were sometimes able to suppress the worst abuses.

The Florida Missions

Christianity came to the American Gulf coast with Juan Ponce de León in 1513. Saint Augustine, with its tiny Spanish population, was founded on the east coast in 1565, but the successful evangelization of the native population was not begun until 1573. After failure by the Dominicans and Jesuits, the Franciscans converted those living in the region south of Carolina. The method of the Franciscans, who were accompanied by no military force, was peaceful persuasion, the Christian example of selflessness and piety. The Franciscans did not take slaves or give the native inhabitants rum. In 1634 there were thirty-five missionaries in charge of forty-four towns with a population of 30,000. The Franciscan missions in Florida were disrupted by the colonial wars between

In 1552 a Spanish friar described the depopulation of the Caribbean islands:

The reason why Christians have killed and destroyed such infinite numbers of souls, is solely because they have made gold their ultimate aim, seeking to load themselves with riches in the shortest time and to mount by high steps, disproportionate to their condition; namely by their insatiable avarice and ambition, the greatest that could be on earth. These islands, being so happy and so rich and the people so humble, so patient, and so easily subjugated, they have no more respect, nor consideration, nor have they taken more account of them (I speak the truth of what I have seen during all the aforementioned time) than—I will not say of animals, for would to God they had considered and treated them as animals—but even less than the dung in the streets.

Bartolomé de Las Casas, *A Short Account of the Destruction of the Indies*

▲ *Quoniambet, depicted here in a 1575 engraving by André Thevet, was king of the Carib tribe. The Spanish attempted to exterminate the Caribs because they were warlike, resourceful, and very difficult to enslave.*

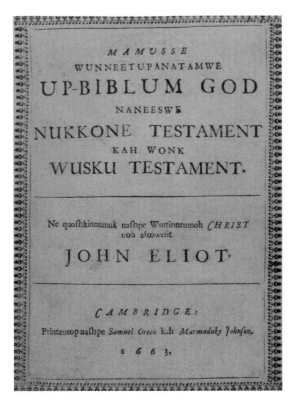

England and Spain. Of the Franciscan centers in Florida, only Pensacola and Saint Augustine would survive as permanent centers of European settlement.

English Colonies

The first English settlement in North America was in Virginia, where the Church of England was established and where there there was more interest in finding clergy to staff parishes than in sending missionaries to the native population. The second was in Massachusetts, where Puritan ministers on the frontier labored fervently to convert the native peoples, an effort that continued into the eighteenth century.

Having abolished religious orders in the 1530s, the English had no pool of dedicated Franciscan and Dominican friars prepared to cross the Atlantic at the command of a religious superior. However, English settlers had a pious concern for the souls of the natives, and American Indian schools were a feature of the colonial colleges. Puritans founded Harvard University in Massachusetts in 1636 for "the education of the English and Indian youth of this Country in knowledge and godliness." John Eliot (1604–1690) was a missionary whose Indian translation of the Bible (New Testament

1661, Old Testament 1663) was printed in the Indian College in Harvard Yard. When the College of William and Mary was founded in Virginia in 1693, its purposes included the education of the native peoples.

In Spanish colonies the greed and ambition of the conquistadores was muted by the self-sacrifice of the Franciscans and Dominicans. By contrast, in English territory commercial interest usually trumped other considerations. Rum and guns, forbidden the native peoples in Spanish missions, were popular trade goods among the English, who sometimes used them to procure slaves. American Indian slaves were an important source of labor in the Carolinas.

South America

From their first province on Hispaniola in 1505, the Franciscans established missions in Cuba, Panama, and Nicaragua. The Franciscans were in Peru by 1532, following the conquest of the Incan Empire by the Spanish explorer Francisco Pizarro. Taking advantage of a civil war raging among the Incas, Pizarro had held the Incan emperor, Atahualpa, for ransom and demanded one room filled with gold and another filled with silver. However, when the rooms were filled, Atahualpa was executed. His death caused another civil war between rival claimants to the Incan throne and inhibited missionary success. The Franciscans were the first missionaries to the Incas; the first Jesuits in Peru were sent by the Spanish king, Philip II, in 1567.

Pizarro also conquered the kingdom of Quito (in what is now Ecuador) in 1534, and soon French Franciscans brought Christianity. From Peru, Spanish traders reached the distant Pacific archipelago that would be called the Philippine Islands. An Augustinian friar, Andrés de Urdaneta, reached the islands in 1565, and from this beginning the tribes of the Philippines were successfully evangelized. Missionaries came to Argentina with the expedition of Pedro de Mendoza, a Spanish soldier, in 1536. Three chapels were built at the site of Buenos Aires, and three in neighboring Paraguay. At Buenos Aires a priest, Juan Gabrielle de Lezceno, opened a school for American Indians to teach them to read and write.

Jesuits in New France and Maryland

The Jesuits evangelized and ministered throughout the Americas. In North America their principal missions were among the native peoples of New France in the Saint Lawrence River valley and the settlers in the tiny colony of English Catholics in Maryland.

Quebec, like most European settlements, was considered by its founders a holy mission to establish Christianity as well as to secure the territory for the French king. Franciscan Recollects arrived in 1615 and ministered to the native tribes without success. In 1623 six Jesuits arrived, but their work was made difficult by warfare between the English and French and by the occupation of Quebec by the English from 1629 to 1632. From 1634 to 1650, the Jesuits conducted a mission to the Hurons that, although partly successful, saw the martyrdom of dozens of missionaries and their converts at the hands of the Hurons, Iroquois, and other American Indian groups. One French Jesuit working among the

Kidnapped by the Iroquois, the Jesuit missionary Isaac Jogues was reluctant to be rescued until he realized he would then be free to make another mission:

He would have escaped a hundred times if providence had not checked him by offering him from time to time through wonderful coincidences the means of opening the gates of paradise to some poor soul.... These opportunities sustained him in his exile. He was unusually distressed because he was constrained to make a resolution that he would escape with the intervention of the Dutch. Had he not seen that it was over with his life, and that he would no longer help those poor barbarians unless he escaped, to come and find them another time, he would never have abandoned them. Our Lord prolonged his life that he might come and present it to him another time—a burnt offering at a place where he had already begun his sacrifice.

The Jesuit Relations and Allied Documents, XXXI, 137

Hurons, Isaac Jogues, was captured by the Ojibwas and tortured but escaped to France with the help of the Dutch. Welcomed as a hero in Paris, Jogues seized the first opportunity to return to New France.

▼ *In this sixteenth-century engraving by Theodore de Bry (1528–1598), hostile Indians armed with bows and arrows massacre some missionaries.*

Maryland, named for the French princess Henrietta Maria, who became the queen of Charles I of England, was given to George Calvert, Lord Baltimore, in a charter of 1612. Calvert was a Catholic, and two priests accompanied his ships the *Ark* and the *Dove* when they sailed from England in the fall of 1633. Between 1634 and 1647 Jesuits established and manned the Maryland missions and did so again after 1660. In imitation of the pattern that had allowed Catholicism to survive in England in the reign of Elizabeth I (1559–1603), the Catholic Church in Maryland was sponsored by the plantation gentry. At the end of the seventeenth century, Saint Marys City was the center of Catholic life in Maryland. The Jesuit enterprise was challenged by the immigration of Virginia Puritans into Maryland, whose charter established tolerance for all Christians. Soon Catholics were a minority in Maryland.

Jesuit Missions to the East

The Portuguese asked Pope Paul III to send Jesuits to evangelize the East. Francis Xavier (1506–1552), a Spanish missionary, was one of the founders of the Jesuit order, a company of priests begun by Ignatius of Loyola in 1534. Francis Xavier left Lisbon in May 1541 and after

more than a year reached the seaport of Goa, in western India. Xavier went on to evangelize Travancore in southwestern India, Melaka (now part of Malaysia), the Moluccas (or Spice Islands, now part of Indonesia), and Sri Lanka, and by 1549 he had reached Japan. Xavier's mission was so successful that it was banned in 1587—the Japanese government feared the missionary work was being done in preparation for the conquest of Japan by foreigners. Although Christianity never died in Japan, Christians were persecuted intermittently between 1597 and 1640, when all foreigners were banished from the islands.

Matteo Ricci, an Italian, joined the Jesuits in Rome in 1571; in the best Jesuit tradition his education included the study of contemporary science. In 1578 Ricci was sent to Goa and then to Macao, in southeastern China, where he learned Chinese. In 1601 he was in Beijing, where his learning in astronomy and mathematics gained him a hearing and many converts. Ricci imitated the practice of the missionary Saint Paul when he was in Athens; Saint Paul had appealed to the fact that his listeners were "very religious" in order to make them open to Christian ideas. Ricci saw that the traditional

▼ *In this eighteenth-century painting by the Mexican artist Antonio Torres, the Jesuit founder Francis Xavier baptizes new converts. The Jesuits attributed 700,000 conversions to Xavier's missionary endeavors.*

On February 15, 1609, Matteo Ricci wrote to his Jesuit superior about his mission's strategy of learning from Chinese culture:

Apart from the fact that we have here in China many good confreres, and many of them theologians, yet each of these has up to now given himself to the study of the Chinese culture in more than a mediocre manner because to know our own culture without knowing theirs would be of little value here. Your excellency will see how important this point is in the beginning of our mission here. In my opinion I reckon this more important than the immediate conversion of ten thousand or more Christians, since I consider this the condition sine qua non [an essential requirement] for the complete and universal conversion of this kingdom.

Letter to Francisco Pasio

Chinese philosophy of Confucianism, which even included a set of rules not unlike the Ten Commandments, shared many of the moral ideals of Christianity. In 1595 Ricci wrote *On the Nature of God,* which encouraged the Chinese to see Christianity as the perfecting of Confucianism and to understand that Christian prayers for the dead were similar to traditional ancestor worship (rites connected with ancestor worship were central to the teachings of Confucius). Ricci and his fellow Jesuit Michele Ruggieri successfully brought Christianity to China, and soon they were joined by Dominicans and Franciscans.

Missions in Africa
Christianity had come to the Roman provinces of North Africa—Egypt, Cyrenaica (now eastern Libya), Numidia (present-day Algeria), and Mauretania (now Morocco and part of Algeria)—in the first century CE, but it did not come to sub-Saharan Africa until the fifteenth century, when the Portuguese began to establish trading stations on the west coast. The port of Luanda, established in 1576, was the center of missionary activity in Angola and the Congo, but growth came slowly. Luanda was the slave port for Brazil, and in Angola the slave trade was even more extensive than in other parts of Africa.

Rivalries
During the sixteenth and seventeenth centuries the work of missionaries was hampered by various rivalries and tensions. These began in 1493 with the difficulties between Christopher Columbus and a Spanish Benedictine, Bernado Buil, who objected to the admiral's administration, and continued throughout the colonial period. Occasionally, as in Maryland, the conflict between Catholics and Protestants was transplanted from Europe to America. In the Spanish missions there was always tension between the missionary priests, who believed the purpose of the conquest and settlement was to convert the native peoples to Christianity, and the royal administrators and military authorities who were there to extract gold and silver. After a country was settled and the missions had become regular dioceses with their own bishops, there was sometimes tension between the bishop and the friars.

▲ *This early-seventeenth-century Japanese paper screen, painted by Kano Naizen (1570–1616), catalogs Portuguese priests in black, Jesuits in black and white, and Franciscans in gray.*

Occasionally there was tension between the orders. In the late sixteenth century the Jesuit mission to Japan was jeopardized by the Franciscans. The Jesuits had made many converts surreptitiously, whereas the Franciscans insisted on preaching publicly and had even built a church in open defiance of the Japanese governor Hideyoshi Toyotomi (also known as Taikosama). When Taikosama learned that Christianity was being practiced against his orders, he had twenty-six people crucified at Nagasaki. The martyrs included Jesuits and Japanese converts as well as Franciscans.

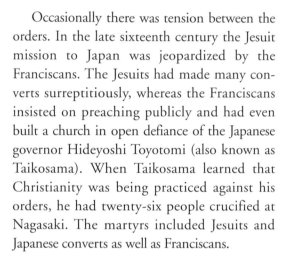

▼ *Christianity was outlawed in Japan under the ruler Hideyoshi Toyotomi, portrayed in this silk painting by an unknown artist. On February 5, 1597, Hideyoshi ordered the crucifixion of twenty-six Christians at Nagasaki—six Franciscan friars, seventeen Japanese converts, and three Jesuit fathers.*

Missionaries and Civilization

In an age when religion was so important, it was inevitable that exploration and missionary activity would go hand in hand. Since Spain and Portugal were most successful at exploration and conquest, their missionaries left the greatest stamp on the New World. The French exploration and settlement of the Saint Lawrence and Mississippi river valleys and the English and Dutch colonization of the Atlantic seaboard of North America also played an important part in establishing Christianity in what would become Canada and the United States.

If civilization's needs often required making Christians by any means, it also required a concern for souls. Sixteenth- and seventeenth-century missionaries showed a remarkable ability to adapt, as they confronted mandarins with scholarship and baptized dying Hurons at their own lives' peril. Their continuing legacy is the worldwide network of Christian churches.

FURTHER READING

Bangert, William V. *A History of the Society of Jesus.* Saint Louis, 1972.

Cronin, Vincent. *The Wise Man from the West.* New York, 1955.

McGratty, Arthur R. *The Fire of Francis Xavier: The Story of an Apostle.* Milwaukee, WI, 1952.

Spence, Jonathan D. *The Memory Palace of Matteo Ricci.* New York, 1984.

James A. Patrick

SEE ALSO

• Columbus, Christopher • Exploration
• Magellan, Ferdinand • Monarchy • Philip II
• Portugal • Preaching • Religious Orders • Spain

Molière

THE PLAYWRIGHT AND ACTOR MOLIÈRE (1622–1673) HELPED TO CREATE THE MODERN FRENCH THEATER AND FOUNDED A TRADITION OF COMIC DRAMA WHOSE INFLUENCE HAS SPREAD FAR BEYOND THE BORDERS OF FRANCE.

Molière was the stage and pen name of Jean-Baptiste Poquelin. Born in 1622, Poquelin was the eldest of six children. His father, Jean Poquelin, was a prosperous Parisian middle-class tradesman (an upholsterer), and an attendant on King Louis XIII (reigned 1610–1643).

Education

Molière probably received his earliest education at one of Paris's many petty (elementary) schools, where he would have learned reading, writing, and—possibly—the rudiments of Latin. Molière's father clearly had high ambitions for his son. He enrolled Molière in the Jesuit-run Collège de Clermont, one of the best schools in France. Students of the college (Molière included) often went on to law school. More important, the students acted in Latin plays, staged to help them gain confidence in public speaking. It is not known for sure whether the young Molière ever performed while at college, but it is very likely he did.

Molière may have already been exposed to theater. His first biographer, Jean-Léonor Le Gallois de Grimarest, recounts that when Molière was nine or ten, his maternal grandfather regularly took him to the Hôtel de Bourgogne, the oldest theater in Paris. Molière may also have seen street theater. Plays—including Italian-style farces—were often performed on the Pont Neuf, a bridge not far from Molière's neighborhood.

► This portrait of Molière (c. 1658) was painted by Pierre Mignard. Mignard painted many of the most illustrious figures of seventeenth-century France, including the tragic playwright Jean Racine, the royal counselor Cardinal Mazarin, and Louis XIV himself.

One contemporary account of Madeleine Béjart's stature as an actress and a charmer comes from a romance written by Madeleine de Scudéry (1607–1701). Using the fictional name Jebar (a close anagram of Béjart), Scudéry describes Madeleine's triumphant portrayal of the heroine Sophonisbe in Jean Mairet's tragedy of the same name:

She was beautiful, she was elegant, she was very witty, she sang well, she danced well, she played all sorts of instruments, she wrote very prettily in verse and in prose and her conversation was very diverting. She was one of the best actresses of her century and her acting had the power to inspire in reality all the feigned passions that one sees represented on the stage. This agreeable actress was called Jebar and, as Abindarrays sought to divert himself and efface the memory of past adventures, he went to the theater where he saw her play the role of Sophonisbe in a manner so touching and so passionate that first he admired her and then he loved her, first his heart was tender with pity, then she stole it from him.

Madeleine de Scudéry, *Almahide*

▼ *This anonymous French portrait of Madeleine Béjart, in oil paint on stone, depicts her as Madelon, one of the leads in Molière's first Parisian hit,* Les précieuses ridicules.

The Illustrious Theater

In 1643 the twenty-one-year-old Molière met and fell in love with Madeleine Béjart, a beautiful red-haired actress. Four years Molière's senior, Béjart also came from a bourgeois Parisian family, though one that was less distinguished than Molière's. The Béjarts had theatrical connections; among Madeleine's aunts and uncles were an actor, an actress, and a poet and playwright.

Madeleine, her older brother Joseph, and Molière founded a theatrical troupe, l'Illustre-Théâtre. The company leased a disused indoor tennis court and borrowed the capital to refit the building as a theater. It was about this time that Molière began using his stage name—a practice common among actors of the day—to create the impression of being an aristocrat and perhaps to protect his father from embarrassment.

The troupe performed a repertoire of melodrama and tragedy. Madeleine Béjart was a gifted tragic player, but Molière was not. His appearance was not imposing, and he stuttered as he spoke his lines. L'Illustre-Théâtre failed to draw large audiences and went bankrupt. As a result, Molière spent several weeks in debtor's prison.

Years in the Provinces

In 1645 Molière and the Béjarts left Paris for the provinces. In the southern region of Languedoc, they acquired a powerful patron, Armand de Bourbon, prince of Conti (1629–1666). His sponsorship brought them financial support and an introduction to other appreciative audiences and patrons. The company found success with both comedies and tragedies, including recent works by the great dramatist Pierre Corneille (1606–1684). Madeleine's careful management assured the troupe's continued prosperity, even after it lost Conti's patronage in 1657 (the prince found religion and rejected the theater and other worldly vanities).

During the thirteen years he spent in the provinces, Molière polished his skills as an actor and, more important, began to write his own comedies. His first work, *L'étourdi (The Blunderer;* 1653) was based on Italian commedia dell'arte, a form of improvised comic theater that originated in the sixteenth century and remained popular into the eighteenth century. Traveling companies played stock characters known as masks since the actors wore theatrical masks. These characters included Pantaloon, the old miser with a flirtatious daughter; Harlequin, Pantaloon's penniless servant; the Captain, a boastful soldier; Pulcinella, a hunchback with an eye for the ladies; Scaramouche, a rakish swordsman; Pagliaccio, the clown; and the Lovers. From Italy wandering groups of actors took their earthy, humorous performances across Europe and became especially popular in France. Molière borrowed heavily from the genre but introduced his own refinements, such as writing in verse instead of prose.

Return to Paris

In 1658 Molière and his players returned to Paris, where they soon secured the patronage of the king's uncle, Gaston, duke of Orléans (1608–1660). At the time there were two theatrical companies in the city: the troupe playing at the Hôtel de Bourgogne performed tragedy, and the Italian troupe at the Petit-Bourbon presented Italian-style comedy. After Molière's company performed for Louis XIV (reigned 1643–1715), it gained the privilege of using the Petit-Bourbon on the Italian troupe's days off. When that theater was razed to expand the royal palace of the Louvre, the company moved to the theater of the Palais Royal.

The company built its success on Molière's new, often controversial comedy. His first successful play, *Les précieuses ridicules (The Affected Young Ladies),* premiered in November 1659. The plot centers on two young provincial ladies who reject the suitors their fathers have found for them and instead fall for two "wits" (their suitors' valets in disguise). The play lampoons the snobbery of certain young women of the middle classes with pretenses to wit and refinement.

A succession of comedies followed, including *Sganarelle* (1660), *Dom Garcie de Navarre, ou Le prince jaloux* (*The Jealous Prince;* 1661), *L'école des maris* (*The School for Husbands;* 1661), and *L'école des femmes* (*The School for Wives;* 1662). These popular and successful dramas brought Molière, Madeleine Béjart, and the rest of the company financial security beyond anything they had ever experienced. Molière also began publishing his plays. The availability of authorized editions put a stop to the market in pirated editions, which were printed by unscrupulous booksellers but were usually of poor quality and full of inaccuracies.

◀ *In this early-seventeenth-century engraving by Jacob Honervogt, a trio of performers act out one of the stock situations in commedia dell'arte. Such performances enjoyed widespread popularity in Molière's day, and their influence appears in his comic drama.*

In 1662 Molière married Armande Béjart, supposedly Madeleine's sister but more probably her illegitimate daughter by Esprit de Rèmond, the count of Modena. Armande was about twenty and had acted with Molière's company most of her life. The marriage proved unstable: the couple suffered a long period of separation, during which time they still acted and associated with one another, but in the end they reconciled.

The same year Louis XIV granted a royal pension to Molière, the first ever paid to an actor. Molière had attained the status of a courtier as well as a theatrical figure. He enjoyed a certain level of familiarity with the king that at first helped but would later disappoint him.

Around this time Molière and his friend the composer Jean-Baptiste Lully (1632–1687) invented the comedy-ballet, an early form of musical comedy. Their three collaborations—*Le marriage forcé* (*The Forced Wedding;* 1664), *La princesse d'Élide* (*The Princess of Elida;* 1664) and *Le bourgeois gentilhomme* (*The Would-Be Gentleman;* 1670)—were performed before the king and his court at, respectively, the Louvre, Versailles, and Chambord.

In 1664 Molière's *Tartuffe* was performed at Versailles and then immediately banned. The church viewed the play as an attack upon reli-

◀ *In this anonymous 1660 engraving, Louis XIV is dressed in a ballet costume. The Sun King patronized the finest artists of his day and used their talents to display and celebrate the grandeur of his regime.*

TARTUFFE

Tartuffe, a charlatan masquerading as a deeply religious man, preys on a rich bourgeois named Orgon. Under Tartuffe's influence, Orgon abuses his family and almost forces his daughter into a hateful marriage with the hypocrite Tartuffe himself. Only when Orgon's wife, Elmire, subjects herself to Tartuffe's advances as Orgon looks on does he come to his senses and recognize Tartuffe for what he is. However, Tartuffe has already woven a web around Orgon. Salvation comes in the form of a royal representative who arrests Tartuffe in the name of the king and thus restores Orgon's peace and property.

The action of *Tartuffe* is usually described as turning on the hypocrisy of the title character, but the major theme has more to do with power than with hypocrisy. Tartuffe himself makes an interesting study in motives. He is a confidence man who uses religion for his schemes and scams. When it suits him, Tartuffe can assume the mask of piety or patriotism. His deceit succeeds so well because Orgon cooperates with Tartuffe's charade. It suits Orgon to have his own family at his mercy. The play establishes an alliance between false piety and tyranny. These two forces sometimes unite to serve libertinism. Molière plays on this connection again in *Don Juan;* in his ultimate descent into degradation, the Don pretends to heed Doña Elvire's plea to convert but only so that he can continue leading his depraved life under cover. By arbitrarily appealing to the "higher authorities" of divine will and self-will, the hypocrite and the tyrant can both exert a near-absolute control over others. However, the would-be tyrant can sometimes become the victim of his own devices, as happens to Orgon when Tartuffe almost gets the upper hand in the denouement of the play. Legitimate authority, represented by the royal agent of the king, can alone assert the reason and justice needed to deliver Orgon from his own folly.

Tartuffe *is one of Molière's masterpieces. The prosperous Orgon falls under the spell of the title character, a scoundrel who passes himself off as a saint. Orgon jeopardizes the happiness of his marriage to Elmire and that of his entire household.*

gion and threatened to excommunicate anyone connected with its performance. Even Louis XIV seems to have shied away from helping Molière against his powerful detractors. It took Molière several years to overcome the play's suppression. Finally, in 1669 the king allowed him to produce a version of the play in Paris, and it proved wildly successful with audiences.

The Misanthrope

The years when *Tartuffe* was suppressed saw the first performances of masterpieces such as *Don Juan* (1665), *The Misanthrope* (1666), and *L'avare* (*The Miser;* 1668). In *The Misanthrope,* Molière reached new dramatic heights. It was usual in a comedy for individual excesses to be remedied by means of society's laughter. Molière turns this convention upside down, with his central character attacking society itself. The misanthrope of the title, Alceste, rails at friends and enemies alike for being insincere. Nevertheless, he falls in love with Célimène, a beautiful young widow who seems to return his affection but also flirts with other men. When Célimène finally agrees to marry Alceste, he rejects her and decides to withdraw from society altogether. The audience is left wondering whether it is nobility of character or sheer contrariness that drives Alceste's misanthropy.

The Miser features another masterful caricature, Harpagon, who loves money above all things. His greed drives him to oppose the marriages of his son and daughter, Cléante and Élise, to their soulmates, Mariane and Valère (also brother and sister). Harpagon finally consents to the marriages, not to make his children happy but to learn the location of his stolen money box, a subterfuge engineered by Cléante's valet, La Flèche. Harpagon's final line sums up his condition. As the young lovers prepare to share their joy with Mariane's mother, Harpagon prepares for a reunion with his "dear money box."

The final years of Molière's life brought bitterness and loss. His father died in 1669, after squandering his fortune. In 1672 Madeleine Béjart died: on her deathbed she renounced her involvement in the theater and reconciled with the church in order to secure a proper burial. The loss of royal support to theatrical rivals was another blow.

Recurring illness had left Molière severely weakened, but he still worked tirelessly. In February 1673 his new comedy *Le malade imaginaire (The Hypochondriac)* opened in Paris with Molière in the title role. After the fourth performance, Molière had a serious pulmonary seizure. He was taken from the theater to his apartment, where he died several hours later. The king had to intervene to have Molière's body buried in consecrated ground, since the church at that time refused a religious burial to anyone involved in the theater.

Long a sufferer from poor health, Molière filled his comedies with jibes at the medical profession:

SGANARELLE. What, sir, you're impious in medicine too?

DON JUAN. It's one of the great errors of mankind.

SGANARELLE. What? You don't believe in senna, or cassia, or emetic wine?

DON JUAN. And why would you have me believe in them?

SGANARELLE. You have the soul of a real unbeliever. However, you have seen that for some time emetic wine has been making quite a stir. Its miracles have converted the most incredulous minds, and not three weeks ago I saw, me, just as I'm speaking to you, a marvelous effect from it.

DON JUAN. And what was that?

SGANARELLE. There was a man who had been in agony for six days; they didn't know what to prescribe for him anymore, and all the remedies weren't doing anything; finally they thought of giving him emetic wine.

DON JUAN. He got well, did he?

SGANARELLE. No, he died.

DON JUAN. That was an admirable result?

SGANARELLE. What? For six whole days he hadn't been able to die, and that made him die right away. Could you ask for anything more efficient than that?

Don Juan, act 3, scene 1

► *In this 1661 engraving by Jean de Gourmont, Molière takes the role of Sganarelle, in the play of the same name. The character is a man who wrongly suspects his wife of infidelity.*

monly employed at the time. His plays, which blended farce, social satire, and high comedy, enriched French literature with a new dramatic form. In his finest works Molière succeeds not only in delighting his audience with outrageous farce but also in opening to them the terrain of the human soul.

Four years after Molière's death, Louis XIV merged the remainder of Molière's troupe with the Hôtel de Bourgogne to form the Comédie-Française, France's national theater, which has operated almost without interruption to the present day.

FURTHER READING

Bloom, Harold, ed. *Molière. Modern Critical Views.* Philadelphia, 2002.

Molière. *The Misanthrope and Other Plays.* Translated by Donald M. Frame. New York, 1968.

———. *Tartuffe and Other Plays.* Translated by Donald M. Frame. New York, 1967.

Scott, Virginia. *A Theatrical Life.* Cambridge, 2000.

Donald Carlson

Legacy

Molière brought a new method of comic acting to the French stage, one that was more natural in style than the highly rhetorical declamation com-

SEE ALSO

• France • French Civil Wars • Literature • Monarchy
• Paris • Popular Culture • Theater

Monarchy

MONARCHY REMAINED EUROPE'S MOST COMMON FORM OF GOVERNMENT THROUGHOUT THE RENAISSANCE. AS INDIVIDUAL DYNASTIES CONSOLIDATED THEIR POWER, THE END OF THE PERIOD SAW THE BIRTH OF THE MODERN NATION-STATE.

A monarchy is a system of government in which political power is concentrated in a single person (*monarchy* derives from Greek words that mean "rule by one"). The actual degree of dominance varied from monarchy to monarchy. Some monarchs had considerable power and influence; others were constrained by formidable aristocracies or even representative assemblies. In addition, different countries developed various rules, traditions, and laws that surrounded and restrained their sovereigns or rulers. In some cases only men could become monarchs. Most states had power-transfer systems based on inheritance, although a few kingdoms and empires elected a sovereign for life.

During the period from 1300 to 1650, various kings and princes endeavored to increase their power and control. These tussles led to almost constant warfare and shifting national borders and also to the demise of some dynasties and the rise of others. Besides fighting with other state sovereigns, monarchs also routinely faced threats from ambitious nobles and constraints by the church. Their struggles to consolidate power resulted in the formation of modern states and powerful central governments with the military and administrative capabilities to regulate large populations and areas of territory.

Types of Monarchies

Monarchies are the oldest form of government. As early as the fourth century BCE, the Greek philosopher Aristotle detailed many of the arguments in favor of monarchy. He asserted that, since a single ruler could make and implement decisions more quickly than a ruling committee, monarchies could be more efficient than democratic systems. A benign and just ruler was perceived as the best means to promote the common interests of the people and to protect the state from external attack or influence. However, there was also the potential for selfish, weak, or inept rulers. Unrestrained monarchs, or tyrants, could not only cause harm among the population but could even bring about the demise of states.

Throughout the Renaissance and into the Reformation, most European governments were

◀ *Feudal nobles could be granted fiefs from different lords; thus, an individual might rule multiple territories with different titles. The French nobleman Louis II (1377–1417), portrayed in this anonymous painting, was duke of Anjou, count of Maine and Provence, and king of Sicily, Naples, and Jerusalem.*

Among the most significant Renaissance monarchs were the Holy Roman emperors. This oil on canvas, after Albrecht Dürer (1471–1528), portrays Sigismund (1368–1437), who was king of Hungary, Rome, Bohemia, and Lombardy before becoming Holy Roman emperor in 1433.

monarchical. The most common form of monarchy was the kingdom, a political unit in which the sovereign (king or queen) held formal sway over a collection of smaller geographic units in a feudal structure. While the monarch ruled the entire kingdom, each of the units was in turn ruled by a lesser authority. A given area might be ruled by a prince or duke if it was large (a territory known as a principality or a duchy, respectively) or by a baron or lord if it was small. Each lesser ruler pledged loyalty and devotion to the monarch in exchange for the right to rule a particular region. Feudalism was at bottom a set of arrangements based on mutual pledges of loyalty and responsibility; the feudal pattern of land ownership was designed to allow a monarch to rule safely by dividing power among trusted nobles. However, a monarch had to be constantly vigilant; powerful nobles might be tempted to wrest control of the country away from the king and become sovereign themselves, as happened in the English civil wars.

The largest political units of the era were empires, collections of kingdoms and smaller states, such as principalities and duchies. Empires were also based on feudal models, but they were considerably larger than the typical kingdom. Founded in 962, the Holy Roman Empire at its height stretched from the Atlantic coast of Europe to the Mediterranean and east to the borders of present-day Russia.

Although there were smaller monarchies throughout Europe, these kingdoms and principalities often faced a difficult time retaining the right to govern themselves because of the power of their larger neighbors. Scotland repeatedly faced interference and invasion from England, including the overthrow of Scottish monarchs; in the early fourteenth century Scotland's independence movement was led by Robert the Bruce. The Renaissance saw the growth of large kingdoms, such as England and Spain, and the decline of smaller monarchies. England was able to incorporate the monarchies of Wales and Ireland during the period, while Spain was born out of the unification of the monarchies of Castille and Aragon. Some smaller kingdoms were able to maintain their autonomy, among them Naples and Portugal.

Robert the Bruce | 1274–1329

Robert the Bruce was born into a noble Scottish family in 1274. He became a leading figure in the Scottish independence movement and later became king of the northern state. Robert inherited the rank and title of earl of Carrick and was initially loyal to the English king, Edward I. However, in 1297 Robert joined a widespread revolt against English rule in Scotland. At the time of the revolt, the nominal king, John de Baliol, was in exile after allowing Scotland to become a fief of the English. When Robert the Bruce joined the campaign for independence, he sought not only to free Scotland of English domination but also to secure the crown for himself and his family.

After several victories under the command of William Wallace, the Scots were defeated in 1297 at the Battle of Falkirk. Nonetheless, Robert the Bruce became one of two guardians appointed to rule Scotland in the absence of a king. He was later replaced as guardian and forced to seek a pardon from Edward II in 1302. Two years later, the death of his father made Robert one of two rival claimants to the throne. He arranged a meeting with John Comyn, Baliol's nephew and brother-in-law, in an effort to resolve his claims to the throne. On February 10, 1306, Robert and Comyn met at Dumfries, and fighting broke out in which Comyn and several of his supporters were killed. As a result of this incident, Robert was excommunicated by Pope Clement V, but his popularity was undiminished, and on March 25 he was crowned King Robert I of Scotland.

Robert initiated a military uprising against the English. After suffering several defeats, he was forced into exile in Ireland. Three of his brothers were captured by the English and executed, and his supporters were scattered. In 1307, however, Robert returned and inflicted a series of defeats on the English. In 1314 he soundly defeated the English at the Battle of Bannockburn. Following the victory, Pope John XXII recognized Robert as the monarch of an independent Scotland (1320). Robert ruled until his death in 1329. His son David ascended the throne, but the English invaded in 1332 and initiated what became known as the Second War for Scottish Independence.

Monarchs and Political Power

Monarchical power came from two main sources. The first was based on feudalism, and the second was derived from the monarchy's relationship with the church. The feudal system was built on a series of personal relationships. Individual aristocrats gave their loyalty and provided resources to the monarchy in exchange for titles, new lands, or other incentives. For instance, following a war or military campaign, a monarch would often distribute conquered lands or wealth as rewards for those who supported the venture or who were politically important. New titles increased the prestige of aristocrats and in turn increased the political control of the monarch. A monarch might elevate a lord to an earl or an earl to a duke as a reward for support. This system of rewards bound nobles to the monarchy and theoretically lessened the likelihood of rebellion.

In England nobles had already rebelled and limited the power of the monarchy. In 1215 a coalition of noblemen defeated King John at the Battle of Runnymede and forced him to relinquish some power by signing the Magna Carta

▶ As ruler of Scotland, Robert the Bruce (1274–1329) helped unify the kingdom through military victories over the English. In this illustration from Seton's Armorial Crests, he is pictured in 1306 with his first wife, the daughter of the earl of Marr.

▲ In this portrait by Anthony Van Dyck, Charles I of England (reigned 1625–1649) is about to go hunting. By the 1600s the power and majesty of the monarchy had reached its zenith.

Tensions between the crown and Parliament in England reached their height during the Stuart monarchy. The conflict resulted in the English civil wars (1642–1651), which in turn led to the overthrow and execution of Charles I and the establishment of the Commonwealth. Even when the monarchy was restored in 1660, Parliament remained the dominant political power in English politics, and the government became a full constitutional monarchy. This state of affairs was confirmed by the Glorious Revolution of 1688, when Parliament forced the abdication of the Catholic king, James II, and offered the throne to his Protestant daughter Mary and her husband, William of Orange. The legacy of this "revolution" was a parliamentary act, the Bill of Rights (1689), which codified the relation of Parliament and the crown.

God-Given Power

Many monarchs argued that in the abstract the source of their power and authority was God. This idea, known as the divine right of kings, regarded monarchical power as divinely bestowed upon individuals and families. The Catholic Church supported this concept in order to help maintain stability within states and to reinforce society's structure and institutions. Consequently, numerous Catholic theologians gave intellectual support to the divine right of kings. The thirteenth-century Italian philosopher Thomas Aquinas even argued that people should have one God and one ruler. Other prominent Catholic thinkers who supported the divine-right theory included Gregory of Valencia and an English Jesuit, Robert Persons, both writing in the late sixteenth century.

The onset of the Reformation undermined belief in the divine right of kings. The German Reformer Martin Luther and the French theologian John Calvin both argued for a greater separation of church and state, and many of the new Protestant sects rejected the hierarchy implicit in monarchical systems. The growth of religious egalitarianism (belief in human equality) reinforced the rise of democracy in many areas.

Conversely, there was also a growth in absolutism, a form of monarchy in which the crown was the source of all law and policies. Unlike the

(Latin for "great charter"). Most of its clauses dealt with very specific offenses and were designed to protect the barons from royal abuses, including unfair imprisonment and the seizure of land by the crown. The charter also restricted the king's rights to raise money. Magna Carta's importance lies in the fact that it paved the way to a constitutional monarchy, one in which the powers of the monarch were circumscribed by a body of accepted law. Even as the Tudor monarchs Henry VIII and Elizabeth I endeavored to increase royal authority in the sixteenth century, their efforts were constrained by the customs and institutions that were founded upon or had grown out of the Magna Carta.

English model and other such systems, in which tradition and common law placed limits on royal power, absolute monarchs ruled with few or no constraints. As the power of the church declined during the Reformation, the church and the papacy no longer served as a check on royal prerogatives, and absolutism became more common in Catholic states. For instance, in the late sixteenth century French kings became increasingly resistant to papal authority and concentrated on expanding their own power through a strong, centralized state administration. This trend peaked with the reign of the Sun King, Louis XIV (1643–1715), who is said to have claimed, "L'état, c'est moi" ("I am the state"). In certain circumstances absolute monarchs became even more powerful in the religious sphere than popes. For instance, Ferdinand of Spain was able to take control of the Inquisition against the wishes of Pope Sixtus IV.

Monarchical Duties

Custom, legal and political traditions, and the power of the nobility determined the duties and powers of individual monarchs. In some states the monarch was ultimately responsible for all areas of government. In others there was a division of labor, and the monarch shared some responsibility with the nobility or career civil servants. As commerce flourished, there was a corresponding expansion in the scope of government. By the sixteenth century many monarchs had to create or expand the royal bureaucracy (the workers and civil servants who ran the government) in order to regulate the growth of trade and industry.

▲ In this portrait by the Flemish artist Paul van Somer, the seventeenth-century English king James I (who was also James VI of Scotland) wears a garter on his left leg. This adornment signifies his position as sovereign of the Order of the Garter, a knightly order that had been created in 1348 to reinforce loyalty to the English throne.

King James I of England was one of the foremost proponents of the divine right of kings. In a speech he made to Parliament in 1609, James outlined arguments justifying his belief that royal authority was bestowed by God and affirmed by the church:

The state of monarchy is the supremest thing upon earth.... Kings are justly called Gods, for that they exercise a manner or resemblance of divine power upon earth. For if you will consider the attributes to God, you shall see how they agree in the person of a king. God has power to create, or destroy, make, or unmake at his pleasure, to give life, or send death, to judge all, and to be judged nor accountable to none: to raise low things, and to make high things low at his pleasure, and to God are both soul and body due. And the like power have kings; they make and unmake their subjects: they have power of raising, and casting down: of life, and of death: judges over all their subjects, and in all causes, and yet accountable to none but God only.

In the Renaissance and the Reformation, pomp and ritual were especially important. As head of state, the monarch granted titles and honors and presided over key events, holidays, and festivals. In some states, the monarch's duties were restricted to this ceremonial role because powerful nobles or regents took over the administrative job of government. Regents—people who ruled during the absence or the minority (childhood) of a monarch—were common at this time, as many monarchs fought wars abroad or died young. Not all regents were officially appointed. In seventeenth-century France a succession of strong cardinals essentially ruled in place of the anointed king: one of the best known is Armand-Jean du Plessis, or Cardinal Richelieu, who controlled Louis XIII and implemented his own domestic and foreign policies.

Most monarchs were not just ceremonial heads of the state but also executive leaders, responsible for the way their country was run. The monarch was assisted by an inner circle of advisers and administrators, generally known as the royal household. In medieval times many of the senior positions within the royal household had been hereditary (passed on from father to son). Gradually this situation changed, and royal household posts went to able civil servants or to loyal nobles as a reward for good service.

Different monarchies used different arrangements, but in a common organization of the household, the body was divided into three main areas headed, respectively, by the chamberlain, the steward, and the master of the horse (sometimes known as the master of the hunt). The chamberlain managed the monarch's personal life, the steward oversaw the monarch's public duties, and the master of the horse supervised the royal stables, lands, and dwellings. Other prestigious posts in the royal household included the marshal or constable, who commanded the army and the constabulary, and the treasurer, who managed the royal accounts. In addition, the sovereign usually had a grand, or privy, council for advice on matters of state.

Military Role

Monarchs served as the head of their military forces. Most medieval kings actively led their

forces in battle. By demonstrating their courage and military might, sovereigns were able to lessen the chance of rebellion at home and forestall invasion by foreign forces. Direct monarchical leadership in battle was less common by the sixteenth century, however, as the medieval code of chivalry declined.

Monarchs remained both the ceremonial and executive head of the military. Even those monarchs who chose not to lead their troops on the field of battle participated in planning and strategy sessions. Monarchs to a large extent deter-

▲ In the first half of the seventeenth century, the French statesman Armand-Jean du Plessis, better known as Cardinal Richelieu, was the most influential and powerful figure behind the French monarchy. This portrait of him was painted around 1635 by an unknown artist working in the style of Philippe de Champaigne.

Queen Elizabeth I visited the English forces at Tilbury Fort before their battle with the Spanish armada in 1588 and made this speech:

My loving people, we have been persuaded by some, that are careful of our safety, to take heed how we commit ourselves to armed multitudes, for fear of treachery; but I assure you, I do not desire to live to distrust my faithful and loving people. Let tyrants fear; I have always so behaved myself that, under God, I have placed my chiefest strength and safeguard in the loyal hearts and good will of my subjects. And therefore I am come amongst you at this time, not as for my recreation or sport, but being resolved, in the midst and heat of the battle, to live or die amongst you all; to lay down, for my God, and for my kingdom, and for my people, my honor and my blood, even in the dust. I know I have but the body of a weak and feeble woman; but I have the heart of a king, and of a king of England, too; and think foul scorn that Parma or Spain, or any prince of Europe, should dare to invade the borders of my realms: to which, rather than any dishonor should grow by me, I myself will take up arms; I myself will be your general, judge, and rewarder of every one of your virtues in the field. I know already, by your forwardness, that you have deserved rewards and crowns; and we do assure you, on the word of a prince, they shall be duly paid you. In the mean my lieutenant general shall be in my stead, than whom never prince commanded a more noble and worthy subject; not doubting by your obedience to my general, by your concord in the camp, and by your valor in the field, we shall shortly have a famous victory over the enemies of my God, of my kingdom, and of my people.

mined the budgets for military operations and weapons. This involvement was especially significant during the military revolution of the period that saw the expanded use of guns, cannons, and increasingly sophisticated fortresses. Monarchs also influenced the training and composition of the officer corps. Several kingdoms, including Sweden and France, created military academies during the period, while Henry VIII of England was one monarch who helped to draft training manuals and codes of conduct. Monarchs also helped to motivate the military. Elizabeth I of England, for example, gave a stirring speech to her navy on the eve of its victory over the Spanish armada (fleet of warships).

Succession and Investiture

A strong tradition of elected monarchs existed among the German peoples of Europe. Monarchies began among the Germans as tribes or clans formed alliances and then chose one leader to rule. By the ninth century many German states had monarchs who were elected for life. Upon the monarch's death, a council of nobles known as electors met to choose a new sovereign. Electors often had special privileges or rank compared with the rest of the aristocracy—

▶ *Queen Elizabeth I, the subject of this painting by Nicholas Hilliard, was an extremely effective monarch. During her forty-five-year rule (1558–1603), she consolidated England's position as a major power.*

▲ Renaissance diplomacy was often personal and involved direct meetings between monarchs. This fourteenth-century French illumination on vellum records a meeting between the French king Charles V and the Holy Roman emperor Charles IV.

for example, they were allowed to travel freely throughout the kingdom. The meetings of electors ultimately formed the basis for the early German Reichstag, the parliament founded in 1009. After an election the Reichstag would present the new monarch with an accord, or contract, that outlined the crown's rights and responsibilities, as well as those of the nobility.

In 1356, at a diet (parliament) in Nuremberg, Emperor Charles IV established regulations for the election of the Holy Roman emperor in his Golden Bull (a bull is an edict or decree). The bull identified seven electors—the archbishops of Cologne, Mainz, and Trier, the king of Bohemia, the count palatine of the Rhine, the duke of Saxony, and the margrave (military governor) of

In 1356 Charles IV described the procedures for electing the Holy Roman emperor. One section of his edict outlines the requirements of the electors:

After, moreover, the oft-mentioned electors or their envoys shall have entered the city of Frankfort, they shall straightway on the following day at dawn, in the church of Saint Bartholomew the apostle, in the presence of all of them cause a mass to be sung to the Holy Spirit, that the Holy Spirit himself may illumine their hearts and infuse the light of his virtue into their senses; so that they, armed with his protection, may be able to elect a just, good, and useful man as king of the Romans and future emperor, and as a safeguard for the people of Christ. After such mass has been performed all those electors or their envoys shall approach the altar on which that mass has been celebrated, and there the ecclesiastical prince electors, before the gospel of Saint John: "In the beginning was the word," which must there be placed before them, shall place their hands with reverence upon their breasts. But the secular prince electors shall actually touch the said gospel with their hands. And all of them, with all their followers, shall stand there unarmed. And the archbishop of Mainz shall give to them the form of the oath, and he together with them, and they, or the envoys of the absent ones, together with him, shall take the oath in common as follows: "I, archbishop of Mainz, arch-chancellor of the holy empire throughout Germany, and prince elector, do swear on this holy gospel of God here actually placed before me, that I, through the faith which binds me to God and to the Holy Roman Empire, do intend by the help of God, to the utmost extent of my discretion and intelligence, and in accordance with the said faith, to elect one who will be suitable, as far as my discretion and discernment can tell for a temporal head of the Christian people, that is, a king of the Romans and prospective emperor. And my voice and vote, or said election, I will give without any pact, payment, price, or promise, or whatever such things may be called. So help me God and all the saints."

The Golden Bull

Brandenburg—and detailed the manner, place, and structure of the election. Significantly, the bull ended papal interference in the election process, although the empire's three senior religious leaders were among the electors. The bull also codified the power and responsibility of the emperor and the rights of the nobility within the empire. The number of electors was increased over the years, and by the fifteenth century the electors' role was more ceremonial, as the Hapsburg dynasty began to operate according to the principle of primogeniture (power passing to the firstborn son). Despite these changes, the bull was used to guide the empire for the next four hundred years.

The Polish-Lithuanian Commonwealth was another example of an elected monarchy. In 1386 the Poles elected Wladyslaw Jagiellon, the duke of Lithuania, as their monarch after he married the Polish queen Jadwiga. Poland and Lithuania were formally united in 1569 through a treaty called the Union of Lublin, which established a system of elected monarchs through a representative assembly, the Sejm.

The most common system of choosing a new sovereign was primogeniture, whereby the oldest male heir automatically became the new sovereign. If there was no male heir in the immediate family, some states bestowed the crown on the oldest female heir. In other countries, however, if there was no immediate male heir, the crown passed to the nearest male relative. Only a few states allowed for direct female succession if a female was the oldest child. Denmark was one of these: the principle of female succession was codified in Danish law in 1665. Margaret I (1353–1412) was queen of Denmark and Norway, and in 1388 she was elected regent of Sweden. Under her leadership a succession of privy councils created the Kalmar Union, which united Denmark, Norway, and Sweden under her grandnephew Erik of Pomerania (although Margaret remained the real power behind the throne during her lifetime).

CHRONOLOGY

1301
The future Edward II becomes the first English heir apparent to be made prince of Wales.

1303
Philip IV of France captures Pope Boniface VIII.

1337–1453
The Hundred Years War results in the loss of all English lands in France (except Calais).

1355
Charles IV of Luxembourg is crowned Holy Roman emperor.

1397
The Kalmar Union unites Denmark, Sweden, and Norway under one monarch (the union lasts until 1523).

1455–1485
In England the houses of York and Lancaster struggle for the throne in the Wars of the Roses.

1479
Castile and Aragon are united by Ferdinand and Isabella.

1610
Henry IV of France is assassinated; Louis XIII becomes king.

1618
The Thirty Years War begins.

1643
Louis XIV becomes king of France.

1689
An English act of Parliament, the Bill of Rights, establishes the rights of the elected Parliament over the crown.

◀ *Margaret (1353–1412), queen of Denmark and Norway and regent of Sweden, presided over the unification of the three nations in 1397. Her tomb is in the Danish royal mausoleum, at Roskilde Cathedral.*

▲ *A depiction of Henry IV being crowned king of England in 1399; it is taken from an edition of Froissart's Chronicles that was illuminated in Bruges between 1470 and 1475. Coronations were lavish events with a serious purpose; they sanctified the new monarch's ascension to the throne and legitimated his or her reign.*

Many states did not have clear laws on succession. Instead they relied on custom, but monarchs occasionally tried to change custom to benefit a favored child or to prevent a relative from another line from assuming the throne. In addition, a monarch would often die without a clear successor, a situation that might lead to a war of succession wherein various contenders fought for the throne. To avoid such conflict, monarchs often designated a successor. In England the sovereign's successor was confirmed by Parliament. Even with such safeguards, when a monarch died without a strong and widely accepted heir—for example, the successor might be very young—civil war often broke out. In England, from 1455 to 1485, the York and Lancaster families fought a civil war over the crown, from which emerged the Tudor dynasty.

During these wars of succession, rivals would often claim to be the monarch as a way to preempt challengers. In response, most states developed complicated and elaborate coronation rituals as a means to affirm the new monarch. Among the most important aspects of these rituals were oaths of allegiance by the major nobles and the consecration of the new sovereign by a church official—either a leading clergyman within the state or a representative of the pope—a custom that led to the widespread tradition of a church leader crowning the monarch.

As the Reformation progressed, an increasing number of states required their monarch to follow a specific faith. Religious disputes between sovereigns and their subjects often led to bloody civil wars, such as the French religious wars of the sixteenth century and the English civil wars a century later. On some occasions sovereigns were forced to change policies or rulings to appease subjects who had different religious beliefs: in 1566 riots by Calvinists in the Netherlands forced their ruler, the regent Margaret of Parma, to abolish the Inquisition.

Church-State Relations

Throughout the Middle Ages the church and most secular monarchs generally worked to reinforce each others' power and authority (although there were numerous individual conflicts). The onset of the Renaissance undermined the church's authority and provided an incentive for monarchs to challenge the church in order to gain political, economic, or social benefits. As a result, the power of the state grew, and the power of religious institutions declined.

A succession of monarchs were able to assert their authority with respect to the papacy. King Philip IV of France forced the pope to relocate to Avignon, an event that led to the thirty-nine-year Western Schism (1378–1417), during which there were rival popes in Avignon and Rome, and to French domination of the church for the next century. In England, King Henry VIII broke with the Catholic Church altogether in 1531 and established a new church with himself at its head. He took this step because the pope had been unwilling to grant him a divorce so that he could remarry and beget a male heir. Henry took possession of church lands in his realm and used them to increase the power of the crown.

▲ *During the Western Schism, the French monarchy managed to eclipse the power of the pope by installing a rival pontiff at Avignon. This page from the Grandes chroniques de France shows the first antipope, Robert of Geneva, being crowned as Clement VII in 1378.*

THE GROWTH OF STATE POWER IN FRANCE

During his reign (1285–1314), King Philip IV, "the Fair," strengthened the French monarchy by creating an efficient and well-organized bureaucracy. Philip's main accomplishment was the professionalization of the government. His reign marked a move from a charismatic monarchy, based on the abilities and personality of a given king, to an institutional monarchy, supported by a powerful and capable government. Hence, the monarchy could continue to function even with a weak or inefficient sovereign.

One of Philip's important legacies was the creation of a professional class of public servants. These law specialists, or legists, were granted a rank equivalent to that of a knight. They owed their status not to their martial prowess but to their merit and ability as civil servants. The legists were charged with developing law and policy and interpreting existing customs and traditions. They codified these customs into law so that Philip's successors had a competent bureaucracy and a well-established legal framework. Philip also created a system of regular meetings of the nobility and other important segments of society. In 1302 the first meeting of the States General (French parliament) was held. Philip used the body to gather support for his policies and to gain endorsement for new taxes or expenditures.

Philip strengthened royal authority at the expense of the church. He taxed the clergy in France and confiscated church land. In order to remove a potential rival source of authority or power, the king also disbanded the Knights Templar in France and seized their wealth, territory, and castles. (The Knights Templar was a politically powerful military order that controlled banking activities in Europe at that time.) Most significant, Philip initiated a long-term struggle over the papacy by having a French bishop made pope (Clement V) and by moving the papal seat to the French-controlled enclave of Avignon. Indirectly, Philip IV helped widen the compass of the Renaissance, since the Avignonese papacy spread Italian culture and humanism into northern Europe. The decline of papal power within the Italian states also accelerated the spread of Renaissance ideas.

Religion affected monarchical politics during the protracted wars of the Reformation. Monarchs used religion as a means to rally support for wars of conquest and suppression, for example, during the Dutch wars of independence (1559–1648) and the Thirty Years War (1618–1648). These conflicts combined elements of civil wars within the German states, religious conflicts between Protestants and Catholics, and wars of conquest, as various coalitions of Catholics and Protestants fought against the Holy Roman Empire of the Hapsburg dynasty. For instance, from 1625 to 1630, the Catholic monarch of France joined with the Anglican king of England in an anti-Hapsburg alliance with the Calvinist Dutch republic. The Treaty of Westphalia (1648), which ended the Thirty Years War, confirmed the nation-state—rather than the church—as the main power in international relations.

Monarchs and Exploration

The kings and queens of Europe played a major role in spurring the Age of Exploration. Monarchs supported the exploration and settlement of new areas for two reasons. First, as rival states conquered new territories, there was a strategic need to gain colonies that would provide wealth and increase state power in the face of threats from these rivals. Second, wealth and resources also boosted a monarch's personal finances. As a result, some states developed colonies that were regarded as royal property rather than land belonging to the state.

In the early 1400s, Prince Henry of Portugal financed a number of voyages to explore Africa. His explorers reached Senegal, Gambia, Guinea, and Sierra Leone and also claimed the Azores, Madeiras, and Cape Verde Islands. Henry, who became known as Henry the Navigator, also established a school of navigation at Sagres, in southwestern Portugal, where great advances were made in the technologies of shipbuilding and navigational instruments. By the time of Henry's death in 1460, the Portuguese had created a variety of major trade routes and were importing goods into Europe. Their success prompted other European states to begin efforts to establish colonies.

In 1492 Ferdinand and Isabella of Spain supported Christopher Columbus in the expedition that led to the colonization of the Americas. Henry VII of England provided financial backing for the Italian-born John Cabot to voyage in search of a northern sea route to Asia. In 1524 the Florentine navigator Giovanni da Verrazano explored the Carolinas and present-day New York on an expedition sponsored by the French, who sought to establish a colonial empire to rival Spain's.

▶ *The decline of the power of the Catholic Church was marked by the Treaty of Westphalia, the peace settlement that ended the Thirty Years War. The signing of the treaty on May 15, 1648, is the subject of this nineteenth-century painting by Claude Jacquand. It is based on an earlier painting by the seventeenth-century Flemish artist Gerard Terborch.*

John Cabot c. 1450–c. 1499

John Cabot was born Giovanni Caboto near Naples around 1450. He became a merchant and settled in Venice and then moved to Spain in 1490. Like his fellow countryman Christopher Columbus, Cabot was interested in exploration and believed that it held the promise of great financial reward. Unable to obtain backing from Spain, he moved to England. The English king, Henry VII, did not want the Spanish monarchy to gain an advantage because of Columbus's discoveries. Like Columbus, Cabot was charged with finding a quick and direct sea route to Asia. Henry VII gave Cabot a royal license to explore the areas of the West in the name of the English monarchy. Cabot's first voyage in 1496 failed because of poor weather. The following year he made a second expedition that succeeded in reaching North America. Cabot spent about a month exploring the area that is now eastern Canada, most probably Newfoundland. He returned to England a hero since many, including the king, were convinced that Cabot had discovered a northern route to Asia. Henry rewarded Cabot with cash and a life pension. The king also authorized another, larger expedition in 1498. Cabot's final voyage was disastrous. Of his five ships, only one returned. Cabot and his son Sebastian died in Canada. Nonetheless, his efforts launched an age of exploration for England.

▲ Henry VII employed the Venetian navigators John and Sebastian Cabot to seek a new trade route to Asia. The father and son are depicted in this fresco by Francesco Grisellini (1717–1783).

Legacy of Renaissance Monarchs

Between the fourteenth and seventeenth centuries, monarchies across Europe consolidated their power and authority. The result was the rise of strong centralized governments and the emergence of powerful nation-states. These new political entities combined the resources of large multistate empires and the citizen loyalty of small city-states. Modern borders began to take shape as weaker and smaller monarchies were overtaken by more dominant kingdoms. In addition, as the power of states grew, there was a decline in the power of the church.

European monarchs went on to extend their realms and authority beyond their own continent. Monarchs initiated the Age of Exploration and European expansion. They funded voyages that led to exploration and settlement in areas of Africa, Asia, and the Western Hemisphere. Foreign colonies were directly responsible to their European monarchs. At the same time, the resources from these new colonies allowed the monarchies of Europe to grow in might and prestige.

FURTHER READING

Bertelli, Sergio. *The King's Body: The Sacred Rituals of Power in Medieval and Early Modern Europe.* Translated by R. Burr Litchfield. Philadelphia, 2002.

Burns, J. H. *Lordship, Kingship, and Empire: The Idea of Monarchy, 1400–1525.* New York, 1992.

Monod, Paul Kléber. *The Power of Kings: Monarchy and Religion in Europe, 1589–1715.* New Haven, CT, 1999.

Tom Lansford

SEE ALSO
- Charles V • Elizabeth I • Ferdinand and Isabella
- Francis I • Hapsburg Empire • Henry IV
- Henry VIII • Ivan IV Vasilyevich • Maximilian I
- Nationalism • Nobility and Rank • Papacy
- Peasants' Revolts • Scotland • Spain • Stuarts, The
- Sweden • Thirty Years War

Monteverdi, Claudio

CLAUDIO MONTEVERDI (1567–1643) IS ONE OF THE GREATEST FIGURES IN THE HISTORY OF WESTERN MUSIC. HIS CAREER MARKS THE TRANSITION FROM THE RENAISSANCE TO THE BAROQUE STYLE.

The impact of Claudio Monteverdi on music has been compared with that of William Shakespeare on literature. Each artist inherited a generally accepted set of rules for producing work in his field, and each departed from established practice by focusing above all on the expression of emotion. Monteverdi turned away from the polyphonic texture of Renaissance music, in which multiple parts of equal importance imitate each other as they weave complex patterns of sound. Instead, he increasingly turned toward what he called a *seconda prattica,* a second, new style of composition that emphasized monody— a single part declaiming a text, with the other parts relegated to an accompanimental role. Monteverdi was also daring in his use of dissonance (discordant sounds) to create emotional tension. He saw his own work as a return to the practice of the ancient Greek theater: drama enhanced by music. His operas constitute the first great flowering of the dramatic potential of music. The works he wrote firmly established opera as a major new genre.

Early Life

Claudio Monteverdi was born in Cremona, in northern Italy, on May 15, 1567. He was the son of a physician and the eldest of five children.

► The Italian artist Bernardo Strozzo painted this portrait of Monteverdi around 1640, when the composer was seventy-three years old.

Little is known about his early years. As a child Monteverdi studied with the composer Marc'Antonio Ingegneri, who was choirmaster of Cremona Cathedral. There is no evidence, though, that Monteverdi was one of the boys of the cathedral choir, so it seems likely that his father paid for private lessons, a fact that suggests he grew up in a music-friendly and reasonably prosperous family. The young Monteverdi apparently received from Ingegneri a grounding in performance as a singer and as a viol (or perhaps violin) player, as well as his first lessons in composition. Monteverdi certainly seems to have been something of a child prodigy as a composer—his first work, a collection of three-part motets (polyphonic choral compositions) called *Cantiunculae sacrae* (Little Sacred Songs) was published in 1582, when he was only fifteen years old. A second collection appeared in 1583.

Life in Mantua

When Monteverdi went to Mantua around 1590, it was as a vocalist and viol player for Duke Vincenzo Gonzaga. Despite his youth Monteverdi appears to have set his hopes on the position of *maestro di cappella* (head of the ducal musicians) when the incumbent died in 1596. The twenty-nine-year-old Monteverdi's ambition was not completely unreasonable. He had good

In this painting by Justus Sustermans, Vincenzo Gonzaga, the ruler of Mantua from 1587 to 1612, wears a cloak of the Order of the Redeemer.

Vincenzo Gonzaga   1562–1612

For all but the few musicians and artists who were independently wealthy, it was vital to find a noble, wealthy patron. By 1592 the young Monteverdi had secured an enviable position at the court of Vincenzo Gonzaga, duke of Mantua, in northern Italy—though it may be safer to say that Monteverdi probably thought himself fortunate at the time. It is plain, however, that long before he was released from service to the Gonzagas, he felt constrained at the Mantuan court and longed to escape to a position that would show his talents to better advantage.

Monteverdi's problem was that the Duchy of Mantua had entered a deep decline by the early seventeenth century. Mantua had been a wealthy city and leading center of cloth production throughout the sixteenth century. Revenue from cloth had allowed the dukes and duchesses of Mantua to play a role as brilliant patrons of the arts and letters. By Monteverdi's time, however, revenues were shrinking, a circumstance aggravated by Vincenzo Gonzaga's extravagant expenditure in every direction but patronage. Most notably, the duke waged several cripplingly expensive and ineffective campaigns against the Turks. Little money was left over for Monteverdi and others like him, although Vincenzo still appears to have had a good eye for quality; for example, he employed the young Flemish painter Peter Paul Rubens during the period when Monteverdi was in Mantua. It is possible to see the Gonzaga family's dwindling resources in Vincenzo's effort to hire the great Italian astronomer and mathematician Galileo Galilei. The pay that the duke offered to Galileo was much lower than he was receiving for the position he already held, and so he demanded more; he never received what he asked for, though, and never entered the duke's service.

credentials and had proven himself to be a prolific and appealing composer. He had already published his first book of madrigals before coming to Mantua, and the pace of his composition does not appear to have slowed during these early years at the duke's court. Monteverdi was deeply disappointed when another court musician, Benedetto Pallavicino, was named *maestro de cappella,* but he won the coveted position in 1601, when Pallavicino died.

As a ducal musician Monteverdi would have played or sung for religious services in the duke's

▲ *The title page from the 1620 Venetian edition of book 6 of the madrigals for five voices. The printing press enabled Monteverdi's compositions to be published quickly and reprinted often.*

chapel, performed for secular entertainments at court, and taken a part in processions and other public events. He also seems to have been free to take private students on the side: in 1599 he married his favorite pupil, the court singer Caterina de Cattaneis Martinelli. The two appear to have had a happy marriage, which produced three children. Caterina's death in 1607 may have increased Monteverdi's desire to leave Mantua—he had already complained of its bad climate, its provinciality, and the stinginess of the duke. Another important reason for Monteverdi's wish to leave must have been the simple belief that he could do better for himself elsewhere. He had won a considerable reputation for his increasingly daring music.

Monteverdi's Madrigals

The progression of Monteverdi's musical thought can be seen best in the eight books of secular madrigals he published in the period between 1587 and 1638, as well as in a ninth book that appeared posthumously in 1651. Madrigals—polyphonic songs in the vernacular (rather than Latin) that usually display a wide range of speeds and rhythms—were extremely popular from the time the first collection was published in 1530 until the mid-seventeenth century. It is impossible to be precise in defining the madrigal since the genre varied widely over time; indeed, nowhere is the development of the madrigal clearer than in the work of Monteverdi. The madrigals included in book 1, completed by the time the composer was seventeen, are not particularly original; the early books in general show a deep musical debt to the Italian composer Luca

THE ARTUSI DEBATE

While Monteverdi's new style fascinated many, it also drew attacks from more conservative musicians. Monteverdi's foremost critic was the theorist and composer Giovanni Maria Artusi of Bologna (c. 1545–1613), whose loud denunciations won Monteverdi more fame throughout the musical world than he could otherwise have hoped for, living as he was in the backwater of Mantua. In both 1600 and 1603, Artusi attacked the "crudities" and "license" of Monteverdi's more novel work. Monteverdi responded to these charges in the introduction to his fifth book of madrigals (1605). This text served as the first great manifesto of the *seconda prattica*—the new method of composition in which words play a dominant part. The point of his innovations, Monteverdi argued, was dramatic, an attempt to express the full range of emotion. He also used this approach to justify the use of dissonance, which Artusi had attacked. The controversy continued over several years, with both Monteverdi and his brother Giulio Cesare responding to Artusi's complaints. In the process, Monteverdi won a reputation as the leader of the "modern" school of musical thought.

Marenzio (c. 1553–1599), the leading Italian madrigalist before Monteverdi. By the fourth madrigal book (1603), Monteverdi was branching out in new directions. The works in this volume were marked by ever-increasing chromaticism—for the composer, the unsupplemented seven notes of a given major or minor scale had become inadequate to his goal: to maximize the dramatic impact of the text. Monteverdi had also begun playing with imitative sound effects and had so far departed from the traditional madrigal polyphony that he introduced passages of declamatory solo singing.

By 1605, when the fifth book of madrigals was published, Monteverdi had moved from a Renaissance to a baroque conception of music. An innovation he added in book 5, the continuo, became the most distinctive feature of baroque music. The continuo is a bass part that is executed by one or more musical instruments and is marked with numbers to show which chords should be played. The use of this device underlined the fact that the music Monteverdi was writing was conceived for a solo voice with an instrumental chordal accompaniment.

Orfeo

In 1607 Monteverdi made another sensational departure when he created his first opera; it was the first work to show the potential of the new genre. This work, *La favola d'Orfeo* (The Legend of Orpheus), was a musical drama in a prologue and five acts, with a libretto by the poet Alessandro Striggio set to music by Monteverdi. The work was composed for Mantua's yearly carnival, apparently at the request of Vincenzo Gonzago, who had probably heard an earlier opera on a visit to Florence.

CHRONOLOGY

1627
His son Massimiliano is arrested by the Inquisition and released the following year.

1632
Scherzi musicali, a collection of light vocal music, is published.

1636
Monteverdi employs the young composers Francesco Manelli and Benedetto Ferrari.

1643
The ballet *La vittoria d'Amore* (now lost) is performed at the Venice opera house.

1643
Monteverdi dies in Venice on November 29.

◄ *Early-seventeenth-century artists in all disciplines, not just music, were preoccupied with emotional states, as may be seen in this painting,* Melancholy *(c. 1622), by the Venetian Domenico Feti.*

▲ *The title page of Monteverdi's opera* Orfeo, *published in Venice in 1609. Thanks to the printing press, the new genre of opera reached a large number of musicians quickly.*

Orfeo retold the ancient Greek myth of the hero and musician Orpheus, his love for Eurydice, her death from a snakebite, and his descent into Hades (the Greek underworld) to rescue her. It had a much greater dramatic impact than earlier operas. Much of the composition consists of a single voice supported by a colorful instrumental accompaniment. A chorus appears only occasionally. *Orfeo* is the first important example of a composer giving full consideration to the effects that can be created with an orchestra. The orchestra for this opera was large by the standards of the time; of particular significance is the fact that Monteverdi specified which instruments were supposed to play the various parts. The directions he provided were much more explicit than the vague annotations that had begun to appear in instrumental music over the course of the preceding two decades.

Orfeo was well received by the private audience that first heard it, and Monteverdi's second opera, produced the following year, was even more popular. *L'Arianna* was based on the ancient legend of the Cretan princess Ariadne. Since opera was invented as a revival of ancient Greek drama, composers and librettists naturally gravitated toward classical themes. In Greek mythology Ariadne helped the hero Theseus to kill the Minotaur, a monster that lived in a labyrinth by her father's palace. She gave Theseus a thread to unwind so that he could find his way out of the maze. In return, Theseus took Ariadne away from Crete. Unfortunately, the only part of the music from Monteverdi's opera that survives is "Arianna's Lament," a haunting melody that was popular throughout the seventeenth century. It has been suggested (with little supporting data) that Monteverdi composed the lament while mourning his wife's death.

Monteverdi's Vespers

In 1608 Claudio Monteverdi returned to Cremona, although the Gonzaga family refused to release him from its service until 1612. This stubborn attitude did not prevent Monteverdi from doing everything he could to win a more prestigious position. The search for a new patron is the unromantic background to one of the most striking collections of sacred music ever made, Monteverdi's *Vespro della Beata Vergine* (Vespers of the Blessed Virgin) of 1610. Monteverdi dedicated this collection (which included music besides the Vespers) to Pope Paul V, apparently in the hope that it would win him appointment to the papal chapel in Rome.

The movements of the Vespers show Monteverdi's impressive versatility, and they may have been intended as an advertisement of his ability to accommodate every musical taste. The work makes use of both the *prima* and the *seconda prattica;* Renaissance and baroque styles are placed side by side. The Vespers proper is accompanied by a full setting of the ordinary of the Mass (the parts of the Mass that do not change from day to day), written in the old style and based on a motet by the early-sixteenth-century Flemish composer Nicolas Gombert. The collection's motets, however, are in the new style. They are set for virtuoso singers with instrumental accompaniment.

Virtuosity in performance became a hallmark of the baroque, and Monteverdi points the way toward the prima donna (leading lady) of the future with the Vespers. The work makes enormous demands on performers. The various pieces have up to ten independent vocal parts, and some sections even require separate choirs. There are also seven vocal solo parts and solos for violin and cornetto. In all cases, the musical setting is intimately related to the needs of the text. Thus, the motet *Nigra sum,* a delicate love song from the Bible's Song of Songs, is performed by a solo tenor, supported by a choir. Similarly, the motet

Duo seraphim (with a text from Isaiah 6:3) starts as a vocal duet, but when the Trinity is mentioned in the text, a third tenor joins in. The more vigorous *Laudate pueri* (Psalm 112) features an eight-part choir and organ. The effect is splendid. Like *Orfeo,* the Vespers is a work that straddles the Renaissance and baroque. Indeed, the two works are closely related, as Monteverdi reuses some music from *Orfeo* in the Vespers.

▼ *This portrait of Paul V (reigned 1605–1621), to whom Monteverdi dedicated his Vespers, was painted by an unknown follower of Caravaggio.*

Monteverdi in Venice

In 1613 Monteverdi won a very prestigious musical appointment—as *maestro di cappella* (musical director) for Saint Mark's Cathedral in Venice. He remained in that position until his death. Freed by several assistants from the need to compose small-scale works for routine ceremonies, Monteverdi produced mostly larger-scale works for ceremonial occasions in this second half of his career. The main exception to this rule was his ongoing experimentation with the madrigal, which saw fruit in the publication of several more books of madrigals. These works show Monteverdi's continuing development as a musician. The sixth book includes some pieces that require a harpsichord accompaniment, while the seventh book consists mostly of solos, duets, and trios with accompaniment—something very unlike the traditional definition of a Renaissance madrigal. The seventh and eighth books also include some short stage works. The part of book 8 (1638) known as the *Madrigale dei guerrieri e amorosi* (Madrigals of Warriors and Lovers) is regarded as the high point of the madrigal genre. In his tenure at Venice, Monteverdi also attracted students from as far afield as England, Germany, and Scandinavia.

The Later Operas

Monteverdi returned to opera in 1627 with a private contract to compose a work known as *La finta pazza Licori* (Licori Who Feigned Madness), a pastoral comedy that was never performed and is now lost. Although he did not write full-scale operas again until 1640, a number of operatic scenes were Monteverdi's vehicle for continuing musical experimentation. The most notable innovations appear in *Il combattimento di Tancredi e Clorinda* (The Combat of Tancred and Clorinda), a ballet with operatic interludes based on an episode of the sixteenth-century Italian poet Torquato Tasso's *Gerusalemme liberata* (1581). This work includes two new string techniques that are still frequently employed in composition: tremolo (frenetic back-and-forth bowing on the same pitch) and pizzicato (plucking rather than bowing stringed instruments for special effect). Both were used to add yet another layer of dramatic impact.

In 1637 Venice opened its first opera house, and Monteverdi again became more active in composing opera. *L'Arianna* was revived in this new venue in 1640. Its success encouraged him to produce no fewer than three full operas, which were first performed in 1641 and 1642: *Il ritorno d'Ulisse in patria* (Ulysses' Return to His Homeland), *Le nozze d'Enea con Lavinia* (The Marriage of Aeneas and Lavinia), which unfortunately no longer exists, and his last masterpiece, *L'incoronazione di Poppea* (The Coronation of Poppea).

Last Years

In 1633 Monteverdi had been ordained a priest, perhaps as a response to a virulent outbreak of the plague. His clerical status does not appear to have affected his musical output. Monteverdi had always composed some religious music and continued to do so until the end of his life. Two col-

▼ Trained as a viol player, Monteverdi was exposed at a young age to new instruments with an expanded range and expressive capability that may have influenced his work as a composer. Carlo Saraceni's painting Saint Cecilia and the Angel (c. 1610) depicts the angel holding the newly developed bass viol.

THE CORONATION OF POPPEA

Monteverdi's final opera, *L'incoronazione di Poppea*, is often described as the greatest opera of the seventeenth century. Its powerful libretto was written by Giovanni Busenello (1598–1659), who has been called the first great opera librettist. Based on the writings of the Roman historian Tacitus, the opera tells the story of Emperor Nero's love for Poppea, a married woman, and how the emperor takes Poppea from her husband, Ottone, who still loves her. Betrayal and corruption are the main themes of the opera, which also includes the suicide of the philosopher Seneca after he is condemned to death.

In *L'incoronazione*, Monteverdi proved himself innovative to the end. The opera pushes realistic character portrayal to a new level. At the same time, figures appear larger than life, especially since Monteverdi made the orchestra smaller and reduced the choir's role. Moreover, this opera was the first to include both comic and tragic scenes. It has been performed frequently since its modern revival in 1937.

▲ The triumphant closing scene from a 1975 production of Monteverdi's *L'incoronazione di Poppea*.

lections of religious music were published, one in 1641 and the other posthumously in 1650. These collections show how difficult it is to categorize Monteverdi's musical output: when he thought it appropriate, the composer continued to produce works in the old style, side by side with works that can be described as baroque. The few masses he produced in this late period remain in the old polyphonic style, perhaps because novelties would not be acceptable to the congregations that heard them. Monteverdi's late psalms and motets, however, were thoroughly "modern"; he appears to have used the motet as a vehicle for musical experimentation, as had so many composers before him.

Beyond these late works, little is known of Monteverdi's end. He made a trip to his home town of Cremona in 1643 and fell ill while returning to Venice. He died there on November 29, 1643.

FURTHER READING

Carter, Tim. *Monteverdi's Musical Theater.* New Haven, CT, 2002.

———. *Music in Late Renaissance and Early Baroque Italy.* Portland, OR, 1992.

Leopold, Silke. *Monteverdi: Music in Transition.* Translated by Anne Smith. New York, 1991.

Monteverdi, Claudio. *The Letters of Claudio Monteverdi.* Translated by Denis Stevens. Rev. ed. New York, 1995.

Ossi, Massimo Michele. *Divining the Oracle: Monteverdi's Seconda Prattica.* Chicago, 2003.

Phyllis G. Jestice

SEE ALSO

- Florence • Italian City-States • Music
- Popular Culture • Rubens, Peter Paul • Venice

More, Thomas

THOMAS MORE (1478–1535) WAS AN
ENGLISH STATESMAN AND PHILOSOPHER
WHOSE PRINCIPLES, ACTIONS, AND
WRITINGS INFLUENCED HIS FELLOW
RENAISSANCE SCHOLARS AND
ULTIMATELY LED TO HIS CANONIZATION.

Thomas More was born in London in 1478. His father, John More, was a well-respected judge. Education was important to the family, and the young More began his education at Saint Anthony's School. When he turned thirteen, More joined the household of the archbishop of Canterbury as a page. Two years later he enrolled at Oxford, where he studied the Greek and Roman classics, French, and history. He studied under the famous Thomas Linacre, who founded the Royal College of Physicians, and William Grocyn, who is credited with introducing the study of Greek to Oxford. Although More devoted considerable energy to his studies while at Oxford, he found time to develop an interest in music and learned to play several instruments, including the violin. He also began to write. His earliest works were comedies, but he also translated some Italian works into English, including the biography of the humanist scholar Giovanni Pico della Mirandola. Drawn to both religion and law, More decided to concentrate on law. In 1494 he returned to London, where he was admitted to the bar in 1501.

More quickly became a noted lecturer and teacher in London. He also met many of the

▶ *This portrait of Thomas More, which perfectly captures its subject's intellect and piety, was made at the school of Hans Holbein the Younger during the early years of More's career.*

Desiderius Erasmus and Thomas More were close friends and collaborators. Erasmus described More in a letter of 1519:

He seems born and framed for friendship, and is a most faithful and enduring friend. He is easy of access to all; but if he chances to get familiar with one whose vices admit no correction, he manages to loosen and let go the intimacy rather than to break it off suddenly. When he finds any sincere and according to his heart, he so delights in their society and conversation as to place in it the principal charm of life. He abhors games of tennis, dice, cards, and the like, by which most gentlemen kill time. Though he is rather too negligent of his own interests, no one is more diligent in those of his friends. In a word, if you want a perfect model of friendship, you will find it in no one better than in More. In society he is so polite, so sweet-mannered, that no one is of so melancholy a disposition as not to be cheered by him, and there is no misfortune that he does not alleviate. Since his boyhood he has so delighted in merriment, that it seems to be part of his nature; yet he does not carry it to buffoonery, nor did he ever like biting pleasantries. When a youth he both wrote and acted some small comedies. If a retort is made against himself, even without ground, he likes it from the pleasure he finds in witty repartees. Hence he amused himself with composing epigrams when a young man, and enjoyed Lucian above all writers. Indeed, it was he who pushed me to write the Praise of Folly, *that is to say, he made a camel frisk [he made a creature reluctant to work—Erasmus himself—eager to work].*

In human affairs there is nothing from which he does not extract enjoyment, even from things that are most serious. If he converses with the learned and judicious, he delights in their talent; if with the ignorant and foolish, he enjoys their stupidity. He is not even offended by professional jesters. With a wonderful dexterity he accommodates himself to every disposition. As a rule, in talking with women, even with his own wife, he is full of jokes and banter.

Letter to Ulrich von Hutten

most famous intellectuals of the time. In 1497 he met the Dutch humanist Desiderius Erasmus, who was on his first visit to England. The two became lifelong friends and worked together on a variety of scholarly projects, including Latin translations of prominent works. In 1506 they published a Latin translation of the works of the ancient Greek satirist Lucian. Erasmus believed that More represented the best of contemporary Christianity and held up his English friend as a model for others. Erasmus was particularly drawn to More's intellect and his ability to reconcile the religious and secular components of his life. More convinced Erasmus to complete his 1509 masterpiece, *Praise of Folly,* which was dedicated to More.

Religious Influences

Although More embarked upon a career of law and public service, he also maintained his religious inclinations. While studying law, More lived in a charterhouse (Carthusian monastery). Although he did not formally join the order, he adopted many of its traditions and rituals. More was especially drawn to the more austere aspects of the monastic life, especially the solitude and freedom from material considerations. More

▲ *Hans Holbein the Younger (c. 1497–1543) painted this portrait of the Dutch scholar Desiderius Erasmus, who was a writer and philosopher as well as More's longtime friend.*

▼ *The seventeenth-century French artist Nicolas Mignard painted this portrait of the Carthusian order's founder, Saint Bruno (1032–1101), praying in the desert. The order's austerity was particularly attractive to More.*

regularly prayed and fasted. He wore a coarse hair shirt, made from goat hair, as a sign of his piety and disdain for secular comforts. During this period More considered becoming a priest or joining one of the monastic orders, either the Carthusians or the Franciscans.

Several factors prevented him from joining a monastery or entering the priesthood. First, he was displeased at the corruption and vice of some church officials who used their office and vocation as a means to gain wealth and influence. Second, More did not believe he could remain celibate. He wanted to eventually marry and perhaps raise a family. Although More remained a deeply religious individual, these factors led him to abandon plans for the priesthood and instead embark on a career in public service. In 1505 More married Jane Colte, with whom he had four children. Jane died in 1511. More remarried a month after Jane's death. His second wife, Alice Middleton, was a widow who was seven years older than More; she soon took over the care of his young children and the management of his household.

Early Career in Public Service

In 1504 More was elected to Parliament. He quickly became noted for his opposition to the efforts of King Henry VII (reigned 1485–1509) to gain parliamentary approval for a one-time appropriation of £113,000—the money was to cover the expenses of his daughter Margaret's marriage to James IV of Scotland. More believed that the sum was excessive and that the increase in taxes would impose hardship on the poor. Through his leadership the appropriation was reduced to £30,000. While the episode brought More public acclaim, it also resulted in royal retaliation. Henry VII had More's father imprisoned in the Tower of London. To secure his release, More had to pay a large fine, leave Parliament, and retire from public life. However, he returned to public service after Henry's death in 1509. In 1510 More was appointed one of London's two undersheriffs (officials who administered court orders). In this post he developed a reputation for his honesty, judgment, and kindness toward the poor.

More's actions as undersheriff attracted the attention of Henry VIII (reigned 1509–1547), who placed him in a succession of important posts. The new king came to value More's service and abilities. In 1515 the king dispatched More as part of a delegation to settle a trade dispute with Flanders. In return for his prior services, including his time as undersheriff and his actions during the mission, the king granted More a pension for life in 1516. The following year More helped to subdue a revolt against foreign merchants and traders in London. In 1518 Henry VIII appointed More as a member of the Privy Council (the body of officials who advised the king on matters of state). A year later More resigned as undersheriff and began to work for the king and government full-time. More accompanied Henry to France to participate in the Field of the Cloth of Gold, a meeting between the English and French monarchs that was known for its opulence and political insignificance since no treaty or agreement could be reached. In 1521 More was knighted for his public service. Over the next decade, More became one of the most powerful political figures in England and a close confidant of Henry VIII. At the same time, his interests in religion and the law continued and resulted in More's main contribution to political philosophy, his 1516 book *Utopia*.

Utopia and Other Works

More wrote a series of poems between 1492 and 1494. Most were lively and dealt with contemporary subjects, ranging from politics to home

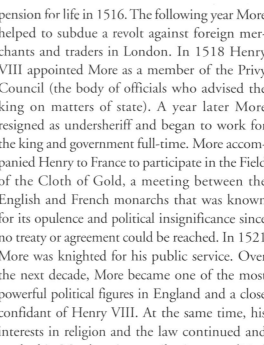

◄ *Although More initially considered becoming a monk, he eventually married and had a large family, presented here in this miniature (c. 1593) by Rowland Lockey.*

decor. From 1513 to 1518, More worked on a long historical study, the *History of Richard III*, in which he harshly criticized the fifteenth-century English monarch. Although unfinished, the work was published by a nephew in 1557 and later influenced William Shakespeare's play *Richard III* (1592–1593). More went on to write a number of religious works, but his most significant book was *Utopia*.

More began writing *Utopia* while on the trade mission to Flanders. The book became his best-known work and influenced a range of later works of political philosophy. More was inspired by the *Republic*, written in the fourth century BCE by the Greek philosopher Plato, which describes different political systems and then advocates an ideal form of politics. Both More and Plato examine their respective societies through the use of a dialogue between characters. Both works favored democracy, although More uses a much broader democratic system than Plato. Unlike Plato, More examines all aspects of his ideal society—not only its politics but also its economics and culture. In addition, while Plato

◀ *The Greek philosopher Plato (c. 428–348 BCE), here represented in an ancient marble bust, influenced a range of Renaissance scholars. Like Plato's* Republic, More's Utopia *was an analysis of the best systems of government.*

In this excerpt from his best-known work, More recounts a conversation with a fictional Portuguese traveler, Raphael Hythloday, who speaks of the problems with the European political system:

For most princes apply themselves more to affairs of war than to the useful arts of peace; and in these I neither have any knowledge, nor do I much desire it: they are generally more set on acquiring new kingdoms, right or wrong, than on governing well those they possess. And among the ministers of princes, there are none that are not so wise as to need no assistance, or at least that do not think themselves so wise that they imagine they need none; and if they court any, it is only those for whom the prince has much personal favor, whom by their fawnings and flatteries they endeavor to fix to their own interests: and indeed Nature has so made us that we all love to be flattered, and to please ourselves with our own notions. The old crow loves his young, and the ape her cubs. Now if in such a court, made up of persons who envy all others, and only admire themselves, a person should but propose anything that he had either read in history or observed in his travels, the rest would think that the reputation of their wisdom would sink, and that their interest would be much depressed, if they could not run it down: and if all other things failed, then they would fly to this, that such or such things pleased our ancestors, and it were well for us if we could but match them. They would set up their rest on such an answer, as a sufficient confutation of all that could be said, as if it were a great misfortune, that any should be found wiser than his ancestors; but though they willingly let go all the good things that were among those of former ages, yet if better things are proposed they cover themselves obstinately with this excuse of reverence to past times. I have met with these proud, morose, and absurd judgments of things in many places, particularly once in England.

Thomas More, Introduction to *Utopia*

divides his society into three hereditary classes, More's utopian society is highly egalitarian.

More critiques the contemporary political, legal, and social system of England and offers an alternative in the form of the state of Utopia (which literally means "nowhere"). Combining a Christian morality (which includes care for those less fortunate) and hierarchy (manifested by the church structure) with social and economic equality so that all have similar opportunities, Utopia has a representative government to ensure equality. Families are grouped together in units under the supervision of a leader known as a *philarch* ("dear leader"), and groups of ten *philarchs* are governed by a chief *philarch*. The people nominate candidates to be the land's leader or prince, and the *philarchs* vote in an election between the four candidates with the highest number of nominations. Councils of political and religious leaders govern all aspects of society and maintain the values and customs of the land. The economic system of Utopia is very similar to that of modern communism in that the people jointly share the wealth and surplus produced by the economy. Since there is joint ownership of property, there is no need for money.

More coined the term *Utopia,* which has since entered the English language to mean a perfect society. Many later political thinkers have described their own utopian systems, including the English philosopher Francis Bacon (1561–1626) and the sociologist and historian H. G. Wells (1866–1946). More's ideas were also incorporated into key political movements of the nineteenth and twentieth centuries, such as socialism and communism.

Rise to Power

Henry VIII came to rely on More for political, personal, and religious counsel. In 1521 More helped the king with his manuscript *A Defense of the Seven Sacraments,* a response to Martin Luther's Ninety-five Theses (the writings condemning the sale of indulgences that Luther had nailed to the church door in Wittenberg on October 31, 1517). In response Pope Leo X granted Henry the title Defender of the Faith.

In 1521 Henry appointed More to the post of deputy treasurer. He had More elected speaker of the House of Commons in 1523 and also granted More several tracts of land in Chelsea. As speaker, More drew on memories of his experiences with the king's father, Henry VII, and campaigned to give members of Parliament the right to criticize the monarchy without fear of retribution. More became increasingly convinced that Parliament should have greater independence of the royal power, and he was not afraid to oppose Henry when he disagreed with the king.

▲ *This woodcut engraving by Ambrosius Holbein prefaced the 1518 edition of More's* Utopia, *published in Basel. In the bottom left-hand corner is the traveler Raphael Hythloday, who supposedly discovered the state of Utopia.*

An unattributed engraving of More's estate in Chelsea. Along with his rise in status and influence came great wealth.

Henry initially valued More's independence and forthrightness. More continued to receive honors and awards for his service. In 1525 he was appointed steward of Cambridge University and chancellor of the duchy of Lancaster. More and Henry became friends and spent hours in conversation walking through the royal gardens of Hampton Court or around More's estate. Henry was particularly interested in how the writings of the great Greek and Roman philosophers could be used to shape government policy. The two also discussed how the church could defend itself from the spread of Lutheranism.

In 1527 Henry asked More to help him gain a divorce, as his marriage to Catherine of Aragon had failed to produce a male heir. More opposed the king's plan to divorce, but Henry continued to look to him for advice. In 1529 More was appointed lord chancellor and so became responsible for reviewing and enforcing all laws, including those that concerned religious matters. Although he was the first layman to hold the position, many contemporary scholars and judges believed that More was the fairest, most competent chancellor in English history. In spite of the power that came with it, the chancellorship was a dangerous post. Henry had already pun-

ished several previous chancellors who disagreed with him. More's predecessor, Cardinal Thomas Wolsey, had been stripped of his office and most of his property and other wealth in 1529 after he failed to gain Henry a papal decree of divorce.

More continued to write, and he participated in the ongoing religious debates over the Reformation. In 1528 he wrote *Dialogue concerning Heresies and Matters of Religion,* in which he argued that the problems within the church were the result of individual actions and misdeeds not widespread structural faults. This work paralleled More's broader religious philosophy, in which he acknowledged deficiencies in church doctrine and policy but thought that reform from within was the best solution.

Fall from Power

As Henry VIII's dispute with Pope Clement VII over his desire for a divorce became more heated, More was increasingly uncomfortable as chancellor. In 1531 he would not add his signature to a letter from prominent politicians asking the pope to annul Henry's marriage. When the pope refused to declare the marriage invalid, Henry established a new church, the Church of England, with himself at its head. He forced

More and others to take an oath that declared the monarchy the head of the church within the bounds of holy law. The king also had Parliament pass legislation that gave the monarchy control of the church's lands and financial resources. More tried to resign, but the king refused the resignation. More was able to step down a year later when Henry decided for a complete break with the Catholic Church.

More tried to return to private life and concentrate on writing. He sought to remain neutral in the religious dispute going on around him but was unable to do so. In 1533 More was indicted on a charge of treason, along with other prominent Catholics. The House of Lords refused to accept More's indictment, and Henry was forced to withdraw the charges.

In 1534 Henry demanded a new, more far-reaching oath to accept recent legislation, the Act of Succession and the Act of Supremacy. The first of these laws acknowledged Anne Boleyn as queen; the second denied the authority of the pope over English Catholics and affirmed Henry as the head of the church. More would not take the oath. In April he was arrested and imprisoned in the Tower of London. While in the Tower he continued to write and exchanged letters with various family members and friends. Many of

▲ This portrait of William Tyndale (c. 1494–1536) adorns the title page of his translation of the Bible, the first in English; his work was significantly influenced by Protestant thinkers, including Martin Luther. Much of More's religious work was written to counter the growing strength of Protestantism in England.

DIALOGUE CONCERNING HERESIES

Dialogue concerning Heresies and Matters of Religion was More's response to the growing number of books printed in English that criticized or undermined the church. In William Tyndale's English version of the Bible, for example, some passages were based on Martin Luther's translations from Latin, which replaced the word *church* with *congregation* and the word *penance* with *repentance*.

More set out to write a work that laypeople in England could use to refute the arguments of the Protestants. It was the first time he had written in English, not Latin. He drew on popular English writers and poets to reinforce his points. In a discussion of pilgrimages, for example, he quotes Geoffrey Chaucer's *Canterbury Tales*.

More's work centers around a dialogue between a Catholic and a Protestant who discuss matters of theology and problems within the Catholic Church. More uses a fictional Protestant character, known as the Messenger, to lay out the main charges and complaints against the Catholic Church and the other character to rebut them. More modeled the Catholic narrator on himself. The book is divided into four parts. In the first two, More describes the church's presence in the world. He writes about church buildings, shrines, miracles, church worship, penance, and pilgrimages. In the final two sections, More explains why the church has the right and duty to punish heretics (people who do not accept church doctrine). Specifically, More attempts to justify the church's efforts to punish the leaders of the growing Protestant movements and to discredit Tyndale's translation of the Bible and the main tenets of Lutheranism.

First published in 1528, *Dialogue concerning Heresies* proved so popular that a second edition was printed in 1531 and a third in 1557.

DIALOGUE OF COMFORT AGAINST TRIBULATION

Dialogue of Comfort against Tribulation is More's most moving and revealing work. While in the Tower of London, More found comfort in writing. He also clearly understood that he was likely to die as a result of his beliefs and his unwillingness to compromise his faith.

As with several previous books, the work took the form of a dialogue between two characters: a wealthy young man, Vincent, and his dying uncle, Anthony. The two discuss mortality, religion, and fear. The work is set in Hungary during the time of the Ottoman invasion, which began in 1521. Vincent is afraid of the advancing Turkish army and of what will happen to himself and his family.

The sage uncle clearly represents More, who uses the book to reassure his family and friends of the power and importance of faith. He makes it clear that his beliefs have dispelled his own fear of dying and that he faces death with humor and serenity. More also uses the dialogue to examine the dilemma of why God allows good people to suffer. He explains that people often forget God during times of prosperity, but it is during times of trial that many turn to religion for strength and courage.

▼ *The arrest and execution of Thomas More is presented in this detail from a sixteenth-century painting by Antoine Caron, which, in the style of the period, replaces the dress of the day with clothing from classical times.*

More's letters contained his core arguments against Henry's split with the pope; the letters were later used as evidence against More. He also began writing his last great work, *Dialogue of Comfort against Tribulation*.

Trial and Execution

On July 1, 1535, More was indicted for treason for his unwillingness to take the oath required for the Act of Supremacy. Much of the evidence against More was fabricated and designed to make it appear that he had actively sought to undermine the monarchy. More denied the testimony of his accusers but did not dispute the basic charge over the oath. After his trial he was found guilty and sentenced to be hanged, drawn, and quartered. The king lessened the sentence to simple execution. More was beheaded on July 6, 1535. In his last words he called himself "the king's good servant, but God's first." More was beatified (declared blessed) by Pope Leo XIII in 1886 and canonized (elevated to sainthood) by Pope Pius XI in 1935.

FURTHER READING

Marius, Richard. *Thomas More: A Biography.* New York, 1984.

More, Thomas. *Utopia.* Translated by Clarence Miller. New Haven, CT, 2001.

Ridley, Jasper Godwin. *Statesman and Saint: Cardinal Wolsey, Sir Thomas More, and the Politics of Henry VIII.* New York, 1982.

Sylvester, R. S., and G. P. Marc'hadour, eds. *Essential Articles for the Study of Thomas More.* Hamden, CT, 1977.

Tom Lansford

SEE ALSO

• Bacon, Francis • Bibles • Chaucer, Geoffrey
• Church of England • Erasmus, Desiderius
• Henry VIII • Humanism and Learning
• Lutheranism • Shakespeare

Muscovy

MUSCOVY AROSE IN THE THIRTEENTH CENTURY AS A SMALL CITY-STATE THAT CENTERED ON THE CITY OF MOSCOW. WITHIN 250 YEARS THE RULERS OF MUSCOVY HAD BECOME THE CZARS OF ALL RUSSIA.

Between 1237 and 1241 the various city-states that made up the region now known as Russia were conquered by the Mongols (Tatars). For the next two hundred years, the Russians were subjects of the Tatar khan (ruler), who was based at Sarai (near present-day Volgograd) on the lower reaches of the Volga River but had troops stationed in most major Russian towns.

The Tatar Yoke

Russia's isolation under the Tatars was made worse by the hostility of its western neighbors, particularly the Swedes and Lithuanians. In 1240 the prince of Novgorod, Alexander Nevsky (c. 1220–1263), led his army to a victory over the Swedes at the Neva River, from which he took his name. Nevsky realized it would be hopeless to resist the Tatars and became the khan's vassal (servant). In 1258 he suppressed an uprising in Novgorod over Tatar taxes.

Other Russian princes followed Nevsky's example. They continued to rule their lands but only after securing the khan's permission, acknowledging that they were his *kholopy* (slaves), and promising to deliver tribute. Loyal service, regular tribute, and feudal deference to the khan were the route to political power—a route followed by Ivan I, prince of Moscow from 1328 to 1341. As the khan's most reliable tax collector, Ivan earned the name Kalita ("moneybag") and was allowed to expand his lands at the expense of other Russian rulers. Ivan's expansion began the process that eventually saw the transformation of the city-state of Moscow into the Russian nation.

▶ In this nineteenth-century painting by Henryk Siemiradski, Alexander Nevsky, prince of Novgorod, receives foreign envoys. Nevsky's son, Daniel, would become the first grand prince of Muscovy.

In 1380 Prince Dmitry Donskoi (reigned 1359–1389) took the first step toward breaking free of the Tatars when he defeated them at Kulikovo Field. Although the Tatars sacked Moscow two years later, they never fully reestablished their rule. Muscovite princes acknowledged the Tatar khan as overlord but acted ever more independently. (In 1480 Ivan III, "the Great," who reigned from 1462 to1505, formally rejected any allegiance to the khan.) As Tatar control declined, Muscovy grew more powerful. Dmitry's successor, Vasily I (reigned 1389–1425), fought to take western Russian lands out of Lithuanian control and reduced the rival Russian principality of Tver to subservience.

▼ *The Battle at Kulikovo Field, fought on September 8, 1380, is the subject of this late-sixteenth-century illumination. The Muscovite prince Dmitry Donskoi was victorious over the Tatars.*

ΤΑΚΟ СΡΑЗΗΒШΕСΑ . ΜΗШΓΑΤΕΛΕСΑΠ.
ΔΛΑΧΟΥ ΗΕΓΟ ΠΟΜΟΓШΟΥ ΒΕΛΗΚΟΜΟΥ Π
ΒΕ ΔΟ ΗΟСΗΟΜΟΥ ΔΜΗΤΡΕΗ . ΗΠΟБΕЖΑ
ΗΗΒЫШΑΠΟΓΑΗΪΗ ΤΑ

Vasily II, "the Blind" (reigned 1425–1462), benefited from the fragmentation of Tatar power by bringing the Tatar principality of Kasimov under his rule. Increasingly, Moscow's authority was seen as the successor to the Tatars' in Russia.

The rulers of Moscow copied the Tatars' administrative and tax system, which had no regard for the subject's ability to pay. They also adopted the Tatars' military system and tactics. Other Tatar customs, such as confining women in the *terem* (secluded women's quarters), became the practice of senior nobles. From the khans the Muscovite rulers learned to govern arbitrarily, without regard to the rule of law, property, or individual rights. Even members of the highest nobility—the boyars, next in rank below the ruling princes—might be flogged on a whim; Muscovite rulers inflicted the same humiliations on the boyars that the khans inflicted on them. Boyars were considered the slaves of the Muscovite sovereign, and they in turn treated their own underlings as slaves.

Starting in the late fifteenth century, writers began occasionally to refer to Muscovite grand princes as czar (that is, Caesar), but the title was not formally adopted until 1547, by Ivan IV, "the Terrible." There are earlier indications of imperial pretensions. In 1472 Ivan III married the Byzantine princess Sophia Palaeologa and adopted the double-headed eagle, the emblem of the Byzantine emperors. Aware of the great changes taking place in Europe as a consequence of the Renaissance, Ivan invited Italian military engineers and architects to Moscow (one of their achievements was the Cathedral of the Assumption in the Kremlin) and attempted to import firearms. Muscovy's hostile western neighbors—notably Sweden and Poland—tried to prevent new technology from reaching Russia and, in fact, enjoyed some success. Other factors, such as religion, also limited Russian acceptance of western ideas.

The Russian Church

More than the Tatar conquest separated Muscovy from western Europe. Russians were members of the Eastern Orthodox Church, which adopted the liturgy of the Greek Church and deferred to the patriarch in Constantinople rather than the pope in Rome. Russia's educated elite was taught not in Latin (the universal language of learning in pre-Reformation western Europe) and not even in Greek. The notoriously ill-educated Russian clergy used Old Slavonic as the church language, a language just sufficiently different from Russian to make religious services unintelligible to the congregation.

The ideas and innovations of the Renaissance caused little excitement in Muscovy, where very few could actually read the Latin correspondence and publications that spread them. The Reformation also had little impact. It was seen by the Muscovites as a quarrel between groups of foreign heretics, and although it sparked a brief upsurge in heresy around the mid-sixteenth century, its main effect was an influx of exiles, many of whom were military men and technical experts. The czars employed some of these foreigners, but there remained barriers to the acceptance of new ideas.

The Russians felt that their church held a unique position. At the Council of Florence (1439), the Greek Orthodox Church had accepted the authority of Rome because it was desperate for help against the Turks. Only fourteen years later Constantinople fell to the Turks. This defeat had important consequences for Russia. It allowed the development of a specifically Russian Orthodox Church, with its own head, or patriarch, from 1589. The rulers of Muscovy had already long seen themselves as the last independent Orthodox sovereigns. From the end of the fifteenth century, the idea began to spread among Russian clergy that Moscow was the "third Rome." The Rome of Saint Peter had fallen to heresy and been overrun by barbarians, as had the second Rome, Constantinople. This turn of events left Moscow as the center of the last truly Christian nation on earth. The clergy argued that there was no possibility of a fourth Rome because all the other European states, Protestant and Catholic alike, were merely heretics. They believed that if Moscow fell to heresy and was conquered by barbarians, the apocalypse (end of the world) must follow.

▲ *Since 1326 the Cathedral of the Assumption in the Kremlin has been the seat of the Russian Orthodox Church. Rebuilt in the 1470s, it was the place of the coronation of the first czar, Ivan the Terrible.*

Around 1510, in an address to Grand Prince Vasily III of Moscow, a monk described the unique nature of the Russian Church:

Your mighty realm, the third new Rome, shines to the ends of the earth in its Orthodox Christian faith brighter than the sun throughout the world. And may your rule, pious czar, know that all the realms of the Orthodox Christian faith have converged into your single realm. You are the only Christian czar in all the world; it befits you, the czar, to rule in fear of God.

Perceive, pious Czar, how all the Christian realms have converged into yours alone. Two Romes have fallen, and the third stands, and a fourth there shall not be. Your Christian realm shall not pass under the rule of another.

Filofei of Pskov, Address to Vasily III

▲ *This jeweled miter, or crown, was one of the symbols of office worn by Patriarch Nikon, head of the Russian Orthodox Church from 1652 to 1658.*

It is not certain whether ideas about the Russian church being the one true church were ever really accepted by the Russian rulers or whether laypeople were even aware of them. There does seem to have been a common view that the purity of the Russian church needed to be safeguarded. This conviction was so deeply held that Patriarch Nikon's seventeenth-century reforms caused sizable problems. Orthodoxy was a force that involved intense cultural conser-

vatism and even xenophobia (dislike or fear of foreigners). People thought that foreigners might infect them with heretical ideas. Even when the czars needed their services, foreigners were kept isolated and had to live outside Moscow in the so-called German quarter—the Russians did not distinguish between foreigners of different nationalities and called them all Germans. Relations between foreigners and ordinary Russians were discouraged, and Russians were forbidden to travel abroad.

Sixteenth-Century Russia

It was Ivan III's successor, Vasily III (reigned 1505–1533), who completed the process of gathering Russia under Moscow's rule. He took Pskov in 1511 and, after three campaigns, Smolensk in 1514. In 1520 Moscow annexed the last independent Russian state, Ryazan. Under Ivan IV the Tatar khanates (regions ruled by the khans) of Kazan and Astrakhan were subjugated. Ivan also approved a private venture by a wealthy family of traders, the Stroganovs, to exploit the weakness of the khan of Sibir (Siberia) and win the wealth of the region by force of arms. A private army of over 1,600 Cossack mercenaries (paid soldiers), led by a fugitive from justice called Yermak Timofeyevich, began the conquest of Siberia. Greed for the region's resources, notably furs, caused a Cossack-led expansion that soon took Russia's borders as far as the Pacific Ocean. The peoples of Siberia, many of them nomadic or semisedentary caribou herders and hunter-gatherers, were ruthlessly exploited. As in the Americas, alcohol and European diseases had a

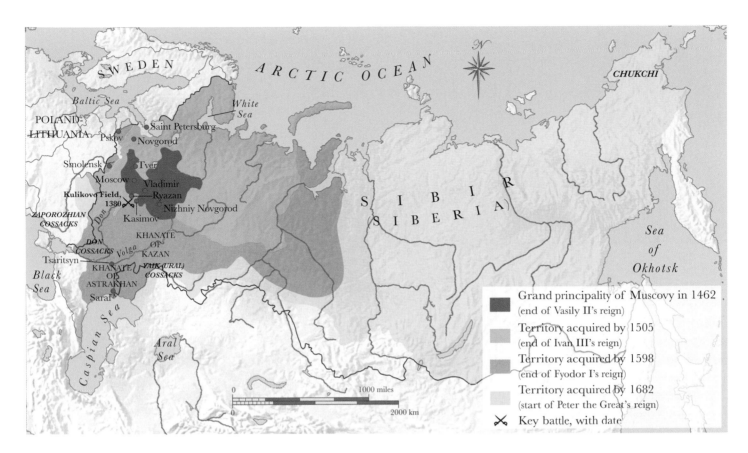

catastrophic impact on Siberia's population and culture. The Siberian peoples were able to put up minimal resistance; only the Chukchi in northeastern Siberia managed to temporarily check the Russian advance in the last stages of the conquest.

In the Livonian war (1558–1583), Ivan IV challenged his western neighbors Poland-Lithuania and Sweden for access to the Baltic, but his war was long, exhausting, and ruinously costly and ended in failure. As the Muscovite state expanded over the generations, the tax burden from constant warfare had multiplied and finally become unsupportable. Ivan compounded Russia's miseries by lashing out at supposed opponents in the reign of terror known as the *oprichnina*. The cost of his wars led to a mass flight of peasants. This exodus impoverished the nobles, whose lands were worthless without cheap labor to work the fields. Landowners required intense effort from their workers in order to make the most of a very short growing season. Forest soil unsuitable for grain production and frequent harvest-time floods also contributed to the low crop yields. Any surplus from the land was very limited, and workers often

went hungry. When the option of escape to newly conquered lands arose and the tax demands became unbearable, many peasants fled central Russia. Their departure was to have dire consequences, as it gave successive Russian rulers in the sixteenth and seventeenth centuries an excuse to curtail peasants' freedom to move. The first steps toward imposing serfdom on the Russian peasantry were taken; they would have a tragic impact over the succeeding centuries.

By the time of Ivan IV's death, Russia had reached crisis point, and the entire economy was in danger of collapse. Ivan was succeeded by his feebleminded son Fyodor I (reigned 1584–1598), who was unable to restore order to the state's finances or to address Russia's needs. A physically weak and unintelligent ruler, he relied on one of his father's close advisers, Boris Godunov, who performed competently enough, given the monumental challenges Russia faced. In 1591 Fyodor's half brother Dmitry died in suspicious circumstances—an epileptic child, he apparently managed to kill himself with his own knife while playing. Fyodor's early death without an heir marked the end of the Rurik dynasty and the start of fourteen years of instability for Russia.

▲ *This map shows the expansion of Muscovy between the fourteenth and seventeenth centuries and the birth of the Russian state.*

The Time of Troubles

Known as the Time of Troubles, the period of Russian history from 1598 to 1612 saw many contenders struggle to be czar. Immediately after Fyodor's death, the throne was seized by Boris Godunov (reigned 1598–1605). Fyodor's regent and brother-in-law, Godunov was also widely suspected of having murdered Dmitry in order to clear his way to the throne. Godunov never really established the legitimacy of his rule, and a disastrous famine (1602–1603) brought the crisis to a head. From nobles to peasants, nearly every section of society was unhappy with Godunov's rule. Cossack bands, living on the outskirts of Russia, were enraged by the attacks on their liberties by the czars, who wanted to bring them into state service. Their numbers swollen by escaped peasants and embittered nobles, the Cossacks were ready to take up arms against Godunov. They did so under the banner of a pretender to the throne, one who claimed he was Ivan IV's son Dmitry and had miraculously survived the knifing of 1591. In reality, this False Dmitry (one of three such) was probably a defrocked monk named Gregory Otrepev. With Polish support he invaded Russia. On the face of it, he took a foolhardy gamble, but his audacity paid off. Godunov's attempts to prove that

◄ *Boris Godunov is the subject of this anonymous eighteenth-century portrait. As de facto ruler, Godunov defeated the Crimean Tatars and recovered territory from Sweden. As czar (1598–1605), he introduced reforms but faced opposition from boyars and the first False Dmitry.*

COSSACKS

The first Cossack bands appeared about the mid-fifteenth century. Initially Tatar mercenaries protecting vulnerable borderlands from raids by other Tatars, they were soon joined by Russians, Poles, and other ethnic groups. Cossacks were often disaffected peasants, eager to exchange the miseries of their daily lives for the adventure, freedom, and chances of wealth offered by pioneering beyond the reach of any government, employment as mercenaries on their own terms, or simple piracy. A distinct Cossack culture emerged that blended Slavic and Tatar elements. Cossacks established their own societies, such as the Yaik (Ural), Don, and Zaporozhian hosts (regions); ignored outside authorities; and played one off against the other at need. Their raids on the Black Sea and on river traffic angered the Tatars, and by ignoring the czars, who often wanted peace, they were a challenge to Muscovite authority. Their makeshift democratic ways and willingness to accept fugitives from Russia, particularly runaway serfs, were another cause of anger in Moscow.

Cossack independence could only survive as long as the Cossacks had lands beyond the effective authority of any state. As the Russians came to dominate their territory, the Cossacks became a frontier people without a frontier. By the late sixteenth century the czars were bringing the Cossacks under control. The Cossacks had to earn their gradually diminishing freedoms as frontier guards and light cavalry in the service of the state. The Cossacks conquered Siberia for the czars, and they were at the forefront of Russian expansion, but their rebellious nature was not tamed easily. Cossacks were involved in the sporadic and bloody revolts that shook Russia as late as the seventeenth and eighteenth centuries, but by the nineteenth century they were loyal servants of autocratic rule.

Dmitry really was dead were simply ignored, and his authority was undermined even further. A number of boyars were only too ready to recognize the False Dmitry simply to destroy Godunov. Even so, the deception would probably have failed but for Godunov's sudden death. The pretender was proclaimed czar in 1605, and Godunov's widow and son were quietly murdered. In the atmosphere of hysteria, Dmitry's own mother was brought from the nunnery to which she had withdrawn and publicly acknowledged the pretender as her long-lost son.

The False Dmitry's Polish entourage and lack of respect for Russian customs soon led to rebellion. Those boyars who had used him to destroy Godunov no longer needed him. Within a year he was denounced as an impostor, killed, and burned, and his ashes were reputedly fired from a cannon toward Poland. A boyar, Vasily Shuysky, ruled as czar from 1606 to 1610, but he proved incapable of ending the chaos. Famine, revolution, anarchy, banditry, peasant flight, and epidemic were depopulating central Russia.

Two more False Dmitrys made claims on the throne, in 1607 and 1611, respectively. Many Russians were desperate to believe in a czar who would cure Russia's ills. The identity of the second pretender is unknown. Often referred to as the Felon of Tushino (he based his court in the village of Tushino, eight miles outside Moscow), the second False Dmitry briefly established rule over considerable areas of Russia but never took Moscow. Once again the mother of the real Dmitry recognized the pretender as her son. The first False Dmitry's widow even recognized him as her husband and bore him a son. In 1610, however, as his cause collapsed, this Dmitry was murdered by one of his supporters. The third False Dmitry, probably a deacon named Sidorka who appeared briefly in Pskov, had no great impact.

Starting in 1610, Swedish troops occupied parts of northern Russia. The Polish army's occupation of Moscow from 1610 to 1612 appeared to spell the end of the Russian state. The Polish king, Sigismund III, seems to have had ambitions to conquer and catholicize the Russians. Two heroes emerged to fight the resistance. Kuzma Minin, a butcher from Nizhniy Novgorod, and Prince Dmitry Pozharsky led the fight for independence and saved Moscow from the Polish invasion.

Demetrius IMPERATOR Moschoviæ, Ejus uxor Marianna MNISZCHOWNA Georgii Palatini Sandomiriensis ex Tarlouna Progenita Filia.

◄ During the Time of Troubles, three "false Dmitrys" made claims to the Russian throne, each declaring himself the second son of Ivan IV. The first, portrayed here by an unknown artist, ruled as czar for little over a year (1605–1606).

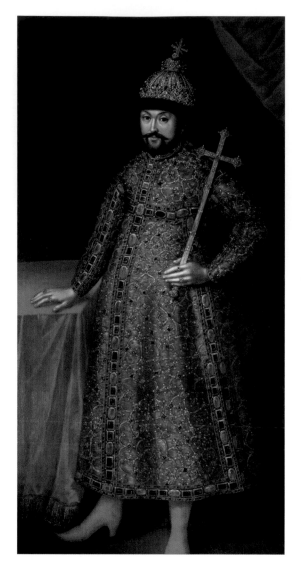

The Romanovs

In 1613 a *zemsky sobor* (assembly of the land) elected a boyar named Michael Romanov as the new czar. The son of Patriarch Philaret and a relative of Ivan IV's first wife, Anastasia, Michael founded the Romanov dynasty that would rule Russia until 1917. During his reign Michael occasionally consulted the *zemsky sobor* but never allowed the assembly to limit his power. Indeed, though internal upheavals continued for some time, very little of the Russian state or society had been changed by the Time of Troubles.

The new, sixteen-year-old czar faced overwhelming difficulties. He was at war with Poland and Sweden, both of which occupied Russian territory; bands of bandits, some of them thousands strong, plagued the land; rumors of new pretenders abounded; and state finances were in an advanced stage of collapse.

The new reign was marked by a cautious rebuilding of the Russian state, in which real power was wielded by the czar's father, Philaret, from the time of his release from Polish captivity in 1619 until his death in 1633. Bandits were amnestied on condition that they fight the invaders. The invaders were eventually bought off with generous terms. By the Peace of Stolbovo (1617), the Swedes returned Novgorod but kept the Baltic coastline, while by the Truce of Deulino (1618), the Poles kept Smolensk. State finances remained chronically weak, despite the draconian measure of imposing extraordinary taxes.

The czar's autocracy (absolute one-man rule) was reinstituted, and the submission of the nobility was assured by the Ulozheniye (law code) introduced in 1649 by Michael's son, Czar Alexis I (reigned 1645–1676). Possibly as a result of a serious revolt in 1648, Alexis moved to strengthen his authority at the expense of his subjects. The Ulozheniye was the tool he used to achieve his goal. It included an attempt to freeze the existing class structure and specify the obligations of each class. Punishments named for particular offenses included flogging, mutilation, and exile to Siberia. Townspeople were forbidden to change residences. The *dvoryanstvo* (nobles whose lands and privileges were dependent on service to the state) had their liberties curtailed, but Alexis was able to keep their loyalty by addressing their greatest grievance— the difficulty of keeping labor on their estates now that Siberia offered peasants a safe haven. Peasant bondage, which had been spreading for many years, was now confirmed in law, at the very time it was being abandoned in western Europe. A century later, as a truly Europeanized nobility emerged, many would find serfdom a national humiliation and would move in the direction of opposition to the autocracy.

Russia took little from the Renaissance and the Reformation and contributed even less: no universities were established, and no memorable literature or secular art produced. Secular music was repressed, there was no vernacular Bible, and xenophobia remained strong. The Romanov czars continued to import Western technology and experts, who were often forbidden to leave if they had valuable skills, but the nation remained

A seventeenth-century scholar sent as an envoy to Moscow from the German duchy of Holstein described the barbarity of Russian people and society:

If a man considers the natures and manner of life of the Muscovites, he will be forced to avow, that there cannot be anything more barbarous than that people.... They never learn any art or science, nor apply themselves to any kind of study: on the contrary, they are so ignorant, as to think, a man cannot make an almanac unless he be a sorcerer, nor foretell the revolutions of the moon and eclipses, unless he have some communications with devils.... And whereas cheating cannot be exercised without treachery, lying, and distrust, which are its constant attendants, they are marvellously well versed in these qualities.... If they fight, it is with their fists, or switches, and the height of their rage is kicking, as much as they can, in the belly and about the sides. 'Twas never yet known that any Muscovite fought with sword or pistol.

Adam Olearius,
The Voyages and Travels of the Ambassadors

medieval in character. Outside commentators remarked on the quaint, exotic, or even barbaric appearance and manners of the elite.

Beyond 1650

The outside world would begin to have a noticeable impact in Russia—and Russia an impact on the outside world—under Peter the Great (reigned 1682–1725). A modernized army and new fleet would win victories over Sweden in the Great Northern War (1700–1721). A new capital (Saint Petersburg) would be built, with new institutions of government and even an academy of science. Yet even then, the boyars were resistant to change. Required to wear western dress and shave their beards, they longed for Peter to die so that they could return to their former lives. Peter, it could be argued, after a lifetime of effort, had only a superficial impact. The process of westernization would prove to be painfully slow and difficult.

▲ *The reign of Alexis I, depicted here on horseback by an anonymous artist, was marked by wars with Poland and Sweden and a peasant revolt. Alexis oversaw the Ulozheniye (1649), a law code that legitimized serfdom.*

FURTHER READING

Crummey, Robert O. *The Formation of Muscovy, 1304–1613.* New York, 1987.

Dunning, Chester S. L. *Russia's First Civil War: The Time of Troubles and the Founding of the Romanov Dynasty.* University Park, PA, 2001.

Ostrowski, Donald G. *Muscovy and the Mongols: Cross-Cultural Influences on the Steppe Frontier, 1304–1589.* New York, 1998.

John Swift

SEE ALSO
• Feudalism • Ivan IV Vasilyevich • Poland • Sweden

Music

THE PURPOSE OF RENAISSANCE MUSIC (WHICH CONTINUES TO CAPTIVATE AUDIENCES) WAS TO DELIGHT AND MOVE BOTH ITS LISTENERS AND ITS PERFORMERS.

◄ One of the best sources of information about how music was performed during the Renaissance is the art of the period. Heavenly musicians are depicted in this detail from Jan van Eyck's oil-painted panel for the Ghent Altarpiece (1426–1427).

Renaissance, which literally means "rebirth," refers to the reawakening of interest in the art, architecture, literature, and philosophy of classical Greece and Rome that accompanied the rediscovery of classical texts. Therefore, strictly speaking, the term "Renaissance music" is a misnomer, since the music of the period that lasted from around 1350 to 1650 was not in fact classical Greek or Roman music reborn. What modern music scholars call Renaissance music, however, has a connection to the humanist thought of the early modern era. The composers of the age strove to create a perfect union between word and sound in order to express the whole range of human emotion in a universal musical language. Music was also a central, though often forgotten element of the education of every well-rounded man and woman of the period. No member of the aristocracy lacked musical training, and a large number of amateur musicians were members of private music clubs throughout Europe. Musicologists normally date the Renaissance period in music from about 1450 to 1600, although these dates vary from country to country—in England, for example, Renaissance music is associated with the Elizabethan era, the second half of the sixteenth century.

Beginnings of the Renaissance

Later medieval music exists in two distinct genres. The first is popular music—ballads, dance music, and other simple monophonic (single-voiced) forms. The other, music of a complex and cultivated style, was performed by professional musicians in churches and royal courts. This elaborate music, which became dominant in the early fourteenth century, was called *ars nova* (new art) by its creators. Because of the manner of its tonal organization, many present-day ears find it alien. It was polyphonic—different voices sang or played different parts—and was composed line by line, and so unsettling dissonances often emerge when the parts are performed together. Frequently, the multiple parts of vocal music involve the performance of different texts simultaneously. It was sometimes impossible for its original auditors to understand all the words.

Compositions were often extremely complicated. Composers took delight in mathematical constructions and concealed meanings that only the most sophisticated listener could pick up. For example, the tenor line might be constructed to spell out the name of a patron or lover. The best examples of this style are found in the work of the French composer Guillaume de Machaut (c. 1300–1377). A cleric employed by King John of Bohemia and then the French court, Machaut spent the last forty years of his life as a canon at the Cathedral of Reims. Most of his twenty-three extant motets (polyphonic choral pieces) follow the pattern of the time: an instrumental tenor line with two voices above it, each singing a different text in a rhythmically complex musical structure. The effect can be stunning, and the flow of sound often fascinating, but aside from specialists few present-day music lovers enjoy or even listen to this music.

Music changed much during the fourteenth century. Composers of the late Middle Ages and early modern era were mostly well-educated and well-rewarded professionals. They started to pay greater attention to harmony and to avoid dissonance between melody lines. There was also a move toward use of a single text so that the words would be comprehensible to listeners.

▲ This manuscript copy of a song by the French poet and composer Guillaume de Machaut is a good example of fourteenth-century polyphonic music notation.

CHRONOLOGY

1452
Lochamer Liederbuch, the earliest collection of German polyphonic songs, is compiled.

c. 1500
New lute-playing technique is introduced.

1524
Johann Walter publishes the first collection of Protestant music.

c. 1540
Modern music notation appears.

1542
The Geneva Psalter is published.

1555
Nicola Vicentino's L'antica musica ridotta alla moderna prattica (Ancient Music Adapted for Modern Practice), the first serious effort to revive ancient Greek music, is published.

1562
Discussions on music begin at the Council of Trent.

1564
Oldest surviving violins by Andrea Amati, developer of the modern instrument, are made.

1581
Music for the oldest surviving French ballet, The Queen's Dramatic Ballet, is performed in Paris.

1588
Nicholas Yonge's Musica transalpina, the first collection of madrigals in England, is published.

1597/8
Jacopo Peri composes Dafne, the first opera.

1605, 1607
William Byrd's Gradualia is published.

1607
Claudio Monteverdi produces his first opera, Orfeo.

1610
Monteverdi's Vespro della Beata Vergine is published.

c. 1620
The Fitzwilliam Virginal Book is compiled.

PARODY: BUILDING BLOCK OF COMPOSITION

Beginning in the mid-fifteenth century with Guillaume Dufay (c. 1400–1474), the most common method for composing polyphony was parody. The composer selected a familiar tune, often a popular song because its musical shape tended to be more pronounced. This tune became the tenor (that is, principal) line of the new composition, often slowed down to the point where it was no longer recognizable. (In the Middle Ages and Renaissance "tenor" did not refer to the tenor vocal range, as it does now.) The other lines were written to complement this tenor line and often imitated elements of the original tune.

Parody was a common device in extended works of religious music, especially from the late fifteenth century, when it became usual to compose the entire ordinary of the Mass—the parts that remain the same each day, namely the Kyrie, Gloria, Credo, Sanctus, and Agnus Dei—as a single unified work. Thus, many masses were based on secular music, and more than fifty existing masses were based on a single chanson, or song, "L'homme armé" (The Armed Man).

Clearly Renaissance composers were not obsessed with originality. In fact, it was considered a compliment to use another composer's tune as the basis for a composition, and many composers were thus honored. At the same time, the original tune can almost never be discerned in the finished composition; so at one level these parody masses can be understood as an insiders' joke.

The Council of Trent (1545–1563) urged composers not to base sacred music on secular themes. Although the great Catholic Counter-Reformation composers obeyed, they continued to write parody masses but drew their tunes from sacred rather than secular sources.

Dufay's Generation

The birth of true Renaissance music is usually associated with the northern French composer Guillaume Dufay (c. 1400–1474) and his contemporaries. These composers are often labeled Netherlandish, Franco-Flemish, or Burgundian since all were born in northern France or the Low Countries and nearly all were connected with the splendid court of the dukes of Burgundy. The Belgian music theorist Johannes Tinctoris, writing in 1477, said that no music older than forty years was worth listening to. He added that the founders of the new style were Dufay, his countryman Gilles Binchois (c. 1400–1460), and the Englishman John Dunstable (c. 1390–1453). The music that these men created turned away from unregulated dissonance. All voices in polyphonic compositions were theoretically of equal importance, usually in a four-part texture. The fifteenth-century Burgundian style was not so much new as it was a fusion of several regional styles. Dunstable, who spent much of his career in France, brought to the continent the English emphasis on major tonality, greater harmonic unity, and fuller sound. Italy and France contributed their forms to the mix. The result was sweeter, fuller, more sonorous music.

Dufay, the greatest figure of the Burgundian school, provides a good example both of early Renaissance music and of the life of a musician employed by the aristocracy. His career began as a choirboy at Cambrai Cathedral, in northern France. Like many of the leading composers of the Renaissance, Dufay became a priest and even

▲ *This sixteenth-century manuscript illumination depicts a meeting that took place around 1440 between the French composers Guillaume Dufay (next to the organ) and Gilles Binchois (holding the harp).*

MUSIC AT THE BURGUNDIAN COURT

During the fifteenth century almost every important musical post in Europe was held by someone from the Netherlands or northern France. Much of the reason for this phenomenon lies in the role of the dukes of Burgundy as sponsors of music composition and performance. The dukes of Burgundy were the greatest art and music patrons of Europe from Philip the Bold's accession in 1363 to the death of Charles the Bold in 1477. Especially in the reign of Philip the Good (1419–1467), the ducal chapel was recognized as the most splendid in Europe. Philip employed between fifteen and twenty-seven musicians for religious purposes, besides a band of minstrels for lighter entertainments. A connoisseur of good music, he paid lavishly to win fine singers and composers away from other courts. He fostered an international exchange of musical ideas and styles, and many foreign musicians visited his court and carried compositions home with them. An extraordinary result of this Burgundian preeminence is that few fifteenth-century Italian composers are remembered at all. The Italian style apparently could not compete with the richer, fuller Burgundian sound for princely patronage.

studied canon law. He soon gravitated to Italy, where he won a position as singer in the papal chapel and also found a ready welcome at various courts. Appreciation for his skill led to a lifetime of financial support. In 1436 Dufay was made a canon of Cambrai Cathedral, an appointment he held in absentia. Rather than at the cathedral, Dufay spent much of his middle years at the Burgundian court, where he won such widespread fame that in 1458 he was invited to Besançon, in eastern France, to arbitrate a musical debate. Perhaps his highest accolade came from the Florentine ruler Piero de' Medici, who in 1467 called Dufay "the greatest ornament of our age." Dufay taught many of the most famous musicians of the next generation, and by the time he died he had become a wealthy man.

The Renaissance Sound

In Dufay's extant music it is possible to trace the move to the Renaissance. Most of the works are motets, brief pieces of religious music in polyphonic settings. The early motets are formulated mathematically, in the highly complex style of *ars nova*. Most notable of these early works are the isorhythmic motets—pieces in which the different chants are repeated according to a meticulously planned system of reiterated notes. Dufay finally stopped composing such works and turned instead to a much more melodic and approachable style, a style that was also characterized by greater concern for the intelligiblity of the texts he was setting. The new sound he created caused a sensation and was soon widely imitated. His music apparently had a strong emotional appeal for both performers and listeners. It is said that Dufay himself asked to have his motet *Ave regina coelorum* (Hail, Queen of Heaven) sung at his bedside while he was dying, in order to ease his soul's passage. Since there was not enough time to gather the choir, the motet was sung at his funeral instead.

For Dufay and his contemporaries, the words of a composition were still usually subservient to the music. Even with all voices singing the same text, words were hard to understand, especially because of the many melismata (running lines of music sung on a single syllable of text). It is

◀ Angel Musicians, *a panel painted during the 1480s by Hans Memling, has very accurate depictions of contemporary musical instruments. This detail illustrates (from left to right) the psaltery, monochord, lute, sackbut, and cornetto.*

seldom clear where the words of Dufay's pieces should be sung relative to the notes; syllables and notes were not yet aligned exactly, as they are in modern musical scores. In other ways, however, the musicians who succeeded Dufay honed a musical style that focused on the meaning of the text. Jean d'Okeghem (c. 1410–1495), for example, added a bass line to choral music, an innovation that created an extraordinary effect of breadth and mystery in his greatest compositions. Okeghem's large-scale requiem mass, probably composed for the funeral of the French king Charles VII in 1461, perhaps catches best the spirit of the later fifteenth century. In this work, the first extant polyphonic setting of a requiem mass, Okeghem began to experiment with simple word painting—for example, he lowers the musical line at the point in the Credo when Christ descends to hell and raises it when Christ ascends.

The High Renaissance

A true union of music with humanist aims was achieved by the French composer Josquin des Prez (c. 1440–1521), whose work influenced music for the next century. Josquin, a Michelangelo-like figure, closed one era of music and opened a new one and is generally regarded

▲ *This depiction of the Flemish composer Jean d'Okeghem conducting a recital of the Gloria is from the sixteenth-century manuscript* Chants royaux sur la conception, couronnés au Puy de Rouen, *a collection of poems about the Virgin Mary composed by Jean Parmentier (1494–1529). In an age of expensive, hand-copied music, the whole choir gathers around a single copy of the score.*

CLEVERNESS AS A COMPOSITIONAL ELEMENT

Although music of the High Renaissance became more natural and expressive in its compositional means, it was still music of great conscious complexity. Nowhere is this description better exemplified than in music composed to honor the great men and women of the age. A Renaissance composer was expected to subtly compliment his patron. As is true in even earlier music, Renaissance musical compliments are often so subtle that only close study of the score will reveal them.

Dufay's five-part motet *Ecclesiae militantis* (On the Church Militant), written in honor of Pope Eugenius IV's election, has a tenor line based on the name Gabriele, the pope's given name. Several of the chansons written by the Franco-Flemish composer Antoine Busnois (c. 1430–1492) include references to his beloved either through puns or acrostics (an acrostic is a verse composition where the first—or sometimes the last—letters of the lines combine to spell out a name, word, or phrase).

Sometimes text and music were crafted so as to present a series of flattering comparisons, both obvious and subtle. The Flemish composer Heinrich Isaac (c. 1450–1517), who served the Florentine ruler Lorenzo de' Medici before becoming court composer to the Holy Roman emperor Maximilian I, was a master of subtle praise. His talent comes across well in the motet *Optime pastor* (Best Pastor), written in 1513 to celebrate a meeting between the imperial chancellor and the new pope, Leo X (a son of Isaac's old patron Lorenzo de' Medici). In the course of the motet, Isaac worked in references to the imperial eagle. The pope is called *medicus* (physician) in allusion to the Medici family. The king of beasts—*leo* (lion)—makes an appearance. There is even reference to war against the Turks, a cause dear to both imperial and papal hearts at the time. The whole is constructed on a tenor line with the text "Give peace in our time, O Lord."

as one of the greatest composers of all time. His renown reached all parts of Europe; the German Reformer Martin Luther, for example, called Josquin simply "the master of the notes." Josquin, a native of Hainaut (now part of Belgium), spent time serving in the chapels of Milan, the papal domains, France, and Ferrara. Musicians flocked to hear him—and to print his works, too: Josquin was the first great composer to have had the advantage of that new invention the printing press. His works were published in many sixteenth-century collections, and indeed, more works were attributed to Josquin than he actually wrote (nearly half the compositions said to be by him are no longer considered his). Even in the sixteenth century, music scholars were well aware of this fact. In 1540 the German composer Georg Forster wrote, "Now that Josquin is dead, he is putting out more works than when he was alive."

Churches took pride in owning and performing Josquin's work. There is an account of the great Flemish composer Adriaan Willaert (c. 1490–1562) visiting the papal chapel and, to his surprise, hearing one of his own motets performed. Willaert made inquiries and was told that it was a work of the great Josquin. When he revealed that it was his own work, the chapel musicians refused to perform it anymore.

What Josquin achieved and passed on to his contemporaries was a perfect wedding of music and meaning in vocal music. With his work text painting, carefully suiting the music to the emotions of the words, became an essential element of composition. At the same time, there was a true fusion of northern and Italian musical styles. Northern music became more chordal and more recognizably modern in its key structure. The composers of this newest style also worked with musical motifs; interweaving a series of points of imitation, they made the different voices echo each other, almost as if they were playing tag. Josquin's style was based on a radical change in compositional method—he wrote all lines of a composition at the same time instead of working on each part separately. Voices became completely equal; they were no longer supported on a slow-moving tenor line.

▲ The job of court musicians was to make their patron look good, whether in his chapel or in public processions. The trumpeters depicted here form part of an idealized procession in a series of 135 woodcuts entitled The Triumphs of Maximilian I (1516–1518), by the German artist Hans Burgkmair.

▲ Music was an important part of a humanist education, and chamber music was a popular pastime, as may be seen in this sixteenth-century Italian oil painting, A Concert, by an unknown artist.

Similarly, the simple chordal motet *Tu solus qui facis mirabilia* (You Who Alone Work Marvels) has had religious significance for many listeners. The music in its spaciousness suggests the awesome greatness of God. Much of the text is chanted homophonically (all the parts supporting the main line), and so the words and their message are easy to hear.

With Josquin, it is also possible to see the composer moving from the role of craftsman to that of creative genius. Like Michelangelo, Josquin had trouble with his patrons. He worked slowly and made many revisions in his search for ways to express new ideas. He was sometimes accused of being overly imaginative.

Word painting and imitative texture were the hallmarks of sixteenth-century music. Word painting was not restricted to ecclesiastical music, although many religious texts are rich in emotional content and lend themselves well to such treatment. Composers also began to imitate street calls and natural phenomena, especially birdsong. A leading practitioner of this sort of double imitation—where musical lines imitate both birdsong and each other—was Clément Janequin (c. 1485–1558). Besides the masterly *Chant des oyseaulx* (Song of the Birds) of 1528, he wrote many other songs imitating larks, nightingales, and other birds.

Music of the Courts

While employing composers and chapel musicians was an important affirmation of status for a Renaissance prince, the primary reason for such patronage was that music entertained. Few composers were so well established that they could ignore their patron's demand for light, pleasant entertainment, and many composers appear to have fitted comfortably into the "entertainment division" of the court. For example, the English composer William Cornyshe (d. 1523) bore the title Master of the Chapel Royal from 1509 until his death, but he also organized pageants and plays to entertain Henry VIII and the lords and ladies of his court.

Court entertainments could be very elaborate. One of the most splendid was a banquet of the Knights of the Golden Fleece in Lille, France, in 1454. The musical entertainment

Josquin's music seldom failed to touch listeners. A particularly fine example of his work is *Absalon, fili mi* (Absalom, My Son), a setting of the lament of King David of Judah and Israel for his dead son Absalom. The motet may have been written in 1497 for Pope Alexander VI after the pope's son, Juan, was murdered. Moving progressively down through the circle of fifths, the voices in this composition communicate the idea of the descent of the soul into death—even to many who have no idea what the Latin text means.

CAREERS IN RENAISSANCE MUSIC

Music could be a richly rewarding field for the musicians who won a place in the choir of a major church or the chapel of a ruler. Such men (service in a church choir was open only to men, although at a much lower social level women performed as minstrels) were highly trained. Their education almost always began as choirboys, and they often received a good general education besides musical training. King Henry VI of England founded the choir of King's College, Cambridge, with an endowment to support fourteen men and sixteen boys. Master of the Boys was a well-paid position for a senior musician, although the position could be abused. For example, Nicolas Gombert (c. 1490–c. 1556), a leading Flemish composer who served the Holy Roman emperor, was accused of molesting a choirboy and condemned to the galleys (forced to row in one of the emperor's warships). Gombert won his release by composing a moving musical appeal to the emperor but was never allowed back at court.

On graduation from the boys' choir, the best singers sought employment at a court or cathedral. The road to promotion was clearly through singing, and even the finest composer was not particularly welcome if he did not have a good voice. The Dutch composer Jacob Obrecht (c. 1450–1505), second only to Josquin in compositional talent, had to work at a series of second-rate positions at Utrecht, Bergen op Zoom, Cambrai, and Bruges. In 1504 he took the risk of going to the court of Ferrara in the hope of improving his career only to die there of the plague within a few months. The fact that a surprising number of musicians also had university degrees suggests that they came from at least comfortably middle-class families. Many composers joined the priesthood as a path to promotion; many such appear to have been genuinely pious, however, including several important Spanish composers, Francisco Guerrero (1528–1599) among them.

The rewards could be excellent for court musicians, who normally received pensions and had security of employment—Renaissance princes would often add musicians but rarely dismiss one except for misbehavior. The most fortunate musicians received sinecure offices (positions with few or no duties and a permanent income). Pope Leo X was so impressed by Jean Mouton (c. 1459–1522), the official French court composer, that he rewarded the man by making him an apostolic notary—that is, clerk to the pope—although the job involved minimal duties.

The world was very different for minstrels. These musical performers were mostly instrumentalists who learned their trade by apprenticeship to a master player. Occupying the lower tier of the musical world, these craftsmen and craftswomen were almost never composers, and their livelihoods were very precarious.

◀ Choirboys played an integral part in religious services. This procession is a detail from Christ's Presentation in the Temple, *the central part of the altarpiece painted for the Benedictine convent in Cologne around 1480 by a German artist known as the Master of the Holy Kinship (fl. 1470–1515).*

Dancing was an accomplishment expected of every gentleman and gentlewoman. At the courts of Europe, there was both show dancing—highly rehearsed performances before an audience that were the precursors of ballet—and dancing by all the courtiers. A large number of dance varieties emerged, each with fixed steps and courtly gestures. Some, such as the volta, required a high degree of athleticism.

Much Renaissance instrumental music consists of dance pieces. Court musicians usually had two sets of instruments to choose between, the high instruments and the low (the names refer to the volume of sound produced, not the pitch). A common high combination was two shawms (a shawm is a double-reed wood-wind instrument that sounds like a very loud oboe) and a sackbut (an early form of trombone), while low instruments included harps, lutes, and flutes or recorders. Pieces of music were often performed in pairs, a slow dance step alternating with a quick one—a slow, stately pavane would be matched to a lively galliard, or a gentle passamezzo would precede an athletic saltarello. The allemande, a moderate-paced dance based on a German folk dance, became popular toward the middle of the sixteenth century.

While much dance music was drawn from minstrel's songs and was probably never written down, several elaborate collections of dance music were published in the sixteenth and early seventeenth centuries. The two most famous were Tielman Susato's *Dansereye* (1551) and Michael Praetorius's *Terpsichore* (1612), named for the ancient Greek muse of dance. Both collections derive from popular music, as harmonized by the editors, who also added works of court composers, including their own.

▼ *This detail—from* A Ball in Flanders, *by the Flemish artist Frans Francken II (1581–1642) —hints at the complex ceremonial of courtly dance.*

included a church built on a large table, with four singers and an organ inside. At one point in the proceedings, a horse was led back and forth with two trumpeters perched on its back playing a fanfare. The most spectacular sight was another table that held an enormous pastry—with twenty-eight instrumentalists playing inside.

The courtiers of Europe also appreciated simpler vocal music, very often a single voice with an instrumental accompaniment. Many important Renaissance composers produced such works side by side with more complex choral music for worship; two of the greatest at the art of the courtly chanson were Heinrich Isaac (c. 1450–1517) and the Swiss composer Ludwig Senfl (c. 1486–1542/3). They produced love songs, mocking songs, comic songs—whatever their sponsors wanted to hear. For example, a popular German chanson, set to music by a number of composers, was *Greiner, Zacker:*

> Grumbler, meddler, snooper,
> How do you like that?
> I want to sit with you at the table
> And kiss your wife on the mouth.

Such simple music could also be put to good use on very elaborate occasions. Some rulers made public spectacles into a fine art, richly accompanied with the best music of the age. Perhaps the high point was reached with the Florentine May carnival, sponsored annually by Lorenzo de' Medici in the late fifteenth century. Lorenzo himself wrote poems to be sung in the great procession at this event, set to music by his own court composer, Heinrich Isaac. Isaac produced songs in praise of Florence and about the various professions of Florence. He even wrote songs that poked fun at mercenaries and their faulty grasp of Italian. In other words, composers were expected to turn their hands to both the sublime and the ephemeral.

The Appearance of National Styles

Heinrich Isaac was one of the most cosmopolitan composers of the Renaissance; he wrote in all available styles and many of the languages of his day. In the course of the sixteenth century, however, developing national styles began to displace the influential Franco-Flemish style of the fifteenth century. It thus becomes easier to recognize different composers on the basis of their style. For instance, Pierre de la Rue (c. 1460–1518) spent most of his life in the Netherlands at the Burgundian and then the Hapsburg court. He never went to Italy, where many composers developed a more text-based style, and so his compositions display less of a link between words and music than those of his more cosmopolitan contemporaries. His harmonies are also less rich. As a rule, German composers tended to be conservative; the Swiss-born Ludwig Senfl, who worked mostly at the Munich court, is a good example. England in the early sixteenth century did not adopt the highly imitative style of the continent, a style in which parts echo each other and the goal is a flow that is unbroken until the final chord. English polyphony was old-fashioned by continental standards.

In Italy the style developed by Josquin, mingling as it did Netherlandish and Italian elements, was all the rage and underwent further regional developments. Of these perhaps the most interesting were to be found in the Venetian school of composition, created by a series of directors of music at Saint Mark's Cathedral. The line of great composers there began with a composer from the Netherlands, Adriaan Willaert. He appears to have been the first to appreciate the full potential of the great

▼ Saint Mark's Cathedral in Venice, the subject of this 1730s oil painting by Canaletto, provided an elaborate ceremonial space that encouraged the composition of full-voiced, resonant music.

Byzantine basilica of Saint Mark's, with its two choir lofts facing each other across the nave. Willaert and his successors developed polychoral music—music for two separate choirs declaiming, alternating, imitating, and briefly joining for climactic moments in triumphant bursts of sound—into a highly elaborated form. Willaert is a notable member of the generation of Josquin's successors. He was one of the first to insist that words be printed directly under notes in musical scores, since in his music it matters

Piper and Drummer (1504), part of the altarpiece Albrecht Dürer painted for the Wittenberg Palace chapel, provides valuable evidence of popular music performance among the lower classes.

immensely that the music fit the text. He was also careful to compose in units of text so that no word or thought was interrupted. Willaert trained his own successor, the Italian Andrea Gabrieli (c. 1520–1586), who in turn trained his successor (and nephew), Giovanni Gabrieli (c. 1556–1612). It was a sign of Italy's growing dominance in the music world that the major German composer of the time, Heinrich Schütz (1585–1672), eventually came to study with the younger Gabrieli.

Reformation and Music

The various Reformation currents had a major impact on the emerging national music styles. In general terms, all the religious movements of the sixteenth century furthered the most important trend already developing in the musical world: making the words of vocal music comprehensible and meaningful to the listener and the performer. The tendency to think of music as a luxury also had a profound effect in the more fundamentalist Protestant lands. The Swiss in particular limited the role of music. The Swiss Reformer Huldrych Zwingli was a good musician, but he was so determined to keep music out of the church that he had the organ cases of Zürich churches nailed shut. The French Reformer John Calvin, who settled in Geneva, issued more comprehensive decrees. He forbade any church singing of texts not in the Bible and discouraged followers from any nonreligious singing outside of church. Calvin also denounced polyphony in church music because it distracted the ear and mind from the text.

An interesting side effect of Calvin's stance was that the Reformed church strongly encouraged the singing of Bible-based hymns, as Martin Luther had already done. Luther was a good musician on the lute and transverse flute. He composed some monophonic hymns, of which the most famous is "Ein' feste Burg ist unser Gott" ("A Mighty Fortress Is Our God"). Luther also encouraged the writing of chorales (simple verse hymns with strong rhyme schemes and simple melodies for congregational singing) and collaborated with other composers, such as Johann Walter (1496–1570), who wrote the first polyphonic settings for chorales.

William Byrd | 1543–1623

The story of the English composer William Byrd illustrates well the disruptions wrought by the Protestant Reformation. From the 1530s on, England rocked back and forth between Protestantism and Catholicism, thanks to several changes of ruler. Elizabeth I (reigned 1558–1603), however, imposed the "great Anglican compromise," which attempted to strike a balance between the two religions. For Elizabeth herself proper religious observance clearly required a chapel royal with well-sung polyphonic music. She does not seem to have particularly cared whether a good musician was Anglican or Catholic. The great composer Thomas Tallis (c. 1505–1585), who served as a member of the Chapel Royal from 1543 until his death, remained a staunch Catholic the whole time. He explored a large variety of styles in the course of his career as English religion changed around him.

William Byrd, another royal singer and composer, was rather less flexible and got into considerably more trouble—though with government officials rather than the queen herself. He fell under suspicion several times, especially in 1580. Several members of Byrd's family were declared outlaws, but Byrd himself was protected by powerful Catholic nobles, including the attorney general. Finally, in 1592 Elizabeth personally intervened and ordered the authorities to stop harassing Byrd. Byrd showed his spirit by writing motets with clearly Roman Catholic messages, such as *Plorans plorabit,* in which he speaks of the "captive flock" of good Christians, by which he meant the persecuted Catholics of England. Several works would have drawn a charge of treason were it not for the fact that the texts he selected were biblical. He could be very blunt; in several settings of the Nicene Creed, he made the word *catholicam* (which appears in the phrase "I believe in one, holy, catholic, and apostolic church") a main point of imitation to stress his support of Catholicism. Nonetheless, he won official approval—in the form of a royal monopoly shared with Thomas Tallis—to publish music in England.

Around 1593 Byrd left court and began the most ambitious project of his life, the *Gradualia,* a two-book collection, published in 1605 and 1607, of music for the principal feasts of the Roman Catholic liturgical year. In all, Byrd composed more than a hundred of these pieces. The compositions are on a small scale, clearly intended for masses celebrated in private households (public celebration of the Roman Catholic liturgy was prohibited by law). Byrd was close to the Jesuits, and this music is filled with a strong Counter-Reformation spirit. In their lucid texture and strong emphasis on textual clarity and open sonorities, the best of Byrd's overtly Catholic works have a transcendent spirit comparable with the mysticism of his Spanish contemporary Tomás Luis de Victoria.

▼ *Both Roman Catholics, the English composers Thomas Tallis (left) and William Byrd (right) served the Protestant queen Elizabeth I. These portraits come from an eighteenth-century Dutch engraving.*

▲ Composers often flattered their patrons with an elaborate dedication in printed works. The title page of Palestrina's Missarum liber primus (First Book of the Missal; 1554) depicts Pope Julius III blessing the work, an indication that it is part of the approved Catholic program for music reform.

Jan Pieterszoon Sweelinck (1562–1621), were able to compose both Calvinist and Catholic vocal music, but most were forced to conform to the religion of the land where they worked, if they had jobs at all. Certainly the establishment of the more puritan forms of Protestantism led to the dismissal of many church musicians. During the reign of the English king Edward VI (1547–1553), choral foundations were abolished, and many liturgical books and organs were destroyed by the government.

The Catholic Counter-Reformation

When the Counter-Reformation formally began with the Council of Trent (1545–1563), among the issues the assembled clerics had to deal with were complaints about church music. The music then used in churches had too secular a spirit, claimed its critics, who were offended especially by the practice of basing masses on secular tunes. They grumbled about complicated polyphony that made it impossible to understand the words and the presence of too many noisy instruments in churches; also, they charged that singers were too often irreverent. A legend arose that the council fathers wanted to go so far as to abolish polyphonic music completely and that church music was saved only because the Italian Giovanni Pierluigi da Palestrina (c. 1525–1594) composed a six-voice mass that showed that polyphony could be both reverent and comprehensible. This story, however, is false. Although the council did issue a vague rule that composers should avoid anything "impure or lascivious" in church music, the council did not aim at radical musical reform. After Trent composers continued to base masses on secular songs and to write elaborate counterpoint.

What the Council of Trent did do was give formal approval to some tendencies that already existed in church music in the mid-sixteenth century, especially in the city of Rome itself. These tendencies can be summed up as a desire for transparency of texture. Church music of this desirable sort had a smooth and mostly step-wise melodic line, regular rhythm, simplified counterpoint, pure major-minor harmony, and a clearly voiced text. This music was also marked by the frequent insertion of homophonic pas-

In 1524 Walter produced the first collection of specifically reformist music, settings of thirty-eight German chorales (hymn tunes), along with five Latin motets. The hymns were an important means of propagating Reformation teachings to a largely illiterate audience and played a vital role in reshaping the experience of worship. The Calvinists, too, used music to win people to their cause. A number of French composers set metrical versions of the psalms to music, including Claude Goudimel (c. 1510–1572), who set the whole psalter to music twice, in 1564 and 1565. The best of these Calvinist composers was Louis Bourgeois (c. 1510–after 1561), whose finest works capture better than any other source the spiritual intensity of the Protestant Reformation. Such psalms were sung at work, at home, and in church.

The arrival of Protestantism imposed severe constraints on church musicians. A fortunate few, such as the Dutch organist and composer

sages—segments in which all voices sing in harmony, with one dominant line of music and text supported by the other vocal lines, which provide a choral accompaniment.

Giovanni Pierluigi da Palestrina, a protégé of Pope Julius III, wrote music that appealed to the Catholic reformers. It was elegantly balanced, with carefully controlled dissonance and sensitive reading of the text. Some, including the composer Michael Praetorius (c. 1571–1621), complained that Palestrina's music was too controlled and rather impersonal. Palestrina seems to have aimed for absolute purity and a sense of spaciousness, perhaps encouraged by the spaces for which he composed—he became choirmaster of the Cappella Giulia, in Saint Peter's, in Rome, in 1550; he later went to Saint John Lateran and finally to Santa Maria Maggiore, both magnificent basilicas. Palestrina was also the first director of music at the Roman seminary established by the Jesuits' founder, Ignatius Loyola. Palestrina,

Carlo Gesualdo   c. 1560–1613

Not all composers of the period had to please a patron or serve the church. The Neapolitan nobleman Carlo Gesualdo was one of the most strikingly original composers of the early period—and one of the most shocking. This prince of Venosa murdered his first wife, Maria, and her lover and is reputed to have gone insane in his later life. Some musicologists have, not surprisingly, suggested that his radically innovative music was a sign of mental derangement.

Gesualdo was a rare Renaissance artist in that he was independently wealthy and so was free to experiment. In some of his secular madrigals he tried out extreme contrasts of harmony and rhythm and also used the full chromatic scale (the twelve-note scale including all the semitones of the octave). Gesualdo was simply carrying a contemporary innovation to an extreme. In the second half of the sixteenth century, composers made wide use of accidentals, ornaments, and rhythmic variation—all in an effort to convey the emotional impact of words more vividly.

who was not himself a priest, had a contract with the Jesuits that included a free education for two of his sons at the new seminary. The vast bulk of Palestrina's musical output consisted of sacred music, including 104 known Mass settings and

▼ Jan Brueghel the Elder's *Hearing* (1617). Only the consort of viols would have been acceptable for church music by Counter-Reformation standards.

about 450 motets. In his youth he wrote eighty-three secular madrigals but later largely disowned them. Besides writing his own compositions, Palestrina supervised the revision of music for the liturgy to conform with the wishes of the Council of Trent.

Spain and the Counter-Reformation

Perhaps the biggest surprise of the Counter-Reformation was the emergence of a distinctive body of Spanish vocal music, which at its best combines the purity of Palestrina with a mystical quality of its own. This development is all the more surprising because Spain produced few composers of note before the mid-sixteenth century. Juan del Encina (1468–1529/30), the most significant Spanish composer of the early sixteenth century, sometimes reached moving emotional heights, as in his songs lauding the successful end of the Spanish *Reconquista* with the surrender of Granada in 1492, but he com-

posed few large-scale works. Cristóbal de Morales (c. 1500–1553), too, pointed the way to the future with some Mass settings of restrained emotion and elegance.

The central figure of Spanish Renaissance music was Tomás Luis de Victoria (1548–1611). After early musical training at Avila Cathedral, the young Victoria moved to Rome in 1567 for further education under the patronage of King Philip II. In Rome, Victoria soon won recognition as both a singer and a fine organist. He served as head of the chapel musicians in several places and in time became a priest and joined the new Oratorian order, founded by the Italian clergyman Philip Neri.

Although he spent much of his career in Rome (he returned to Spain around 1595), Victoria has been called the essence of Spanish Catholicism. His output was limited—about twenty masses, about forty-five motets, a series of hymns, and no secular music at all—but some

▼ *El Greco's* Angelic Concert *(c. 1610) catches the mystical fervor of Spanish music of the Counter-Reformation.*

MUSIC PUBLISHING

Europeans' experience of music was transformed by the printing press. The first music was printed around 1473 in the form of liturgical books with plainsong (monophonic choral music, such as Gregorian chant). Polyphonic music was slow to follow because of the technical difficulties of making notes line up with the musical staves, a problem multiplied in multipart music. The first printed collection of part music was the *Harmonice Musices Odhecaton A,* published by Ottaviano dei Petrucci in Venice in 1501. In the late 1520s the French publisher Pierre Attaignant developed a method of printing music with a single impression (small bits of broken line were printed with each note, instead of first printing the stave and then the music on top), a method that simplified the process. Around 1540 a simpler notational system was developed with smaller note values that looked much like modern notation.

The form in which most early printed music appeared was the partbook. In a typical partbook the soprano singer, for example, would have only the music for her own part. To save money, partbooks were often printed with several parts on the same page but facing in different directions; thus, a group of singers or players could gather around the music laid out on a table and each read his or her own part. Such publications were intended for home use. They reflect a growing taste for musical performance in middle- and upper-class homes, a taste fostered by the accessibility of inexpensive scores.

Thanks to the new technology, musical styles had a very widespread influence. The Spaniard Cristóbal de Morales was one of the first important composers of requiem masses. His *Missa pro defunctis* was published in Rome in 1544, while he was a member of the papal choir. The work became widely known in Europe. It even survives in New World cathedral archives, in Guatemala, Peru, and Mexico.

Music publishers provided comprehensive collections to connoisseurs starved for new music and also performable religious music to churches. Heinrich Isaac's greatest creation was the *Choralis Constantinus,* a collection of more than three hundred polyphonic settings of the propers of the Mass—the specific readings for all the Sundays and major feast days of the year. This enormous work did not find a publisher until the early 1550s, when it was produced in three oversized volumes in the German city of Constance. By that time religious controversy was altering church music, and some of these huge collections were attempts to fill newly perceived religious gaps. Georg Rhaw (1488–1548), the leading music publisher in Lutheran Germany, issued a collection of 123 polyphonic chorale arrangements and motets, the work of leading German and Swiss composers, in 1544. For Luther's new eucharistic service, a new kind of music was needed.

of his works, including the Christmas motet *O magnum mysterium* (Oh, Great Mystery), continue to have wide appeal and are still frequently performed in churches. Victoria's works are structurally clear, with a strong internal logic. He uses music to reinforce the text and often moves from an imitative style to a homophonic one to emphasize particular words or phrases. For many his work epitomizes religious music. Victoria has often been likened to the painter El Greco, Spain's great adoptive son, as has Palestrina to the brighter, lighter, and less intense artist Raphael.

▶ *This page comes from a partbook, the English composer John Dowland's* Songes or Ayres *(1597). When laid flat on a table, the musicians could gather round it and read their own part. The page includes a lute tablature on lines 2, 4, and 6—a tablature is a type of musical notation that indicates the string and fret to be used rather than the tone to be sounded..*

▶ *The title page of* Theatrum instrumentorum *(Theater of Instruments), in the second volume of Michael Praetorius's* Syntagma musicum *(1614–1620). The work includes detailed illustrations of a wide array of instruments, as well as information about their range and proper use.*

Musical Instruments and Their Players

The musical world of Europe was enriched by the development of several new musical instruments during the Renaissance and by a series of improvements to existing ones. Two typical Renaissance instruments—the viol and the sackbut—were invented in the early fifteenth century. The sackbut, a mellower and lighter ancestor of the trombone, became a key instrument for dancing and public occasions and as accompaniment to the lower vocal parts in sung music. The viol, which comes in a variety of sizes at different pitches, is a bowed six-string instrument. It produces a purer, thinner sound than modern bowed instruments, such as the violin, not least because it has frets, which prevent the player from amplifying the texture by adding vibrato (vibrato is the slight, rapid change in

pitch produced by stopping the string with a shaking movement of the hand). The viol consort (a family of different-sized viols that play together) became especially popular for chamber music, to judge by the number of partbooks published for viol players. Often consort pieces were quite simple compositions that could be performed with pleasure by amateurs. By the end of the Renaissance, virtuoso wind and string music was also being published. A collection of such music, *Der Fluyten Lust-hof* (The Flute's Pleasure Garden) by Jacob van Eyck, was published in Amsterdam in 1644.

Matched consorts of instruments, such as viols, recorders, or violins, were usually commissioned as a group by a rich patron who wanted an instrumental ensemble with a uniform timbre—an idea still pursued by modern-day early music performing groups. For example, the Italian violin maker Andrea Amati made no fewer than thirty-eight instruments of the violin family for King Charles IX of France between 1564 and 1574. Henry VIII of England was sent a consort of krummhorns (capped-reed wooden instruments that sound much like the kazoo) as a diplomatic present.

Besides their use in private homes and at court, string and wind instruments were used as a matter of course in churches—the chapel music of the Renaissance was not normally performed a cappella (without instrumental accompaniment). Instruments doubled the voices or sometimes substituted for them. The instrumental resources of a church could be large. In 1616, Saint Mark's Cathedral in Venice had on its payroll sixteen players of brass and string instruments. The city of Venice also employed six players who accompanied the doge (Venice's

The soft-voiced lute was usually employed as a solo instrument or served as accompaniment for a single singer, as it does in The Lute Player (c. 1595) by Caravaggio.

chief magistrate) in processions; they sometimes also played in church. These were highly qualified musicians, as their records of service show: they enjoyed good pay, tenure, and pensions, besides being able to add to their income by playing elsewhere in their free time.

Lutes and Keyboards

For much of the early modern period, the most important musical instrument was the lute, which came into being as a solo instrument at the beginning of the sixteenth century. A lute is plucked like the guitar, but its semicircular belly creates more resonance. Lutes commonly have fifteen to seventeen strings, with the same pitch often doubled for greater reverberation. Until about the year 1500, the lute was played by plucking the strings with a quill. The shift to playing with the fingertips made it possible to produce three or four lines of music at the same time and also created a sweeter, mellower sound. The lute flourished especially in Italy, although it was used throughout Europe. The earliest printed lute music, from Italy, was published between 1507 and 1511, but the first really

important year for instrumental music publication was 1536, when the Spanish composer Luis Milán (c. 1500–after 1561) published *El maestro* for the vihuela (an instrument midway between a guitar and a lute). This work is not just a collection of music but a how-to book, with technical information on how to play, choose good strings, tune the instrument, and perform the rhythms. The pieces themselves are arranged in order of difficulty. Soon lute music, written in tablature (a special form of notation that tells the lute players where to place the fingers on the frets), was being published in Venice, Milan, and Nuremberg. Ever more amateur musicians appeared, and the ability to play the lute or vihuela became a mark of education and culture. The greatest lutenist of the era was the Englishman John Dowland (1563–1626), who was hailed throughout Europe as a performer and a composer.

The keyboard flourished for the first time during the Renaissance. The clavichord and harpsichord, both invented in the fourteenth century, were not widely used until the fifteenth. Over the course of the fourteenth century, the

▼ *Saint Cecilia, the patron saint of music, was a popular figure in Renaissance art. In this painting by the sixteenth-century Flemish artist Michiel van Coxie, Saint Cecilia plays a harpsichord.*

organ developed from a portable instrument that the performer pumped with one hand while playing with the other into a large instrument that was installed in a growing number of churches. From the late fourteenth century, pedal keyboards were added, and they allowed the organ to produce a greater range and complexity of sound. In the early fifteenth century the organ developed further with the addition of a second keyboard and multiple ranks of pipes that could be connected and disconnected when the player pulled levers or handles called stops. However, sixteenth-century organs rarely had more than six to eight stops and typically had only one keyboard and no pedals. Thus, organists produced a sound much lighter than that available to later composers and organists such as Dietrich Buxtehude (1637–1707) and Johann Sebastian Bach (1685–1750).

New styles in keyboard music began to appear around 1550, including textless instrumental forms not intended for dancing, such as the ricercar (a slow-moving polyphonic composition) and the toccata (a brilliant piece in a free style that exploited the capabilities of the instrument with runs and trills). Both forms originated in improvisation. The greatest pioneer in Italian organ music was Annibale Padovano (1527–1575), a native of Padua who made the ricercar a serious compositional form. By 1600 keyboard music, which had become much more demanding, produced virtuoso performers such as Girolamo Frescobaldi (1583–1643) and Jan Pieterszoon Sweelinck, who was famous throughout northern Europe for his keyboard playing and improvisatory skills.

Ends and Beginnings

By the seventeenth century Italy had succeeded the Netherlands as the center of European musical life. Italy continued to hold that position for the next two centuries. A new style of music developed on the peninsula in the latter part of the sixteenth century; this development marked the end of the Renaissance and the beginning of the baroque era. From 1573 on, a circle of musicians, the Florentine Camerata, met to discuss literature, science, and the arts. One of the best-known members of the circle was Vincenzo Galilei (c. 1520–1591), a theorist, lutenist, and composer and the father of the astronomer Galileo Galilei. The Camerata produced a new vocal style, accompanied monody (single-voiced declamatory singing), which they based on what they knew of ancient Greek music. In 1581 Galilei's *Dialogo della musica antica et della moderna* (Dialogue between Old and New Music) became the manifesto of the new style.

The modern music championed in Florence was the culmination of a decades-long trend. Musicians had been turning from elaborate polyphony and toward a more immediate, direct, and declamatory style. The movement away from polyphony can be seen in the work of late Renaissance composers, such as the Fleming Orlando di Lasso (1532–1594), who gave his music structure less by means of imitation than the manipulation of harmony. The Italians went farther in the process, especially in the preferred secular vocal genre, the madrigal. A vast number of madrigals were produced in sixteenth-century Italy, most of them sentimental or erotic. Toward the end of the century, composers of madrigals increasingly emphasized expressiveness and distorted the proportions of the music for dramatic effect. Some parts were moved into the background as accompaniment to a single, main voice.

The most influential figure of the late Renaissance and early baroque was Claudio Monteverdi (1567–1643), some of whose work—especially the first operas—rejected the polyphonic fabric of Renaissance music for single-voiced declamation, with instruments relegated to a role as accompaniment. During the first half of the seventeenth century, most of

Europe's musicians embraced the baroque style. Only in fringe countries, especially England, Poland, and Portugal, did composers continue to compose unaccompanied choral music as late as 1650 and employ significant elements of Renaissance musical style.

▲ The subject of this portrait, by an unknown artist working in the mannerist style of Alessandro Allori, is believed to be the Italian musician Vincenzo Galilei, a founder of the Florentine Camerata, a select group of humanist musicians who pioneered the style of music known as the baroque.

FURTHER READING

Atlas, Allan W. *Renaissance Music: Music in Western Europe, 1400–1600.* New York, 1998.

Brown, Howard Mayer. *Music in the Renaissance.* Englewood Cliffs, NJ, 1976.

Carter, Tim. *Music in Late Renaissance and Early Baroque Italy.* Portland, OR, 1992.

Fallows, David. *Dufay.* New York, 1988.

Reese, Gustave, ed. *The New Grove High Renaissance Masters: Josquin, Palestrina, Lassus, Byrd, Victoria.* New York, 1984.

Phyllis G. Jestice

SEE ALSO

• Burgundy • Calvinism • Church of England
• Lutheranism • Monteverdi, Claudio
• Popular Culture • Reformation
• Schütz, Heinrich

Nationalism

NATIONALIST SENTIMENTS BEGAN TO EMERGE IN EUROPE IN THE LATE RENAISSANCE. THEY EVENTUALLY TRANSFORMED MEDIEVAL SOCIETIES INTO THE FIRST NATION-STATES.

A nation-state is generally defined as a political community with clearly delineated boundaries whose people speak the same language and are united by culture and traditions. During the period extending from 1300 to 1650, very few of the states of western Europe met all of these conditions. England perhaps came the closest, though only if Wales is considered to be a completely separate political unit.

The sense of nationhood, as the term is nowadays understood, derives from a combination of

▼ *In this seventeenth-century engraving by Robert Vaughan, the English gentleman is presented as a paragon of virtue. An Englishman would not have appeared so to people of other nations.*

elements, including language, culture, ethnicity, a sense of political community, loyalty to a monarch, and a shared religion. This combination was largely absent during the period in question. Most people had a strong sense of local identity but cared little about the world beyond their village or town.

Unless they lived on routes to sites of international pilgrimage or in some university towns, most people's knowledge of other nations was limited to what they learned through trade or warfare, and national stereotypes were formed from such experiences. Italians, familiar throughout Europe as bankers and merchants, were thought of as rich traders who preferred to pay others to fight for them; Spaniards were considered proud and avaricious; the French, brave but foolhardy, quick to attack but then equally quick to retire in confusion; the Germans were drunken brawlers; and the English were known for drink, violence, and killing their kings. No nation was really considered trustworthy by any other.

The religious changes and divisions of the sixteenth century sometimes heightened a people's sense of belonging to a wider community, one distinct from others, but religious controversies divided as many as they united.

Nations

In the Middle Ages *nation* was used to describe people held to belong to the same ethnic group, *people* to describe a political community. The most obvious sign of belonging to a nation was language: the German nation consisted of those people who spoke one of the many varieties of the German language.

Students at universities that attracted scholars from other countries were divided into "nations," although these might combine different language groups—Scandinavians could be included in the German nation, for example, or the Portuguese with the Spanish. Delegates attending international church councils were also categorized according to nation. At the Council of Constance (1414–1418), delegates were divided into nations for procedural purposes,

William Shakespeare's history plays reflect the development of English patriotism during the reign of Elizabeth I. In *Richard II*, one of a series of plays chronicling the fifteenth-century Wars of the Roses, John of Gaunt describes England as

This royal throne of kings, this scepter'd isle
This earth of majesty, this seat of Mars,
This other Eden, demi-paradise;
This fortress built by nature for herself
Against infection and the hand of war;
This happy breed of men, this little world;
This precious stone set in the silver sea,
Which serves it in the office of a wall,
Or as a moat defensive to a house,
Against the envy of less happier lands;
This blessed plot, this earth, this realm, this England.

Richard II, act 2, scene 1

John of Gaunt's high opinion of England and all things English was by no means universally shared. The following comments, which were made by an anonymous Venetian author writing at the beginning of the sixteenth century, offer another perspective on the patriotism expressed by John of Gaunt and other Englishmen:

The English are great lovers of themselves and of everything belonging to them; they think that there are no other men than themselves, and no other world but England. . . . They have an antipathy to foreigners, and imagine that they never come into their island, but to make themselves masters of it, and to usurp their goods.

Italian Relation of England

with the German nation including prelates from Denmark, Sweden, Norway, Hungary, and Poland. Although the nations at Constance were formed for administrative convenience, for political reasons the French objected to the English forming a separate nation; in response, the English turned to arguments about nations being based on common language or blood or the habit of acting together in support of their claim to nationhood.

Language and Nation

A common language was one of the main defining characteristics of a nation, although no language yet had a standard spoken form and the development of generally accepted written forms was still a work in progress in the sixteenth century. In Spain, Castilian became the prevailing form of Spanish in the thirteenth century, and only Catalan and Portuguese survived as separate literary languages. In France the language of the royal court and Paris became accepted as the cultured form of French from the late fourteenth century and gradually spread to other areas of the kingdom. There was no agreed-upon written version of German until the late seventeenth century. In Italy many championed the Tuscan language, favored by the fourteenth-century Florentine writers Dante, Petrarch, and Boccaccio, but there were still those who preferred written forms of Italian closer to their own regional dialects.

◄ *This marble representation, created by the Venetian brothers Jacobello and Pier Paolo dalle Masegne around 1400, depicts a group of students from the University of Bologna. Along with other universities, it attracted students from all over Europe. These schools tended to group their students by place of origin.*

National histories both expressed national sentiment and helped develop it. In France the *Grandes chroniques de France* (Great Chronicles of France), compiled from the twelfth century in the monastery of Saint-Denis, provided a widely read account of national history, including the mythical descent of the French from a Trojan called Francus. In the sixteenth century these Trojan origins were disputed by historian-lawyers, who wanted to prove that French law and custom had no foreign models. The Protestant François Hotman, for example, used history to support the claim that the French, or Gallican, church had always been independent of the papacy; these arguments were important during the French wars of religion (1562–1598).

The Swiss Confederation was an association of communes with no common language and little else linking them. Confronting questions about the legitimacy of their state, apologists stressed Swiss success on the battlefield and the role of peasant associations in the Swiss government. The *Weisse Buch von Sarnen (White Book of Sarnen),* published about 1470, brought together many popular legends about Swiss struggles against their Hapsburg overlords during the thirteenth century. The chronicles, which mention the legendary hero William Tell, helped to foster a sense of Swiss statehood.

▼ *This 1514 pen-and-ink drawing by Urs Graf the Elder depicts a Swiss lancer. In the late fifteenth and early sixteenth centuries, companies of Swiss mercenaries were the best infantry in Europe. Their reputation and achievement shaped the image and identity of the Swiss at home and abroad.*

Throughout Europe, local dialects remained so distinct that people from different regions often did not understand each other. Even when a standard literary language had been developed, its impact on the majority of people (who were illiterate) was limited.

States, Dynasties, and Nations

State boundaries in Renaissance Europe were not determined by the divisions between language groups. They were frequently redrawn because of the accidents of inheritance and patterns of marriage between ruling families or the fortunes of war. For some areas of Europe, it is very hard to draw a clear map.

The political geography of the German-speaking lands was particularly complex, as they consisted of principalities, city-states, and the estates of independent imperial knights. Most, but not all, were technically part of the Holy Roman Empire, which from the fifteenth century on was increasingly thought of as the German Empire. When the emperor-elect Maximilian addressed himself to the German "nation" in 1495, for example, he was addressing the estates of the empire—those states that were subject to imperial taxes and laws and that might be represented in the imperial assembly, the diet. The Holy Roman Empire included much of northern Italy (although no Italian was expected to attend imperial diets) and many French speakers on the empire's western edge. The dukes of Burgundy were able to build up their state in the fourteenth and fifteenth centuries because the border between the kingdom of France and the empire was so difficult to define as to be almost indeterminable, with a swath of territory divided into counties and duchies over which the emperor and the king of France had only marginal control, if any.

Some Frenchmen spoke of the natural boundaries of France, but there was no agreement where they were. Some claimed that France should extend to the Rhine River in the east; others placed the natural boundary on other rivers farther west, such as the Saône and the Rhône. Much of what was recognized as the kingdom of France was not under the control of the king until the late fifteenth century. A most significant fact is that a large part of southwestern France, Gascony, had been ruled by the king of England since the twelfth century. After Edward III of England claimed the throne of France as his by inheritance in 1337, the prolonged conflict that became known as the Hundred Years War began. Not until 1453 did the forces of the French king Charles VII drive the English from their last stronghold in France, Bordeaux. Provence, in the south of France, came to Charles's son Louis XI as heir to the Angevin dynasty only in 1481. Other lands, too, were claimed for the French crown by conquest or inheritance. Some, such as the duchy of Burgundy, were regarded as integral parts of the lands of the kingdom. Those lands not treated as France included the kingdom of Naples, claimed by Charles VIII as part of the Angevin inheritance and seized in 1495, and the duchy of Milan, claimed as an inheritance by his cousin and successor Louis XII and conquered between 1499 and 1500.

Whether lands that came to a ruler by inheritance or conquest were incorporated into his other lands or treated as a separate state depended on the circumstances. If the newly acquired state had a long tradition of independence, well-established political institutions, or perhaps a long-standing rivalry with other states under his rule, the inhabitants might rebel to prevent the loss of a separate identity.

Spain, for instance, was not one kingdom but a union of the kingdoms of Castile and Aragon.

Aragon itself included Catalonia and Valencia, both of which cherished their particular identity and institutions. The kingdoms of Castile and Aragon came together as the inheritance of the descendants of Queen Isabella of Castile and King Ferdinand of Aragon, who were married in 1469. Though the monarchs reigned jointly, their lands were not brought under a single administration. When the kingdom of Granada (the last territory held by the Muslims in Spain) fell to Isabella and Ferdinand in 1492, it became part of the kingdom of Castile.

▲ A portrait of the Hapsburg emperor-elect Maximilian by Bernhard Strigel (1460–1528). Maximilian's marriage in 1477 to Mary of Burgundy and the union in 1496 of their son Philip with Joan, who inherited the Spanish kingdoms, brought much of Europe and the Americas under Hapsburg rule.

ITALIA

Although what is now Italy consisted of a large number of independent states in the fifteenth century, there was still a feeling among Italians that they were a nation. Italian national sentiment was based on a shared language and cultural and political traditions and pride in being the heirs to the ancient Romans. Italians considered themselves culturally superior to the barbarians north of the Alps and celebrated the beauty of their countryside, cities, buildings, and works of art.

The Italian wars that began in 1494 brought invasion and occupation by French, Spanish, German, and Swiss troops. Calls to unite to free "Italia" from foreign domination had little effect, as individual states pursued their own short-term interests. When Spanish control was established in the mid-sixteenth century, Italians still took consolation in feelings of cultural superiority.

Ferdinand and Isabella's grandson, Emperor Charles V, provides the most striking example of how widely scattered lands could be brought under one ruler through the chance of inheritance. As well as Spain, Charles's inheritance from Isabella included the newly acquired lands in the Americas; from Ferdinand, Charles inherited the kingdom of Naples (conquered by Spanish troops between 1500 and 1504). Through his other grandparents, Mary of Burgundy and Maximilian, Charles got title to the lands that the Valois dukes of Burgundy had acquired in the Netherlands (all these territories had kept separate identities) and the Hapsburg lands in Austria.

Political communities that owed allegiance to a single ruler did not necessarily regard themselves as having anything else in common. Officials brought from one part of the ruler's dominions to administer another could be resented as intruders. Shared loyalty to a prince was not enough in itself to create a political community, let alone form a nation, but nationalist feeling could be focused on a ruler, as Elizabeth I became a focus of loyalty for the English. Some monarchs, such as the kings of Poland, were elected and so had to earn the loyalty of their subjects.

A republic might generate intense loyalty among its citizens, particularly those citizens who enjoyed access to the reins of power. Few were as proud of their state and its traditions as the Venetians. Even those excluded from political office could feel loyalty to a republic if they thought they were governed justly. If the subjects of a republic had no hope of becoming citizens, however, it was unlikely they would identify with its interests. A citizen of Vicenza or Verona,

▶ *The historic rivalry between the republics of Pisa and Florence left a legacy of bitterness after Pisa came under Florentine rule in 1406. When the Pisans rebelled in 1494, the Florentines could not subdue them until 1509, after years of warfare. This 1569 fresco by Giorgio Vasari and his workshop shows the Pisans' defeat at San Vincenzo.*

even after generations of Venetian rule, could never be a Venetian. The citizens of the subject towns of the republic of Florence, particularly those of Pisa, were given little reason to feel loyal to the republican government.

Nationalism and War

There has often been a close association between nationalism and war. Major victories or defeats in war are treated as landmarks in the history of nations and can remain a focus for patriotism and national feeling for centuries. Memories of the heavy defeat of the Serbs by the Ottoman Sultan Bayezid I at the Battle of Kosovo in 1389, for example, still underpin the claims of Serbian nationalists that the territory of Kosovo belongs to Serbia. The experience of warfare contributes to the rise of national feeling by encouraging populations to identify themselves as a community with a common enemy. On the other hand, nationalist sentiment can make a significant contribution to military strength by arousing fighting spirit and a sense of shared honor and purpose among troops. In Renaissance Europe national military traditions became a source of pride, with different nations becoming associated with different military techniques or forces: for example, the French were known for their dashing cavalry, the English for their skilled longbowmen, the Swiss for their disciplined companies of pikemen, and the Spanish for the stubborn endurance of hardship shown by their infantry.

Wars in Renaissance Europe were often fought to further the dynastic ambitions of princes or for reasons of high policy that had little to do with the interests of ordinary people. Princes would try to encourage their subjects to see their rulers' private quarrels as their own concern, too. Subjects were made to feel that they had a duty to support their prince and that, in fighting on his behalf, they were defending not only his honor but also, at least to some degree, their own. A republican government might try to convince its people that they held a common interest in the outcome of war, even if the issues at stake might only be, for example, fulfilling the terms of an alliance that meant little to most of the population. Such propaganda often had only limited effect. War inevitably brought increased taxation, but it could still be difficult for governments to raise enough money to pay for soldiers or for ships and sailors if they were needed. Indeed, it was often hard to find enough good men willing to fight. If troops were conscripted, communities sent, not their best fighting men,

but those they felt they could best do without—petty criminals and people without property, for whom the dangers and privations of a soldier's life would be better than slow starvation at home. Whether conscripts, militia, or mercenaries, most soldiers served for pay, not patriotism, and if they were not paid, they were liable to desert.

Even so, victory in battle could be a cause for national celebration. The English, for example, took great pride in the victory of Henry V over the French at Agincourt in 1415. Military glory was important to monarchs, who were still expected to lead their army in person if they could. A display of courage and leadership in war won the admiration and loyalty of a monarch's subjects and made them more willing to make further sacrifices to continue the war. Prowess in war helped forge a strong bond between the monarch and the nobility, who also looked for glory fighting at the king's side.

Invasion or the threat of invasion could rally the people behind their government, especially if the conflict was between traditional enemies. Owing to the nature of warfare at the time, however, there were few pitched battles. Most military campaigns consisted of siege warfare. Soldiers ravaged the countryside to gather supplies, booty, and hostages for ransom and to destroy any crops or buildings that could be useful to the enemy. Civilians frequently suffered more than soldiers—often at the hands of their defenders as well as the enemy. Even if civilians fought back, it was rarely for patriotic reasons. More often they tried to appease whichever side had the upper hand and, reasonably enough, wanted peace at any price.

▲ A depiction of Joan of Arc that decorates an illuminated letter from a late-fifteenth-century manuscript. Joan's conviction that Charles VII was the true king of France helped inspire renewed resistance to the English at a critical stage in the Hundred Years War.

CLAIMS TO FRANCE

English kings from Edward III to Henry VIII claimed to be the legal kings of France. During the Hundred Years War some of the French, particularly in areas of France that had long been subject to the kings of England, were prepared to accept the legitimacy of English claims. Some even called themselves English, though others accepted the English king as their sovereign while still regarding themselves as French. Most, however, detested the English for the destruction the wars brought to the kingdom and supported the Valois as the rightful kings of France. In 1429 Joan of Arc rallied support for Charles VII as the true heir of France, even though he had been disinherited by his father. Charles VII's victories reinforced the crown's claims to sovereignty over all France and laid the foundations for a strong French monarchy with loyal subjects.

Nationalism and Religion

Religious differences and disputes about the administration of the church reinforced nationalist sentiment before and after the Reformation. The power of religious dissent as a focus for a nation had already been shown in the early fifteenth century in Bohemia. The Hussites—followers of the Czech reformer Jan Hus (1372/3–1415)—appealed to those who were Czech by birth and language; most of those who opposed the Hussites in Bohemia were German speakers. After Hus was condemned and burned by the ecclesiastical Council of Constance in 1415, the Czech nobility protested on behalf of the Czech crown against his execution. They denounced Czech Catholics who sided with the enemies of Hus as betrayers of the Czech crown and language.

The Roman Catholic Church had always accomodated national or regional divisions. Throughout Europe there was a sense that benefices (church offices, especially when regarded as property or a source of revenue) should be given to local clergy and not used to provide income for faraway members of the papal court and bureaucracy. Rulers wanted to use benefices to support their own officials, many of whom were clergy (lawyers gradually replaced clergy in government positions in Renaissance Europe). Some major benefices yielded large incomes and had lands and fortresses of great strategic importance attached, such as the bishopric of Durham in the north of England and the patriarchate of Aquileia in northeastern Italy. Who held such benefices was a matter of political consequence.

There could also be resentment about the income from benefices or about money from taxes on the clergy being sent to Rome. Some governments used legislation to try to control the resources of the church and limit the pope's powers. In France there was a strong local tradition that stressed the independence of the French church. Adherents of this tradition, called Gallicanism, defended their "liberties" against the king as well as the pope. In the fifteenth century popes came to separate agreements with a number of princes. The Concordat of Redon (1441), made with the duke of Brittany, for

▲ *The teachings of the Czech reformer Jan Hus—particularly his calls for the creation of a national church and a Czech Bible—aroused nationalist sentiment among the Czechs. This depiction of his 1415 execution as a heretic comes from the fifteenth-century Chronicle of Ulrich von Richental. The civil war that broke out in Bohemia in 1419 was closely tied to Hus's execution.*

example, stipulated that the pope would nominate to Breton bishoprics only men of whom the duke approved.

A local church could also be associated with a desire for reform or with taking a stand against the claimed corruption of Rome. This attitude was common among Venetians, for example. The Spanish saw the *Reconquista*—the gradual reconquest of the Iberian Peninsula from the Moorish princes and peoples who had settled there—as their nation's crusade against Islam. Intolerance toward the remaining Muslims, the Jews, and those whose conversion to Christianity was suspected of being insincere was justified on the grounds of protecting Spain's Catholic faith.

Heresy (dissent from church doctrine) had traditionally been seen as subversive of the political order as well as the religious. Divisions brought about by the Reformation heightened the feeling among both Catholics and Protestants that religious unity was important to the state. Conformity to the religion chosen by the ruler was a test of political loyalty. In late-sixteenth-century England, where the monarch was head of the established church, Catholics were suspected of treachery and of putting loyalty to the pope before loyalty to the monarch. In France many Catholics could not accept that Protestants should be left in control of certain areas of the kingdom.

GERMAN NATIONALISM AND PROTESTANTISM

In the fifteenth century expressions of German nationalist sentiment were often linked with calls for reform of the church in Germany. In 1445, for example, there were calls for a national church council, in 1447 there was a concordat between the pope and the German princes, and in 1448 the Concordat of Vienna was concluded between the pope and the German nation, represented by the emperor. In popular literature there were calls for reform of the German church, and it was even suggested that Mainz, not Rome, should be the central seat of the Catholic Church. The German Reformer Martin Luther's appeals to political powers—for example, "To the Christian Nobility of the German Nation" (1520)—were rooted in this tradition.

Luther's translation of the Bible was not the first German translation, but it was the first to be widely available: an estimated half million copies were printed before his death in 1546. This translation not only made the Scriptures accessible to laymen but also provided a model of written German that contributed greatly to the development of a standard language. Luther and other Protestant authors wrote thousands of pamphlets in German; Catholics also wrote treatises in German, but far more Protestant literature was printed.

Although Protestantism in German-speaking lands was associated with concepts of the German nation and contributed greatly to the development of a standard written German language, religious differences also led to bitter new quarrels between German states, quarrels that reinforced the political divisions among them. The Peace of Augsburg (1555) established the principle that the religious denomination of all the people of a given state was that of their ruler. It was many decades before this compromise was accepted as final, and in the meantime religious conflict continued to plague the German states.

▼ *The German Reformer Martin Luther's translation of the Bible was of great significance in the development of a standard form of the German language. A woodcut printed on the title page of the 1546 edition of his New Testament, published in Wittenberg, depicts Luther and Elector John Frederick of Saxony beneath the cross.*

Religious differences brought added bitterness to both international conflicts and civil wars and made them harder to resolve. Alliance between a Protestant and a Catholic state was extremely unusual. It was expected that Protestants would seek Protestant allies and Catholics, Catholic allies. Strengthening nationalist sentiment while deepening the divisions between nations, religious allegiance became an integral part of political allegiance.

FURTHER READING

Allmand, Christopher, ed. *The New Cambridge Medieval History.* Vol. 7, *C. 1415–c. 1500.* New York, 1998.

Guenée, Bernard. *States and Rulers in Later Medieval Europe.* Translated by Juliet Vale. New York, 1985.

Marcu, Eva Dorothea. *Sixteenth-Century Nationalism.* New York, 1976.

Thomson, John A. F. *Popes and Princes, 1417–1517: Politics and Polity in the Late Medieval Church.* Boston, 1980.

Christine Shaw

SEE ALSO

• Augsburg, Peace of • Burgundy • England
• Established Churches • Ferdinand and Isabella
• France • Holy Roman Empire • Italian City-States
• Languages, Vernacular • Monarchy • Switzerland

Nobility and Rank

NOBLEMEN AND NOBLEWOMEN HELD A HIGH PLACE IN EUROPEAN RENAISSANCE SOCIETY. THIS STATUS WAS TYPICALLY CONNECTED WITH A COMBINATION OF SEVERAL FACTORS: THEIR BIRTH, CHOICE OF SPOUSE, OCCUPATION, WEALTH, AND PROPERTY.

▼ *Dress was an important indication of a person's rank and role in society. This scene, painted by the Italian artist Pietro Vannucci (c. 1450–1523), known as Perugino, depicts a palace courtyard, with richly costumed courtiers and a priest dressed in a somber habit.*

Throughout Europe during the Renaissance and the Reformation, there was an acute consciousness of social status, but assessing a person's exact position in society could be difficult. A person was usually considered of the same rank as his or her birth family, but it was also possible to move up or down in society. The status of different social groups—for example, merchants—varied from place to place. One of the most contentious questions concerned the definition of nobility itself: who counted as noble, what made a person noble, and whether a noble in one society was considered noble in another.

There were wide differences in the proportion of the population that was accounted noble in various parts of Europe. In Poland, Hungary, and the Spanish kingdoms, about 10 percent of the population belonged to the nobility. Many were poor, with little to distinguish them in their way of life from their commoner neighbors. In France and Germany about 1 or 2 percent of people belonged to the nobility. In England only a tiny percentage were nobles—by definition, the peers who sat in the House of Lords and their immediate families—but there was a much larger number of gentry, who would have a claim to be considered the equivalent of nobles elsewhere in Europe. In England, France, and Germany there were poor nobles and gentry, too, although it was questionable whether an elevated status could be maintained in poverty, particularly if an impoverished noble was forced to turn to an ignoble occupation in order to earn a living.

Most nobles had titles, such as count, marquis, duke, or even prince. In some societies all members of the family—or at least all the males—bore the title, while in others only the eldest son inherited it. Formal hierarchies of noble ranks did not always reflect the relative esteem in which the families were held. A count of ancient lineage (descent) might be respected more than a recently ennobled duke.

There were sometimes practical advantages to being a noble, such as exemption from certain taxes or the right to be better treated if prosecuted for a crime. Some offices, such as military commands and diplomatic appointments, were considered to be particularly suited for nobles. For many nobles, however, the most important advantage of their status was the respect they received from others.

Becoming a Nobleman or Noblewoman

The easiest and most common way to become a member of the nobility was to be born to noble parents; indeed, to many, nobility of birth was the only true kind. Few would challenge the claim to nobility of a person born into a family of wealthy, titled landowners with a long history of social preeminence.

How long a family had been noble was intrinsic to its prestige. Some families could boast that their nobility was so ancient that there was no record of when it began. Others claimed descent from historic figures, ancient Roman families, or even legendary heroes, and they devised elaborate genealogies (family trees) to bolster these claims.

Letters of ennoblement from a prince, with or without the grant of a title, constituted a clear claim to noble status but did not necessarily earn the holder or his family recognition of the claim. Much depended on the reasons for the grant and the personal circumstances and reputation of the new noble. Although the prince was the fount of honor (he had the exclusive right to confer new titles of nobility), some argued that he could really provide only external recognition of inherent noble qualities. If the title had in effect been bought, little honor would come to the new noble.

In some societies, notably France or some Italian city-states, holding certain offices in gov-

▲ *A knight was generally regarded as a member of the nobility. Investiture with knighthood for service to a prince, as illustrated in this anonymous early-sixteenth-century French work, was especially honorable.*

TREATISES ON NOBILITY

Many treatises on the nature of nobility were written, published, and widely circulated in Renaissance Europe. Often they rehearsed the debate found in classical authors about whether true nobility was based on birth or merit (that is, virtue). Those who regarded nobility as an inherited characteristic argued that the ancestors of nobles had passed on superior qualities to their descendants—virtue was inherited with noble blood. Those who argued that true nobility was based on the qualities of the individual could pose the awkward question, When did a noble's ancestors become noble, and on what grounds?

Although these arguments had gone on for centuries, treatises were often rooted in real social tensions and conflicts. Defenders of the idea that nobility derived from office holding supported the argument based on virtue; members of the landed nobility concerned about threats to their status from wealthy upstarts argued for the primacy of nobility of birth. Academics argued, fruitlessly, about the nobility of holders of higher university degrees. There were assertions of the validity of nobility conferred by military prowess—an ancient association. There were debates about the validity of nobility conferred by a prince; ennoblement for outstanding services, especially in war, was one thing, but how valid could a title of nobility be if it were simply bought? The question of nobility remained contentious, even when the authors and readers of the treatises did not confront the challenge expressed in the question posed during the Peasants' Revolt in England in 1381: "When Adam delved and Eve span, who was then the gentleman?"

ernment conferred noble status. Sometimes only the holder of the office could claim to be a noble, and he could not pass on the status to his heirs. Nobility through office was contentious and not necessarily recognized by others.

Another way to acquire status was to purchase land, especially the kind of property, such as a fief (feudal estate), that came with a title or powers of jurisdiction. Owning such land was not enough in itself to gain recognition of nobility, but it could be an element in a claim for recognition.

Some claimed that holding a university doctorate conferred noble status, although the only people likely to accept the argument were others with doctorates.

Recognition of noble status sometimes was acquired gradually, perhaps over two or three generations, as a family's importance came to be accepted by those who knew them. Buying a fief, an office, or even a title was only a start; members of the family would have to live in a way that was appropriate to the nobility.

Types of Nobility

Just as there were various ways of becoming noble, there were various types of nobility. In most areas of Europe, owning land was the most widely recognized way of being part of the nobility. There were great variations in wealth and power among the landed nobility, from the magnate with thousands of acres of land and several fine houses or castles to the petty rural noble who struggled to feed his family and rarely left his neighborhood. However different their circumstances, magnates and petty rural nobles shared important values and interests and felt a greater affinity with each other than with men from other social groups. One strong bond was the tradition of pursuing a military career. The local minor nobility was also often linked to the great nobles of the land by networks of patronage and clientage (whereby minor nobles offered their services as retainers to powerful nobles in return for support).

The landed nobility often had close associations with towns and townsmen. If they could afford it, many had at least one town house where they spent part of the year. Hostility seldom existed between landed nobles and their urban counterparts. The latter, however, were quite distinct in the way they had become noble and also in their way of life. Urban noblemen often acquired status through the offices they held or the offices that previous generations of

◀ *No one would have disputed the claim to nobility of a man such as the duke of Lancaster—a powerful, wealthy landowner, of royal blood, with a prestigious title, and a member of the most important English chivalric order, the Order of the Garter. This depiction of the duke is from the* Book of the Founder Knights of the Garter *(c. 1430).*

their family had held. In many Italian cities holding offices in civic government or sitting in the legislative council were associated with noble status, as had been the tradition in Venice since the late thirteenth century: all adult male Venetian nobles had the right to sit in the Great Council. By the mid-sixteenth century, the association between civic office and noble status was a widespread feature of the government and society of Italian towns. During the Italian wars of the first half of the sixteenth century, Italian townsmen had become more likely to claim noble status and assert their right to respect from French and Spanish occupying forces. Even Italians, however, questioned whether a man considered noble in his own town because he had a right to sit in the council could be considered noble elsewhere.

Noblesse de Robe and Noblesse d'Épée

In France those who acquired nobility through holding, buying, or inheriting government offices formed the *noblesse de robe* (nobility of the robe). The traditional nobility was known as the *noblesse d'épée* (nobility of the sword), a name that reflects the significance of its military role.

In the first half of the fourteenth century, a man holding a law degree and a post as a royal official could claim to be a nobleman, but as the numbers of lawyers and officials grew and more attention was paid to the legitimacy of such claims, the nature of the process changed. By the late fifteenth century, the growth of the royal administration and similar princely ones, such as that of the duke of Brittany, led to the creation of many more full-time, permanent positions that conferred prestige and the opportunity to make a living from salaries and fees. From the late fourteenth century it had become accepted that officials, first in the lower offices and gradually in the higher offices as well, could sell their posts or pass them on to their heirs. From the later fifteenth century the crown began to monopolize the sale of royal offices, and this practice became an important source of revenue for the king.

About the same time, some offices came to be regarded as conferring nobility, although only the holders of the most important posts, such as chancellor, could pass on their status to their heirs. Other offices had to be held for two or three generations before the holding family was considered noble. By the late sixteenth century

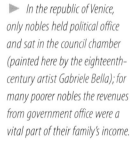

▶ *In the republic of Venice, only nobles held political office and sat in the council chamber (painted here by the eighteenth-century artist Gabriele Bella); for many poorer nobles the revenues from government office were a vital part of their family's income.*

NOBILITY AND RANK IN THE CHURCH

According to some theories of rank, all clergymen were superior to all laymen. For example, there was a widespread idea that all clergy belonged to the First Estate, the nobility to the Second Estate, and everyone else to the Third Estate. In practice, social status within the clergy was a reflection of social rank in lay society. Many poor parish priests, some scarcely literate, lived much as the peasants or urban poor around them did. Members of noble families who entered the church were not expected to serve as parish priests even at the beginning of their career. They began by holding positions, such as canon of a cathedral or a wealthy collegiate church, where they had few duties and often did not need to be resident. Many German collegiate churches took clergy only from knightly or other noble families.

There was much social differentiation between orders of monks, friars, and nuns. Noble parents who sent their daughters to be nuns in order to avoid paying dowries wanted them to live among their social equals. Certain monasteries were regarded as more suitable for nobles than others. Membership in religious orders was, however, the best way for able boys from poorer families to gain an education and make a career. Some boys from obscure backgrounds became cardinals or even popes, Sixtus IV (reigned 1471–1484) and Pius V (reigned 1566–1572), for example.

Many bishops came from noble families. A wealthy see was a desirable post for a noble cleric, particularly if some secular jurisdiction was attached to it, such as the territory governed by the bishop of Durham, England. In England bishops and, until the Reformation, some abbots sat as members of the House of Lords. After the Reformation the Protestant Church of England kept much of the hierarchy of the Catholic Church. Other Protestant churches, such as the Calvinists, lacked wealthy and prestigious benefices and did not attract as many noble clerics.

the *noblesse de robe* had become very powerful and much more difficult to enter. At the time the relative status and merits of the nobilities of the robe and of the sword were hotly argued, and it remains uncertain whether the *noblesse de robe* ever successfully challenged the preeminence of the *noblesse d'épée.* The divisions between them and the differences between their values and ways of life were not always clear. Some members of the *noblesse d'épée* studied law, for example, and held royal office; some of the *noblesse de robe* pursued a military career. In Germany, too, where all ranks of the nobility were very conscious of their status, many nobles held administrative offices under the princes of the empire. Holding such a post could signally enhance the fortunes of a noble family. Service to a prince was not scorned or seen as a sign of economic difficulties or political submission.

Living Nobly

A man's occupation and how he and his family lived were crucial to their acceptance as noble by others. Whether or not they lived nobly was a test applied when, for example, a French townsman was claiming the tax privileges of a nobleman. If he won exemption from tax, the burden on his neighbors increased, and so claims to noble status were scrutinized carefully. In France and elsewhere in Europe, living nobly generally entailed the avoidance of manual labor or trades that were considered demeaning. For example, a tanner, however prosperous, had little hope of acceptance as a member of the nobility.

Above all, a nobleman defended his honor. Certain incidental characteristics, however, were regarded as signs of true nobility. Appropriate manners, dress, and behavior were important. A nobleman was expected to spend freely even if he had little money. A family could be ruined as its members, unable to bring themselves to turn to occupations that might be thought dishonorable, tried without sufficient means to maintain a way of life suited to their rank. Charitable foundations were formed specifically to give discreet aid to poor nobles and gentlefolk so as not to

▶ *Pierre Séguier, painted here astride his horse by Charles Le Brun, was chancellor of France for most of the period between 1635 and 1672. As such, he was the highest member of the* noblesse de robe, *but despite his great wealth and status, he was not accepted as the equal of the highest ranks of the* noblesse d'epée.

The practice of fighting duels to avenge insults or defend one's honor became widespread in some parts of Europe, chiefly England, France, and Italy. It is estimated that, during the late sixteenth and early seventeenth centuries, several thousand men were killed in duels each year. There were regulations for the conduct of duels, which were usually fought with swords rather than firearms. Only noblemen or gentlemen could fight duels because only they had the kind of personal honor that could be defended in this way. Although many societies banned or strictly regulated dueling because of concern for the loss of life, a gentleman could not refuse a challenge to a duel without risking the deep dishonor of being branded a coward—unless the challenger was a social inferior, who, by the codes of dueling, was not qualified to fight one. In such a case, to fight the duel would dishonor the gentleman. Sometimes a duel was preceded by an exchange of letters. In the letters, which might well be made public, doubt could be cast on whether the opponent was really worthy of taking part in the duel. An unworthy challenger who defied a noble might be attacked by the noble's servants because of the implied insult of presuming to be the noble's equal.

▶ This fourteenth-century German manuscript illumination depicts a tournament where single combat is taking place between two suitors. Such chivalric entertainment developed into the serious—and sometimes lethal—duel; medieval tournament rules formed the basis of an agreed-upon code of conduct practiced by duelers.

humiliate them further. It was accepted that an impoverished nobleman had a claim to better treatment than one of the ordinary poor, that he should be helped to live decently rather than barely subsist.

Those who struggled to attain recognition of noble status had to be especially careful. They risked social ridicule if they were thought to be aspiring to a status they did not merit or could not maintain. Those who proudly felt they were living nobly might be seen as mere parvenus by jealous or scornful neighbors.

Nobles and Merchants

How far nobles could engage in trade without losing their status varied across Europe. In some societies, particularly in great trading cities, such as Venice, it was acceptable for nobles to be merchants. Even in regions where nobles were not expected to be merchants, it was usually acceptable for them to sell surplus produce from their lands, sometimes on a large scale, and perhaps to own trading ships or exploit the mineral wealth of their estates. There were many ways in which nobles could make money from commerce and industry without appearing to demean themselves. There was, however, a general distinction between wholesale and retail trade.

Wholesale trade, particularly if it was large scale and international, was an honorable way to make money, whereas retail trade was seen as the equivalent of manual labor. When enquiries were being made into noble status, testimony that a man—or his father or any other close relative—had been seen standing in a shop serving customers was strong, perhaps conclusive evidence that his family was not noble.

Many nobles regarded direct involvement in trade as unfitting for people of their status; they criticized merchants for being obsessed with making money, while nobles thought principally of honor. Merchants could be just as contemptuous of nobles; they criticized nobles as wastrels who led violent, idle lives. Nevertheless, many merchants aspired to noble status, if not for themselves then for their children. They might buy land, send their sons to study law or pursue a military career rather than join the family business, or marry their daughters into noble families. Marriage to a rich merchant's daughter was a recognized solution to the problem of noble families suffering economic difficulties (nobles were much less likely to marry their daughters to a merchant's son, because a wife's status was more influenced by her husband's social standing than a husband's by his wife's).

The links between trade and acquiring social status are very significant. Trade was the best way to accumulate wealth, and wealth from trade could be used to buy social recognition and status, but association with trade could also fatally compromise claims to nobility.

Court Society

Royal courts in Renaissance Europe were increasingly important as cultural and political centers and as social centers for the nobility. Court rituals became more complex to express more elaborate hierarchies of courtiers. Members of prominent noble families were usually regarded as a prince's natural companions when he was at leisure, such as when hunting.

High noble rank did not, however, always equate with political influence and power. In many courts, particularly in the sixteenth century, princes were becoming reliant on secretaries of comparatively lowly birth, whose knowledge of state secrets and ease of access to the prince might cause envy and resentment among high-born courtiers. Many nobles still claimed that they should be the natural coun-

◄ *In this fifteenth-century illumination from the* Triumph of Love, *produced by Apollonio di Giovanni's workshop, nobles wear luxurious fabrics and furs. Dressing appropriately, especially at ceremonies and court entertainments, could be extremely costly.*

selors of the prince. As nobles grew more dependent on offices, pensions, grants of privileges, and military commands, competition for the ruler's favor increased. Nobles who learned the arts of the courtier and exploited the networks of patronage and faction within court society could reap rich rewards.

It is possible that princes deliberately summoned the nobility to court and kept them there to make them more dependent, so that their time and efforts would be spent competing for favor rather than building up their power in the provinces. This tactic has been seen as a prime feature of centralized government. On the other hand, there was a practical limit to the number of nobles that could be at court, and evidence suggests that the majority rarely went there, if ever. Princes did not have the resources to govern their lands alone; they needed the assistance of the nobles. A wise ruler was more likely to harness the power of the nobles than to work to suppress their influence.

Even if the nobility lost some of its political power by the seventeenth century, it was still socially and culturally powerful. The importance attached to noble status and to distinctions of rank was, if anything, greater in the seventeenth century than in the fourteenth century.

FURTHER READING

Dewald, Jonathan. *The European Nobility, 1400– 1800.* New York, 1996.

Huppert, George. *Les Bourgeois Gentilshommes: An Essay on the Definition of Elites in Renaissance France.* Chicago, 1977.

Stone, Lawrence. *The Crisis of the Aristocracy, 1558– 1641.* Oxford, 1965.

Christine Shaw

SEE ALSO

• Burgundy • Chivalry • England • Feudalism
• France • German Towns • Households
• Italian City-States • Monarchy • Portugal
• Spain • Venice • Women

SUMPTUARY LAWS

Sumptuary laws were statutes regulating elaborate dress and other forms of display, such as banquets. These laws were in place throughout Renaissance Europe, in both monarchies and republics, Catholic states and Protestant ones. Sumptuary laws were created partly for economic reasons (to curb what was viewed as a waste of resources) and partly for moral reasons (on the grounds that extravagance was sinful). Another motive was to preserve social hierarchies and distinctions. Prostitutes were forbidden to wear certain jewels or fabrics lest they be mistaken for women of high status. Only people of a certain level of wealth or social standing were permitted to wear silk or particular types of furs, and there were regulations on how many garments a person could own. Upper limits were set for dowries according to the social status of the bride. There were even regulations governing the conduct of social festivities. In German towns, for example, tradesmen were not allowed to join in dances with the urban aristocracy; even women from lower social ranks who had married into the aristocracy might be barred from dancing in places reserved for aristocrats. Such laws were difficult to police and enforce. They were often revised, a fact that suggests that people were reluctant to obey them and attached great importance to outward displays of rank.

Painting and Sculpture

THE PERIOD FROM 1300 TO 1650, ONE OF UNRIVALED ARTISTIC INNOVATION, WITNESSED THE DEVELOPMENT OF MATHEMATICAL PERSPECTIVE AND THE RISE OF NATURALISTIC PORTRAITURE.

The division of the period extending from 1300 to 1650 into the Renaissance and the Reformation, though commonplace within many branches of history, is not recognized in the visual arts. Historians of art have adopted different terms to characterize the major styles and style changes: Renaissance (early and High), mannerism, and baroque. Understood rightly, these terms afford an overview of art in Europe following the medieval period.

Classical Heritage

When artists of the later Middle Ages, such as the Florentine painter Giotto di Bondone (1266/7 or 1276–1337), began to explore the possibilities of a new, more naturalistic type of representation, they drew inspiration from the works of earlier artists. In Italy especially, the classical past could be seen all around. In seeking to imitate Roman and Greek modes of representation, artists were by no means entering uncharted waters. Throughout the Middle Ages many great men—kings, popes, and thinkers, as well as artists—had sought the refinements of classical culture. Something was different, however, about the intellectual and artistic climate of Italy by 1300; this time, in borrowing from the aesthetics of the ancients, artists would come to acquire a deep understanding of their techniques and theories and also of the outlook that underpinned them.

Naturalistic depiction of the human figure and the introduction of illusory perspective were among the first areas to attract interest. These and other techniques were increasingly systematized during the fifteenth century. Theoretical understanding of such techniques was stalled by the Black Death, an epidemic of bubonic plague that devastated Europe in the mid-fourteenth century. As the most talented artists typically resided in the plague-ravaged cities, the death toll among painters and sculptors would have been high; the Sienese Lorenzetti brothers, Pietro (c. 1280–c. 1348) and Ambrogio (c. 1290–1348), for instance, would likely have contributed a great deal to the understanding of illusory perspective had they survived.

▲ The Sienese artist Ambrogio Lorenzetti's Presentation (1342) uses a perspectival system that incorporates a number of vanishing points (the floor, for instance, recedes into the distance less quickly than the vaulted ceiling). Such experimentation helped pave the way toward the understanding of perspective.

▶ *In his* Well of Moses, *sculpted for the Charterhouse of Champmol in Dijon, France, Claus Sluter combined carefully naturalistic characterizations of Old Testament prophets (such as David, viewed here) with a dramatic interplay of light and shadow in order to create a heightened sense of animation.*

Following the Black Death, the European artistic community was busy relearning techniques. The decades on either side of 1400 witnessed the ascendancy of a style known as international Gothic. Derived largely from the principles of manuscript illumination, works in this style exhibit sumptuous materials, copious surface decoration, and careful attention to detail. It appeared throughout much of Europe north of the Alps; Italian painting was not really part of this movement. By 1425, in central Italy at least, the art of classical antiquity had reasserted itself as the primary inspiration for painters and sculptors. Here the art-historical road divides: Italian painters and sculptors continued to rediscover and revive the classical past, while northern European artists and patrons, less strongly linked to ancient Rome, created a visual culture more firmly rooted in the world as they saw it.

Claus Sluter c. 1340/50–1406

Probably born in Haarlem, the Dutch sculptor Claus Sluter entered the service of Duke Philip the Bold of Burgundy in 1385 and became the duke's court sculptor in 1389. All of Sluter's surviving works are connected with the Burgundian court, from where, along with the French royal court in Paris, the international Gothic style spread. Sluter is the most influential sculptor associated with this style. Sluter's work has a stately grandeur and precise attention to naturalistic detail that is typical of international Gothic art. His carving in deep relief and bold use of contrasting areas of light and shadow make his figures almost lifelike. Sluter's three important surviving works are the sculptural group on the entrance to the chapel of the Carthusian monastery of Champmol (founded by Duke Philip in 1383), the *Well of Moses* within the monastic complex, and the tomb of Philip the Bold.

PAINTING IN FLANDERS AFTER VAN EYCK

Though many of the more superficial aspects of Jan van Eyck's style and techniques were copied throughout northern Europe even into the sixteenth century, none of his emulators achieved anything like his status. The most important Flemish painters to follow van Eyck show his influence but pursued their own talents. Rogier van der Weyden (c. 1399–1464) represents a strand of Flemish painting that emphasizes the sorrow and frailty of the human experience. While his portraits exude an unstudied informality and an attempt to portray—rather than to enhance—reality, van der Weyden's religious works focus on the humanity of Christ, also a preoccupation of the later artists Hans Memling (c. 1430/5–1494) and Hugo van der Goes (c. 1440–1482).

Other important painters, such as Petrus Christus (c. 1420–1472/3) and Dirck Bouts (c. 1400–1475), focused on the formal conception of their compositions. In their works the concern with surfaces and actual visual experience is coupled with a more theoretical approach to the depiction of three-dimensionality. The lack of evidence of direct contact with Italy leaves the possibility that by the mid-fifteenth century certain Flemish painters were independently exploring artistic modes of expression generally associated with classical ideals.

Northern Naturalism

From the beginning of the fifteenth century, Gothic tastes prevailed north of the Alps, but they were increasingly tempered by influences from Flemish art. In urban, industrial Flanders the fifteenth century was a time of considerable economic expansion. Wealthy Flemish merchants commissioned paintings, illuminated manuscripts, and funerary sculpture, and their tastes and aspirations are reflected in the style and content of Flemish art. Hardworking and often of relatively humble origins, Flemish merchants understood their social status in terms of the material goods that they were able to acquire with their newly won wealth and paid great heed to outward appearance. Generally speaking, Flemish art of the fiteenth century delights in

▶ *Dirk Bouts's* Last Supper *(1464–1467), in Saint Peter's Church, Louvain, Belgium, is one of the earliest northern European panels to utilize single-point perspective (its central panel is shown here). Although the work does not exhibit a system of perspective that unifies the space throughout the composition, a single vanishing point is present within each of the distinct rooms.*

In 1401 the artists Filippo Brunelleschi and Lorenzo Ghiberti created panels depicting the sacrifice of Isaac for the door of the Florence baptistery. Brunelleschi's panel (left) displays attention to detail and a sense of drama but is fundamentally Gothic in its conception. The relative stasis and calmness of Ghiberti's panel (right) and its attention to the human form are an early illustration of the artistic ideals of the Renaissance.

surfaces. Brilliantly colored and richly textured works catalog in careful detail people and the houses, places of work, decor, furniture, and clothing that advertise their place in society.

The dominance of the craft guilds in fifteenth-century Flanders ensured that technical standards were maintained at a high level, and the best painters became expert in showing the minutiae of their world—the pile of an expensive Persian carpet or the shimmer of a silk gown, even the parched, wrinkled skin of an aged bishop. By 1430 artists such as Jan van Eyck (before 1395–1441) and his brother Hubert had perfected the use of luminous, slow-drying oil-based glazes, which were more suited to realism than the fast-drying, matte egg tempera favored by earlier painters. Northern naturalism was unaffected by the Italian Renaissance until much later in the century, under the influence of the German Albrecht Dürer (1471–1528).

Wealth in Italy

Over the fourteenth and fifteenth centuries the Italians, like their northern counterparts, developed a new sense of their own place within the world order, one that was also underpinned by an emergent individualism. Whereas Flemish painters captured the spirit of contemporary Flanders, Italian artists sought to explore their affinity with classical Rome. Fifteenth-century Italians saw themselves as the heirs of the ancient Romans, celebrated for their nobility, patriotism, and intellectual and moral sophistication. Artists and their patrons throughout Italy were surrounded by the physical remains of ancient Rome (buildings, sculpture, and tombs) and were increasingly familiar with the great works of classical literature, philosophy, and scientific investigation.

The first public commission to reflect the emerging taste for classically inspired art was one for new doors for the baptistery in Florence's cathedral (1401). The reliefs submitted by the architect Filippo Brunelleschi (1377–1446), who later designed the spectacular dome for the cathedral, and Lorenzo Ghiberti (c. 1378–1455), the sculptor who won the commission, both depicted Abraham's sacrifice of Isaac within a Gothic quatrefoil. Brunelleschi's relief is rather busy and highly dramatic, with the main figures—in their stances and drapery folds—echoing the narrative tension of the moment when Isaac is spared through divine intervention. Ghiberti, in contrast, lends a sense of calm by avoiding the most dramatic moment and making the action psychological rather than physical, as seen in Abraham's purposeful stare and furrowed brow. Ghiberti's relief also shows a new interest in the human form: the folds in Abraham's drapery suggest a real body beneath, while the figure of Isaac has been called the first naturalistic nude figure since classical antiquity.

Sculptors after Ghiberti continued to explore both the classical ideal of physical form and the depiction of the psyche and intellect. In the decades just after 1400, the Florentine sculptor Donatello (c. 1386–1466) experimented with classical stances to create a sense of movement and shifts of weight within his figures. With his statue *David* (1430–1432), Donatello reintroduced freestanding, plurifacial sculpture (sculpture viewable from all sides) into Europe after an absence of nearly a millennium. Like Ghiberti, Donatello is interested in the psychology behind the drama. His *David* shows self-awareness—

▲ *Antonio Pollaiuolo's bronze statue* Hercules and Antaeus *(c. 1475) captures the hero Hercules and the giant Antaeus at the height of their struggle. The two figures' awkward poses give the piece a strong sense of dynamism.*

pride in his body and his deed; this interest in the way the inner self may be portrayed in the outer form became a cornerstone of Renaissance art. About five years earlier (around 1425), the painter Masaccio (Tomasso Guidi; 1401–1428) was at work on a fresco cycle in the Brancacci Chapel of the Church of Santa Maria del Carmine in Florence. His figures of Adam and Eve as they are expelled from Eden, while perhaps slightly less anatomically convincing, evoke the same sense of self-awareness (Adam and Eve express despair rather than pride) found in Donatello's *David*.

Masaccio was a great innovator; the true-to-life quality of his work must have stunned his contemporaries. To suggest space and depth, Masaccio employed a single vanishing point and aerial perspective (whereby things farther away from the viewer appear out of focus and muted in tone). Both techniques had been used in Roman painting. Brunelleschi is credited with rediscovering mathematical single-point perspective, but Masaccio appears to have introduced aerial perspective without knowledge of antique models. Masaccio's paintings are often lit by a single light source from within so that depth and volume are suggested through the contrast of light and shadow (a technique known as chiaroscuro). Masaccio involves the viewer by grouping his figures into an open circle with the viewer as the implied missing figure or by arranging his vanishing point so that it appears at the spectator's eye level.

The Italian humanist art theorist and architect Leon Battista Alberti (1404–1472) discussed perspective in his treatise on painting, *De pittura* (1435). Alberti states that painters should strive to imitate nature, which can be understood in purely mathematical terms. He stresses the importance of draftsmanship and artistic talent and recommends controlled use of color, naturalistic depiction of light and dark, and careful planning of composition. Alberti also discusses the necessity of portraying psychological states through gestures, facial expressions, and subtle coloring. He believed that painters should tell a story clearly and beautifully and at the same time reveal the rich variety of life and humanity. Alberti was a huge influence on painters of the

PORTRAITURE IN THE EARLY RENAISSANCE

Naturalistic portraiture, explored by Tuscan painters of the early fourteenth century, appears first in illuminated manuscripts and then in painted panels and sculpted images from around 1400. Many of the earliest portraits are in profile, a method of portraiture that echoes the images on Roman coins and allows a good likeness—it avoids the necessity for foreshortening posed by frontal views. Flemish painters from van Eyck onward preferred to paint subjects in three-quarters or full-frontal poses. In Italy frontal views gradually replaced profiles from around 1475.

The equestrian portrait was reintroduced in the 1440s by Donatello—his statue of Erasmo da Narni (known as *Gattamelata*) astride his horse was erected in the Piazza del Santo in Padua in 1453. Italian busts, again inspired by Roman models, became popular from the middle of the fifteenth century.

▲ The three-quarters view and close attention to surface detail found in Hans Memling's Portrait of an Old Woman (c. 1480) are typical of Flemish portrait paintings of the fifteenth century.

quattrocento (fifteenth century), including Paolo Uccello (1397–1475) and Piero della Francesca (c. 1420–1492).

New Directions

Whereas artists of the early fifteenth century explored life's static qualities and depicted a world underpinned by the classical ideals of rational order and balance, later artists tended to portray life as a dynamic force. Artists such as Antonio Pollaiuolo (c. 1431–1498) and Andrea del Verrocchio (1435–1488) looked for ways of capturing movement and change. Other artists, including Sandro Botticelli (1444–1510), sought to depict the inner life of their human subjects. The ordering of their compositions, figures, color harmonies, and details was designed to express emotion, psychological motivations, and spirituality. In contrast, Domenico Ghirlandaio (1449–1494) and other society painters painted religious scenes populated by wealthy Florentines and portraits of the same people in all their finery. Ghirlandaio was the most financially successful Florentine painter of his generation. He tried to understand the world by recording his surroundings—Florence, its architectural wonders, and its noble citizenry.

Unlike their Flemish contemporaries, Italian artists of the quattrocento recorded their surroundings in order to express philosophical concerns—their patriotism, their pride in their classical heritage, and their understanding of man's place in the universe, for example. To an Italian artist of the period, the accurate rendering of a facial expression or cascading silk gown explains the reality of what lies beneath; to a northern artist the visual experience is a reality in itself.

▶ *Michelangelo's* Creation of Adam *is part of the fresco he painted on the ceiling of the Sistine Chapel, in Rome, between 1508 and 1512. With its classically inspired nudes and carefully balanced composition, it reflects the basic tenets of High Renaissance painting. The dynamic tension created by the tiny gap between God's finger and Adam's illustrates the artistic genius of Michelangelo.*

Rome and the High Renaissance

The High Renaissance is so called because during it, the advances and experimentation of the fifteenth century had been fully assimilated and, for a short time, contemporary art rivaled the art of fifth-century-BCE Athens. The High Renaissance spans less than thirty-five years. It begins in the mid-1490s with the collapse of Medici rule in Florence and the invasion of Italy by Charles VIII of France, and it ends in 1527 with the sack of Rome by the French. During this time Rome, under a series of powerful popes, was transformed into a glittering center of artistic and architectural excellence. Florence and Venice contributed greatly to the High Renaissance, but its epicenter was Rome.

Many of the most recognizable images in Western art—among them Michelangelo's *David* and Leonardo's *Mona Lisa*—date from the High Renaissance, and the style can be summed up in the careers of four major artists: Leonardo da Vinci (1452–1519), Michelangelo Buonarroti (1475–1564), Raphael Sanzio (1483–1520), and Titian (Tiziano Vecelli; 1488/90–1576). The works of all four, although they differ greatly, embody the classical ideals of the Renaissance. These artists, who are among the most important conceptual thinkers in the history of Western art, pushed their forms to the limit. Gone is the concept of the artist as a specialist (in perspective or portraiture, for instance);

in its place appears a completeness of vision that transcends formal boundaries.

A full generation older than Michelangelo, Raphael, and Titian, Leonardo is often described as a man before his time, and he developed new skills throughout his career. He spent most of the High Renaissance in Milan rather than in Rome or Florence, but his studies of anatomy, physics, and other sciences—and their application to his art—make him a true "Renaissance man." Leonardo's conception of the individual components within a composition as subordinate to the whole and his exploration into the way that technique and composition may be used to convey emotional states pave the way for the younger Renaissance masters.

Of the four artists Raphael wears his mantle of genius most easily. His career is the only one to be more or less contained within the High Renaissance. Known for his tender Madonnas, clear color palette, and logical approach to both subject matter and composition, his work exhibits little of the strife seen throughout the lengthy career of Michelangelo. Michelangelo struggled constantly with other artists, with his own problems, with his definitions of artistic standards, and with his theoretical ideals. If the transformation of the artist from talented craftsman to divinely inspired creator is the defining theme of the High Renaissance, then Michelangelo should be seen as its supreme exemplar.

UNDERSTANDING RENAISSANCE COMPOSITIONS

The arrangement of the various figures and objects within a work of art is known as its composition. In Italian painting of the trecento (fourteenth century), the important figures and main action of the scene generally appear in a line across the bottom—such placement was a medieval convention that continued despite the introduction of illusory perspective. During the early Renaissance, mathematically based systems of perspective became more visually convincing. As artists became ever more concerned with verismilitude, they began to place figures within, rather than in front of, the three-dimensional "space." Leon Battista Alberti devoted a large portion of his treatise on painting to defining and understanding composition (both of individual figures and groups of figures). Early Renaissance painters strove for a composition that was clear and uncluttered but also allowed for the depiction of various actions, gestures, and stances. Painters used geometrical shapes to place figures within and not just in front of the illusory space—a figure was given prominence, for example, by placing it at the top of the semicircle or triangle that formed the basis of the composition.

Leonardo added a new sense of dynamism to Renaissance art by introducing the pyramid into artistic composition. Its implied three-dimensionality gives compositions based on the pyramid a sculptural and spatial mass never achieved by the two-dimensional triangle. Mannerist artists of the later sixteenth century would prefer rounded or serpentine compositions, which gave their works a fluidity and elegance.

◄ *In his* Resurrection *(1463), Piero della Francesca groups his figures into a series of interlocking triangles; the largest incorporates all of the figures, with the risen Christ at its apex, a second utilizes Christ's bent knee as its apex, and the two subgroups of sleeping soldiers form two smaller triangles toward the bottom of the fresco.*

Titan is perhaps less universally recognized as a member of this group. The best-known painter of the Venetian school, Titian enjoyed great fame during his lifetime. He trained under Giovanni Bellini (c. 1430–1516) alongside the short-lived genius known as Giorgione (c. 1477–1511). Titian's painting incorporates the vivid colors, the pageantry, and the emphasis on human emotions for which Venetian painters had long been celebrated, but he surpasses his contemporaries in his mastery of his chosen medium (oil paint) and in the sheer exuberance of his approach. Titian carefully organized his compositions and built up his fields of jewel-like colors. He gives the impression of capturing a moment in time, but there is nothing static or staged about his compositions. His monumentality and grandeur are born not of stately calm or intellectual order but of the radiant glory and dynamism of human life.

Titian's Legacy

The lush colors, sensuous nudes, and dramatic gestures popularized by Titian had a great impact on post-Renaissance painting throughout Europe. The work of Titian and his Venetian contemporaries—who all favored the subtle modulation of fields of color to achieve volume and depth in their figures—falls firmly within the *colorito* camp in the Renaissance debate as to the relative merits of color over line. The *disegno* (drawing) camp found its most influential proponent in Michelangelo, though the stark contrast between the two sides of the debate was recently softened when the restoration of the Sistine Chapel ceiling revealed a subtle use of color and a much more adventurous palette than art historians have traditionally assigned to Michelangelo. Arguments over the relative merits of color and line have informed theoretical debate within the art world ever since.

Titian, again more by accident than by design, served as the conduit of yet another development that had a major impact on the history of painting. The Venetian preference for oil on canvas, as opposed to tempera on panel, became so prevalent throughout Europe (largely thanks to the works of Titian) that nowadays a painting, unless described otherwise, is generally assumed to be painted in oils on canvas. Like Leonardo, Titian was largely absent from the Florence-Rome axis on which the fame of Raphael and Michelangelo so securely rests, but more than any of the others, Titian set the course for European artistic tastes for much of the next two centuries.

◀ *Titian's best-known work is probably* The Assumption of the Virgin *(1516–1518), a massive panel that stands nearly twenty-three-feet (7 m) tall. Its three-part composition is carefully ordered; Titian uses various devices, such as fields of color and extended arms, to bind the various levels one to another.*

VENETIAN PAINTING OF THE HIGH RENAISSANCE

Though his father had introduced Renaissance ideals into Venetian painting, it was Giovanni Bellini who laid the foundations for Venetian painting of the High Renaissance. His mature works display a poignant sweetness and piety coupled with a startlingly free use of color and imaginative interpretation of the world. Whereas Tuscan painters emphatically embraced scientific approaches to the rendering of natural forms, Venetian depictions are seen through the prism of human experience—Bellini and his contemporaries sought to depict the world experientially, not intellectually. Emotion in Venetian painting is conveyed not through specific gestures or facial expressions (as set down by Alberti) but rather through the work as a whole—its palette, compositional details, atmosphere, and scale.

By 1500 Bellini had begun to exploit color, rather than line, as a means of suggesting volume and space. He abandoned linear perspective; his "intuitive" landscapes allow the viewer to "feel" rather than see the reality of the space. Despite this new, almost antitheoretical approach, works from Bellini's studio at this time exhibit a grandeur and internal harmony similar to those of the High Renaissance in Rome and Florence. For Bellini's student Giorgione, feeling and mood became the keynotes of his work. Venetian painters had always approached traditional subject matter, both classical and religious, with greater imaginative freedom than their counterparts to the south, but Giorgione initiates a new kind of painting, one in which the atmosphere or mood supersedes the narrative. Giorgione also championed the use of sfumato (subtle modulation from light to dark, perfected by Leonardo), which greatly heightens the atmospheric qualities of his compositions and adds a new sensuousness to his figures. Freed from the painter's traditional role as storyteller, Giorgione embarked on an exploration of the (often tense) relationship between humanity and nature. The early death of Giorgione and that of Bellini six years later left Venetian painting largely in the hands of the young Titian. The lessons he had learned from his master and his fellow pupil, married with his inherent color sense, genius for composition, and exuberant depiction of emotion, secured his position as one of Europe's most eminent painters right up to the time of his death in 1576.

◀ X-ray studies of Giorgione's The Tempest (1505–1510) reveal a nude woman originally painted where the soldier now stands. Such studies help art historians to better understand how Giorgione allowed his composition to develop during the painting process.

Mannerism

Strictly speaking, the period dominated by mannerism (from the Italian *maniera*, which means "manner" or "style") begins with the death of Raphael in 1520. While High Renaissance artists had looked to nature for their inspiration, mannerists sought perfection and inspiration from art itself, especially the art of classical antiquity and the High Renaissance. Through stylization and artifice, mannerist artists created work that was highly refined and self-consciously intellectual.

Figures executed in *la maniera*, be they sculpted or painted, are often depicted in tortuous poses that emphasize their exaggeratedly long limbs, small heads, and elegant gestures. Mannerist painters frequently employed a serpentine mode of organization based on the circle. They consciously left a void at a composition's center, the most important area in the painting of the High Renaissance. Mannerist sculptors often focused on intense physical strain and abandoned the athletic innocence and noble determination evident in Michelangelo's *David*.

Mannerism originated in Italy, where its most famous practitioners include the Florentines Jacopo Pontormo (1494–1557), Benvenuto Cellini (1500–1571), and Il Bronzino (Agnolo di Cosimo; 1503–1572). The Holy Roman emperor Rudolf II brought mannerism to central Europe through artistic patronage at his court in Prague, while German and Dutch artists encountered the new style when they traveled to Rome to study its antiquities. The Florentines Cellini, Il Rosso (1494–1540), and Francesco Primaticcio (1504–1570) brought mannerism to France when they came to decorate Francis I's new palace at Fontainebleau. Jean Clouet (c. 1485–c. 1540) and Bartholomeus Spranger (1546–1611) are among the Flemish artists most associated with mannerism. By 1600 mannerism had more or less run its course and was replaced across Europe by a complex group of styles known collectively as the baroque.

Rise of the Baroque

Baroque art (the origin of the term *baroque* is unclear) was the bold visual statement of a turbulent culture. There is no single baroque style, but each variant reflects some characteristic of the period's cultural landscape. The Counter-Reformation, the Catholic Church's response to the rise of Protestantism, was a major influence on baroque art. As a form of propaganda, the church commissioned religious works that

◀ *In Parmigianino's* Madonna with the Long Neck *(c. 1535), the elongation of the Virgin's neck and fingers and of the limbs of the sleeping Christ and the figures to the left add to the sense of mannerist elegance. Also mannerist is the ambiguous depiction of depth and scale in the open space behind the Virgin.*

would make a strong appeal to believers' emotions. The basic ingredients of baroque religious art—naturalistic and emotionally dramatic depictions suffused with wonder—are also found in secular art. In religious art the sense of wonder derives from contemplation of the divine; in secular art it owes more to contemplation of the infinitely complex natural world that contemporary scientific advances were beginning to open up. Political and societal developments of the period also influenced the visual arts. The (typically Catholic) absolute monarchy sought to advertise its power and grandeur on a monumental scale, while the emerging middle classes (often Protestant) were, for the first time, rich enough to be patrons (middle-class tastes usually tended toward realism). Finally, the

ROMANO'S PALAZZO DEL TÈ

In 1525 Federigo II, duke of Mantua, commissioned the Roman architect Giulio Romano to build the Palazzo del Tè, a summer residence for the duke and his court. A masterpiece of mannerist artifice, the palace occupied Romano for the next ten years. Its architecture draws on classical models but in startling ways. The interior painted decoration, largely executed by Romano himself, exhibits the same antiestablishment approach. The Salon of the Giants contains a fresco depicting the struggle between the gods and invading giants atop Mount Olympus. In the collapsing columns and piles of rubble, it is tempting to see an allegory of Romano's attempt to upend the rules and theories laid down by the artists and architects of the High Renaissance.

▲ In his floor-to-ceiling decorative schemes within the Palazzo del Tè, Giulio Romano provides an important model for the extravagant interior designs favored by baroque artists and sculptors. In this scene the Olympian gods watch the fall of the Titans.

baroque period is characterized by freedom of personal expression and individualism—idiosyncrasy of style is a hallmark of the baroque artist.

Baroque art has its roots in Rome, the center of Catholic reform and revitalization during the Counter-Reformation. Italian baroque sculpture is dramatic, full of movement and intense emotion, often large in scale, and complex in form and iconography. Italian baroque painting is perhaps slightly more restrained, though like its sculptural counterpart, its secular subject matter is frequently classical and it remains firmly grounded in the technique and theory perfected by the masters of the High Renaissance. However, baroque artists searched for new ways to communicate meaning visually by engaging the viewers' senses (and not merely their intellect). In baroque churches and secular buildings architecture, sculpture, and painting are often fused into grandiose and complex decorative schemes. Such extravagant artistic syntheses afford even an uneducated viewer a sensory experience of the unseen heavens, of abstract concepts, such as divine ecstasy, or of the

◀ *A detail from Veronese's* Feast in the House of Levi *(1573). Certain of its aspects—the festive atmosphere, a servant with a bleeding nose, an apostle cleaning his teeth with a toothpick—contravened the church's stance on religious imagery.*

noble virtues of the ancients. The baroque in Italy encompassed a wide variety of individual styles, from the restrained classicism of Annibale Carracci (1560–1609) to the dynamic drama of Gian Lorenzo Bernini (1598–1680) and the stark realism of Caravaggio (1573–1610).

In baroque art the Catholic Church found the ideal vehicle for the expression of intense spirituality. The baroque style, whose origin and inspiration was Italian, became inextricably linked with Catholic Europe and thus made little impression on those areas under the sway of Protestantism (such as Holland and England). However, despite the many religious commissions available, baroque artists increasingly employed their skills in aid of secular political powers as well. The grandiose compositions, dramatic poses, and large scale of baroque paintings and sculptures mirrored the pomp and ceremony of the royal courts and the first families of the nobility. The painter who best exhibits the bold sumptuousness of baroque art and whose work was sought by religious and secular patrons from all over Europe was not Italian but Flemish. Peter Paul Rubens (1577–1640) would become an international art celebrity, much as the German Albrecht Dürer had been just over a century earlier. Trained in Flanders before falling under the spell of classical antiquity and the Italian masters, Rubens, a staunch Catholic, executed commissions for royal courts and religious institutions all over Europe. Rubens's full-blown baroque style influenced many notable artists, including his pupil Anthony van Dyck (1599–1641) and the young Spanish painter Diego Rodríguez de Silva Velázquez (1599–1660).

▼ Painted in 1621 by the Italian artist Il Guercino (Giovani Francesco Barbieri; 1591–1666), this dramatic panel in the baroque style, with its bold architectural trompe l'oeil and monumental figures, vividly depicts an allegorical image of Night.

▲ *In his* Martyrdom of Saint Bartholomew *(c. 1639), José de Ribera depicts the gruesome scene of the flaying of the apostle Bartholomew in Armenia with an almost journalistic sense of visual detail.*

way in which this high baroque style was interpreted by the native artists of each region varied greatly. As a result, it is at times difficult to identify exactly what unifies baroque painting and sculpture of the seventeenth century. The appeal of baroque art to the senses, however, remains a constant factor.

In Spain, for example, the baroque style of Bernini and Rubens was largely ignored, and pride of place given to the native preference for stark realism as an expression of deep religious fervor. Often exhibiting strong contrast between light and dark—not unlike the so-called tenebrist style championed in Italy by Caravaggio—Spanish painting of the period deals with harsh realities and raw emotion, born no doubt of the contemporary atmosphere of religious zeal. José de Ribera (1591–1652) and Francisco de Zurbarán (1598–1664) are among its better-known exponents. Though heavily influenced by native Spanish artistic traditions, Diego Velázquez largely abandoned the visions and images of physical torture so prevalent in Spanish painting of his time. His interests centered on what his eye could see and, furthermore, exactly how his eye could see. Court painter to Philip IV of Spain throughout his career, Velázquez was familiar with and to some extent influenced by the works of the Italian masters, notably Titian, and those of Rubens. Velázquez's own contributions to Western painting, however, are significant; his free brushwork, his deep understanding of light, shadow, and color gradation, and his mastery of optical realism have astonished succeeding generations of painters.

French baroque art exhibits a strong sense of classicized restraint. The French painter Nicolas Poussin (1594–1665), who spent most of his life in Italy, believed that art should depict only worthy subjects (often drawn from classical sources) executed in a style that was idealized but rational and orderly. He was deeply inspired by the Italian landscape and its ancient ruins, and his landscapes represent an attempt to impose the ideals of ancient Rome onto its natural surroundings. Claude Lorrain (Claude Gellée; 1600–1682), another Frenchman who preferred Italy, painted classical landscapes similar to Poussin's but in a less idealized style. Where Poussin

Spanish and French Baroque

Trends in baroque art often match roughly to geographical and cultural divisions—one speaks of Spanish or French baroque—though terms such as *Rubenesque* or *Caravaggisti* indicate the extent to which the work of individual artists affected the evolution of the style. The courtly style of Rubens, with its rich colors, ample and sensuous figures, and highly charged emotional drama, spread quickly throughout Europe. The

◀ *Nicolas Poussin's* The Ashes of Phocion Collected by his Widow *(1648) was inspired by Plutarch's history of the Athenian general Phocion, who was condemned to death by the mob. Poussin's landscape, full of classical architecture, recedes into the distance in an orderly progression of interlocking planes.*

became the champion of French academic painters, Claude would be held up as a forerunner of the romantic style so popular in the first half of the nineteenth century.

Alongside the intellectual classicism of Poussin and Claude, there existed in France a more humble classicism in the works of painters such as Georges de La Tour (1593–1652) and Louis Le Nain (1593–1648). Though Le Nain specialized in scenes of peasant life and La Tour is known for his dramatically lit religious subjects, both artists exhibit an interest in light and shadow inspired by Caravaggio and a simple grandeur in their orderly compositions.

The Dutch School

Dutch painting of the seventeenth century bears little resemblance to the baroque style as practiced in much of Catholic Europe. A devout Protestantism that frowned on the use of religious imagery, accompanied by a similar distaste for classical themes, robbed Dutch painters of much of the subject matter so frequently used by painters working for Catholics. Owing to the staunch republicanism of the region, the courtly commissions so prevalent in France, Spain, the Italian peninsula, and (to a lesser extent) England and Germany were also nonexistent within Holland. Equally important in any explanation of the unique style of Dutch painting must be the strong tradition of visual observation of everyday life present in Netherlandish art from the late Middle Ages onward. Dutch artists, though able to command huge prices for their best works, never developed the persona of the divinely inspired artist as seen in the High Renaissance and popularized by Catholic baroque artists.

▲ The objects depicted in this oil painting—Willem Kalff's Still Life with the Drinking Horn of the Saint Sebastian Archers' Guild, Lobster, and Glasses (c. 1653)—were highly prized, but the painstaking optical realism of their painted images was also greatly valued.

Two of the most important Dutch artists of the seventeenth century are Rembrandt van Rijn (1606–1669) and Frans Hals (1581/5–1666). Rembrandt's artistic ability and tragic personal life lend his art a timelessness that has since led to countless lesser works being assigned to the artist's own hand. The brutal honesty with which Rembrandt treats his subjects, be they leading lights in Dutch society or biblical figures, and his subdued palette give his works a pathos rarely seen in the works of such a heroic age. Hals, a lifelong resident of the city of Haarlem, is the portraitist's portrait painter. Working in a society that shunned finery and extravagance, which baroque artists in Catholic societies painted vividly, Hals depicted his subjects in plain, often black garments against simple backgrounds. His earlier works display a vivacity and informality rarely seen in portraiture of the period; his later works, ever more restrained in palette and detail, display the same interest in catching the sparkle of an eye or the hint of a smile, but they focus less on youthful optimism and more on the care-worn realism that comes with maturity. His limited palette and exuberant brushwork inspired many later painters, including Édouard Manet (1832–1883) and Vincent van Gogh (1853–1890).

Countless lesser-known painters, known as the Little Dutch Masters, are perhaps more characteristic of seventeenth-century Dutch art as a whole—they include Willem Kalff (1619–1693) and Jan Vermeer (1632–1675). These painters should not be seen necessarily as less gifted than other artists (Vermeer, in particular, has always enjoyed great esteem and popularity) but rather as artists who worked for local dignitaries, typically in a single location, within the strict codes of practice established for Dutch painters. In most cases the price of a Dutch painting did not reflect the artist's skill or materials but instead was tied to its subject matter. History paintings (usually of classical subjects and thus considered estimable)

and portraits were assigned the highest values because of the skills necessary to execute them well; other types of paintings, including genre scenes, landscapes, and still lifes, commanded lower prices. Most painters specialized in a single type of work, and for the first time many painters made a living from the sale of their paintings, as opposed to depending upon paid commissions from artistic patrons.

Regardless of the subject matter they chose, Dutch painters shared an ability to depict their surroundings in what they believed to be an honest way. This "honesty" takes many forms and is often coupled with a reminder of the temporary nature of human life. The exactitude with

THE DUTCH CARAVAGGISTI: PAINTERS OF THE NIGHT

Caravaggio's use of strongly contrasting areas of light and shadow, a style of painting known as tenebrism, greatly heightens the dramatic interest within his works. A small group of Dutch artists from Utrecht fell under Caravaggio's spell and changed the face of Dutch painting. Hendrik Terbrugghen (1588–1629), Dirck van Baburen (c. 1590–1624), and Gerrit van Honthorst (1590–1656) were among several painters who visited Italy sometime around 1610 and encountered the works of Caravaggio and those of his student, Bartolomeo Manfredi (1580–1620/1). Upon their return to Utrecht, they specialized in dramatically lit night scenes, often of religious subjects but also secular. Their innovative technique spread throughout Holland, where it influenced such Dutch masters as Frans Hals and Rembrandt, and into France, where it greatly affected the work of Georges de La Tour.

◀ A reworking of Caravaggio's original, this painting, The Calling of Saint Matthew (c. 1620), by Hendrik Terbrugghen is typical of the work done by the Dutch artists known as the Caravaggisti.

Jan Vermeer   1632–1675

Jan Vermeer was born in 1632 in the Dutch city of Delft, where he lived (rather reclusively) until his death in 1675. He appears to have supported his large family by acting as an art dealer; there is little evidence that his own works sold well during his lifetime. Only in the 1850s did Vermeer's painting begin to receive the attention that it deserves. A number of his surviving works depict well-to-do ladies in their well-appointed homes, but careful observation reveals that all is not as it seems. Figures are often shown behind a chair or table, literally blocked from escaping the strictures of their lifestyle. Vermeer gives no compositional emphasis to his ladies; they are painted with the same care as his carpets, jugs, and loaves of bread. The unifying factor of his compositions is the even light—often entering from a window at the side—that pours over the surfaces of the various "objects" (including human figures). Vermeer's interest in the qualities of light, reflection, and shadow is illustrated by his careful attention to the painted surface as a depiction of exactly what the eye sees; this impulse to chart the visual world is perhaps hinted at by the maps that frequently adorn the walls in his paintings. So Vermeer's surviving body of work, though small (just over thirty paintings), is instantly recognizable as the work of a pioneering artist.

which a flower painter executed his blooms, for instance, is tempered by the fact that often his arrangement contains flowers that were not all available at the same time of the year; thus, viewers are forced to question the visual realism of the painting in terms of the reality of their world. Remarkably lifelike images representing Dutch delicacies, such as glistening half-peeled lemons and freshly caught fish, are painted with a loving naturalism that is denied both by the viewer's knowledge of the putrefaction that would set in with the passing of real time and by visual reminders of the passing of time within the composition, such as an hourglass or a skull. Still other Dutch painters concentrated on different types of reality. Rembrandt looked to psychological states of mind (the inner self) to determine what is real. For Hals and for Vermeer, the understanding of how the eye sees—how it distinguishes light from shadow as well as one color from another—was paramount.

Setting the Stage for Future Debate

The numerous technical advances and the regional permutations of the visual arts in Europe from the fourteenth century until the end of the baroque period have influenced art history, theory, and criticism up through the modern day. In terms of understanding how painting and sculpture have developed, especially since 1500, it is helpful to think in terms of one prevalent style gradually giving way to the next. However, this approach to art history masks the extent to which developments within painting and sculpture are so often the result of the work of a single artist—or even of a single painting or sculpture. Art historians must be careful to avoid, for example, interpreting Jacopo Pontormo's works as fitting into a preconceived definition of mannerist style; his works help to *define* that style rather than *follow* it according to previously determined rules. Another problem with the art-historical canon is that it encourages one to experience a work of art as representative of a certain style instead of on its own merits. Michelangelo's

◄ *Jan Vermeer's interest in the qualities of light is demonstrated in* Young Woman with a Water Jug *(c. 1662) through the care with which he explores how different surfaces reflect light.*

David and Leonardo's *Mona Lisa* deserve their reputations as masterpieces of art not because they best represent the artistic aspirations of the High Renaissance but because of the way they continue—despite a cultural gap of five hundred years—to affect the viewer emotionally and intellectually. Such qualities in a work of art define timelessness.

FURTHER READING

Harris, Ann Sutherland. *Seventeenth-Century Art and Architecture.* Upper Saddle River, NJ, 2005.

Hartt, Frederick. *History of Italian Renaissance Art: Painting, Sculpture, Architecture.* 5th ed. New York, 2002.

Murray, Linda. *The High Renaissance and Mannerism.* New York, 1985.

Snyder, James. *Northern Renaissance Art: Painting, Sculpture, the Graphic Arts from 1350 to 1575.* 2nd ed. Upper Saddle River, NJ, 2004.

Caroline S. Hull

SEE ALSO

- Bernini, Gian Lorenzo • Bosch, Hieronymus
- Botticelli, Sandro • Bruegel, Pieter • Caravaggio
- Dürer, Albrecht • Eyck, Jan van
- Gentileschi, Artemisia • Giotto • Michelangelo
- Raphael • Rembrandt • Rubens, Peter Paul
- Velázquez, Diego Rodríguez de Silva

▲ For cityscapes, such as View of Delft *(c. 1660–1661), pictured here, Vermeer is believed to have used a camera obscura (a forerunner of the modern camera) to study the visual effects of light and distance, as well as to help him develop the composition.*

Palladio, Andrea

ANDREA PALLADIO (1508–1580)
DESIGNED PALACES IN VICENZA,
CHURCHES IN VENICE, AND
COUNTRY HOUSES IN THE LATTER
CITY'S MAINLAND TERRITORY. HIS
POPULARITY WAS SUCH THAT HIS
DISTINCTIVE ARCHITECTURAL STYLE
ACQUIRED INTERNATIONAL RENOWN.

Andrea Palladio was born Andrea di Pietro della Gondola in Padua, in the Italian province of Veneto, on November 30, 1508, to Pietro della Gondola, a hatmaker, and his lame wife, Marta.

Palladio remained poor most of his life—his income did not reach the level subject to taxation until he was fifty, and in 1564 he had difficulty finding four hundred ducats for his daughter Zenobia's dowry.

In 1521 Palladio was apprenticed to a local stonecutter, Bartolomeo Cavazza, but in 1523 he withdrew from the apprenticeship and went to Vicenza, about forty miles west of Venice. He enrolled in the guild of stonemasons there in 1524 and for the next fourteen years worked as an assistant in one of the principal stonecutting shops of the city, owned by Giovanni da Pedemuro and Girolamo Pittoni. In the Pedemuro workshop Palladio would have fashioned window frames and mantelpieces, and he may have had some part in the design and construction of the high altar in the cathedral between 1534 and 1536. Like Bernini and Michelangelo, Palladio learned firsthand what stone and marble could become. In 1534 he married Allegradonna Marangon, the daughter of a carpenter; they had five children. Two sons perpetuated the family interest in building—Leonida, who served as his father's assistant, and Marc'Antonio, who worked with the sculptor Alessandro Vittoria in Venice.

Perhaps Palladio would have remained a footnote to the architecture of the Veneto had he not been called on in 1528 by Count Gian Giorgio Trissino (1478–1550) to help complete his villa in Cricoli, a suburb of Vicenza. Palladio was thirty when Count Trissino became his patron. The name Palladio, by which he was known after 1540, was taken from Trissino's book *Italy Liberated from the Goths,* in which the angel Palladio explains the divine significance of geometrical forms in architecture.

Trissino encouraged Palladio to study in his informal residential academy, where architecture, art, and literature were discussed and where Palladio learned something of the aristocratic humanism typified by the Florentine scholar and

◀ *This portrait by Orlando Flacco depicts Andrea Palladio in middle age, when he had risen from the ranks of the nameless stonecutters to become one of the Venetian republic's premier architects.*

▶ *Count Trissino was Palladio's mentor in the 1530s. A humanist whose interests included history, literature, and art, he is portrayed in this oil painting by Vincenzo di Biago Catena holding a book, a symbol of his scholarly attainments.*

1508
Andrea Palladio is born in Padua on November 30.

1528
Is employed as a stonecutter by Count Trissino.

1530s
As much of Venice's commercial nobility migrate to the Veneto to be gentlemen farmers, Palladio gets a steady market for villas and country palaces.

1539
Sebastiano Serlio visits Vicenza with parts of his architectural treatise, *Tutte l'opere d'architettura e prospetiva.* Palladio later imitates its use of illustrations in his own *Four Books of Architecture.*

1541
In Rome, begins his sketchbooks of plans and elevations of ancient Roman buildings and fanciful reconstructions of Roman ruins.

1542
Is awarded the contract for the Palazzo Thiene, one of his first city palaces.

1559
Begins one of his most imitated designs, Villa Foscari at Malcontenta, with its riverfront porch of six columns.

1570
Becomes the most sought after architect in the Veneto, following Jacopo Sansovino's death on November 27.

1571
Builds Loggia del Capitaniato, employing giant half columns applied directly to the facade, across the square from his earlier Basilica (1549) in Vicenza.

1579
Is commissioned to build the chapel at Maser.

1580
Dies at Vicenza or Maser on August 19.

architect Leon Battista Alberti (1404–1472). Trissino's academy went with him to Padua, Ferrara, and Venice from 1538 to 1541. In Padua, Palladio met the architect Luigi Alvise Cornaro and the Barbaro brothers, Daniele and Marc'Antonio. Palladio later collaborated with Daniele Barbaro in the publication of the first illustrated edition of Vitruvius's *Ten Books of Architecture.* In 1555, through Trissino's patronage, Palladio became a founder of the Accademia Olympica in Vicenza, an association that was dedicated to the fostering of learning.

THE INFLUENCE OF CORNARO

Palladio, who was with Trissino when the count was exiled to Padua (1538–1540), there came under the influence of Luigi Alvise Cornaro (1475–1566). Having grown wealthy through land reclamation, Cornaro had taken up architecture in the 1520s. Assisted by the painter-turned-architect Giovanni Maria Falconetto, Cornaro showed Palladio that every facade did not have to bear the ancient orders (columns with a characteristic base and capital), that triangle-shaped roofs, called pediments, could be used in domestic architecture as well as in churches, and that rooms should be designed with consideration for the placement of furniture. Cornaro was interested in homes for citizens, not palaces. A building beautiful and comfortable was to be preferred to one supremely beautiful but uncomfortable. Palladio never developed an architecture for ordinary citizens, but the practicality of his villas and the freedom with which he adapted classical forms owes something to Cornaro's short *Trattato dell'architettura (Treatise on Architecture),* written between 1550 and 1553.

REGINA VIRTVS

I QVATTRO LIBRI
DELL'ARCHITETTVRA
Di Andrea Palladio.

Ne' quali, dopo vn breue trattato de' cinque
ordini, & di quelli auertimenti, che sono
piu necessarij nel fabricare;
SI TRATTA DELLE CASE PRIVATE,
delle Vie, dei Ponti, delle Piazze, dei Xisti, et de' Tempij.
CON PRIVILEGI.

IN VENETIA,
Appresso Bartolomeo
Carampello.
1581.

▲ *The title page of Palladio's* Four Books of Architecture *displays a broken segmental (circular) pediment and the Latin phrase* Regina Virtus *("virtue is queen"). Shown here is the book's second edition, published in Venice in 1581.*

Sanmicheli, Sansovino, and Serlio

From the 1540s Palladio began to undertake architectural commissions; his first palaces were built in Vicenza—including the Palazzo Chieracati—and over the next two decades, his country houses appeared throughout the Veneto. When Palladio began his career as an architect in the Veneto, the local standards of good design had been set by Jacopo Sansovino (1486–1570), Michele Sanmicheli (1484–1559), and Sebastiano Serlio (1475–1554).

Jacopo Sansovino had come to Venice after the sack of Rome in 1527. Palladio first documented visit to Venice was in 1548, and there he would have seen Sansovino's library of Saint Mark's. In the preface to his *Four Books of Architecture,* Palladio credited Sansovino with the introduction of the "beautiful manner" in the library, which he called "the richest and most adorned edifice that has been made since the ancients." Sansovino was also the architect of several rural palaces, including the Villa Garzoni in Pontecasale, near Padua.

Palladio would have known the works of Sanmicheli through the Pedemuro workshop in Vicenza. The palaces built by Sanmicheli in Verona during the 1530s, Palazzo Canossa and Palazzo Brevilacqua, would have offered precedents for Palladio's early palaces in Vicenza.

The great reputation of Sebastiano Serlio, who like Sansovino had fled to Venice after the sack of Rome, rested on his treatise on architecture, *Tutte l'opere d'architettura e prospetiva,* the fourth book of which was published in Venice in 1537, with the first book following in 1540.

Palladio and Rome

Palladio traveled as far as Nîmes in France in search of ancient architecture, but it was the remains of baths and temples, carefully sketched and measured on his visits to Rome in 1541, 1545, 1546, and 1554, that inspired his development as an architect. Count Trissino, whom Palladio accompanied on his first two visits, knew Roman architecture, since Trissino had been exiled to Rome from 1510 to 1516 for siding with the League of Cambrai against Venice when the Veneto was invaded in 1509. Trissino provided the knowledge and the useful introductions that made Palladio's interests fruitful. On his Roman journeys Palladio filled his sketchbooks with drawings of the monuments that could be seen aboveground.

When Palladio first visited Rome in 1541, he would have found a city still recovering from the sack of 1527. He would have seen the famous works of the architect Donato Bramante—such as the house of Raphael and the tempietto in the Church of San Pietro in Montorio (the only modern building Palladio included in his *Four Books of Architecture*)—and the city's great palaces, including the Palazzo Massimi, the Palazzo della Cancelleria, the Palazzo Farnese,

Although it is difficult to discover much academic loyalty to antique forms in Palladio's work, he opened his *Four Books of Architecture* (1570) with an appeal to the authority of the first-century-CE Roman architect Vitruvius:

Guided by natural inclination, I gave myself up in my most early years to the study of architecture; and as it was always my opinion that the ancient Romans, as in many other things, so in building well, vastly excelled all those who have been since their time, I proposed to myself Vitruvius for my master and guide, who is the only ancient writer of this art, and set myself to search into the relics of all the ancient edifices, that, in spite of time and the cruelty of the Barbarians, yet remain; and finding them much more worthy of observation, than at first I had imagined, I began very minutely, with the utmost diligence to measure every one of their parts; of which I grew at last so solicitous an examiner (not finding anything that was not done with reason and beautiful proportion) that I have very frequently not only traveled in different parts of Italy, but also out of it.

Introduction to *Four Books of Architecture*

and especially the Palazzo Farnesina, with its splendid painted ceilings.

Palladio's work suggests that the Roman buildings that most influenced him were Raphael's Roman palaces, the Palazzo Jacopo di Brescia and the Villa Madama, and Bramante's house of Raphael. Bramante's pupil, Antonio da Sangallo the Younger, was the architect of Saint Peter's in 1541 and was striving to overcome years of inaction by reverting to the plan proposed by Baldassare Peruzzi, who favored a nave in the shape of an elongated Latin cross. When Palladio returned to Rome in 1545, he may have seen Michelangelo's designs for the three palaces that would make up his project for the Capitoline Hill. In 1554, when Palladio visited Tivoli and Palestrina as well as Rome, Michelangelo, at the zenith of his career, had been the architect of Saint Peter's since the death of Sangallo in 1546, and Giulio Romano's villa for Pope Julius, with its dramatic semicircular courtyard, was new. On this last journey to Rome, Palladio produced *Antiquities of Rome*, the first reliable handbook to locate and describe the Roman monuments; in 1556 he would publish *Description of the Churches*. Although he used classical forms freely, his designs almost always drew on his knowledge of Roman architecture.

▶ *Designed by Raphael around 1518, the Villa Madama in Rome was an inspiration to later Renaissance architects, including Palladio. Its domed loggia, or portico, photographed here, influenced Palladio's Venetian churches of the 1570s and 1580s.*

Palladio in Vicenza

During the 1540s Palladio established himself as an architect when he designed and built palaces for the local gentry. The Casa Civena (1541–1542), the Palazzo Thiene (after 1546), and the Palazzo da Porto Festa (1548) all show the influence of Palladio's favorite Roman model, Bramante's house of Raphael. In each the rusticated (rough-surfaced) ground-floor facade carried a series of arches, this first story providing a base for columns that embellish the second and third stories above. With these palaces to his credit, Palladio was asked to make a proposal for the construction of an encircling loggia (galleried porch) for Vicenza's centuries-old regional meeting hall, the room in which the council sat. The authorities had already consulted Sansovino, Serlio, Sanmicheli, and Romano. After submitting a wooden model of one bay of the proposed structure to the council, Palladio was finally awarded the commission in 1549, although the building was not completed until 1617. Called the Basilica since the 1550s, its two identical stories were composed of a series of windows that over time would be called Palladian or Venetian windows—each window is an arched opening flanked by two smaller openings that rise only to the spring line of the arch, a device that ingeniously enabled the architect to employ identical arches spanning different distances—the difference in the width of bays being made up by expanding or compressing the spaces flanking the arched opening. Palladio's reputation was established with the design for the Basilica, and commissions for palaces and villas followed. Palazzo Chieracati, designed for Girolamo Chieracati, one of the supervisors of the Basilica, was completed in 1552. A long, two-story block with a loggia across the ground floor, an invisible roof, and statues thrown against the sky at the top of every column, the building is an urban palace that bears the stamp of Michelangelo's Capitoline project in Rome.

Villas and Country Palaces

In his architecture Palladio displayed mastery of a distinctive style unlike anything that had gone before. Palladio called the site on which a build-

▼ *In 1549 Palladio designed what came to be known as the Basilica, a two-story colonnade that wrapped around Vicenza's medieval meeting hall.*

▲ *Palladio's hilltop Villa Rotonda, begun in 1550, is one of the most influential buildings in the world. Each of its four porches faces a different direction.*

(1556–1563) are of this type—the main block and flanking structures stretched dramatically across the terrain.

Another Palladian pattern was the tightly designed central plan with secondary structures set away from the villa proper. Sometimes these were not farms but rural palaces. The most famous of Palladio's villas, at least in eighteenth-century England, was the Villa Rotunda near Vicenza. A superbly assertive design, this domed villa sits atop a hill overlooking the fields, perfectly symmetrical around both axes, with pedimented porches facing the four compass points. At Villa Rotonda, with the stables and secondary structures tucked beneath the hill, the dramatic clarity of the design was uninterrupted.

Perhaps the most widely imitated of Palladio's characteristic designs was the lengthwise-oriented block with a two-story porch of four (Villa Pisani, 1553–1555) or six columns (Villa Cornaro, 1560–1565) carrying a triangular pediment, centered and sometimes recessed. The one-story variation was represented by the Villa Foscari (before 1560), the central pavilion of the Villa Badoer (1556–1563), and the Villa Emo (c. 1558).

Palladio's designs fall into recognizable patterns, but there are also surprises, buildings for which no precedent can be cited. One example is the Villa Thiene (before 1550), where the central block—the only part of the building constructed—was to be subordinated to two grander flanking structures. Another example is the Villa Poiani (1545–1550), whose facade has almost no classical references. In each of these compositions, there is a unity, a clarity, and a kind of peacefulness that set Palladio's designs apart from the tension and lack of clarity that threatened the mannerist designs of the late 1500s.

ing was placed a theater, and a sense of drama may be said to derive from the placement of the villa among the fields from which the wealth of the Veneto grew. Although each of his villas is distinctive, Palladio turned again and again to one of several patterns. More than once Palladio designed villas in which a two-story central block was connected with flanking secondary structures arranged symmetrically by long screens or curtain walls, with the main block and secondary buildings laid out along a horizontal axis. This arrangement provided stables and other farm buildings near the villa but out of sight. The Villa Godi (1538–1542) and the Villa Badoer

VASARI ON PALLADIO

In 1566 Giorgio Vasari, the author of *Lives of the Painters,* visited Palladio in Venice, and in the second edition of *Lives,* Vasari included a sketch of Palladio as an appendix to his essay on Sansovino. Of Palladio he wrote, "As he is still young and devotes himself unceasingly to his art, we can expect greater things from him every day." Vasari knew of most of the villas and palaces, and he was aware of Palladio's new projects in Venice, the convent of Santa Maria della Carità and the Church of San Giorgio Maggiore. Palladio was fifty-eight when Vasari visited, and during the next twenty-two years he would build a career in Venice around his designs for two churches.

▲ The Church of San Giorgio Maggiore seems to float on the waters. Located across the lagoon from Sansovino's library and Saint Mark's Cathedral, Palladio's church defines the lagoon as the center around which Venice is built.

Palladio in Venice

From 1560 Palladio worked in Venice, and he finally moved there in 1570. In the last two decades of his life, he designed two important churches, San Giorgio Maggiore and Il Redentore, and also published the *Four Books of Architecture* (1570). When one approaches Venice by sea, the city is dominated by the domes of Saint Mark's, the campanile (bell tower), and Sansovino's library, but when one stands in Saint Mark's Square looking seaward the scene is dominated by Palladio's grand San Giorgio Maggiore, the monastic church built in 1560 on the Isola di San Giorgio. Farther south is Il Redentore (the Church of the Redeemer), built in 1576 on the Isola Giudecca by the Venetian senate in fulfillment of a vow made when the city was saved from plague.

Both churches have a bold temple-front facade composed of columns elevated either by an entrance stairway (Il Redentore) or on plinths (San Giorgio Maggiore)—devices that allowed the facade, with its columns and pediment, to retain the proportions of a Roman temple. Like

all of Palladio's designs, the Venetian churches were characterized by originality and clarity. San Giorgio Maggiore is crowned by a spherical dome, located not over the altar but at the transept (where the aisles cross at right angles). The aisles terminate in apses (semicircular projections of the building). Il Redentore is also a domed central space joined to a nave, with a short transept that ends in semicircular apses. The glory of Il Redentore is the screen of Corinthian columns (decorated at the top with carved leaves) behind the altar, which separate it from the choir and allow the composition to terminate in a sea of light.

Il Redentore was not Andrea Palladio's last design. In 1579 he was asked to create a theater for the Accademia Olympica, the academy in Vicenza that he had helped to found in 1556. Palladio's farewell to Vicenza was an architectural fantasy: the proscenium was a triumphal arch, extended laterally in a three-story series of bays, each originally intended to frame the statue of an ancient hero. The nobility of Vicenza decided to replace these ancients with themselves—a vain

AN ARCHITECTURAL LEGACY

Palladianism became the hallmark of English architecture after Inigo Jones (1573–1652) acquired a copy of Palladio's *Four Books* on his trip to Rome in 1613. Jones covered the title page of Palladio's *Four Books* with his signature alternating with his imitation of Palladio's. Jones, who saw himself as the English Palladio, introduced Palladian architecture to England. After Jones designed the Prince of Wales's house in Newport, the Queen's House, and the banqueting hall at Whitehall, Palladianism was taken up by Jones's pupil John Webb and by Christopher Wren. The wealthy English architectural amateur Lord Burlington spent ten days in the Veneto in 1719 and made careful notes in his own copy of the *Four Books*. He acquired a large number of Palladio's drawings, became the sponsor of English Palladianism, and encouraged the publication of Isaac Ware's translation of the *Four Books* in 1738.

In France the garden front of the palace of Versailles (1669–1685) by Louis Le Vau and Jules Hardouin-Mansart displays Palladian idioms borrowed from the Villa Chieracati, among other sources. The influence of Palladio was also evident at Potsdam, in Prussia, in Georg Christian Unger's Langer Stall palace (c. 1780).

Palladio was the only architect of the Renaissance who built many country farmhouses for gentlemen. Like the Veneto, England in 1700 and Virginia in 1800 depended on agriculture, and their landowners needed suitable houses. In England the Villa Rotonda was copied by Colin Campbell at Mereworth Castle in 1723 and by Lord Burlington at Chiswick in 1729. In Virginia, Colonel Isaac Coles wrote General John Hartwell Cocke on February 23, 1816, "With Mr Jefferson, I conversed at length on the subject of architecture. 'Palladio,' he said, 'was the Bible. You should get it and stick close to it.'"

The Palladian country house on the pattern of Villa Pisani and Villa Cornaro—the two-story block with a four- or six-columned porch carrying a triangular pediment—has been built in the United States a thousand times, and the architecture of universities, country clubs, and motels often shows Palladian influences. Perhaps because of the historical association between landowning, wealth, and the Palladian villa, the Palladian country house is often favored by the very wealthy. In 2004 a Palladian country house was built in a Texas city at a cost of $31,000,000.

▼ *At Il Redentore (the Church of the Redeemer) in Venice, Palladio used semicircular transoms (windows set above the cornice) to flood the building with light.*

touch, perhaps, but a solid indication of the way that they saw themselves: as part of a living tradition rooted in the classical past. Palladio died in Vicenza in 1580.

FURTHER READING

Ackerman, James S. *Palladio.* London, 1966.

Boucher, Bruce. *Andrea Palladio: The Architect in His Time.* New York, 1994.

Holberton, Paul. *Palladio's Villas: Life in the Renaissance Countryside.* London, 1990.

Palladio, Andrea. *The Complete Illustrated Works.* Edited by Guido Beltramini and Antonio Padoan. New York, 2001.

Tavernor, Robert. *Palladio and Palladianism.* New York, 1991.

Whitehill, Walter Muir, and Frederick Doveton Nichols. *Palladio in America.* Milan, 1976.

James A. Patrick

SEE ALSO

• Architecture • Bernini, Gian Lorenzo
• Bramante, Donato • Michelangelo • Raphael
• Rome • Venice

Papacy

THE OCCUPANT OF THE PAPAL CHAIR, BESIDES BEING SPIRITUAL HEAD OF THE ROMAN CATHOLIC CHURCH, WAS INVOLVED IN EVERY ASPECT OF SECULAR LIFE IN RENAISSANCE EUROPE. PAPAL PATRONAGE SUPPORTED MANY IMPORTANT ARTISTIC AND SCHOLARLY ENTERPRISES OF THE ERA.

At the beginning of the Renaissance, the pope was the religious leader of all Christians except those who belonged to the Greek Orthodox Church, which did not recognize the authority of the papacy.

The pope, with the support of an ever-growing diplomatic and managerial staff, was the bishop of Rome and the spiritual leader of the Catholic Church. A clergyman, the pope was elected to office and served for the duration of his life. His pronouncements were binding in matters of faith and morality. He also made or confirmed the appointments of cardinals, archbishops, bishops, and all the other administrative officers of the church.

The pope was assisted by the college of cardinals, a group of clergymen that could number as many as seventy, although it was often smaller. In theory the cardinals owed loyalty only to the pope, but in practice many of them represented the interests of secular rulers, such as the Holy Roman emperor, the king of France, and the governing families of Italian city-states. Some cardinals lived in Rome and advised the pope on policies—if he chose to use their services—and served other functions. Many cardinals lived in large palaces and had their own large retinue of secretaries and servants. The most important function of the college of cardinals was to choose a new pope at the death of the incumbent. The college always elected a clergyman from its own ranks.

Below the cardinals were archbishops and bishops, the spiritual leaders of specific territories called dioceses. A diocese might range in size from a large city, home to many thousands of Catholics, down to a few square miles in the countryside that contained only several hundred. The pope appointed both archbishops—who were usually in charge of the larger and more important dioceses—and bishops.

Ranked below the bishops in the church hierarchy were priests, who performed the everyday religious functions of Catholic ritual: celebrating mass, preaching, baptizing children, hearing confessions, and burying the dead.

The clergy consisted of secular clergy and regular clergy. *Secular* derives from the Latin word *saeculum* (literally, "generation" or "age") and describes those clergy who lived in the world—the parish priests, who were subject to the authority of a bishop. The regular clergy were those who lived according to a rule (in Latin, *regula*). These priests were members of religious

▼ *Funding and planning the rebuilding of Saint Peter's Basilica in Rome was a major project of the Renaissance papacy. Prominent in this view of Saint Peter's Square is the colonnade created by Gian Lorenzo Bernini between 1656 and 1667.*

orders who lived communally in monasteries and took perpetual vows of poverty (which the secular clergy did not take), chastity, and obedience. The regular clergy were often in charge of orphanages, hospitals for the sick and dying, and refuges for the poor and outcasts of society. Clergymen were exempt from military service, did not hold civil office, and were not taxed, although civil governments sometimes obtained money from the church in other ways.

Over the centuries the Catholic Church had developed a large organizational structure to deal with the many people and issues it considered to fall under its jurisdiction. It had its own court system, which usually decided marriage disputes (that is, cases in which there was doubt that a legal marriage existed). Diocesan courts often heard the types of cases that are heard by modern civil courts. In order to sustain the apparatus of a court system, lawyers and an appeal procedure were required. Eventually, all complicated court cases and many other matters were referred to Rome for arbitration by the various tribunals based in the city or by the pope himself.

The Origins of the Western Schism

The Renaissance papacy emerged out of the divided and weak papacy of the late Middle Ages, which was buffeted by conflict among the major political powers of Europe and riven by internal disputes. One of the most difficult periods for the papacy began with the election of Clement V (reigned 1305–1314). At the time of his election, Clement was not in Rome—he was crowned in Lyon, in his native France. When he arrived in Rome to take up his duties, he found the city in turmoil owing to violent disagreements among noble families. The fighting made it very difficult to administer the affairs of the

papacy, and so in 1309 Clement moved the papal seat to Avignon, a city in southern France that the papacy had controlled for some time.

As disorder continued in Rome and the Papal States, subsequent popes, most of whom were French, became comfortable in Avignon, and the papal court flourished there. However, some believed that the combination of French popes and a papal seat in a French city placed the papacy excessively under the influence of French kings. Prominent figures, including the Italian poet and scholar Petrarch (1304–1374), reminded the popes that their historic seat was in Rome and urged them to return. Some popes were prepared to listen to the criticisms and wished to return to their ancient home, partly because they believed that only from the proximity of Rome would they be able to restore order to the Papal States and establish proper government.

▲ Something of the splendor of the Renaissance papacy is captured in this sixteenth-century painting by Francesco Salviati, which depicts Pope Paul III (reigned 1534–1549) enthroned between the allegorical figures of Peace and Fertility.

This illustration from the fifteenth-century chronicle of Ulrich von Richental depicts the Council of Constance (1414–1418). At this council the church's leading bishops and cardinals ended the Western Schism by deposing three rival popes and electing Martin V, the figure in the upper right wearing the elaborate papal crown.

Gregory XI (reigned 1370–1378), accompanied by papal officials and all but six of the cardinals, finally returned to Rome in 1377. With Gregory's death, however, a new problem arose. The people of Rome put intense pressure on the cardinals, most of whom were French, to choose an Italian as the next pope, and the cardinals duly elected Urban VI (reigned 1378–1389). At first, all seemed well, but within two months it became clear that Urban's approach to his papal duties differed markedly from that of his predecessors. Urban may have been mentally unstable or simply rash and imprudent, but the fact is that almost all the cardinals declared his election invalid on the grounds that they had been intim-

idated by the Roman populace (the truth of this claim remains a subject of debate). The cardinals left Rome and elected a Frenchman, Robert of Geneva (1342–1394), as Clement VII, in opposition to Urban. Christendom now had a pope and an antipope, each recognized by some cardinals and rulers but neither possessing enough spiritual, legal, political, or military support to win acceptance by a majority. Thus began a formal fracture, or schism, within the church. Extending from 1378 to 1417, it is usually called the Western Schism to distinguish it from the Great Schism, the East-West split of 1054.

The situation soon worsened for the papacy and for the church as a whole. Both popes sought support from political rulers, and both usually had to pay a price in return for such support. The concessions they granted included allowing monarchs to select the holders of church offices—a privilege that was traditionally the prerogative of the pope—and giving up revenues that were normally received by the papacy. While such concessions weakened the material authority of the papacy, the existence of two popes also weakened its spiritual authority, since the pronouncements of one pontiff on religious issues could now be contradicted by the other.

The deaths of Urban VI and the antipope Clement VII did not end the Western Schism; instead, rival groups of cardinals elected two successors. Many people, including the majority of the cardinals, soon realized that the obvious solution was for both popes to resign and allow the cardinals to choose a new pope, but neither pope wished to surrender his position. Moreover, each had an entourage of officials who would lose their positions in the event of a resignation, and each was supported by governments that stood to lose the benefits they had enjoyed from the rivalry between the popes. Therefore, the two popes excommunicated each other and, whenever possible, imprisoned each other's supporters. When a third claimant to the papacy came forward, the situation became even more complicated.

The solution of a double resignation gradually won widespread approval. A general church council (a meeting of all the bishops) met in Constance, Switzerland, from 1414 to 1418. The council deposed the two major claimants to the

THE BORGIAS

Numerous legends have grown up about the crimes of the Borgia family. Most of them stem from accounts of the real and alleged misdeeds of Pope Alexander VI (born Rodrigo Borgia) and his children, Cesare and Lucrezia. According to the legends, Rodrigo and his children rose to and retained power against a background of murder and incest. However, the Borgias' enemies often exaggerated their crimes.

The Borgias were a Spanish family (in Spanish, their name is spelled Borja) whose first prominent member was Cardinal Alfonso de Borja (born in 1378), a pious and able clergyman who moved to Rome in 1432 and eventually reigned as Pope Calixtus III from 1455 to 1458. Calixtus's followers included his nephew Rodrigo Borgia (1431–1503), whom Calixtus appointed a cardinal when Rodrigo was only twenty-five. Rodrigo was a skilled administrator, an adept collector of lucrative benefices (church offices whose income he received without performing the duties they entailed), and a lover of women—of the eight or nine illegitimate children he fathered by different women, two were born after he became pope. As Pope Alexander VI (reigned 1492–1503) he used his position to advance the interests of the Borgia family. The sons became military commanders, and the daughters were married to important political leaders.

The most notorious of the Borgias was Rodrigo's son Cesare (1475–1507), who was made a cardinal when his father assumed the papacy. Cesare soon renounced the cardinalate to become a military commander; he ruthlessly put down rebellions in the Papal States and gained control over large territories. The measures of cruelty and deception that he used were praised by the political thinker Niccolò Machiavelli in his book *The Prince* (written in 1513). However, it is unlikely that Cesare murdered his brother and committed incest with his sister Lucrezia, as his enemies charged.

The sudden death of Pope Alexander brought a reversal of fortune for Cesare. The new pope, Julius II (reigned 1503–1513), was a bitter enemy of the Borgias. Cesare, who no longer had any support, was killed in an obscure battle when he was only thirty-one.

According to the enemies of the Borgias, the beautiful Lucrezia (1480–1519) committed incest with both her father and her brother. The truth of the matter is that Lucrezia was used as a pawn in order to further the interests of the Borgia family. Her first marriage was annulled, and her second husband was assassinated, possibly by Cesare. Her third marriage, to Alfonso d'Este of Ferrara, with whom she had seven children, was a success, and Lucrezia was much loved by the people of Ferrara.

Not all of the male Borgias were ruthless politicians. One of Rodrigo's grandchildren, Francesco Borgia (1510–1572), became a Jesuit. Elected general (leader) of the Jesuits in 1565, Francesco was eventually canonized. Whether saints or sinners, the Borgias made significant contributions to public life in Renaissance Italy.

papacy, and the third claimant resigned. A new pope, Martin V (reigned 1417–1431), was then chosen. Universally recognized as pope, he lived in Rome together with papal officials and many cardinals. The other two popes faded from history.

Thus, a long and complicated story that had begun when the papacy moved to Avignon in 1309 finally ended. The Renaissance papacy really began in 1417. During the Renaissance all but two of the popes were Italian, and Italians increasingly dominated the major papal offices.

Reconquering the Papal States

One of the first tasks awaiting the pope upon his return to Rome was to reassert his authority over the Papal States, territories that stretched from east to west across central Italy. This task was a matter of necessity; rulers who could not control

◀ *Cesare Borgia, the subject of this contemporary portrait by an unknown artist, was the illegitimate son of Pope Alexander VI. A brilliant and unscrupulous opportunist who used force and deceit to gain control of much of the Papal States, he swiftly fell from power when his father died in 1503.*

THE POPE'S ELEPHANT

All roads led to Rome, even for an Asian elephant. Because of the central role of the papacy in politics, the major rulers of Europe visited the pope to discuss policy. When they came, they brought gifts. The king of Portugal, Manuel I (1495–1521), gave the pope an elephant.

Voyages of discovery to Asia and the Americas had brought explorers into contact with unfamiliar species of animals. After Portuguese explorers returned from India with reports of Asian elephants, Manuel I arranged for two young calves to be shipped to Portugal. During a voyage that lasted between four and five months, the elephants consumed huge quantities of food and water. They arrived in Lisbon in the summer of 1511.

The king decided to give one of the elephants to the pope in the hope that such an impressive gift would win him some concessions. After landing at the port of Civitavecchia, the elephant and its entourage walked the fifty-two miles to Rome and, on March 19, 1514, made a triumphant entry into the city. According to some accounts, as the elephant reached Pope Leo X, it knelt before him. It then filled its trunk with water from a nearby trough and sprayed the pope and his advisers. The pope was greatly amused.

The elephant, named Hanno, made its home in the grounds of the Vatican Palace and was greatly admired. Unfortunately, after only two years it fell ill and died. The saddened pope ordered Raphael and other artists to make sketches of the elephant so that a suitable memorial painting of the great beast might be made. Although the painting was created, it has since disappeared. Nevertheless, some very good drawings of the elephant, made by Raphael or Giulio Romano, do survive.

▼ *During the reign of Julius II, the so-called warrior pope, much of the territory encompassed by the Papal States was reconquered. Julius also commissioned many works of art; this portrait is a copy by Titian of an earlier work by Raphael.*

their own subjects did not prosper during the Renaissance. It was also a matter of money, since the rebellious territories paid no taxes. Over the course of a hundred years and especially at the end of the fifteenth century and during the first years of the sixteenth, the papacy fought to reestablish control. When necessary, it used military force against rebellious barons and cities.

In 1503 the cardinals elected Julius II pope because of his strength of character and because they believed that he would defend the interests of the church. Julius, sometimes called the warrior pope, did not disappoint. He personally led a military expedition that forced the rebellious cities of Bologna and Perugia to acknowledge papal rule. In 1509 he joined an international alliance that defeated Venice in war. Venice was forced to give back to the papacy territories that it had earlier taken. Although the pope was criticized for fighting, his military and diplomatic efforts helped the papacy. By around 1515 the Papal States were under control once more, and later in the sixteenth century the papacy gained some new territories.

The Reformation

Just as the papacy mastered the political problems in Italy, a new challenge appeared. In the autumn of 1517, Martin Luther (1483–1546) began to criticize the papacy for sponsoring the sale of

ADORNATA·FVIT·CONSILIO·D·IOANNIS·IACOBI·PASTORIS·HVIVS·ECCLESIÆ·ANNO·DNI

◄ *Martin Luther, who initiated the Reformation, is depicted preaching, administering the Eucharist, and baptizing in this unattributed 1561 painting, which adorns the front of a church altar in Torslunde, Denmark.*

indulgences by an unscrupulous indulgence seller in Saxony, in eastern Germany. The theological foundation of the doctrine of indulgences was the belief that, after death, a sinner who is not so evil as to be condemned to hell but not yet deserving of the rewards of heaven must suffer a temporary period of punishment in purgatory. If, however, the sinner while still on earth confesses his sins, truly repents, and then does a good deed (in the case that angered Luther, that deed was the contribution of money toward the rebuilding of Saint Peter's Basilica in Rome), he may be granted an indulgence—a shortening of his time in purgatory. Luther rejected the doctrine of indulgences. To his surprise others agreed with him, partly because there was widespread but previously unrecognized discontent with the papacy in Germany. Luther quickly developed a broader religious platform that combined sharp attacks on the papacy with a rejection of important features of Catholic doctrine.

The Reformation caught the papacy by surprise. At first, it did not take Luther's attacks seriously. Luther was an obscure professor at the University of Wittenberg, a new and minor insti-

tution whose Saxon location placed it far from the intellectual and political centers of Europe, such as Paris and Rome. Pope Leo X (reigned 1513–1521) delayed taking action against Luther because he did not want to antagonize Frederick of Saxony (reigned 1486–1525). Frederick was an elector, one of the seven men who would choose the next Holy Roman emperor, and the pope wanted Frederick to vote against the Hapsburg king of Spain, Charles I (reigned 1516–1556), whom the pope opposed. Since Luther was Frederick's subject and a popular professor in the university Frederick had founded, Leo feared that action against Luther would anger Frederick. Only after the election in 1519 (in which Frederick voted for Charles, who won and became Emperor Charles V), did the papacy move against Luther. On June 15, 1520, Leo issued a bull demanding that Luther renounce his views and burn his books. Instead, Luther burned the papal bull. By this time it was too late to stop Luther, who had many followers and enjoyed political protection. Other religious leaders soon joined the challenge against Rome, and important German princes supported them.

REGIN THER EIVS Æ·KΞ INÆ VXOR

► Catherine of Aragon is the subject of this portrait by an unknown artist. The work dates from about 1530, the period during which Catherine was fighting efforts by Henry VIII to divorce her.

An Embattled Papacy

The papacy also suffered political and military reverses in the 1520s and 1530s. In May 1527 the unpaid, leaderless, and undisciplined troops of the Holy Roman emperor, Charles V, sacked Rome. For months the troops plundered the city and tortured, killed, or held to ransom many of its inhabitants. Pope Clement VII (reigned 1523–1534) and thirteen cardinals were imprisoned in Castel Sant'Angelo, a Roman fortress. They were finally allowed to leave the city in December 1527 but only after paying an enormous ransom. The pope did not return to Rome until October 1528. Thus, for a crucial eighteen-month period there was little the papacy could do about any matter of church business, including combating the spread of Reform.

Another blow came from England. In 1529 King Henry VIII demanded that Clement VII annul Henry's marriage to Catherine of Aragon (1485–1536). Henry wanted the pope to declare that the marriage, which had produced one living daughter and several babies who had died at birth, had never been a valid one. If Henry's demands were met, he would be free to marry Anne Boleyn, with whom he was infatuated. He hoped that Anne would produce the male heir that he desperately wanted.

Clement was in a difficult position. The legal grounds for granting the annulment were weak, but the pope might have overcome his scruples had it not been for powerful political opposition. Catherine of Aragon opposed the dissolution of her marriage, and she had the support of her nephew—the Holy Roman emperor Charles V. After the sack of Rome, the pope was in no position to anger Charles by granting the annulment. Besides, he needed the support of Charles in various diplomatic and political affairs. Although Clement sent representatives to England in the summer of 1529 to hear Henry's arguments, he reserved judgment in the matter for himself.

Frustrated, Henry took matters into his own hands. He established the Church of England, appointed himself its head, and ordered it to sever all ties with the papacy. The Church of England obediently permitted Henry's divorce, and in January 1533 the king married Anne Boleyn. At first, the English church continued to follow Catholic doctrines and deviated from Rome only in refusing to accept the authority of the pope. However, the Church of England became more strongly Protestant during the reigns of Henry's children, Edward VI (1547–1553) and Elizabeth I (1558–1603).

◄ The figure on the left of this unattributed engraving is Matteo Ricci, a Jesuit missionary in China; the figure on the right is an official of the Ming dynasty. Ricci's success in China owed much to his belief that missionaries should, as far as possible, adapt to local customs.

THE WORLD-TRAVELING JESUIT MISSIONARIES

The papacy helped to set in motion one of the most important religious and cultural movements of the Renaissance, the spread of Christianity to the non-European world. In turn, Europeans for the first time began to learn about the peoples and customs of the rest of the world. The most important missionary group was the Society of Jesus.

As a student at the University of Paris between 1528 and 1535, Ignatius of Loyola, a Spaniard, met regularly with six other men from Spain and France for prayer. Together the men wondered how they might spend their lives serving God and helping others. They decided to create a new religious order, which they called the Society of Jesus (its members are known as Jesuits). Unlike other religious orders, the Jesuits decided that they would not require their (exclusively male) members to pray together or live in a monastery. They wanted to be free to go anywhere that they were needed at a moment's notice. These unusual ideas provoked questions and some opposition from religious authorities, but Pope Paul III (reigned 1534–1549), who trusted Loyola and his followers, gave the Society of Jesus official recognition in 1540. In addition to the customary vows of poverty, chastity, and obedience, the Jesuits added a special vow to obey the pope "concerning missions," in which they pledged that they would be available to go anywhere to spread Christianity. This vow took the Jesuits around the world.

Francis Xavier (1506–1552), one of the original seven Jesuits (he was later canonized), undertook important missionary work in South and East Asia. Xavier sailed for India in 1539, and after converting thousands of Indians to Christianity, went on to the Spice Islands (the present-day Moluccas, part of Indonesia). From the Spice Islands he traveled in 1549 to Japan, a country that was totally unknown to westerners at that time. There, he again converted many people to Christianity. He then set sail for China but died on the island of Macao, just off the mainland, in 1552. Another Jesuit, Matteo Ricci (1552–1610), did work as a missionary in China, where he adopted Chinese dress and customs, translated European works into Chinese and Chinese works into Latin, and argued that Christian and Confucian views were compatible. The Jesuits also went to Brazil in 1549, to Mexico and other parts of Latin America later in the sixteenth century, and to New France (present-day Canada) in the early seventeenth century. The visionary Jesuits insisted that missionaries learn and respect local languages and customs. They also accepted into the society the native men of the countries in which they worked at a time when other European religious orders would not do so.

Paul III ▮ 1468–1549

The pontificate of Pope Paul III marked the transition from the Renaissance papacy to the Counter-Reformation papacy. The contradictory nature of his character still amazes: Paul III was at once an extravagant and worldly Renaissance churchman and a dedicated, reforming Counter-Reformation pope.

Paul III was born Alessandro Farnese in 1468, the son of a noble family from the Papal States. He was a well-educated and cultured man who loved Renaissance art and learning. His first promotion came about as a result of a papal misdemeanor: his sister was one of the mistresses of Pope Alexander VI. In the Renaissance it was customary for a powerful man to help the family of his mistress; Alexander VI thus became Alessandro's patron and made him a cardinal in 1493. Unlike many who were appointed to high office on grounds other than merit, Cardinal Alessandro Farnese served the papacy well. He was an able man who earned his keep by undertaking complicated diplomatic missions. He was also a cardinal who wore his vows lightly and lived in grand style. He collected the income from many church offices without fulfilling the duties of those offices. He also fathered several children before finally becoming a priest and taking the vow of celibacy in 1519.

After he became pope on October 13, 1534, Paul III at first continued to behave as he had done before. He used his office to shower riches and offices on his son and grandsons. He made two grandsons cardinals at the ages of sixteen and fourteen, and he created the duchy of Parma and Piacenza in northern Italy for his son, who was not a good ruler and was soon assassinated.

This conduct notwithstanding, Paul III endorsed and supported the Counter-Reformation. He brought to Rome and elevated to the cardinalate churchmen who sought to end the pattern of behavior of which he himself was guilty. In 1536 he appointed a reform commission of eminent churchmen; its report strongly criticized the very abuses that Paul practiced on a grand scale, including nepotism (awarding offices to undeserving relatives) and pluralism (holding two or more church offices and collecting their income without fulfilling their duties). Paul's most important achievement was to convene the Council of Trent (it eventually ran from 1545 to 1563). By the end of his pontificate, the church was so firmly committed to the Counter-Reformation that it would not turn back.

▲ This depiction of the inaugural session of the Council of Trent, held on December 13, 1545, was painted in 1711 by Niccolò Dorigatti.

The Counter-Reformation

With significant parts of Germany and Switzerland becoming Protestant and the Church of England split from Rome, the papacy seemed to be losing its authority and influence. Yet in the 1540s a remarkable recovery began.

Before the beginning of the Reformation, a number of individuals and groups had pledged both to better their own spiritual lives and to work to eliminate abuses and problems in the Roman Catholic Church. The term Counter-Reformation is often used to describe the transformation and improvement of the Catholic Church. New religious orders of both men and women were particularly important in renewing and energizing the church. One of the most important was the Society of Jesus (the Jesuits), which pledged itself in particular to missionary activity and the education of boys.

At first Rome procrastinated. It was reluctant to endorse and support Catholic reform efforts, partly because of the serious political problems that it faced and partly because it still hoped that differences with Protestants could be overcome and Christendom reunited. The situation changed in the 1540s. Despite sincere efforts by dedicated individuals on both sides to bring Catholics and Protestants together, the divisions

were too deep for reconciliation. As the papacy came to realize the permanence of the split, it moved forward on several fronts to improve the church. It joined or led efforts for internal reform in order to improve the educational and moral quality of clergymen and to eradicate abuses within the church.

The change began during the pontificate of Paul III. His most important decision was to convoke a general church council to clarify Catholic doctrine and to draft a program for renewal of the church. The council, which brought together numerous bishops, cardinals, and theologians, convened at Trent, a German-speaking city in northern Italy. Paul III, who wanted reconciliation as well as renewal, even invited Protestants to attend, but they refused;. The Council of Trent opened in 1545 and accomplished a good deal in its first session, which lasted from 1545 to 1547, especially in drafting statements defining the core Catholic beliefs. Forced to adjourn because of strong political differences between Paul III and Charles V, the council met again in 1551 and 1552 and, after another long delay caused by fighting in Germany, from early 1562 to the end of 1563.

▲ *This Japanese screen, probably painted in the last decade of the sixteenth century, depicts Portuguese Jesuit missionaries in Japan.*

plaints that the fact that the clergy as a whole were poorly educated had contributed to the growth of Protestantism.

During the forty years immediately following the Council of Trent, a series of strong, reform-minded popes implemented its decrees. Even more important, there was a new desire and dedication both in Rome and far beyond to make the church more spiritually disciplined. Major efforts were made to improve education, not only for the clergy but also for the general population: new schools for boys and girls gave equal emphasis to education and religious training. For those who could not attend regular schools, groups of laymen and laywomen organized catechism schools that met on Sundays and religious holidays. These schools taught prayers, the rudiments of Catholic belief, and a little reading and writing to both boys and girls.

The papacy also moved to halt the spread of Protestantism. When it realized that reconciliation with the Protestants was impossible and that the hostility and proselytizing efforts of Protestants would not stop, it took steps to guard Catholics against heresy. Paul III established the Roman Inquisition in 1542 to seek out and punish Protestants worshiping in secret in Catholic lands. Eventually there were local branches of the Inquisition in most major centers in Italy but not in France, where the monarchy would not accept the Roman Inquisition, or Spain, which had its own Inquisition. Other measures against Protestants followed. For a long time there had been confusion about exactly which books were heretical and which were not. In 1564 the papacy issued an Index of Forbidden Books to resolve this problem. On this list were books written by Protestants—and by some Catholics who criticized the papacy—that were not to be printed or read by Catholics. The move was quite successful in preventing the printing of Protestant books in Catholic countries, but it never completely stopped the smuggling of Protestant literature into Catholic lands. Later in the sixteenth century the papacy gave political support and sometimes financial support to governments that fought Protestantism.

The papacy and the Catholic Church as a whole made a significant recovery from the

The Council of Trent did not bridge the differences with Protestants, but it made clear the doctrinal positions of Catholicism. It reaffirmed and clarified Catholic teaching on a number of issues about which many people had been confused. The council also decreed substantial reform in church practices. A major problem had been the widespread failure of bishops actually to reside within and minister to their dioceses; the Council of Trent decreed that such absenteeism must stop. It insisted that parish priests, too, must reside within their parish and be good preachers and pastors. In order to improve the quality of the clergy, the council ordered every diocese to establish a seminary for the training of priests. This move came in response to com-

THE ROMAN INQUISITION

As Catholic hopes for reunion with Protestants faded and Protestants tried to convert Catholics to their cause even in Italy, Pope Paul III set up a tribunal called the Roman Inquisition to find and punish heretics. The Roman Inquisition, established in 1542, should not be confused with the Spanish Inquisition, which operated in Spanish territories and was controlled by the Spanish monarchy. For a long time the Roman Inquisition was considered by many to have been a cruel and ruthless instrument of persecution and injustice. However, recent research based on the records of the Inquisition itself demonstrates that this view is not just. The Inquisition's goal was the reconciliation of the heretic with the church. Thus, it tried to persuade the heretic of the error of his ways and thereby to bring him back to Catholicism. The Inquisition followed rules of law, based its process on evidence, and gave the accused the right to defend himself. The Roman Inquisition used torture only very sparingly, and most of its sentences were mild: they included prayers, penances, and a short period of house arrest. Prison sentences were often commuted. It was not common for the Roman Inquisition to issue death sentences; they were imposed only when a heretic who had previously renounced his heresy then returned to his heretical beliefs and refused to change his views. At that point the Inquisition decided that the heretic could not be converted and saved and therefore had to be removed from society.

The Roman Inquisition prevented travesties of justice. The inquisitors were trained investigators, usually with law degrees, who were not swept away by popular hysteria. They viewed accusations of witchcraft with caution and sometimes with outright skepticism. As a result, inquisitions did not participate in the periodic witch hunts that tended to occur in times of crop failures or other troubles. Wherever the Roman Inquisition was active, there were few if any witch trials, and many women were spared a terrible fate.

▼ *Giordano Bruno (1548–1600) was one of the relatively small number of people put to death at the behest of the Roman Inquisition. An Italian philosopher, he was executed for refusing to recant his many heretical views. This nineteenth-century statue of Bruno, the work of Ettore Ferrari, stands in the Campo de' Fiori in Rome, where Bruno was burned at the stake.*

threat posed by the Reformation. After 1555 the church lost no more territories to Protestantism. By 1600 Rome had regained its moral authority and had won back for Catholicism a few areas of Europe. The papacy also avoided repeating the mistake of becoming involved in the political battles in Italy, a mistake that had caused it much trouble early in the century.

Civic Challenges to the Church

By the early seventeenth century, Europe was changing again. Although the upheaval caused by the split of the continent into Catholic and Protestant states had mostly ended, rulers still found reasons to go to war. Civil governments, both Catholic and Protestant, were becoming more powerful. They wished to exert greater control over the lives of citizens and organizations within their borders. In order to do so, they had to restrict the power of other institutions in the state, especially the church. For centuries the church had enjoyed special privileges in society. For example, clergymen accused of crimes were tried in church courts rather than civil courts. It was not that church courts were necessarily more lenient than civil courts but rather that this privilege affirmed that churchmen were to be differentiated from laymen because they served God

and provided spiritual services for the populace. This attitude began to change in the late Renaissance, as civil governments made unilateral changes that restricted church rights. The papacy increasingly had to defend what it felt were its legitimate rights not against Protestants but against the governments of Catholic states. Resolutions were hard to reach, and the legal and jurisdictional battles would continue throughout the seventeenth and eighteenth centuries—with the papacy usually losing.

The first major battle between the papacy and a Catholic state occurred at the end of the Renaissance. In the late sixteenth century the government of the republic of Venice, the most important state on the Italian peninsula, passed laws asserting civil jurisdiction over lands owned by ecclesiastical organizations, such as monasteries. The Venetian government passed another law that gave it the power to tell church organizations where and when they might build churches. It then arrested two clergymen accused of crimes and prepared to try them in civil courts rather than hand them over to church courts. The ensuing confrontation with the church eventually led Pope Paul V (reigned 1605–1621) to impose an interdict on the Venetian republic in 1606. The crisis escalated as the Venetians and the papacy threatened to go to war.

Within a few months the two sides began to extend feelers for peace, and in April 1607 the pope lifted the interdict. Although both parties

▲ An unattributed bust of Pope Pius IV, who had a significant impact on the Counter-Reformation by concluding the Council of Trent, supporting religious scholarship, and issuing the Index of Forbidden Books.

Pius IV ▮ 1499–1565

Some of the popes who have attracted less attention than those who led more colorful lives actually accomplished a lot more. Giovanni Angelo de' Medici was a cardinal from Milan, a lawyer by training and a scholar who loved to quote from memory long passages from the classics. He was not viewed as a significant figure before he became Pope Pius IV. After a long and contentious conclave (a meeting at which cardinals secluded together choose the next pope), he was elected in December 1559 as a compromise choice. Although the cardinals did not expect much of him, Pius did a great deal for the church. The Council of Trent had been in recess for ten years when he reconvened it in January 1562. By the end of 1563, it had passed major reform legislation, most notably the decree that required every diocese to establish a seminary for the training of priests. After the council Pius created a permanent commission of cardinals to make sure that its decisions were implemented. He also promulgated the Index of Forbidden Books, a list of those books—mostly ones written by Protestants—that Catholics were not to read or print. He made excellent appointments and promoted artistic and scholarly projects in Rome. Among the latter was a program of papal support for the editing and printing of works by major patristic (early-Christian-era) and medieval Catholic authors, plus basic liturgical works, which were to be prepared according to the highest humanistic historical and philological standards. Pius died on December 9, 1565, having achieved a great deal in six years without generating much controversy.

pronounced themselves satisfied with the outcome, it was clear that Venice had won and the papacy had lost. The pope had tried to get the laws changed and failed. From that point forward, governments of Catholic states increasingly brought the Catholic Church within their territory under civil control. This issue did not arise in Protestant states, where governments had always controlled the church.

Paul V's failed interdict brought the papacy full circle. In the early fifteenth century the papacy had been weak compared with civil governments. Its power then rose during a period when it played a significant role in international diplomacy, politics, and war. The papacy joined alliances and even went to war to defend its interests. However, after Paul V's failed attempt to get the Venetians to fall into line by using an interdict, the influence of the papacy in international politics steadily declined. Governments increasingly made war and peace without consulting or involving the papacy, and they dominated the Catholic Church inside their borders.

The Papacy as Patron of Learning

Throughout the Renaissance the papacy gave support to scholars in many fields by appointing them to positions in the papal bureaucracy or paying them to carry out certain projects. The papal administration, the Roman Curia, was certainly in a position to offer employment to scholars. The curia communicated in Latin, the language in which the humanists were so skilled. By the second decade of the sixteenth century, the bureaucracy had nearly two thousand positions for which humanists were supremely qualified—although humanists did not, of course, fill all of those positions.

▲ *Saint Mark's Square in the center of Venice has changed little since the early seventeenth century, when the city was embroiled in a challenge to the authority of the papacy. In this painting by Louis de Caulery (c. 1580–1621/2), the ducal palace can be seen on the right, and Saint Mark's Basilica in the background.*

The Renaissance papacy created the Vatican Library (the official title is Biblioteca Apostolica Vaticana). One of the premier libraries in the world, it is particularly famous for its important manuscripts in the humanities and religious studies. Pope Nicholas V, who supported learning and collected books, had the idea of establishing a library open to all. In 1450 he set aside three rooms in the Vatican Palace and donated his own collection, which formed the nucleus of the new library. One room was for Latin manuscripts (of which there were around 800), another for Greek manuscripts (around 350), and a third for documents reserved for the pope's use—in effect, the papal archive. Established as it was before the invention of printing, the original collection held only handwritten manuscripts.

Nicholas V's immediate successors did not do much for the library. However, Sixtus IV (reigned 1471–1484), the pope who built the Sistine Chapel, did. He added a fourth room, separated the archive from the library, and appointed a humanist scholar, Bartolomeo Sacchi (called Platina, after his northern Italian birthplace), the first Vatican librarian. Sixtus also greatly enlarged the collection. At the time of his death, the library had over 3,600 manuscripts and printed books.

Many other popes and cardinals gave manuscripts and printed books to the library during the Renaissance. The Vatican Library continued to grow and to be of great use to scholars, some of whom traveled from far away to examine the precious manuscripts. Readers could even borrow manuscripts for home use, a practice that is no longer permitted. In the 1580s Pope Sixtus V (reigned 1585–1590) erected the large and imposing building that still houses much of the library and its reading rooms. Funds he provided also enabled eight scholars to study and work in the library.

In the second half of the sixteenth century, a deepening mutual suspicion and hostility between Protestants and Catholics resulted in access to the library being restricted to scholars in the Vatican itself. The restrictions were not lifted until 1883, when Pope Leo XIII (reigned 1878–1903) opened the library to all qualified scholars. Hundreds, possibly thousands of scholars from all over the world still use the Vatican Library every year, especially to study its unrivaled collection of ancient, medieval, and Renaissance manuscripts. It has over 75,000 manuscripts written in Greek, Hebrew, Arabic, Coptic, Syriac, Persian, Latin, and other languages. Possibly its most famous holding is the fourth-century manuscript known as Codex B, the earliest surviving complete Greek text of the Bible.

Humanists and other scholars also found employment as secretaries, advisers, and pedagogues in the households of popes and prelates, especially the twenty or so cardinals who lived in Rome. When a newly appointed cardinal or bishop came to Rome, he would bring along one or more secretaries and advisers. In addition, the University of Rome offered professorships. Very few of the scholars were Romans, although many of them were from Italy. Most of the positions that they found in Rome were not overly demanding. They provided income and security while leaving ample time for study and writing. Although some scholars left after a few years, the majority never returned to their home city or country. As a result, Renaissance Rome became a very cosmopolitan place where learning flourished.

Pope Nicholas V (reigned 1447–1455) brought humanists to Rome to translate or retranslate Greek classical and patristic texts into Latin. He believed that this program of translation

◀ *The sumptuously decorated walls and ceiling of a corridor in the Vatican Library, which was built by Pope Sixtus V in the late sixteenth century.*

In this work Melozzo da Forli (1438–1494) records the appointment of the humanist Bartolomeo Sacchi, called Platina, to the post of Vatican librarian by Pope Sixtus IV.

would make a large body of Greek material accessible to western Christians and aid in the spiritual renewal of the Catholic clergy. Cardinals were also major supporters of learning. Cardinal Bessarion (1403–1472), a Greek prelate and scholar who sought unity between the Catholic and Orthodox churches, settled in Rome in 1440. His household became a center for scholarly activity. Even scholars who criticized the papacy did not necessarily render themselves ineligible for papal support. For example, Lorenzo Valla (1407–1457), a brilliant humanist, attacked the papacy in his earlier works but was nevertheless appointed to teach at the University of Rome during the pontificate of Nicholas V. To be sure, Valla and other humanists did not criticize the papacy while they were living and working in Rome.

Popes also helped many scholars who lived far from Rome. When such men sent copies of their books with lavish dedications to the reigning pope, the pope generally responded with praise and money, a gift, or occasionally an annual pension. Northern European humanists, such as Desiderius Erasmus (c. 1466–1536), also received financial support in return for dedicating their books to the pope. However, when Erasmus attacked papal and clerical abuses, such as simony (the sale of church offices), nepotism, and militarism, the flow of papal gifts stopped.

By the early sixteenth century Rome had the largest concentration of scholars to be found anywhere in Europe, with the possible exception of Paris. Then times changed. Adrian VI (reigned 1522–1523), who came from the Netherlands, did not support scholars as freely as his predecessors had done. (Adrian VI was the last non-Italian pope before the election of John Paul II, a Pole, in 1978.) Clement VII was so preoccupied with the military and diplomatic problems of Italy and the Lutheran religious rebellion that he had little time for scholars. When the troops of Emperor Charles V sacked Rome in 1527, some humanists died, and many fled Rome, never to return.

▲ *Pope Gregory XIII is the subject of this portrait by Lavinia Fontana (1552–1614), an artist from the pope's birthplace, the northern Italian city of Bologna.*

As the papacy entered the age of the Counter-Reformation, it viewed scholars differently. It no longer supported a wide variety of individuals and projects but only those viewed as important to the religious mission of the church. Popes from Pius IV onward promoted only those projects—and the humanists who carried them out—that were directly related to the history and theology of Catholicism or those that advanced papal claims in scholarly battles with Protestants. Pius IV brought to Rome Paolo Manuzio (1512–1574), a talented humanist and an important publisher, and paid him a large amount of money to establish his printing press in the city. Among the subsidies given by the papacy to Manuzio were sums to cover the costs of printing the edited works of such early church fathers as Saint Gregory of Nyssa and Saint Jerome and the decrees of the Council of Trent. The program of papal support for sacred scholar-

ship continued through the rest of the sixteenth century. Gregory XIII (reigned 1572–1585) supported the preparation of the first edition of the *Martyrologium Romanum* (Roman Martyrology; 1584), a historical account of early Christian martyrs. The program culminated in the preparation and publication of the Vulgate, the traditional Latin text of the Bible, in 1592.

Calendar Reform

In the last quarter of the sixteenth century, the papacy tackled the long-standing problem of reforming the calendar. Europe was still using the Julian calendar introduced by the Roman statesman Julius Caesar in 45 BCE. Although the Julian calendar calculated days, weeks, months, and years in much the same way as the modern calendar does, its year was eleven minutes, fourteen seconds too long. As the centuries passed, the discrepancy between the Julian calendar and the movement of the sun had steadily built up, and by the sixteenth century the calendar was ten days behind. Various astronomers had noticed the inaccuracy over the centuries, but little was done until Pope Gregory XIII appointed a commission to solve the problem. The commission prepared a new calendar based on better astronomical knowledge than had been available in the ancient world. The pope promulgated the new calendar, called the Gregorian calendar, in October 1582. To make up the ten days that the Julian calendar had lost, the Gregorian calendar changed October 5, 1582, to October 15, 1582.

Catholic countries immediately adopted the Gregorian calendar. Protestant countries were slow to overcome their hostility to anything issuing from the papacy—England did not adopt the Gregorian calendar until 1752—but they eventually followed the Catholic lead. Russia and parts of eastern Europe where the Greek Orthodox Church—which does not recognize the authority of the papacy—was dominant refused to make the change. Russia accepted the Gregorian calendar only after the Russian Revolution, which fell in October 1917 according to the Julian calendar and in November 1917 according to the Gregorian calendar.

THE POPES OF THE RENAISSANCE: A SELECTION

1370–1378	Gregory XI
1378–1394	Urban VI; antipope Clement VII; Western Schism begins
1417–1431	Martin V; Western Schism ends
1431–1447	Eugenius IV
1447–1455	Nicholas V
1455–1458	Calixtus III
1458–1464	Pius II
1464–1471	Paul II
1471–1484	Sixtus IV
1484–1492	Innocent VIII
1492–1503	Alexander VI
1503–1513	Julius II
1513–1521	Leo X
1523–1534	Clement VII
1534–1549	Paul III
1549–1555	Julius III
1555–1559	Paul IV
1559–1565	Pius IV
1566–1572	Pius V
1572–1585	Gregory XIII
1585–1590	Sixtus V
1590–1592	Three short-term popes
1592–1605	Clement VIII
1605–1621	Paul V
1621–1623	Gregory XV
1623–1644	Urban VIII

The Gregorian calendar is not perfect. The Gregorian commission believed that it would "lose" one day over 22,000 years. More recent research shows that it loses one day in 2,500 years. However, the Gregorian commission did its work so well that it will be a long time before the calendar has to be adjusted again.

The Papacy as Patron of the Arts

The list of works of art commissioned and paid for by the papacy during the Renaissance includes some of the masterpieces of Western civilization. Among the most important papal patrons was Julius II, who commissioned Michelangelo Buonarroti (1475–1564) to paint the ceiling of the Sistine Chapel. Michelangelo worked on the ceiling paintings between 1508 and 1512, and

his *Creation,* along with his *Last Judgment* (1536–1541) in the same chapel, are among the best-known works of the Renaissance. Julius II also hired Raphael (1483–1520) to decorate many rooms in the Vatican Palace with his magnificent frescoes, of which *The School of Athens* (1513), which celebrates Plato, Aristotle, and other ancient philosophers, is the most famous.

The city of Rome benefited greatly from the projects undertaken and financed by the papacy. The first Renaissance popes inherited a medieval city with narrow twisting streets, crowded houses, empty spaces, and ancient Roman ruins. The papacy created a more ordered city with many new buildings, open squares, and better streets. Julius II in particular rebuilt whole sections of Rome. He laid out broad, straight streets and leveled areas of the city in order to create large squares. During the sixteenth century several popes erected monuments—obelisks long before brought from Egypt, for example—in the middle of these open squares. A bridge was built over the Tiber River to bring the two halves of the city together. The popes restored churches and tore down old buildings in order to build new ones. They vastly enlarged the Vatican Palace, where they lived and where many papal officials worked. Wealthy cardinals built large and sumptuous Renaissance palaces to house themselves and their entourages.

◄ *One of the most magnificent Renaissance buildings in Rome, the Farnese Palace was begun by Cardinal Alessandro Farnese (later Pope Paul III) in 1514; Michelangelo Buonarroti was among the architects involved in its construction. The frescoes pictured here are by Giovanni dei Vecchi (1536–1615).*

THE BUILDING OF SAINT PETER'S

The most important building project of the papacy was the new Basilica of Saint Peter, the pope's own church as well as the most important church in Catholic Christendom. Many of the leading Renaissance architects worked at Saint Peter's.

According to legend, in the first half of the fourth century, the Roman emperor Constantine built the original Saint Peter's Basilica over the tomb of Saint Peter, the leader of the Twelve Apostles. Since the remains of an ancient Roman cemetery have been located under the current church, the legend may be true, even though no grave has been identified as that of Saint Peter. By the Renaissance, however, the church was old, undistinguished, and in dire need of repair. It was not adequate for the ceremonial demands of the papacy, nor did it measure up to the high standards of contemporary architecture. It lacked space and grandeur.

Pope Julius II commissioned Donato Bramante (1444–1514) to design a new Saint Peter's according to the principles of Renaissance architecture, which followed classical models. Bramante's design was for a symmetrical and balanced church. However, both Julius II and Bramante died before much work could be done, and so Raphael (1483–1520) was brought in. He proposed a new design but also died before his plans could be implemented—as did his successor, Antonio da Sangallo the Younger (d. 1546). Progress stalled.

In 1546 Pope Paul III entrusted the building of Saint Peter's to Michelangelo Buonarroti (1475–1564), who had no training and little experience as an architect. He rejected the plans of Bramante and Raphael and imposed a simpler design, a Greek cross with a magnificent large, high dome and cupola. The design was accepted, and work began. After Michelangelo's death other architects carried out his wishes and built according to his plan.

The beginning of the seventeenth century was marked by a general upsurge in religious fervor among Catholics and a rise in papal prestige. Pope Paul V and his advisers believed that Michelangelo's design was insufficiently grand. They decided to elongate one of the four sides in order to create a large nave and to add a large porch in the front and a grand facade. Carlo Maderna (1556–1629) directed this part of the construction, which was finished in 1617. After extensive decorative work was done in the interior, the church was dedicated in 1626. The building that resulted is not only an an architectural monument but also the largest church in Christendom, capable of holding thousands of worshipers. Gian Lorenzo Bernini (1598–1680) added the magnificent colonnade in Saint Peter's Square in 1656 and 1667.

With all the false starts and changes in design, Saint Peter's might have emerged as an architectural mess. Some critics still believe that Michelangelo's plan should not have been altered. However, in the opinion of most, Saint Peter's expresses well the religious spirit and vitality of a papacy and church that survived the Reformation and emerged confident and strong.

Late in the sixteenth century the popes financed the excavation and exploration of the vast network of catacombs under the city, where the tombs of early Christians are located. Nor did the popes overlook the practical engineering projects that made Rome habitable. They repaired the ancient aqueducts that brought freshwater into the city from the nearby mountains. Once abundant water was available, they built fountains across the city. Although the popes and their builders admired and imitated Rome's classical buildings, they nevertheless pillaged the Colosseum and other ancient ruins for stone to be used in new constructions. The Renaissance papacy made Rome into a major European capital with the broad streets and open spaces necessary for the staging of grand processions. The city became a favorite destination of pilgrims and tourists from the rest of Europe.

A Splendid Legacy

At the beginning of the Renaissance, the papacy was weak. Church councils undermined its spiritual authority, and domineering princes limited its political power. The papacy could not even control all of its own territories. In the fifteenth century the popes gradually built up their authority by becoming involved in Italian and European political affairs. However, just as the papacy gained political and religious security, the Reformation challenged its authority, and the sack of Rome in 1527 damaged the city. Although the papacy could not win back the

Protestants and never again enjoyed as much political influence as it did in the fifteenth century, it did much to reform itself and the Catholic Church in the second half of the sixteenth century. The popes recovered a great deal of their religious prestige and authority; they regained some of their political authority, too. In art, scholarship, and architecture the popes of the Renaissance left a magnificent legacy.

FURTHER READING

Black, Christopher F. *Church, Religion and Society in Early Modern Italy.* New York, 2004.

D'Amico, John F. *Renaissance Humanism in Papal Rome: Humanists and Churchmen on the Eve of the Reformation.* Baltimore, 1983.

Grafton, Anthony, ed. *Rome Reborn: The Vatican Library and Renaissance Culture.* Washington, DC, 1993.

Levillain, Philippe, ed. *The Papacy: An Encyclopedia.* 3 vols. New York, 2002.

Minnich, Nelson H. "Papacy." In *Encyclopedia of the Renaissance.* Edited by Paul F. Grendler. 6 vols. New York, 1999.

Partner, Peter. *The Pope's Men: The Papal Civil Service in the Renaissance.* Oxford, 1990.

Pastor, Ludwig von. *The History of the Popes from the Close of the Middle Ages.* Translated and edited by F. I. Antrobus et al. 29 vols. Saint Louis, 1891–1933.

Stinger, Charles L. *The Renaissance in Rome.* Rev. ed. Bloomington, IN, 1998.

Paul F. Grendler

SEE ALSO
• Bernini, Gian Lorenzo • Bibles • Borgia, Lucrezia
• Bramante, Donato • Calendars • Charles V
• Clement VII • Florence, Council of • Henry VIII
• Heresy • Holy Roman Empire
• Humanism and Learning • Italian Wars • Leo X
• Lutheranism • Michelangelo
• Painting and Sculpture • Paul V • Pius II • Raphael
• Reformation • Renaissance • Rome
• Trent, Council of

▲ *This tomb, in the catacombs of Saint Sebastian in Rome, dates from the second century. In the late sixteenth century the popes supported the exploration and study of the catacombs, where many early Christians are buried.*

Paris

AS THE CAPITAL OF FRANCE AND THE LARGEST CITY IN NORTHERN EUROPE, PARIS BECAME BOTH A CENTER OF THE RENAISSANCE AND A BATTLEGROUND IN THE RELIGIOUS WARS DURING THE SIXTEENTH CENTURY.

By the beginning of the fourteenth century, Paris was one of the largest cities in Europe, with a population of between 80,000 and 120,000. The city had long been a major regional trade center, and it was home to a leading European university as well as several important church foundations. However, the key to its expansion in the Middle Ages was the rise of the French monarchy. From 1000 through 1300, the kings of France steadily increased their power and authority, and as part of this long-term process, they created a more professional system of government and based it in Paris.

Famine, War, and Plague

The fourteenth and fifteenth centuries were punctuated by a series of disasters—some natural, others with a human cause—that had profound effects on the city. In the region of Paris, as in Europe more generally, the long-term growth in population after 1000 had by 1300 placed significant strains on the food supply. Overpopulation in the countryside helped to fuel the growth of Paris's population during the 1200s as poor rural workers migrated to the city to find work, but the increase in the local population left the city vulnerable to food shortages. In 1314 a poor wheat harvest brought on by unusually cold temperatures and heavy rainfall in the Paris region began a period of chronic food shortages that lasted until 1317. At the height of the crisis, contemporary observers described the dead as littering the streets of Paris, since what little food was available cost more than the poor could afford. Food shortages continued to afflict the city into the 1340s.

▼ *In this sixteenth-century painting,* Scène Galante at the Gates of Paris, *by an unknown Flemish artist, the Cathedral of Notre-Dame dominates the city skyline behind the revelers.*

Around 1360 a monk provided the following eyewitness account of the impact of the Black Death as it spread through Paris:

In 1348 the people of France, and of virtually the whole world, were assailed by something more than war. For just as famine had befallen them, as described in the beginning of this account, and then war, as described in the course of the account, so now pestilences broke out in various parts of the world. . . . As a result of that pestilence a great many men and women died that year and next in Paris and throughout the kingdom of France, as they also did in other parts of the world. The young were more likely to die than the elderly, and did so in such numbers that burials could hardly keep pace. Those who fell ill lasted little more than two or three days, but died suddenly, as if in the midst of health—for someone who was healthy one day could be dead and buried the next. Lumps suddenly erupted in their armpits or groin, and their appearance was an infallible sign of death. Doctors called this sickness or pestilence an epidemic. Such an enormous number of people died in 1348 and 1349 that nothing like it has been heard or seen or read about. And death and sickness came by imagination, or by contact with others and consequent contagion; for a healthy person who visited the sick hardly ever escaped death. . . . To be brief, in many places not two men remained alive out of twenty. The mortality was so great that for a considerable period more than 500 bodies a day were being taken in carts from the Hôtel-Dieu [the main hospital] in Paris for burial in the cemetery of the Holy Innocents.

Chronicle of Jean de Venette

The 1320s brought new difficulties as ongoing territorial disputes edged the kings of France and England toward war. The conflict that came to be known as the Hundred Years War lasted from 1337 until 1453. With war came the destruction of crops, the cutting of trade routes, and chronic inflation. Until its close, the Hundred Years War had a disruptive effect on Paris, a key battleground, as rival factions sought to control the machinery of government located there.

In 1348 the Black Death arrived in France. No precise figures exist for the number of Parisians who died of the plague, but contemporary chroniclers estimated that nearly one-half of the city's population was dead by 1350. Periodic outbreaks of the plague and other epidemic diseases continued to kill large numbers of Parisians into the seventeenth century.

The severe disruptions of the first half of the fourteenth century led to significant political change in the second half. In 1356 the French royal army was nearly annihilated at the Battle of Poitiers, and the French king, John II (reigned 1350–1364), became a prisoner of the English. During this period of royal weakness, political factions opposed to the monarchy seized effective control of Paris. The region around the city experienced a violent peasant uprising known as the Jacquerie in 1358 and the ravages of English troops between 1360 and 1365.

Peace returned to Paris only when Charles V (reigned 1364–1380) regained control of his capital. Concerned by the unstable political situation, Charles sought to strengthen the city's defenses by constructing a new wall, rebuilding the Louvre fortress, and constructing the fortress

▲ The recovery and growth of Paris in the sixteenth century is reflected in this map of 1576, which shows the spread of the city on both banks of the Seine River.

after 1392, increasingly lost control of the political situation in France. Paris became the battleground for a struggle between two rival factions: the Armagnacs, led by the king's brother Louis, duke of Orléans, and the Burgundians, led by the king's uncle, Duke John the Fearless. In November 1407 Louis was assassinated by John's men, and the struggle between the two parties dominated the political life of Paris for the next twenty-eight years. The opening decades of the fifteenth century proved a low point in Paris's fortunes, as the city became the focus of political struggles and suffered from the ravages of warfare, lawlessness, and recurring food shortages.

A key moment in the struggles occurred in 1419, when John met the same fate as his rival Louis at the hands of a courtier of Charles VI. John's assassination led the Burgundian faction to support the claim of Henry V, king of England (reigned 1413–1422), to the throne of France. The support Henry received from the Burgundians, together with his stunning victory at the Battle of Agincourt in 1415, led to the Treaty of Troyes, in which Henry was named to succeed to the French throne when Charles VI died. The English forces and their Burgundian allies also occupied Paris. They remained in control of the city until 1437.

Recovery and Growth

After years of fighting, the Burgundians transferred their loyalty back to the French crown, and in 1437 Charles VII (reigned 1422–1461) was able to reclaim Paris. Within two decades the city started to recover its prosperity. Although the kings of the later fifteenth century spent little time in residence there, Paris experienced a renewal during the period. Peace in the countryside and the resulting recovery in trade played a role in the city's return to prosperity, but equally important was the reestablishment and growth of the royal governmental institutions. Paris's recovery continued during the sixteenth century as its population grew from fewer than 200,000 to more than 300,000 by the opening decades of the seventeenth century. It was not only by some margin the largest city in the kingdom but also the largest in northern Europe.

▲ *In this illumination from the Très riches heures du duc de Berry, a renowned fifteenth-century book of hours, the peasants in the foreground are sowing the winter grain. Towering over the fields is the Louvre, a fortress that was renovated into a palace by Charles V in the fourteenth century (although it retained many of its military features).*

of Saint Antoine, later known as the Bastille, to protect the eastern part of the city. Together these projects significantly increased the area of the city and surrounding suburbs that was protected by permanent defenses.

English Rule of Paris

The period of relative peace in Paris during the reign of Charles V proved only temporary; Paris fell back into disorder under Charles VI (reigned 1380–1422). In the early fifteenth century the king, who had begun to suffer bouts of insanity

Renaissance Paris

During the first half of the sixteenth century, Paris became a key center of the Renaissance in northern Europe. In part, royal patronage drove this development. Francis I (reigned 1515–1547) and his successors rebuilt the royal fortress known as the Louvre and turned it into a Renaissance palace. Catherine de Médicis (1519–1589), Henry II's wife and a member of Florence's preeminent family, began construction of the Tuileries, a second palace beside the Louvre. The monarchy also played a role in making Paris a leading center of Renaissance learning. In 1535 Francis I founded the Collège de France, an institution dedicated to teaching the classical languages and humanistic thought, the disciplines that lay at the heart of the Renaissance approach to education. During this same period the printing industry developed in the city and played an important role in the spread of ideas.

Renaissance Paris continued to flourish until the 1560s, when the threat of new Protestant ideas in this strongly Catholic city and the outbreak of civil war led to a change in the intellectual climate.

◀ By the time Reinier Zeeman (c. 1623–1667) painted this view of the Louvre, the medieval fortress had been torn down and replaced by the familiar palace in the Renaissance style.

THE LOUVRE

Perhaps the most dramatic alteration to the Parisian landscape during the Renaissance was the transformation of the Louvre from a defensive bastion into a royal palace. The first stone for the Louvre was laid in 1202. Its original design centered on a formidable tower placed at a strategic position along the Seine from where the city's wall could be defended and protection could be provided from an enemy flotilla on the river. The tower's thick stone walls were broken only by thin arrow slits.

During the reign of Charles V, the Louvre was remodeled so that it could also serve as a royal residence. Windows replaced many of the arrow slits, and decorative pointed roofs were added to its turrets and towers. Despite the refurbishment French monarchs preferred to live in other palaces in Paris.

It was only during the reign of Francis I that the Louvre was transformed into the chief residence of French monarchs in Paris. In reconstructing the Louvre, Francis also created perhaps the most important example of Renaissance architecture in his capital. He razed the old bastion, which had lost its original purpose as a defensive structure owing to both the continued expansion of Paris and the increase in the power of the monarchy—which no longer needed a defensive fortress in its capital. Francis replaced the structure with an elegant palace that incorporated Italian Renaissance architectural features but retained a distinctly French look through its steep roof and decoration. From the reign of Francis I, the Louvre became the French monarchy's chief residence in Paris, and successive monarchs continued to expand the original palace until 1663, when Louis XIV completed the building work.

▲ *Henry II, the subject of this contemporary portrait by an unidentified French artist, was the first monarch to persecute Protestants systematically in Paris.*

tion any books that contained Luther's subversive propositions. In 1525, for the first time, Protestants were burned in Paris for the crime of heresy. The city's population on the whole supported these actions. The vandalizing of a statue of the Virgin Mary by Protestants in 1528 caused public outrage.

Despite the strong support for Catholicism among a majority of Parisians, Protestant ideas spread in secret among some members of the university, a few royal judges, and a number of merchants. Several followers of Protestantism at the university, including John Calvin (1509–1564), were forced to flee Paris in 1533 after the university's newly installed rector, Nicholas Cop, gave a sermon that appeared to support Protestant doctrine. However, systematic persecution by the royal judges began only in the 1540s, when Francis I's son, Henry II (reigned 1547–1559), became king. In the Parisian parliament Henry set up a special chamber, known as the burning chamber, to try heretics. His action was in part a response to the growing organization of Protestants in his capital, where informal meetings for the reading of scripture and prayer had developed into full services that included the sacraments. In 1555 the first Protestant minister was appointed in Paris. In 1557 local Catholics discovered a service taking place and attacked the participants; the authorities ultimately arrested 130 of the Protestants attending the service. Most recanted their beliefs in order to secure their freedom, but seven were executed for heresy. Despite this setback the Protestant community continued to organize itself, and in May 1559 the first national Protestant church meeting took place in secret in the French capital.

Following Henry II's death in 1559, the wars of religion broke out in France. Within Paris the majority of the population remained firmly Catholic. During times of conflict, the authorities and town militia sought to drive professed or suspected Protestants from the city. Paris also consistently opposed royal efforts to secure peace through toleration of the Protestant minority. The city's populace, supported by clergy who preached the dangers of tolerance, opposed each successive bid for peace in the 1560s. Ultimately

The Wars of Religion

Paris's importance to the Reformation lay in the solid support for the Catholic faith from the theologians at the University of Paris, the royal judges based in the city, and the population as a whole. From the first the university theologians defended Catholic dogma against Protestant challenges. In April 1521 they condemned as heretical 104 propositions made by Martin Luther (1483–1546), the German who set the Reformation in motion. Five months later, the royal courts supported the decrees of the university by ordering that people turn in for destruc-

A Catholic judge wrote the following eyewitness account of the Saint Bartholomew's Day Massacre.

In the mean time Guise, with Aumale and Angolesme [noblemen of the Catholic faction], return into the City, where the King's Guards did commit outrages upon the lives and fortunes of the Protestant Nobles and Gentlemen, even of those that were their familiars, and well known to them. This work being assigned to them in particular, while the people incited by the Sheriffs, wardsmen and tything-men that ran about, did furiously rage with all manner of licentiousness and excess against their fellow-Citizens, and a sad and horrid face of things did every where appear. For the streets and ways did resound with the noise of those that flocked to the slaughter and plunder, and the complaints and doleful out-cries of dying men, and those that were nigh to danger were every where heard. The carcasses of the slain were thrown down from the windows, the Courts & chambers of houses were full of dead men, their dead bodies rolled in dirt were dragged through the streets, bloud did flow in such abundance through the channels of the streets, that full streams of bloud did run down into the River: the number of the slain men, women, even those that were great with child [pregnant], and children also was innumerable.

Jacques-Auguste de Thou, *The History of the Bloody Massacres of the Protestants in France in the Year 1572*

▼ *The Saint Bartholomew's Day Massacre of August 24, 1572, is recorded in this detail from a contemporary painting by François Dubois.*

this opposition manifested itself in one of the most dramatic events of the religious wars, the Saint Bartholomew's Day Massacre. On August 24, 1572, while Charles IX (reigned 1560–1574) and his council ordered the assassination of several leading Protestant figures in Paris, rumors of a Protestant coup spread among the people. The royal authorities quickly lost control of the situation, and mob violence ensued. More than two thousand Protestants were massacred. Those who survived either fled Paris or recanted.

In the aftermath of the massacre, the city became a focal point for Catholic resistance to the toleration of Protestants. The most radical Catholic leaders in Paris, including several prominent and influential preachers, became members of the Catholic League, a group that opposed the policy of compromise with the Protestants, a policy advocated by the French crown. Opposition in Paris came to a head in May 1588, when, on the so-called Day of the Barricades, the Catholic League drove King Henry III (reigned 1574–1589) from Paris and seized effective political control of the capital. Over the next six years Paris played a leading role in the league's rebellion, and the gates of the capital were closed against the French monarchs and their forces.

The assassination of Henry III in 1589 and the accession of the Protestant Henry IV (reigned 1589–1610) failed to change the political situa-

tion; Paris continued to refuse to open its gates. Henry IV began a long and bitter siege but was forced to abandon it when troops from the Spanish Netherlands marched to relieve the city. Only after Henry IV abandoned the Protestant faith and sought to return to Catholicism in 1593 did resistance to his rule weaken significantly in Paris. He finally gained control of his capital in March 1594.

Despite the inauspicious start to his reign, Henry IV ultimately became a popular ruler in Paris. He immediately set about repairing the damage that the city had suffered during the religious wars and made moves to revive its flagging economy. A key project was the completion of the Pont Neuf, a bridge across the Seine that Henry III had begun. In the Edict of Nantes (1598), which granted Protestants a legal standing in France, Henry IV specifically identified Paris as a Catholic city and restricted Protestant worship in the region to the town of Charenton, well outside the city limits.

Paris in the Seventeenth Century

With the reestablishment and, later, the expansion of the royal government under Henry IV and Louis XIII (reigned 1610–1643), Paris grew in size and importance. Royal judges continued to meet in the old royal palace on the Île-de-Cité, but Louis XIII's first minister, Cardinal Richelieu

HENRY IV AND THE REBUILDING OF PARIS

When Henry IV triumphantly entered his capital in March 1594, he must have been struck, as many contemporaries were, by its state of disrepair. Henry's siege of Paris in 1590 had caused further damage to a city that was already scarred by the wars of the previous thirty years. Construction and even the repair of the city's buildings had largely been neglected as disruptions in trade and the ravages of war undermined the city's wealth. Even the basic infrastructure, including the streets and the primitive drainage system, had largely collapsed.

The *Mercure française* recorded after Henry's death that "as soon as he [Henry] was master of Paris, one saw nothing but stone masons at work." Henry wanted not merely to repair his capital but to rebuild it to reflect his ambitions for France. Like his predecessors, he built his own addition to the Louvre, this time a magnificent gallery, 1,640 feet (500 m) long, along the Seine River that linked the Louvre and Tuileries palaces. He also took up Henry III's uncompleted project for a stone bridge across the Seine. The bridge, named the Pont Neuf and completed in 1607, became a key artery for traffic in Paris.

The Place Royale (now known as the Place des Vosges) was perhaps Henry's most visionary project in that it provided a model for town planning in Paris over the next two centuries. Henry transformed an empty site in the heart of the city into an impressive town square. His intention was to attract skilled silk workers to the capital, but ultimately the elegant town houses, all built to the same design, became residences for the fashionable and wealthy. The Place Royale was completed two years after Henry's death, but his even more ambitious plan for a massive semicircular space, provisionally named the Place de France, in the east of the capital was never realized. Nonetheless, his vision of elegant new public spaces became a model for his successors, who carried out similar projects in Paris and helped to give the city its distinctive character.

(1585–1642), built his Paris residence near the Louvre and actively encouraged other important members of court to do likewise. As a result, the geographic center of the city gradually shifted toward the Louvre district. At the same time the triumph of Catholicism in Paris led to the rebuilding of churches and the establishment of new religious orders associated with the Catholic Counter-Reformation. To cope with the growing population, new neighborhoods were constructed. This process included the transformation of two small muddy islands in the Seine into the fashionable Île-Saint-Louis.

By 1650 Paris had established itself as the political and economic capital of France. Over the previous three and a half centuries the city had experienced both rapid growth and contraction. The decision of French monarchs to settle in Paris and focus their increasingly sophisticated bureaucracy in the capital ensured that the city's influence would continue to spread throughout the realm and beyond.

FURTHER READING

Diefendorf, Barbara. *Beneath the Cross: Catholics and Huguenots in Sixteenth-Century Paris.* Oxford, 1991.

Horne, Alistair. *Seven Ages of Paris.* New York, 2002.

Thomson, David. *Renaissance Paris: Architecture and Growth, 1475–1600.* Berkeley, CA, 1984.

Eric Nelson

SEE ALSO

- Agincourt, Battle of • Agriculture • Burgundy
- Catherine de Médicis • Disease • England • France
- Francis I • French Civil Wars • Henry IV • Heresy
- Humanism and Learning • Hundred Years War
- Population • Reformation • Religious Orders
- Renaissance • Trade • Universities • Warfare

▲ *In this work by an unknown artist, the Place Royale, Henry IV's most important building project, is the setting for festivities to mark the wedding of Louis XIII to Marie-Louise of Austria in 1615.*

Paul V

ALTHOUGH PAUL V (1552–1621) VIGOROUSLY ASSERTED THE SUPREMACY OF THE PAPACY, HIS PONTIFICATE WAS ALSO THE FIRST IN WHICH THE POPE WAS NO LONGER A CENTRAL FIGURE IN INTERNATIONAL POLITICS.

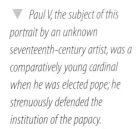

▼ Paul V, the subject of this portrait by an unknown seventeenth-century artist, was a comparatively young cardinal when he was elected pope; he strenuously defended the institution of the papacy.

Pope Paul V was born Camillo Borghese. His father, Marcantonio Borghese, was a lawyer, and his mother, Flaminia Astelli, came from an old Roman family. Marcantonio moved his family from Siena to Rome in Camillo's youth, and Camillo thus thought of himself as a Roman. He studied law at the University of Perugia and on his return to Rome became a priest and worked with his father as a lawyer in the curia (the papal bureaucracy). In 1588 Camillo was appointed vice-legate in Bologna, where he stayed for five

years. His only direct experience of the world outside the Papal States was during a diplomatic mission to Philip II of Spain in 1593. Appointed a cardinal in 1596, Camillo became a member of the Roman Inquisition (the body charged with rooting out heresy). In May 1605, while still one of the youngest cardinals, he was unexpectedly elected pope (he was chosen as a compromise candidate to break the deadlock between the main factions in the College of Cardinals).

Physically imposing, serious, hardworking, and pious, Pope Paul V had a strong sense of his responsibilities. He thought of his papal duty primarily in terms of protecting the political and legal rights of the church. In order to collect documentary evidence of these rights, he founded the Vatican archives to bring together the scattered records of previous popes. He asserted the independence of the church, the clergy, and ecclesiastical property from the control of secular authorities and was inclined to see lay politicians who disagreed with this view as heretics; he expected papal commands to be met with obedience, not argument. In forming his policies, he paid little attention to the advice of his cardinals.

Paul wanted the decrees of the Council of Trent (1545–1563) to be enforced throughout the Catholic Church and encouraged the efforts of reforming bishops. Among the saints canonized during his pontificate were Francesca Romana (1384–1440), who had long been venerated by the Romans, and Carlo Borromeo (1538–1584), an exemplar of the ideals of the Counter-Reformation. Paul also tried to end two long-running doctrinal disputes within the church but was unable to reach a definitive conclusion. Neither the Jesuits nor the Dominicans were declared right (or wrong) in their dispute over the roles of divine grace and free will in determining human actions. On the controversial issue of the Immaculate Conception (whether the Virgin Mary had been preserved from sin from the moment of her conception), Paul simply forbade further discussion. He did, however, back the order of the Inquisition that Galileo Galilei (1564–1642) should cease to propagate the idea that the earth, not the sun, moved in orbit.

CHRONOLOGY

1552
Camillo Borghese is born in
Rome on September 17.

1588–1593
Serves as vice-legate in
Bologna.

1593
Is sent on a diplomatic mission
to Philip II of Spain.

1596
Is made a cardinal on June 15.

1605
Is elected pope on May 18 and
takes the name Paul V. Decides
in September to demolish the
remainder of old Saint Peter's
Church in Rome.

1606
Places Venice under interdict.

1607
Revokes the interdict against
Venice in April.

1611–1612
Founds the secret archives of
the papacy, housed in the
Vatican.

1615–1617
The new Saint Peter's Basilica is
completed.

1621
Paul V dies on January 28.

▲ *The Dutch artist Abraham van Cuylenborch painted this view of the Villa Borghese in the mid-seventeenth century. The villa now houses a magnificent art collection, and its grounds have become the most famous park in Rome—a lasting testimony to the wealth Paul V's family acquired during his papacy.*

PAPAL NEPOTISM

The sixteenth century saw the emergence of the cardinal-nephew, a cardinal who was a close relative of the pope and who acted as the pope's representative and sometimes as a kind of chief minister. The most powerful cardinal-nephews could deal with all aspects of the affairs of state of the papacy, particularly those concerning the administration of the Papal States and relations with other governments.

Paul V's cardinal-nephew was his sister's son, Scipione Caffarelli (1576–1633), who was given the name Borghese when he was made a cardinal at the age of twenty-seven in July 1605. Scipione Borghese handled the autocratic pope with much tact and did not develop independent policies, as some cardinal-nephews did. He was rewarded in the considerable authority the pope gave him and in a decree of 1618 that, defining the responsibilities of the cardinal-nephew, confirmed the position as a recognized office within the administration of the church. Borghese accumulated many other offices and amassed great wealth, which he used to buy land around Rome and to construct and embellish the Villa Borghese and its extensive pleasure grounds (the villa stood just outside the city). He also gathered an impressive collection of works of art.

Like many other popes, Paul V sought to enrich his family. He educated the only son of his two brothers, Marcantonio, and bought fine estates for him in the kingdom of Naples (through which estates Marcantonio gained the title prince of Sulmona) as well as in the Papal States. Paul did not try to set up his beloved nephew as the ruler of an independent state, as Leo X, Clement VII, and other previous popes had done with their relatives, but he nonetheless established his family as one of the wealthiest in Rome.

The Venetian Interdict

Paul V's concern to protect the autonomy of the church, its clergy, and its assets from the intervention of secular government brought him into dispute with Venice. As a result of the confrontation, Venice was placed under interdict. In effect, the Venetian clergy was prohibited from celebrating and the laity from attending Mass or any other public religious ceremony. This proved to be the last occasion on which a pope placed an entire state under interdict.

The Venetian republic had a long tradition of closely supervising the clergy and religious institutions within its territory, a policy that had repeatedly brought the Venetians into conflict with the papacy. Two pieces of legislation, extending to all Venetian territories laws that had long been in force in the city of Venice itself, angered the pope. The first, of 1603, prohibited the building of any new church without the permission of the government; the second, of 1605, forbade the grant of new lands by laymen to the church for longer than two years, after which the land had to be sold to a layman. Paul was also annoyed by two cases in which clerics were prosecuted by the lay courts. These prosecutions contravened the principle that members of the clergy were exempt from lay jurisdiction.

In December 1605 the pope wrote to warn the Venetian government that it would be excommunicated and all Venice's territories placed under interdict unless the government revoked several laws that, in his opinion, infringed the rights of the church. The excommunications and interdict were duly issued in April 1606. The Venetians tried to prevent the publication of the interdict and insisted that the clergy should continue to perform its religious duties as usual. A large number of the clergy did so, more or less willingly, and some were punished for refusing. Many Venetians backed the stance of the government.

▲ *Paolo Sarpi's fame as a critic of the papacy's supposed manipulation of the Council of Trent is signaled in the inscription on this portrait, which refers to him as the "disemboweler" of the council. The name of the artist and the date of the painting are unknown.*

Paolo Sarpi ■ 1552–1623

Paolo Sarpi was appointed as an official theologian by the Venetian government. His job was to contest the validity of the interdict and refute the arguments put forward on behalf of the papacy. In Rome, Sarpi came to be seen as the main instigator of Venice's defiance, but in practice he was only giving effective expression to opinions held by many Venetians.

Sarpi was a member of the Servites, an order of mendicant friars who lived a monastic life but also worked in the community. He studied theology at the University of Padua and was also interested in science, philosophy, and the study of history. He was excommunicated in January 1607 because of his writings, which were burned in Rome. Attempts were made to assassinate him, but he remained an unrepentant critic of papal power. In his most famous work, the *History of the Council of Trent* (1619), he argued that the popes had manipulated the council to defend the primacy of the papacy—and had set this goal above the reform of the church. Regarded as a saint by many Venetians, Sarpi, despite his unconventional personal religious views and his well-known contacts with Protestants, was kept on as official consultant to the Venetian government until his death in 1623. Opinion is divided over whether he was at heart a Catholic reformer, a Calvinist, or an atheist; to Paul V he was a dangerous heretic.

The quarrel aroused great interest in other states. While Paul's election to the papacy had been seen by some as a diplomatic success for the French, the French king, Henry IV (reigned 1589–1610), was sympathetic to Venice. The Spanish, anxious to recover their long-standing position as the main ally of the papacy, supported Paul V, although in fact many Spanish officials agreed with the basic tenets of Venice's position in the dispute. Neither the French nor the Spanish wanted to go to war over the issue, and both tried to mediate, as did other powers. In February 1607 the Venetians agreed to allow the mediation of François de Joyeuse, a French cardinal, although they maintained their refusal to accept the validity of the interdict. Paul V, concerned about the support the Venetian position was attracting and the interest the Protestants were taking in the dispute, agreed to lift the interdict and excommunications in April 1607 in return for formal Venetian revocation of the protest against the papal decrees. The two clerics whose prosecution had become part of the dispute were handed over to the French for Henry IV to decide what should be done with them. This settlement was generally seen as a defeat for the papacy.

Paul V's Role in European Politics

The unfavorable outcome of the dispute with Venice intensified Paul V's cautious approach to becoming involved in the quarrels of the major European powers. Desiring to remain neutral in ongoing disagreements between France and Spain, he encouraged negotiations for marriage alliances between the Spanish Hapsburgs and the Bourbon kings of France. He was less enthusiastic about proposals for a Spanish match with the prince of Wales, since he was involved in a prolonged dispute with the prince's father, James I of England. The dispute related to an oath of loyalty to the king that Catholics in England had been required to take following the 1605 Gunpowder Plot—a conspiracy by Catholic extremists to blow up the Houses of Parliament when James I was present. Paul declared that it was unlawful for Catholics to take the oath; they would, he was sure, prefer torture and death.

▲ *Paul V was one of the popes who extended and embellished the papal summer palace on the Quirinal Hill in Rome. The palace is pictured here in a work by the Italian artist Canaletto (1697–1768).*

BUILDING WORKS IN ROME

Paul V made an important contribution to the construction of papal Rome. In the ancient Basilica of Santa Maria Maggiore, his favorite church in Rome, he built a large, sumptuous chapel, the Cappella Paolina, with frescoes by Guido Reni and an altar decorated with agate and lapis lazuli. In front of the church, a bronze statue of the Virgin was placed on a gigantic marble column.

Paul greatly extended the pope's summer palace on the Quirinal Hill. The ancient aqueduct of the emperor Trajan, which brought water to Rome from near Lake Bracciano but had become derelict, was repaired and rebuilt and became known as the Acqua Paola. The monumental fountain of the Acqua Paola in Trastevere was one of many around Rome built for Paul V; among others were the fountain in Saint Peter's Square and that in the Belvedere courtyard of the Vatican.

Throughout his pontificate, Paul put great amounts of money and effort into the completion of the new Saint Peter's. It was he who made the decision to demolish the remains of the old basilica, and he also approved radical changes to the plans for the new building, which was completed in 1615. Paul's name is emblazoned on the gigantic inscription across the facade.

▼ Paul V is buried in the Cappella Paolini (pictured below), the magnificent chapel he had built in the Basilica of Santa Maria Maggiore in Rome.

Paul V did not in general encourage Catholics to make war on Protestants, but he did give subsidies to the Holy Roman emperor and to the Catholic League of Germany in the opening stage of the Thirty Years War (1618–1648). The crushing victory of the Catholics over the leader of the German Protestant forces, the elector Palatine of the Rhine, at the Battle of White Mountain, near Prague, in November 1620 was greeted with great joy by the pope in early December. His dreams of witnessing a great Catholic restoration in Germany cheered the last weeks of his life. He died on January 28, 1621.

FURTHER READING

Bouwsma, William James. *Venice and the Defense of Republican Liberty.* Berkeley, CA, 1968.

Magnuson, Torgil. *Rome in the Age of Bernini.* Vol. 1, *From the Election of Sixtus V to the Death of Urban VIII.* Translated by Nancy Adler. Atlantic Highlands, NJ, 1982.

Reinhard, Wolfgang. "Papal Power and Family Strategy in the Sixteenth and Seventeenth Centuries." In *Princes, Patronage and the Nobility: The Court at the Beginning of the Modern Age, c. 1450–1650,* edited by Ronald G. Asch and Adolf M. Birke. London, 1991.

Christine Shaw

SEE ALSO

• Clement VII • Galilei, Galileo • Henry IV
• Leo X • Lombardy • Papacy • Rome
• Thirty Years War • Trent, Council of • Venice

Peasants' Revolts

POPULAR UPRISINGS OF THE RURAL
WORKING CLASSES TOOK PLACE ACROSS
EUROPE IN THE LATE MIDDLE AGES.
THE BEST-KNOWN OF THESE VIOLENT
PROTESTS IS THE ENGLISH PEASANTS'
REVOLT OF 1381.

The fourteenth century was a period of great social instability. In total, the first outbreak of the Black Death in 1348 and the recurrent epidemics in the following decades wiped out one-third of Europe's population. The result was widespread social and economic dislocation. The greater opportunities for personal freedom and social mobility that presented themselves to the lower classes provoked a reaction from ruling classes determined to preserve the status quo. The souring of relations between social classes led eventually to rebellion.

The vast majority of Europeans were peasants (small-scale agriculturalists). Some were freemen, who owned or rented their property. Many were serfs (also known as villeins), who occupied land in return for providing their labor or some other service to the landowner and were tied to some degree to both lord and land. In the aftermath of the plague, far fewer people were available to work the land, and the result was competition for workers and a sharp rise in wages. For the first time peasants were in a position to dictate terms and conditions to landlords. In several instances the landlords responded with attempts to keep workers in their "proper station." In England the Statute of Laborers (1351) set a maximum wage for each trade and tried to restrict the movement of peasants from their villages in search of better pay and conditions elsewhere. Attempts to tie peasants to the land were also catalysts for revolt in Hungary and Spain in the fifteenth century. In England and several Italian city-states, sumptuary laws regulated the style and cost of clothes that people wore. The goal of these laws was to prevent social mobility—it became a felony for a prosperous peasant to look and live like those who held a more elevated position in society. Antagonism between the peasantry, thwarted in their ambitions to improve their lot, and the propertied elite, who were themselves under financial pressure and fearful of change, was thus a significant factor in increasing discontent.

The collapse in population led to long-term economic changes in the countryside. The price of food fell as a result of declining demand, and the value of land plummeted. Many noblemen switched from cultivating crops to raising sheep, a less labor-intensive process that left agricultural workers unemployed and led in turn to villages being abandoned. Other landlords gave up working their estates and leased them out for a fixed rate (known as a farm) or sold off part of their land to prosperous peasants. These modest freeholders suffered when agricultural prices dropped even lower in the late fourteenth century, at the same time that taxation in several states rose to previously unknown levels.

▶ The illuminations in the Luttrell Psalter, produced around 1340, depict the everyday life of the English peasantry before the upheavals wrought by the Black Death. In this scene peasants are stacking sheaves of corn.

In addition to the social dislocation, economic problems, and other instabilities caused largely by the plague, another pressing factor was war, particularly in England and France. The Hundred Years War brought utter devastation to several regions of rural France and inflamed widespread anger against the knightly class, whose raison d'être (in theory at least) was to defend society. Escalating taxes, levied to finance the war, further impoverished people. When the war was going badly, people targeted their resentment at local officials and the government, who stood accused of incompetence or corruption even when protesters maintained loyalty to the king.

The Peasants' Revolt and Its Participants

The spark that ignited the Peasants' Revolt of 1381 was a universal poll tax (head tax) of one

◀ *The French peasant uprising known as the Jacquerie began in May 1358 near Compiègne, in northeastern France, and lasted for around three weeks. In this illumination from the* Chronicle of Saint-Denis *(1375), French knights are depicted slaughtering rebel peasants.*

PATTERNS OF PEASANT REVOLTS

The English Peasants' Revolt of 1381 is the classic example of late-medieval social rebellion—a short, violent episode of popular outrage against a backdrop of political weakness, economic crisis, and increasing class dislocation. Revolts in France during this period were inspired also by the ever-increasing taxation made necessary by the largely unsuccessful pursuit of the Hundred Years War. The uprising known as the Jacquerie (1358) erupted at a time when French fortunes were at their lowest; bands of brigands and mercenaries were ravaging the countryside, and the king, John II (reigned 1350–1364), was held captive in England. Small-scale rebellions against local lords and tax officials were swiftly put down, and fearful of renewed insurgency, the nobility dealt out brutal reprisals. The French uprising of 1381 and 1382 closely resembled the Peasants' Revolt in that both were directed against the regency administration of a king who was still a minor and both were caused largely by a perception that taxation was unfairly imposed and imprudently managed.

Other English uprisings had similar causes and followed patterns almost identical to those of the 1381 revolt. Jack Cade's rebellion (1450) raised grievances of unfair taxation, government corruption, and military failures in France. Thousands marched on London, where a week of lynching and looting petered out in the face of false promises of reform. The Cornish Rebellion (1497), a protest against Henry VII's war taxation, ended swiftly after a skirmish outside London and the capture and execution of the leaders.

Elsewhere, the Bobâlna Revolt in Hungary (1437) was sparked by taxation demands in Transylvania but spread widely and raised more general grievances over enforcement of feudal ties and restrictions of movement. The Rebellion of the Remences (named after the Catalan word that means "serfs") appealed to John II of Aragon (reigned 1458–1479) for an end to serfdom and to the abuse by the nobility of its traditional powers. The peasants rose against the landowners in 1462, and a peasant army fought alongside the king in his own conflict with the Catalan nobility (1462–1471) but received little from him in return. A subsequent revolt in 1485 ended serfdom, but rural society remained firmly feudal. Revolts that took place in Slovenia and Croatia in 1515 and 1573, respectively, serve to highlight resentment among peasants in many parts of Europe about their position in society, even into the late sixteenth century.

Peasants' revolts might be defined as uprisings in which peasants made up the vast majority of insurgents and that were caused by grievances that affected mainly the rural working class. However, this unstable period also witnessed insurgencies among city dwellers, particularly in the heavily urbanized areas of Flanders, Italy, and northern France. Other revolts were prompted mainly by religious fervor; examples include the Pilgrimage of Grace in England (1536), the Peasants' War (1524–1526) in the Holy Roman Empire, and the Hungarian uprising of the crusading army of George Dózsa (1514).

shilling per person over the age of fifteen. This tax was crippling to the poorest peasant families, whose income might be no more than twenty shillings a year, and so there was mass evasion of the poll tax before disquiet boiled over into violence in the summer of 1381. As King Richard II of England (reigned 1377–1399) was then only fourteen years old, the country was ruled by a council of nobles, clergymen, and other officers of state, the most prominent of whom was the king's eldest uncle, John of Gaunt. The government's response to the virtual "tax strike" was to send out special local commissioners to attempt to enforce payment. The revolt began on May 31, 1381, when tax officials were driven out of the village of Fobbing in Essex, east of London.

Contemporary sources differ in their presentation of the exact chronology of events over the following two weeks, but all are in agreement that news of the revolt spread quickly throughout the southeast, as did other, similar uprisings. The chief justice of the county of Essex, Robert Belknapp, was driven out of the town of Brentwood on June 2 by rioters who killed a number of his soldiers. Within a week the wildfire of revolt had overtaken the counties around the capital. Dissidents in towns throughout Kent rose up in a series of attacks directed initially against local officials and their records; in one incident large quantities of documents were seized from the house of the Dartford coroner on June 5 and ceremoniously burned in the streets. There are also early examples of actions aimed against perceived "traitors" and "evil counselors" surrounding the young king. On June 6 a mob attacked Rochester Castle and released an imprisoned serf who worked the lands of Simon Burley, the king's tutor, while the ransack of the palace of the archbishop of Canterbury, Simon Sudbury, on June 10 must have been connected also to his other role as chancellor (chief administrative officer of the kingdom and holder of the great seal). The Kent rebels joined up with the Essex bands en route, in the manner of an invading army, before they converged with banners and slogans on the suburbs of London on June 12.

There is general agreement among scholars that the term "peasants' revolt" is something of a misnomer that was perhaps first attached to the

▲ When the fourteen-year-old Richard II appeared before an angry mob of London peasants in 1381, his kingly aura sufficed to persuade them to lay down their arms and go home. This anonymous panel portrait of Richard, painted around 1395, is installed in Westminster Abbey, London.

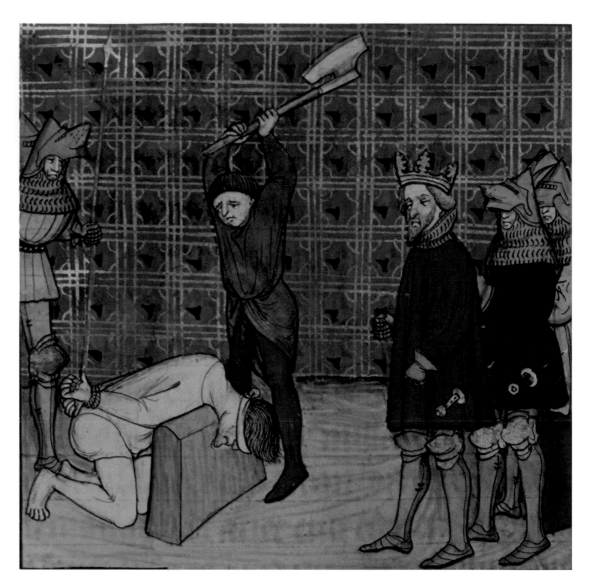

► *The violent attacks on nobles and their families that took place during the Jacquerie met with bloody reprisals. This anonymous fourteenth-century French manuscript illumination depicts the execution of one of the rebel leaders.*

1381 rising as a term of abuse. A proportion of those involved—and certainly the more prominent of the leaders—were key figures in their communities. There were townsfolk, some clergymen, even a few knights and members of the gentry, not just laborers and peasants. It would be wrong also to imagine that all the rebellious peasants were at the bottom of the social scale. There was a wide range of wealth within peasant society. Among the rebels historians have identified quite successful peasants, tenant farmers with up to twenty acres of land. Those of free and servile status were equally represented, and there were also landless cottagers and day laborers—workers who might lodge in a communal room and not even have their own tools.

Once it began, the rebellion became more organized, with local contingents coordinated in their movements. Despite the serious nature of

the rebels' developing agenda, an air of revel also emerged, quite possibly because the uprising coincided with the midsummer lull in the agricultural year, when people traditionally organized festivities and communal games. The march on London brought to the fore some notable leaders, among them John Ball, a roaming preacher who had been arrested several times for his inflammatory sermons. The most famous was Wat Tyler, an Essex man, probably a tiler by trade, who had served as a soldier in the French wars. The Peasants' Revolt provided a rare opportunity for somebody to rise to prominence in the role of a popular demagogue. For both Ball and Tyler, though, the moment in the spotlight was brief.

"Carnival of Anarchy"

"Carnival of anarchy" is the phrase first used by the distinguished Victorian historian Charles

The following text is an excerpt from a sermon by a radical priest that, according to the French chronicler Jean Froissart, was delivered to the rebels at Blackheath.

Good people, things cannot go right in England and never will, until goods are held in common and there are no more villeins and gentlefolk, but we are all one and the same. In what way are those whom we call lords greater masters than ourselves? How have they deserved it? Why do they hold us in bondage? If we all spring from a single father and mother, Adam and Eve, how can they claim or prove that they are lords more than us, except by making us produce and grow the wealth that they spend? They are clad in velvet and camlet [fine woolen cloth] lined with squirrel and ermine, while we go dressed in coarse cloth. They have the wines, the spices and the good bread: we have the rye, the husks and the straw, and we drink water. They have shelter and ease in their fine manors, and we have hardship and toil, the wind and the rain in the fields. And from us must come, from our labor, the things that keep them in luxury. We are called serfs and beaten if we are slow in our service to them, yet we have no sovereign lord we can complain to, none to hear us and do us justice. Let us go to the King—he is young—and show him how we are oppressed, and tell him that we want things to be changed, or else we will change them ourselves. If we go in good earnest and all together, very many people who are called serfs and are held in subjection will follow us to get their freedom. And when the King sees and hears us, he will remedy the evil, either willingly or otherwise.

John Ball (1381)

Oman (and adopted by others since) to describe the activities of the rebel hordes upon reaching London in mid-June 1381. On June 12 groups from Kent and Essex had reached the suburbs, where they were joined by bands from counties all over the southeast—from Surrey, Sussex, Suffolk, Norfolk, Buckinghamshire, and Hertfordshire. The Essex men based themselves at Mile End, outside Aldgate, whilst those from Kent set up camp on Blackheath, on the southern bank of the Thames River. There the assembled crowd listened to the radical sermon of John Ball that has become distilled in folklore into one powerful couplet:

> When Adam delved [dug] and Eve span,
> Who was then a gentleman?

In other words, all people were created equal and provided for themselves by their own labors. God did not dictate that some should be servants and some lords and masters—as humankind had done. The couplet was not Ball's creation; it has been traced back to the 1340s and so was likely already to have been a populist slogan, known and adopted by the rebels on the march and consequently incorporated by Ball into his sermon. The sentiment of the catchphrase, though, vividly illustrates the degree of social change for

which some of the rebels hoped. One chronicler claims that 30,000 peasants were camped at Blackheath; another puts the figure as high as 60,000. These figures are quite formulaic and improbable; they probably represent "a great number," and modern historians estimate that, in fact, the crowd totaled 7,000 to 10,000 people—still a remarkable number.

▲ *In the center of this illumination from the chronicles of Jean Froissart, John Ball rides at the head of the rebels toward the ranks of soldiers.*

There followed two days of destruction and brutality in London. When supporters within the city unbarred the gates, the rebels swarmed across London Bridge. Their anger at the king's counselors was demonstrated by attacks on or destruction to their properties—including John of Gaunt's Savoy palace; Lambeth Palace, the London home of the archbishop of Canterbury, Simon Sudbury; and the base of the Knights Hospitaller, attacked because the order's prior, Robert Hales, also served as treasurer of England, the chief financial official of the kingdom. In a state of panic, the council agreed that the teenage King Richard II should hear the rebels' case; a meeting took place on June 14. Wat Tyler presented the rebels' demands, namely, the arrest of corrupt "traitors" responsible for the implementation of the poll tax, an abolition of the tax itself, increased freedoms for the populace, and a free pardon for all involved in the rebellion. Having been granted charters of liberties, many rebels set off back to their homes, satisfied by the king's promise that all of their requests would be considered. However, Tyler and a hard core of supporters remained in the capital. Four hundred of their number broke into the Tower of London that afternoon, humiliated the king's mother, Joan of Kent, and dragged out from the sanctuary of the tower's chapel Sudbury, Hales, and several other members of the king's council, whom they beheaded on Tower Hill. Several hundred Flemish merchants and a number of Londoners were also massacred that afternoon.

On June 15, the following morning, the rebels secured a second audience with the king at Smithfield. On this occasion demands reached revolutionary heights: complete equality of all people before the law, the abolition of all serfdom and lordship, an end to tithes, and the disestablishment of the church. Wat Tyler shocked the king's company by his overfamiliar manner, and in a fit of rage, the mayor of London, William Walworth, drew his dagger and knocked Tyler down. Tyler was then killed by several of the king's men, and with his death any effective resistance was at an end. Richard presented himself to the angry mob, declared that he was their king and their captain, and relied on little more than

▶ The climactic events of the Peasants' Revolt of 1381 are depicted in this illumination from a fifteenth-century chronicle of English history. At the left, Wat Tyler, the rebel leader, is about to be struck down in front of the king. On the right, Richard II addresses the rebels.

John of Gaunt, duke of Lancaster | 1340–1399

John, the third surviving son of Edward III (reigned 1327–1377), was born in the city of Ghent (in modern-day Belgium); his nickname is a mispronunciation of his birthplace. His father provided for him financially by marrying him to Blanche, heiress of Henry, duke of Lancaster. On his father-in-law's death in 1362, John was granted the title. With this vast inheritance John became the richest man in England after the king. He held more than thirty castles and a luxurious palace called the Savoy on the banks of the Thames in London (a famous hotel and theater bearing the same name now stand on the site).

John of Gaunt was an active politician at home and abroad. He laid claim in 1372 to the Spanish kingdom of Castile in the name of his second wife, Constance, and led a number of military expeditions there. He also fought regularly in France in the campaigns of the Hundred Years War and in 1390 was created duke of Aquitaine for life by his young nephew, Richard II. During the 1370s Gaunt effectively took over government in England from his ailing father, Edward III, and also became the leading figure in Richard II's administration while the king was a minor unable to rule in his own right. Gaunt successfully acted as a mediator between political factions in the 1380s, as unease increased at King Richard's authoritarianism and the influence wielded at court by his favorites.

However, Gaunt was also the target of much popular criticism by contemporaries. His prominence in government in the decade prior to the Peasants' Revolt of 1381 made him an obvious scapegoat for all that went wrong or was unpopular. The loss of many of England's French possessions in this period was laid at his door, and he was among those whom the rebels identified as being responsible for the imposition of the poll tax. Gaunt was not attacked physically during the revolt, but his Savoy palace was devastated in a carefully organized and directed assault on June 14. His luxurious possessions were not looted but deliberately destroyed before being burned and thrown into the river (the twenty-first-century historian Alastair Dunn called this event "almost an act of iconoclasm"), perhaps in a belief that tax revenue had been embezzled to pay for them.

▼ *John of Gaunt, duke of Lancaster and the most powerful man in England in the 1470s, is portrayed here in a contemporary manuscript illumination.*

the aura of monarchy to woo them into dispersing on promise of a general pardon.

Aftermath of the Peasants' Revolt

The Peasants' Revolt of 1381 was arguably the most serious challenge to social order in medieval European history. The events at Tower Hill and Smithfield—not to mention the burning of records of existing landlordism—came close to denying the main economic and jurisdictional bases of what historians have called feudalism.

The crown's immediate response was harsh; it reflected the depth of the shock that the authorities felt at the revolt. One week after Smithfield, Richard II marched out of London and announced that all the concessions he had made were given under duress and were consequently null and void. About five hundred Essex rebels were killed in battle with the royal army at Billericay on June 23, and county sheriffs were ordered to take whatever measures necessary to crush the remaining pockets of unrest. Over the next three months an estimated 1,500 rebels were executed, John Ball among them. By the end of September 1381, a few weeks after it began, the Peasants' Revolt was over.

> John Ball's speech to the rebels at Blackheath had a lasting influence on radicals and reformers down the centuries. Pictured here is the frontispiece to the first edition (1887) of William Morris's socialist fantasy A Dream of John Ball.

When Adam delved and Eve span Who was then the gentleman

The Legacy of Revolt

The long-term consequences of the Peasants' Revolt of 1381 are hard to quantify, given that the rising came to such an abrupt end and that none of the rebels' demands were met. Biographers of Richard II have argued convincingly that it had a considerable effect on the king himself. The bravery displayed by the king and his success in dispersing the mob must have given the impressionable teenager an intoxicating blast of the potential power of monarchy; that sense remained with him for life and may well have engendered his later absolutism.

The revolt also gave historical prominence beyond all possible expectation to its leaders. The sermon of John Ball in particular inspired later writers in their reflections on social injustice, perhaps the most notable case being the writings five hundred years later of William Morris (1834–1896), the radical politician and founder of the Arts and Crafts movement. In *A Dream of John Ball*, a socialist fantasy tale first published in 1887, Morris promoted a vision of a craftsmen's idyll totally at odds with the industrialized world of Victorian Britain. Wat Tyler's name would be championed or feared as a political bogeyman during the so-called enclosure riots of the mid-sixteenth century and the English civil wars, as well as in the rise of utopian socialism, the Kent uprising of the 1830s, and the labor movement in the nineteenth century. After a career of little more than a week, Tyler became a talisman for popular resistance down the ages.

As far as the majority of the rebels of 1381 and subsequent uprisings were concerned, peasants' revolts themselves brought no tangible benefit, although, ironically, the widespread social and economic changes that provoked them arguably did. Owing to the fact that it took until the late sixteenth century for the population to recover to the level it had reached before the Black Death, demand for labor would continue to outstrip supply. Market forces and increasing opportunities for choice and mobility among the laboring classes arguably did far more to bring about a complete end to serfdom, raise wages, and provide greater autonomy for workers than did peasants' revolts throughout Europe. Whatever the cause, though, the world was changing forever, despite the best efforts of the existing ruling classes to halt the change.

FURTHER READING

Dunn, Alastair. *The Great Rising of 1381: The Peasants' Revolt and England's Failed Revolution of 1381*. Charleston, SC, 2002.

Forquin, Guy. *The Anatomy of Popular Rebellion in the Middle Ages*. Translated by Anne Chesters. New York, 1978.

Froissart, Jean. *Chronicles*. Edited by G. Brereton. Baltimore, 1968.

Fryde, E. B. *Peasants and Landlords in Later Medieval England*. New York, 1996.

Hector, L. C., and Barbara L. Harvey, eds. *The Westminster Chronicle, 1381–1394*. New York, 1982

Hilton, R. H. *Bond Men Made Free: Medieval Peasant Movements and the English Rising of 1381*. New York, 1973.

Holmes, George. *Europe: Hierarchy and Revolt, 1320–1450*. 2nd ed. Malden, MA, 2000.

Kaeuper, Richard W. *War, Justice, and Public Order: England and France in the Later Middle Ages*. New York, 1988.

Rachel C. Gibbons

SEE ALSO

• Agriculture • Disease • Feudalism

• Hundred Years War • Literature • London

Petrarch

THE ITALIAN POET, RHETORICIAN, AND CLASSICAL SCHOLAR PETRARCH (1304–1374) IS SOMETIMES CREDITED AS THE FOUNDER OF HUMANISM, THE PHILOSOPHICAL AND METHODOLOGICAL SYSTEM THAT SHAPED THE RENAISSANCE.

Francesco di Petracco (also known as Francesco Petrarca or, most commonly, Petrarch) was born in Arezzo in 1304. His father had been exiled from Florence after a civic dispute that occurred slightly more than two years before Petrarch's birth. He later settled with his mother in Incisa, a Tuscan village near Florence. His subsequent mastery of the heavily idiomatic Tuscan dialect is largely attributable to this period spent in Incisa.

In 1312 Petrarch's father moved the family west to Pisa, but the following year they uprooted again to the French city of Avignon, which at that time was the papal seat. Petrarch was to remain in Avignon with only occasional (though sometimes lengthy) absences until 1353, when he was nearly fifty. After 1353 he lived in Italy, where at differ-ent times he made his home in Milan, Venice, and Padua. In the course of his studies and in the service of his artistic patrons, he traveled widely in Europe.

Petrarch is best known for his poetry in Italian, most notably *Il canzoniere,* a collection of sonnets that he worked on during a period of almost forty years. He is also recognized for his accomplishments as a rhetorician, classical scholar, moral philosopher, and writer of Latin verse and prose. A devout Christian, he nonetheless vehe-mently opposed the Scholastic philosophy that underpinned the medieval church's theology. Scholasticism depended for its minutely detailed argumentation on the thinking of the Greek philosopher Aristotle (384–322 BCE). Petrarch, however, was noteworthy as an early proponent of the philosophy of Plato (c. 428–348/7 BCE), another great philosopher of ancient Greece, at a time when Platonism was not widely taken up and had virtually no institutional support.

Education

While Petrarch's family was living at Carpentras, near Avignon, Petrarch became the pupil of

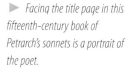

▶ *Facing the title page in this fifteenth-century book of Petrarch's sonnets is a portrait of the poet.*

▲ This 1409 illustration of the city of Avignon with the papal palace appears in a manuscript by the French poet Pierre Salmon. Petrarch came to detest the clamor and intrigues of the papal court and retreated to Vaucluse, a quiet valley where he wrote some of his most famous works, including Africa.

From 1320 to 1326, Petrarch studied at the University of Bologna, which was then the greatest center of learning in Europe. If, by sending his son to Bologna, Petrarch's father hoped to wean the young scholar off literature and onto law, the plan backfired spectacularly. More than just a prominent university town, Bologna was an active and vibrant center of intellectual activity, and the teenage Petrarch seems to have been very much in his element. At Bologna he made many friends who would prove influential later in his life. There he also encountered new literary forms, including lyric poetry written in regional Italian dialects rather than in Latin.

The *Canzoniere*

Petrarch's first known work, a comedy called *Philologia,* no longer survives. He wrote it around the time he ended his studies at Bologna. The following year, 1327, he saw for the first time the woman who was to inspire his greatest achievement. Identified only as Laura, she became the muse for a sequence of poems on which Petrarch worked for much of the rest of his life. Called variously the *Rime sparse* ("scattered rhymes") or *Rerum vulgarium fragmenta* (a wryly dismissive title, used privately by Petrarch himself, that means something akin to "fragments in the vulgar tongue"), the famed collection is most familiarly known as the *Canzoniere* (Songbook).

Most of the 366 poems that make up the *Canzoniere* are sonnets, although it also contains madrigals, ballads, canzones, and sestines. Each poem is both a lyrical achievement in its own right and one component of a carefully designed scheme. At one level the *Canzoniere* explores Petrarch's experience of unrequited love and his grief at Laura's early death, but the peoms also chronicle his soul's journey from sin through penance to salvation. The two interpretations are synthesized in the final sonnet, in which the suffering soul ascends toward a vision of Laura as the Virgin Mary in heaven.

The *Canzoniere* had a profound influence on Petrarch's literary successors. By choosing to write in the Tuscan dialect rather than in Latin, Petrarch, like Dante (1265–1321) before him, was instrumental in establishing the vernacular as an acceptable vehicle for literary expression.

Convenole de Prato, from whom he chiefly learned grammar and rhetoric. Petrarch pursued a classical education until 1319, when, at around age fifteen, he was sent to Montpellier to study law. Petrarch, in common with many later Renaissance figures, entered the legal profession at the request of his family but had little taste for the law, preferring instead classical literature, poetry, and philosophy. A widely credited story relates how Petrarch's father, upon discovering that his fifteen-year-old son was neglecting his legal studies and reading classical literature, burned all young Petrarch's books except for one by Virgil and another by Cicero.

Laure de Noves   1310–1348

Petrarch's life and works were profoundly influenced by his long-standing infatuation with a woman he identifies only as Laura. Laura's true identity remains a matter of conjecture; Petrarch never betrayed the secret and left only scant clues. It is generally accepted that she was not a construct of Petrarch's fertile imagination and that she was a married woman, but the rest is speculation. Whoever she was, Laura served as Petrarch's muse; she was the inspiration for hundreds of his poems, and it was in the course of extolling Laura's virtues that he perfected his particular version of the sonnet form.

One leading candidate for Petrarch's Laura is Laure de Noves, a native of Avignon, where Petrarch spent a great deal of time during childhood and as a young man. Six years Petrarch's junior, Laure married Hugues II de Sade in 1325. Petrarch saw her two years later for the first time. She died in 1348 at age thirty-eight.

There is no way of knowing whether or not Laure de Noves was Petrarch's Laura or even if she and Petrarch ever spoke to each other. She is not mentioned even once in all of Petrarch's letters, and the figure of Laura appears only a few times in Petrarch's writing outside of his poetry. A story about a humanist scholar named Maurice Sceve does, however, provide some evidence that points to Laura's identity. On a visit to Avignon some years after the death of Laure de Noves, Sceve discovered a lead box inside her tomb. The box contained a medal bearing an image of a woman ripping out her own heart. Underneath the medal was a sonnet written by Petrarch.

◄ *The woman portrayed here is Laura as an unknown sixteenth-century Italian painter imagined her. The true identity of Petrarch's muse remains unclear.*

PETRARCH'S DREAM OF ROME RESTORED

Civil strife precipitated the flight of Pope Clement V (reigned 1305–1314) from Rome to Avignon in 1309, and with the departure of the papacy, the status of Rome declined. For Petrarch, a lover of classical civilization, the restoration of Rome to its former preeminence became a lifelong desire. His aim was not merely a restoration of Rome's political fortunes but also a revival of the civic values embodied by the Roman orator Cicero, who had employed his renowned eloquence and wisdom in the service of the state.

In 1340 Petrarch was offered the ancient title of poet laureate by both the University of Paris and the city of Rome; he chose to receive the symbolic laurel wreath in the capitol. The grand ceremony took place on Easter Sunday, April 8, 1341. In accepting the title once bestowed upon Virgil, another of his heroes, Petrarch revived a role that had been in abeyance for 1,300 years.

In the 1340s Petrarch became friendly with Cola di Rienzo (1313–1354), a Roman official who dreamed of restoring a popular republic and actually led a short-lived rebellion in 1347. Petrarch's friendship with Rienzo cost him the patronage of Cardinal Stefano Colonna, but undaunted by the overthrow and eventual death of Rienzo at the hands of a mob, Petrarch continued to press the case for the restoration of Rome. While working as an emissary for the duke of Milan in the 1350s, he obtained two audiences with the Holy Roman emperor, Charles IV (reigned 1355–1378), during which he tried to persuade the emperor to move his court from Prague to Rome. In his letter "To Posterity" (*Epistolae seniles*, 1373), Petrarch refers to the continued residence of the papacy in Avignon as a "shameful exile." He had been overjoyed by Pope Urban V's reestablishment of the Holy See in Rome in 1367 and was equally disappointed when Urban returned once more to Avignon in 1370, shortly before the pope's death: "Had he lived but a little longer, he would certainly have learned how I regarded his retreat. My pen was in my hand when he abruptly surrendered at once his exalted office and his life. Unhappy man, who might have died before the altar of Saint Peter and in his own habitation!" The primacy of Rome was not convincingly reasserted until the election of Pope Martin V in 1417 brought an end to the Western Schism, but Petrarch did not live to see this event.

Some modern critics have doubted the existence of Laura, Petrarch's muse, but the debate is irrelevant; Laura lives and breathes in Petrarch's verse, which is markedly less stylized than the work of most poets of the previous generation. In the *Canzoniere,* Petrarch also popularized the particular form of the sonnet that came to bear his name. The Petrarchan sonnet, which was probably invented in Italy in the thirteenth century, has a fixed rhyme scheme *abbaabba* for the octave, while the sestet follows a variety of formats, most often *cdecde.*

Later during the Renaissance, poets across Europe seized upon Petrarch's innovations; more than 1,400 works in a similar style were produced in Italy alone during the sixteenth century. Among the most notable of Petrarch's imitators was the English poet Philip Sidney (1554–1586), who wrote his sonnet sequence *Astrophel and Stella* around 1582. William Shakespeare (1564–1616) also showed Petrarch's influence when he addressed his own collection of sonnets to an unknown beloved (Shakespeare, however, used a different rhyme scheme in his sonnets).

Works in Latin

Although Petrarch's most enduring and influential literary achievement, the *Canzoniere,* was written in the vernacular, he wrote most of his works in Latin. In 1338 he began *Africa,* an epic account of the Roman commander Scipio's victory over Hannibal in the Second Punic War (218–202 BCE). Around the same time he began *De viris illustribus (Of Famous Men),* twenty-four biographies of great figures of the ancient world whose lives, he believed, could provide moral guidance for contemporary Italian society. It was through these and other Latin works that Petrarch won respect during his own lifetime.

Intended for use in private meditation, *Secretum meum (My Secret Book)* was never published while Petrarch was alive. In it, through three imaginary dialogues with Saint Augustine of Hippo (354–430), Petrarch explores his sense of personal crisis, which arises from the conflict between his worldy ambitions and his spiritual obligations as a Christian. The poet draws consolation from his reading of Augustine's *Confessions* and works by the classical Roman poets Virgil

(70–19 BCE) and Ovid (43 BCE–17 CE) and is ultimately able to achieve inner peace.

Influenced by his hero, the Roman orator and statesman Cicero (106–43 BCE), Petrarch became a prolific writer of letters, many of which he collected and published. His first collection, *Epistolae familiares* (Familiar Letters), begun in 1359, eventually comprised 350 letters in 24 books. In his preface to the collection, Petrarch explains that the letters are "written in a familiar style to friends . . . sometimes referring to matters of public or private interest, sometimes relating to bereavements, which form, alas! an ever recurring theme. . . . Sometimes, when it was not inappropriate, there may be a bit of simple narration or a few moral reflections, such as Cicero was accustomed to introduce into his letters." These letters and those of a later collection, *Epistolae seniles* (Letters in Old Age), offer a fascinating insight into Petrarch's daily life, his state of mind, and the environment in which he lived.

Manuscript Hunter

In his own time Petrarch was renowned for his achievements in locating manuscripts of classical texts as well as for his literary output. From early youth he had been fascinated by the poets and philosophers of classical Rome, especially Cicero. During extensive travels in France, Germany, and the Netherlands while he was in the employ of Cardinal Colonna, Petrarch was able to devote considerable time to the search for lost works. His first discovery, in Liège in 1333, was the text of a speech by Cicero, *Pro Archia* (In Defense of Archias). From Petrarch's transcript of the text, all the copies in circulation in Italy during the Renaissance were produced. In 1345 he proclaimed the discovery of a manuscript of Cicero's *Ad Atticus* (Letters to Atticus). Although Petrarch is widely credited with the discovery of this work in the cathedral library of Verona, it is likely that some Veronese scholars were aware of its existence. Whether or not Petrarch actually discovered the manuscript, it was undoubtedly through him that the work became widely known.

Petrarch eventually amassed a large collection of classical works and inspired other scholars to begin their own searches for ancient manuscripts. Through systematic and painstaking study of different versions of a text, he was able to identify errors introduced by copyists over the centuries and to produce a version as close as possible to the original Latin text. Other scholars followed his lead, and thus one of the defining activities of the Renaissance humanists was established. The Renaissance itself, the "rebirth" of Western culture, was based upon a new understanding of the literature and philosophy of classical Rome. Later humanists also made great advances in the study of classical Greek texts. Although Petrarch appreciated the importance of learning Greek in order to further his work, he never mastered more than the basics.

Petrarch as Philosopher

In addition to his more prominent literary accomplishments, Petrarch is credited as a moral philosopher. He was notable for his opposition to

▼ *An illuminated page from a fourteenth-century edition of Petrarch's allegorical poem* Trionfi *(Triumphs). Begun in 1351, the* Trionfi, *like the* Canzoniere, *is written in the Tuscan vernacular. It charts the progress of the soul through life in a manner loosely reminiscent of Dante's Divine* Comedy.

Petrarch's thinking was greatly influenced by Cicero, who in turn followed many of the teachings of Plato, widely regarded as the founder of Western philosophy. Therefore, it is hardly surprising that Petrarch's sympathies lay with Plato, despite the prevailing opinion in fourteenth-century Italy that the philosophy of Aristotle, Plato's famously rebellious pupil, was not only superior to Plato's work but also, what is at least as significant, more congruent with the teachings of the church.

Petrarch wrote, "Plato is praised by the greater men, whereas Aristotle is praised by the greater number." This comment on Aristotle's popularity reflects the fundamentally Aristotelian character of Scholastic philosophy, which dominated medieval theology and remained influential through the beginning of the Renaissance. However, despite his identification of Aristotle as inferior to Plato, Petrarch did give Aristotle significant credit as a moral philosopher and particularly admired Aristotle's *Nicomachean Ethics*. Petrarch also suggested at various points in his own work that Aristotle's writings—which survived in numerous translations that had come down through the church and the work of such Arab scholars and commentators as Ibn Rushd (Averroës)—were likely far superior in the original Greek.

Petrarch and Scholasticism

Petrarch was in many ways a revolutionary. This quality is most evident in his opposition to the Scholasticism that underpinned medieval Catholic doctrine. Scholasticism was the product of the church schools, which were run by various different orders within the church, and its adherents were consequently referred to as Schoolmen.

Petrarch objected to Scholasticism on several grounds. He objected to its reliance on a hair-splitting method of enquiry that derived from Aristotle. He also believed that excessive dependence on Aristotle and other pagan (pre-Christian) philosophers had forced the church into logical balancing acts. One example was the double-truth theory, which, by distinguishing religious from philosophical truth, papered over profound disagreements between church teaching and pagan philosophy instead of effectively

▲ *For many scholars Petrarch's status as the father of Renaissance humanism derives largely from his advocacy of Plato over Aristotle. This depiction of Plato, which dates from the seventeenth century, was produced by an unknown French artist.*

the prevailing belief in the superiority of Aristotelian over Platonic teaching. Even so, his standing as a philosopher is grounded at least as much in his influence on later Renaissance figures as it is on the value of the philosophy itself. Petrarch's philosophical works embody no clear and consistent methodological or philosophical approach; they are concerned with his various personal interests, inclinations, and feelings rather than with any particular way of looking at the world. Among his most popular writings are *De vita solitaria* (*On the Solitary Life;* 1356) and *De remediis utriusque fortunae* (*On the Remedies of Good and Bad Fortune;* 1366).

In a letter to Tommaso da Messina, Petrarch expounds his views on the logicians who claimed to be following in the footsteps of Aristotle:

These logicians seek to cover their teachings with the splendour of Aristotle's name; they claim that Aristotle was wont to argue in the same way.... But they all deceive themselves. Aristotle was a man of the most exalted genius, who not only discussed but wrote upon themes of the very highest importance. How can we otherwise explain so vast an array of works, involving such prolonged labor, and prepared with supreme care amid such serious preoccupations ... and within the compass, too, of a life by no means long?—for he died at about sixty-three, the age which all writers deem so unlucky. Now why should these fellows diverge so widely from the path of their leader? Why is not the name of Aristotelians a source of shame to them rather than of satisfaction, for no one could be more utterly different from that great philosopher than a man who writes nothing, knows but little, and constantly indulges in much vain declamation? Who does not laugh at their trivial conclusions, with which, although educated men, they weary both themselves and others? They waste their whole lives in such contentions.

Ad familiares

▲ *This portrait of the ancient Greek philosopher Aristotle was painted by the Flemish artist Justus van Ghent around 1450. Many humanists of the Renaissance—and indeed, many Reformers—followed Petrarch in rejecting the heavily Aristotelian Scholasticism that dominated medieval theology.*

addressing them. To Petrarch's mind, this failure to address inconsistencies had the effect of undermining church teaching, however indirectly. Third, Petrarch seems to have personally disliked the commentators upon whom the church relied for its application of Aristotelianism to theology.

Petrarch held up earlier models against the Scholastics. His favorite Christian thinker was Augustine of Hippo; indeed, it seems that the first book Petrarch purchased was Augustine's *City of God.* Petrarch saw in Augustine a man of faith who set little store by the intricate and (in Petrarch's view) oversubtle reasonings of Aristotle; a man whose first interest lay not in unraveling the mysteries of nature but in understanding humanity's relationship with God.

Father of the Renaissance

Many of the hallmarks of Petrarch's work came to characterize Renaissance scholarship. Petrarch was a student of the classical world and, despite his lack of facility in the Greek language, a thoroughgoing advocate of the ideals of ancient Greece. He was also, like many of the great poets and artists who followed him, a devout Roman Catholic. He personally embodied what is arguably the central tension, if not an outright contradiction, in Renaissance thinking: he loved the pagans of antiquity, whose work he sought to emulate, but he loved the church even more. For this reason, Petrarch is often identified as the father of the Renaissance. His approach came to typify the age that followed him, an age that admired the classical world, embraced the humanistic conviction that "the proper study of mankind is man," and loved the church, which would itself ultimately promote the rebirth of classical culture under its wide aegis.

FURTHER READING

Mann, Nicholas. *Petrarch.* New York, 1984.

Musa, Mark, trans. *The Portable Petrarch.* New York, 2004.

Wilkins, Ernest H. *Life of Petrarch.* Chicago, 1961.

Daniel Horace Fernald

SEE ALSO
- Aristotle • Boccaccio, Giovanni • Florence
- Florence, Council of • France • Italian City-States
- Languages, Classical • Languages, Vernacular
- Literature • Renaissance

Philip II

A HARDWORKING MONARCH WHO DID NOT TOLERATE DISSENT, PHILIP II (1527–1598) RULED THE SPANISH KINGDOMS AND AN EXTENSIVE OVERSEAS EMPIRE FOR OVER FORTY YEARS. HIS REIGN IS REGARDED AS MARKING THE DAWN OF SPAIN'S GOLDEN AGE.

The son of the Holy Roman emperor Charles V (reigned 1519–1556) and Isabella of Portugal (1503–1539), Philip of Spain was born at Valladolid on May 21, 1527. At age sixteen he assumed responsibility for the government of the Spanish kingdoms as his father's regent. Following his marriage in 1554 to Mary I of England (reigned 1553–1558), Philip briefly assumed a prominent role as Mary's consort; he even rode at the head of an English army after the defeat of the French at the Battle of Saint Quentin (1557). Philip had inherited the Netherlands upon his father's abdication in 1555, and the following

▶ A 1551 portrait of Philip II by Titian. Philip became an important patron of the Venetian artist, from whom he commissioned a series of paintings on mythological subjects between 1550 and 1562.

year he also became ruler of the Spanish kingdoms. He spent two years in the Netherlands after the Battle of Saint Quentin and in 1559 returned to Spain, where he stayed for the rest of his reign.

The Centralization of Power

An extremely hard-working and dedicated monarch, Philip concerned himself with the minutiae of government and administration. When Charles V had established Philip as his regent in 1543, he had given his son the following advice: "Depend on no one but yourself. Make sure of all but rely exclusively on none. In your perplexities, trust always to your Maker. Have no care but for him." As a result, Philip never relied on a chief minister; in fact, he was deeply suspicious of some of his more able and loyal servants. He lacked the ability to delegate or to distinguish between trivial and important matters. Decision making was therefore slow, and the process was further complicated by the sheer size of the empire. It took ten days for news of a decision to reach Spanish authorities in the Netherlands and sometimes years to reach the Spanish colonies in the New World.

Philip headed a series of governmental councils that had been established by his predecessors. The most important was the council of state. He worked from *consultas* (reports or memoranda) submitted by his ministers. In 1561 he established Madrid as his capital city and the administrative center of his empire. In spite of the apparent wealth of the empire, it proved difficult in practice for Philip to raise enough income from across his territories to match his expenditure, especially on military and foreign affairs. As a result, the king declared the state bankrupt in 1557, 1575, and 1596.

Philip's centralized style of government and the perceived dominance of the kingdom of Castile provoked opposition. In 1566 a rebellion broke out in the Netherlands that was to continue beyond his reign. Two years later the Moriscos (Muslim converts to Christianity) in Granada rose up against the king's economic measures and efforts to force them to assimilate into mainstream Christian society. The rebellion was

crushed in 1570. Philip held back from expelling the Moriscos from Spain, although their outright expulsion was eventually ordered by his son. In 1591 and 1592 the Aragonese rebelled against Philip's intervention in their internal affairs.

Relations between Church and State

Religion was of primary importance to Philip. He made the following declaration to Pope Pius V in 1566: "Rather than suffer the least damage to religion and the service of God, I would lose all

REVOLT OF THE NETHERLANDS

Philip's centralizing policies provoked discontent by tending to exclude leading nobles in the Netherlands from decision making. Policies intended to suppress heresy aggravated the situation, since they aroused the anger not only of Protestants but also of nobles, who saw the measures as a threat to their rights and privileges. Philip's regent in the Netherlands, Margaret of Parma (1522–1586), briefly relaxed the religious laws in 1566. The result was a wave of Protestant preaching followed by the seizure and ransacking of Catholic churches. These events marked the start of the revolt of the Netherlands.

The Protestant success was short-lived. The duke of Alba replaced Margaret of Parma as governor of the Netherlands and straight away instigated a policy of strong government and repression of dissent. Nevertheless, armed resistance to Spanish rule flared again in 1572 with the seizure of the ports of Brill and Flushing. William of Orange (1533–1584) became the figurehead of the revolt. Philip reacted to events in the Netherlands with alternating policies of repression and conciliation that reflected the varying ascendancy of different factions and interests at the Spanish court. However, during the early years of the revolt, the Netherlands was not Philip's first priority, and the military campaign lacked the necessary funds.

The provinces of the Netherlands were united against Spain in 1576 as a result of the sack of Antwerp by mutinous unpaid Spanish troops, but by the end of the decade, they had divided over religion. The southern provinces, where Catholicism was dominant, were reconciled with Philip; the northern provinces continued to reject the king's authority and eventually formed what became known as the United Provinces. The revolt was not resolved until after Philip's death. The truce agreed upon in 1609 lasted only until 1621, when the conflict was reignited as part of the wider Thirty Years War (1618–1648).

1527
Philip is born at Valladolid on May 21.

1543
Becomes regent of Spain; marries his cousin Maria of Portugal.

1554
Becomes king of Naples; marries Mary I of England.

1555
Becomes ruler of the Netherlands following the abdication of Charles V.

1556
Becomes king of Spain on the abdication of his father.

1559
Peace of Cateau-Cambrésis ends conflict with France.

1566
Revolt of the Netherlands begins.

1580
Philip annexes Portugal and becomes king.

1588
The Spanish armada fails in its mission to invade England.

1598
Peace of Vervins ends Spanish intervention in the French wars of religion; Philip dies.

▶ *Popularly known as* The Dream of Philip II, *this painting, whose official title is* Adoration of the Name of Jesus, *is by the Spanish artist El Greco (1540–1614). Philip II is depicted kneeling at the center of the foreground with Doge Mocenigo of Venice and Pope Pius V, fellow leaders of the crusade established by Pius in 1571 to counter the growing threat of Islamic activity in the Mediterranean (the crusade culminated in a Christian victory against the Turks at the Battle of Lepanto).*

my states and a hundred lives, if I had them; for I do not propose nor desire to be the ruler of heretics." Notwithstanding his Catholicism, Philip's dealings with the papacy were often tense and uneasy. King and pope were frequently divided on foreign affairs—the Neapolitan Pope Paul IV (reigned 1555–1559) even pursued an anti-Spanish foreign policy. The fact that the Catholic Church in Spain was firmly under the control of the crown also strained relations; the decrees of the Council of Trent, for example, were introduced only insofar as they did not limit royal authority. However, during Philip's reign the Catholic Church in Spain asserted its authority through the Spanish Inquisition, which eradicated support for Protestantism and ensured uniformity of belief among Catholics.

Foreign Policy

The long-held interpretations of Philip's foreign policy were that it was restricted by financial considerations or else merely responsive to events. A more affirmative view, however, has also been advanced: that Philip's policy was in fact deter-

Don Carlos 1545–1568

The tragic story of Don Carlos, the son of Philip II and his first wife, Maria of Portugal (1527–1545), has been the subject of much controversy. It was seized upon by those of Philip's enemies who propagated the so-called Black Legend, which characterized Spaniards as cruel and bloodthirsty. Maria died four days after giving birth to Carlos, and in his early years the prince saw little of his father, who spent much of this period abroad. Historical evidence suggests that Carlos had a relatively stable upbringing, but he made poor progress in his studies and seems to have inherited the mental instability that ran in the royal family. From 1560 on he also began to suffer from fevers, possibly as a result of contracting malaria. A fall down the stairs in 1561 left him with serious head injuries that rendered him temporarily blind and unable to walk. After the fall he was prone to violent tantrums and bizarre behavior—including cruelty to animals—that made him the subject of court gossip.

The Cortes (the representative assembly) of Castile had recognized Carlos as heir to the throne in 1560, and Philip encouraged him to attend meetings of the council and be involved in affairs of state. Philip had promised in 1559 to send Carlos to replace him as ruler in the Netherlands, but the king came to realize that his son was unsuitable for the task. When the duke of Alba was appointed governor of the Netherlands in 1567, Carlos threatened to kill the duke and may even have attempted to stab him. Carlos also threatened to kill the king and started planning to escape from court, possibly to the Netherlands.

In January 1568, having taken advice from his ministers, Philip personally led an armed guard that arrested and imprisoned Carlos. The king ordered that his son's name not be mentioned, forbade mourning or weeping, and disbanded the prince's household—actions that were later used by the king's opponents to discredit his character. In prison the prince's condition continued to deteriorate. He undertook hunger strikes and finally starved to death on July 24, 1568. Philip explained his own actions in a letter to Pope Pius V: "I saw the grave risks that would arise were he to be given the succession and the obvious dangers that would accrue; and therefore, after long and careful consideration, and having tried every alternative in vain, it was clear that there was little or no prospect of his condition's improving in time to prevent the evils which could reasonably be foreseen."

mined by a kind of grand strategy—in the first place to defend Catholicism; in the second to protect the Mediterranean from Turkish expansion; and finally to maintain his vast empire.

When Philip became king of Spain, the country was still at war with France. After the decisive defeat of the French forces at Saint Quentin in August 1557, Philip himself led the entrance of the triumphant troops into the captured city. Hostilities were ended in 1559 by the Peace of Cateau-Cambrésis, through which Elizabeth of Valois (the daughter of the French king, Henry II) became Philip's third wife.

Initially Philip pursued a policy of neutrality toward England, where the Protestant Elizabeth I succeeded his late wife Mary in 1558. His main concern during the early years of his reign was the expansion of the Ottoman Turks into the Mediterranean. The Turkish advance threatened Spanish possessions in Italy and the communications that ran between those possessions and the Iberian Peninsula. In 1571 an alliance of Christian naval forces under Spanish command achieved a great victory over the Turks at the

▶ *Don Carlos, the son of Philip II and Maria of Portugal, is the subject of this portrait by the sixteenth-century Spanish artist Alonso Coello Sanchez.*

▼ *The Escorial, the monastery and royal mausoleum founded by Philip II, is pictured here in a seventeenth-century painting by an unknown Spanish artist.*

Battle of Lepanto. From that point forward, both sides in the conflict had pressing internal issues and therefore maintained peace with each other through a series of truces.

The removal of the Ottoman threat led to a reorientation of foreign policy that was bolstered by the influx of silver from the colonies in South America. Following the death of the king of Portugal in 1578, Philip conquered the neighboring state and annexed its empire. Pacific islands that had formerly belonged to the Portuguese were renamed the Philippines in his honor.

The assistance Elizabeth I of England gave to the rebels in the Netherlands sparked war with Spain in 1585. Philip sent the armada, a great fleet, to conquer England in 1588, but the ships that survived the English counterattack were scattered by storms, and many sank on the journey home. The conflict between the two countries was not concluded until 1604. Philip also intervened in the French wars of religion by providing financial support for the Catholic League and sending troops to France after the succession of the Protestant king Henry IV in 1589. However, the embroilment in French affairs diverted resources from the Netherlands, and Philip was finally forced to conclude the Peace of Vervins in 1598.

Philip died at the Escorial on September 13, 1598. Some events, such as the ongoing conflict in the Netherlands, may have tarnished his reputation, but he is generally regarded as a successful monarch, the king whose reign inaugurated Spain's golden age.

FURTHER READING

Kamen, Henry. *Philip of Spain.* New Haven, CT, 1997.

Parker, Geoffrey. *The Grand Strategy of Philip II.* New Haven, CT, 2000.

———. *Philip II.* London, 1978.

Woodward, Geoffrey. *Philip II.* Harlow, UK, 1992.

Andrew Spicer

SEE ALSO

• Armada, Spanish • Charles V • Italian Wars
• Lepanto, Battle of • Thirty Years War

Philosophy

FROM 1400 ON, PHILOSOPHERS LOOKED AFRESH NOT ONLY AT THE NATURE OF THE UNIVERSE BUT ALSO AT HUMAN RELATIONSHIPS, WHETHER WITH GOD OR ONE'S FELLOWS.

For about a thousand years before 1400, philosophy had been pursued mostly by thinkers who were also professional theologians. After 1400 learned amateurs who were neither churchmen nor university philosophers began to write about philosophical topics. The intense interest in philosophy during the Renaissance is evident in Raphael's great fresco *The School of Athens* (1509). The central figures are two classical Greek philosophers: Plato (c. 428–348/7 BCE), who is pointing upward to the heaven of ideas, and Aristotle (384–322 BCE), who gestures toward the world of humanity and nature below. These poses illustrate the core philosophies of the two great thinkers. Plato envisaged a realm of ideas (also called forms or essences) that lay above or at least outside the world of physical matter that is experienced by the senses. For Aristotle these same ideas existed within matter; nature had a reality of its own. Although both Plato and Aristotle would, strictly speaking, be considered philosophical realists, their different ideas laid the foundation for divergent views of humankind and the world.

Although the study of Aristotle never entirely ceased in the West, the philosophy of Plato and of his third-century-CE follower Plotinus, who established the tradition known as Neoplatonism, dominated the thousand-year period from the Christianization of Europe to the Renaissance. Perhaps Christian thinkers were attracted by Plato's notion that ultimate reality lay beyond the world known to the senses. Perhaps the dominance of Platonism was due simply to the fact that Platonic texts were more readily obtainable than Aristotelian writings. By 1200, however, Aristotle's works had become available again in the West through the work of scholars at the university in Naples and through Arabic translations brought into Muslim Spain. During the thirteenth century the philosophies of Aristotle and Plato existed in a friendly dialogue. Both held the world to be knowable because the mind could

► The founding fathers of the Western philosophical tradition are portrayed in this detail from The School of Athens, *a fresco created for the Vatican by Raphael (1483–1520) between 1509 and 1511. Plato, on the left, points upward to the realm of ideas while Aristotle gestures toward the world of matter below.*

▲ *This detail from the Dome of Paradise, a fresco painted around 1375 by the Italian artist Giusto Menabuoi, depicts Christ surrounded by angels and those elected for salvation. The large figure beneath Christ is the Virgin Mary. In realist thought God was at the top of a hierarchy in which all creation was simultaneously linked together and yet distinct from the levels above and below.*

grasp the forms that underlay things in the world. Both held the cosmos to be alive, and both taught that virtue was essential to happiness. Platonism and Aristotelianism belonged to the school of thought known as realism. In the Middle Ages two of the greatest exponents of philosophical realism were Thomas Aquinas (c. 1225–1274), who put forward interpretations of Aristotle that challenged the readings offered in Thomas's Arabic sources, and Bonaventure (1221–1274), whose works drew on traditional Platonic philosophy.

The Impact of Nominalism

Realist thought of the late Middle Ages was founded on three basic notions: participation, hierarchy, and mediation. By participation the realists meant that all human beings, for example, shared in a form or idea called humanity. Individual men and women were concrete instances of the idea of humanity. The realists also

viewed the natural world as being hierarchically structured: all creatures could be ranked on a kind of ladder or chain of being. The beings that made up this ladder—God, angels, people, animals, and plants—were not absolutely separate from one another. Each had the positive attributes of the lesser creature below and added one further attribute. At the bottom of the chain, rocks, for example, merely existed. Above rocks, animals possessed existence and also—like the humans above them—bodily life. Humans had bodily life and rational intellect. Angels were, like humans, rational created beings, but were also, like God, pure spirits. Mediation described the partial sharing of natures that bound one level in the interconnective chain of being to another.

This participatory, hierarchical, mediated world was destroyed by nominalist philosophers, particularly William of Ockham (c. 1285–1349). Gluing the world of philosophical realism together were the ideas (or forms) that existed in their pure intellectual form in God and served as a kind of underlying pattern for his creation. To the nominalists these ideas seemed to limit the power of God, for, according to the realist view, God was required to act through the ideas—as though he were subject to them rather than the author of them. For nominalists, the ideas and the words that represented them were not realities but conveniences constructed by the human mind. If the nominalist contention were true, the intelligible and reliable late-medieval world as it was generally understood would crumble; nothing but the unknowable and all-powerful will of God would relate creature to creature—or even cause to effect. If the ideas were not realities, the words that described the ideas had no particular reference in reality. In the hands of the nominalists, words ceased to be windows into reality and became nothing more than arbitrary names (in Latin, *nomina*), or a kind of conventional code.

This new philosophy was essentially a theological defense of the power of God, and its chief impact was in its use of theological ideas to solve philosophical problems. The advent of nominalism inaugurated a three-hundred-year period during which the disciplines of theology and philosophy were poorly defined and often confused. Calvin's theme of the sovereignty of God was a

As chancellor of the University of Oxford, on March 29, 1518, Thomas More urged the masters to teach Greek—that is, teach Plato—instead of sticking stubbornly to the Latin Aristotelianism that had dominated the university for three centuries.

To whom is it not obvious that to the Greeks we owe all our precision in the Liberal Arts generally? …Take philosophy, for example, if you leave out Cicero and Seneca, the Romans wrote their philosophy in Greek, or translated it from Greek.

theological version of nominalism. For Calvin a sovereign God acted immediately, without the mediation of ideas, in ways that not only transcended but lay beyond the bounds of human reason. For Luther, God could consider the unjust and unholy just and holy without violating reason.

Philosophers since Aristotle had accepted some version of the doctrine that events and creatures were the result of not one but several causes; The material cause of a house, for instance, is the wood it is made from; the house's formal cause is its plan; its efficient cause is the carpenter; and its final cause is the purpose for which it is made—the provision of shelter. Nominalists abandoned the doctrine of the four causes in favor of the idea that the smallest possible number of causes should be used to explain any event. In practice, this idea—known as Ockham's razor, after William of Ockham—led to the conclusion that the only necessary cause was the efficient cause. God was obviously the one necessary efficient cause of every being, and his powerful and all-sufficient relation to each left a world of unrelated objects waiting to be reintegrated into some intelligible pattern. (This task was eventually accomplished by mathematics in its triumphant march from Copernicus to Galileo to Newton). When the Renaissance began, the common philosophical ideas that had formed the West were under sustained attack from the nominalists, and the field was open to new ideas about humankind, God, and nature.

Marsilio Ficino and the Platonic Revival

As the threat to Constantinople from the Muslim Ottoman Empire grew during the first half of the fifteenth century, scholars from the eastern part of Christendom moved west. Among the scholars who attended the Council of Florence in 1439 were George Gemistus Plethon (c. 1355–1452), a fervent Platonist who had written a work in imi-

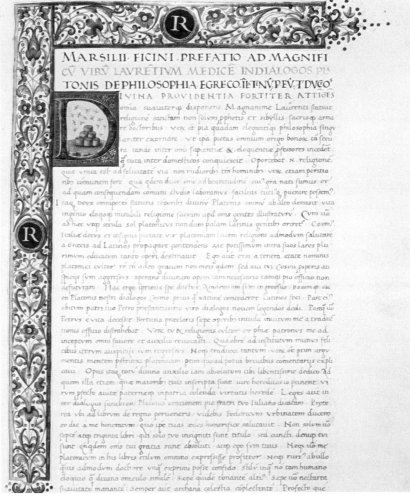

tation of Plato's *Laws,* and his disciple Bessarion (1403–1472). Inspired by Plethon's reading of Plato, Cosimo de' Medici, the leader of the Florentine republic, encouraged an informal academy to pursue its studies of Plato. Cosimo's successor, Lorenzo de' Medici, transformed the informal group into the Florentine Academy in imitation of the original Academy established by Plato in Athens. The academy's leading scholar was Marsilio Ficino (1433–1499), who translated Plato and Plotinus and published a Platonic theology in 1482. Platonism became fashionable across Europe, and it became essential for scholars to know some Greek.

▲ *A manuscript of Plato's dialogues, translated by Marsilio Ficino around 1480 and dedicated to Lorenzo the Magnificent.*

Opposing Views of Human Nature

According to the prevailing view in the Middle Ages, humans were fundamentally good—even though they were often evil in their actions—because each person was related to God. Similarly, humankind was glorious because it bore God's image, but without God's grace every person was a lost sinner, doomed to everlasting death because of the flaw of original sin (committed in the Garden of Eden). As the Renaissance and Reformation matured, this view fell apart. The pessimistic doctrines of Martin Luther (1483–1546) and John Calvin (1509–1564) and their followers insisted upon humankind's utter depravity and the complete powerlessness of people to effect what mattered most—their own salvation.

Opposing the Lutherans and Calvinists were the humanists, who argued optimistically for people's absolute ability to control nature and determine their own future. In his treatise *On the Dignity of Man* (c. 1487), the humanist scholar Giovanni Pico della Mirandola (1463–1494) presented a new understanding of human possibilities when he imagined God's first words to Adam: "We have made you a creature neither of heaven nor of earth, neither mortal nor immortal, in order that you may, as proud shaper of your own being, fashion yourself in the form you may prefer. It will be in your power to descend to the lower, brutish forms of life; you will be able, through your own decision, to rise again to the superior orders whose life is divine."

Pietro Pomponazzi and Petrus Ramus

Pietro Pomponazzi (1462–1525) was the first important European philosopher whose thought lay outside the circle of the theological concerns that characterized philosophy even in the late Middle Ages. Pomponazzi studied at Padua, in northeastern Italy, and taught philosophy there between 1487 and 1509 before accepting positions at Ferrara and finally at Bologna. Although the study of Aristotle would never die out completely, Pomponazzi was the last great sixteenth-century Aristotelian; he was familiar with the available texts of Aristotle and with the commentaries of Thomas Aquinas and the Arabian Ibn Rushd (known in the West as Averroës; 1126–1198). In his best known work, *On the Immortality of the Soul* (1516), Pomponazzi argued that, though the soul's immortality might be a revealed truth, natural reason and hence philosophy offered no convincing proof of it. His approach to theological and philosophical questions was influenced by his interest in medicine.

Within two decades of Pomponazzi's death, a movement hostile to Aristotle had made the philosopher unpopular. The movement's most determined representative was Pierre de la Ramée (usually known by his Latin name, Petrus Ramus; 1515–1572). A native of Picardy, in France, Ramus violently attacked Aristotle in two works: *Objections to Aristotle* and *Aristotelian Institutes* (both 1543). In 1544 King Francis I forbade Ramus to teach in France.

Philosophy and the Reformation

From the second century CE to 1500, Christian theology had been built on a philosophic foundation. The fathers of the early church taught that grace did not destroy nature but perfected it; sim-

▼ An anonymous sixteenth-century engraving of Petrus Ramus, the French humanist, mathematician, and philosopher who began his academic career with a thesis proposing that "all Aristotle's doctrines are false." This position eventually led to the condemnation of his works by the University of Paris.

MAGIC AND SCIENCE

In the sixteenth and seventeenth centuries, astrology—the attempt to predict the future by calculating and analyzing the positions and movements of the stars—was not clearly distinguished from astronomy, nor was chemistry from alchemy, nor mathematics from magic. Fifteenth-century Platonism, with its vision of the kinship between immortal souls and God and of the divinity of creation, posited a kind of pantheistic view of the universe, one in which the power of God could be felt in every natural force. To some scholars the notion that mysterious divine power was immanent in the natural world seemed to suggest that a profound understanding of nature might also bring the ability to control it. In the fifteenth century Marsilio Ficino had translated *Hermes Trismegistus*, a Greek manuscript of Egyptian origin that viewed nature as being susceptible to magical powers. The Italian philosopher Giordano Bruno (1548–1600), who was eventually condemned for heresy by the Roman Inquisition, developed a vision of an infinite universe shot through with the spirit of God. In magic the Platonists hoped to find a means of controlling nature; in Giovanni Pico della Mirandola's words, "Magic is the practical part of the science of nature."

Magic still lingered at the edge of philosophical consideration in the sixteenth century. The English philosopher and politician Francis Bacon (1561–1626) directed the third part of his *Advancement of Learning* (1605) against what he called "fantastical learning"—the various attempts to control nature not, as he himself recommended, through knowledge and experimentation but through alchemy or magic. Perhaps he had in mind John Dee (1527–1608), a mathematician educated at Trinity College, Cambridge, who staunchly denied that he practiced magic but nevertheless pursued a career that led him to seek the philosopher's stone—a mythical chemical or preparation that possessed the power to turn base metals into gold—and to invoke the angels to achieve his effects.

ilarly, philosophy was made perfect, not destroyed, by theology. Nature and philosophy—the science that investigated nature—were alike considered created phenomena that provided a universal starting point for thought. Neither invaded the intellectual domain of sacred doctrine or theology—the science that led to knowledge of God without relying on the Bible or church tradition.

During the Reformation several factors influenced the Reformers' denial of the significance of philosophy. The most important religious movement of the fourteenth and fifteenth centuries was the *devotio moderna* ("modern devotion"). Its leading authorities, who included John Tauler (c. 1300–1361), criticized the philosophers, whom they sometimes called rationalists, for devoting their lives to considering highly technical questions, questions that did not direct humankind to God, in preference to pious meditation. A parallel movement, nominalism, had tended to reduce philosophy to a kind of theology in which natural causality was in doubt, since God was the immediate cause of every event.

The great Reformers of the sixteenth century held that human reason was utterly corrupted by the fall of man, and so philosophy, the fruit of human reason, was rejected or viewed with suspicion. Luther's angry rejection of Aristotle laid

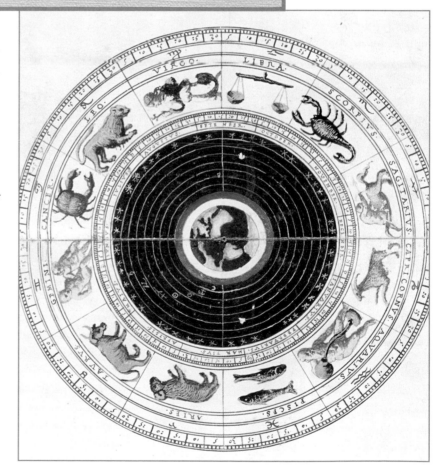

▲ During the Renaissance no clear distinction separated the disciplines of astrology, science, and philosophy from one another. This sixteenth-century astrological chart, which represents a universe with the earth at its center and includes depictions of the signs of the zodiac, is in fact a detail from a scientific work—a portolan map used for navigation at sea.

down a position to which Protestant thinkers would occasionally appeal for the next two centuries. Luther wrote, "One should learn philosophy only as one learns bad arts, that is to destroy them." Calvin was a classicist, but although he wrote that philosophy was sometimes useful, his doctrine of total depravity nevertheless cast doubt upon its usefulness.

▲ *The disobedience of Adam and Eve, the subject of this painting by the German artist Lucas Cranach the Elder (1472–1553), precipitated the fall of man, a biblical story that resonated powerfully with those who saw human nature as essentially corrupt.*

Machiavelli and Hobbes

Political turmoil in Italy and England called forth two works that were to revolutionize political philosophy. Niccolò Machiavelli (1469–1527) wrote *The Prince* (1513) during the troubled times that beset Florence in the early sixteenth century, and just over a century later Thomas Hobbes (1588–1679) wrote his *Leviathan* (1651) in the middle of the Puritan revolution in England. Machiavelli, a Florentine statesman, saw Florence—as Hobbes later saw England—threatened with descent into the revolutionary chaos that often arises as a result of weak government. Machiavelli proposed that Florence would never have peace without a strong ruler determined to use any means to establish his authority.

Hobbes and Machiavelli lived and wrote during turbulent times—the Italian states were embroiled in almost perpetual warfare, the Holy Roman Empire was in conflict with France, Muslim armies were invading Europe, and much of Europe was in the grip of violent social and religious unrest that would erupt into war in Germany and England. No doubt influenced by endemic strife and upheaval, Machiavelli anticipated and Hobbes reflected not the optimism of Pico della Mirandola but the pessimism that belonged to the Reformers Luther and Calvin. Both Machiavelli and Hobbes turned their backs on the Aristotelian tradition that considered friendship the basis of the city; on the medieval theory of kingship, according to which the king was responsible to God for ruling justly; and on the classical theory that viewed law not simply as an instrument of punishment but as the rule and measure of human acts, a social norm without which civilized life could not exist. For both Hobbes and Machiavelli, men were perpetual adversaries; they had to be controlled by the

The following passage typifies the arch pragmatism recommended by Niccolò Machiavelli in 1513 in arguably the most influential work of political philosophy of the Renaissance:

Everyone admits how praiseworthy it is in a prince to keep faith and to live with integrity and not with craft. Nevertheless our experience has been that those princes who have done great things have held good faith of little account, and have known how to circumvent the intellect of men by craft, and in the end have overcome those who have relied on their word.

The Prince

◀ *The English philosopher Thomas Hobbes is the subject of this engraving, made by Jean Charles François (1717–1769) from a portrait by Jean-Baptiste Pierre (1713–1789).*

prince, whose will was law. Hobbes, for example, believed that men were so nearly equal that each conceived the idea of seizing what he desired from his neighbor. Since violent self-interest was the essential characteristic of every person, it was the duty of a prince to secure peace by intimidating his subjects.

Bacon's New Philosophy of Science

Through his *Advancement of Learning* (1605) and *Novum organum* (1620), Francis Bacon (1561–1626) directed scholars away from concerns rooted in metaphysics and theology and toward the world of nature. At age twelve Bacon began his studies at Trinity College, Cambridge, where he spent two and a half years before studying for three years in Paris. He became a lawyer, entered Parliament, and was later elevated to the peerage. He served as solicitor general (1607), lord keeper of the seal (1617), and lord chancellor (1618). His political career ended in 1621, when he was charged with bribery. By 1605 he had started writing a series of works that he believed would give philosophy a new beginning; it was these works that brought him lasting fame. The *Advancement of Learning* was the first book that

▲ For Francis Bacon, portrayed here in a contemporary painting attributed to William Larkin, the philosopher's quest for truth began in recording the details observed while studying the natural world. The philosopher's job was to identify patterns among the details and formulate axioms of increasing generality until overarching truths were reached.

true but unattempted way" (*Novum organum*, book 1). Both projects would have a revolutionary future. In his *Enquiry concerning Human Understanding* (1748), the Scottish philosopher David Hume (1711–1776) would declare knowledge of the world of nature to consist of matters of fact, assertions known immediately from the senses. The attempt to express metaphysical propositions in nonverbal symbols that imitated mathematics would be developed by John Venn in *Symbolic Logic* (1881) and by Bertrand Russell in the *Introduction to Mathematical Philosophy* (1919).

Perhaps Bacon's most enduring legacy was his insistence that nature is not simply to be known but is also to be used to promote human comfort. People of the Middle Ages had viewed nature with wonder and been content merely to describe it. Beginning with Bacon, philosophers saw their task as discovering ways to manipulate nature. Bacon insisted that in the past philosophers had failed to produce new knowledge and that philosophers should pursue their work without great (and undue) respect for the philosophies of the past. He was an early advocate of the idea that knowledge is cumulative, an idea upon which the doctrine of progress would be built. However, this concept of cumulative knowledge created a puzzle for Bacon's successors, for while progress in things technical and scientific is apparent, attempts to show that knowledge of human nature has changed for the better with the passing of time have been less successful.

The seventeenth century was seen as an age of progress. If the sixteenth century had been the age of classical academies founded for the study of the humanities, from Ficino's Florentine Academy to the Arcadian Academy founded in 1689 in Rome in memory of Queen Christina of Sweden, the seventeenth century was the era of scientific societies. The model was the Royal Society, founded in London in 1660 for the purpose of advancing scientific enquiry.

Galileo

Galileo Galilei (1564–1642), Francis Bacon's near contemporary, is most often remembered for his confrontation with the Roman authorities over the Copernican proposal that the sun rather

turned the attention of the learned away from a brand of philosophy closely allied to theology and instead toward the project of advancing human comfort and convenience by wresting secrets from nature. His attempts to reform philosophy, represented most completely by the *Novum organum,* sought to link knowledge to the world as it was experienced empirically (regardless of system or theory) by the senses and to give philosophy the certainty that had previously belonged only to mathematics. He advocated a painstaking method to discover the truth, which began with the senses and particulars, "ascending continually and most gradually, till it arrives finally at the most general axioms, which is the

than the earth was the center of the cosmos. Important as this proposition—given evidentiary support by Galileo's telescope—was, Galileo's philosophy of nature was also revolutionary, for it was he who proposed that the universe can be read only by mathematicians: "Philosophy is written in that vast book that stands ever open before our eyes, I mean the universe: but it cannot be read until we have learned the language. . . . It is written in mathematical language, and the letters are triangles, circles, and other geometrical figures" *(The Assayer).*

The idea that nature is a book to be read by humankind goes back in the West at least to Saint Augustine of Hippo (354–430), who wrote that, in the book of nature, human beings encounter God's creative power, since "the very forms in things cry out 'God made me.'" For Galileo, however, the world was to be described in terms of number or quantity rather than in terms of qualitative differences observable by the senses, such as color and sound. Reality was geometry—a world abstracted from the senses but knowable immediately to the intellect.

Descartes and Idealism

Although Pomponazzi, Bacon, and other philosophers before René Descartes (1596–1650) had suggested that the thinking of the past constituted no foundation for philosophy, it was Descartes who proposed to begin philosophic thought anew in a systematic way. His approach combined Bacon's notion of progress with Galileo's belief that mathematics was the language of reality. His warrant for setting this revolution in motion was a moment of revelation that came to him in 1619, while he was meditating in a warming room in Bavaria; the sudden insight convinced him that he was destined to found a new philosophic system.

▲ *Pictured above is the frontispiece to a seventeenth-century manuscript copy of Galileo Galilei's work* The Operation of Geometric and Military Compasses. *Galileo's approach to philosophy was shaped by his study of mathematics.*

In the third of a series of six meditations, which together form a work published in 1642, René Descartes investigates the nature of his own existence by searching his own mind:

I shall close my eyes, I shall stop my ears, I shall call away all my senses, I shall erase even from my thoughts all the images of corporeal things, or at least (for that is hardly possible) I shall esteem them as vain and false; and thus holding converse only with myself and considering my own nature, I shall try to reach a better knowledge of and a more familiar acquaintanceship with myself. I am a thing that thinks, that is to say, that doubts, affirms, denies, and knows a few things, . . . that also imagines and perceives, for as I remarked before, although the things which I perceive and imagine are perhaps nothing at all apart from me and in themselves, I am nevertheless assured that these modes of thought . . . certainly reside in me.

Meditations on First Philosophy

Descartes's philosophy began with a search for certainty. Almost all earlier philosophers had aimed for insight, a sympathetic understanding of the human condition that produced familiar questions to be revisited by every new generation of philosophers. Descartes believed that, rather than reflect on more or less permanent questions, philosophy should produce new and better answers, perhaps on the model of the emerging natural sciences. He began with doubt, testing everything that claimed to be knowledge by asking if its existence could be doubted. Only one fact withstood the test—his own existence as a thinking being. Therefore, Descartes concluded that he could not be mistaken in asserting his own existence. The famous Latin phrase *"Cogito, ergo sum"* ("I think, therefore I am") was the basis of Cartesian philosophy, and within this sure framework Descartes discovered other clear and distinct ideas. Chief among these was the idea of a perfect God; Descartes argued that God must exist, for if he did not, he would not be perfect. This position established, Descartes called upon God to guarantee that he would not be deceived with regard to his knowledge of existing things.

The revolutionary character of Descartes's philosophy was in part the conviction that knowledge of the world did not necessarily involve an investigation of the world of real objects. The journey to truth might be a journey within the philosopher's mind.

Descartes did not think that the world was known through innate ideas, but he did believe that what humans know of the world is not things themselves but the ideas they form of things. In his philosophy it is difficult to bridge the gap between the known ideal world and the world of real things, between geometry and matter (which Descartes called "extension"). After Descartes philosophers would tend to assume the existence either of a mental world of ideas (this view was held, for example, by Immanuel Kant [1724–1804]) or would be drawn to the conclusion that reality is a world of things known by the impressions they make on the senses (the position taken by Hume).

Cambridge Platonists

The seventeenth century saw the development at Cambridge of a school whose work built on the study of Plato and Plotinus. Called the Cambridge Platonists, this group included Benjamin Whichcote (1609–1683), Nathaniel Culverwell (1619–1651), Ralph Cudworth (1617–1689), and Henry More (1614–1687). The most famous aphorism of the Cambridge Platonists was "the spirit of man is the candle of the Lord." Inspired by the idealism of Descartes, the Cambridge Platonists believed that reason presided even over revelation, for reason was itself in some way divine—as Henry More explained in his ethical treatise *An Account of Virtue* (1666): "The height of virtue is this, constantly to pursue

▲ *René Descartes, whose conclusion "I think, therefore I am" laid the foundations for a new school of philosophical thought, is commemorated in this statue created by Augustin Pajou (1730–1809).*

In 1768 the English philosopher Edward Herbert proposed five principles of a rational religion:

1. *That there is a supreme God.*
2. *That a chief worship is to be given unto him.*
3. *That the best worship of him consists in virtue, piety, and charity conjoined with faith in, and love of God.*
4. *That if we transgress or fall from the rules thereof, that we must repent from the bottom of our heart, and return to the right way, since without it repentance will be but vain.*
5. *That there is both reward and punishment here and hereafter.*

A Dialogue between a Tutor and his Pupil

that which to right reason seems best. For indeed she herself is even absolutely and simply the best, not only as she is so constant to divine reason, which does nothing partially for the sake of this or that particular; but as she generously dictates, like to a common parent, such laws as tend in their own nature to the happiness of all mankind."

Deism and Philosophy

Deism was the system that proposed a religion based on reason and rejected as superstition the biblical account of the creation of the world, the fall of man, and redemption through the sacrifice of Jesus Christ. Named from the Latin word *deus* ("god"), deism was propagated in France by Pierre Charron (1541–1693) and in England by Edward Herbert, Lord Cherbury (1583–1648). It appealed to those intellectuals of the seventeenth and eighteenth centuries who found the Christian account far-fetched, bloody, and particularistic (historically specific). Herbert made deism into a kind of rationalist religion by proposing universal principles that were independent of revelation. The deism of Lord Herbert of Cherbury and the thought of the Cambridge Platonists had much in common.

Spinoza and Pantheism

The Dutch Jewish philosopher Baruch Spinoza (1632–1677) was influenced by his reading of Giordano Bruno, Thomas Hobbes, and Descartes. In 1656 Spinoza's independence of thought resulted in his expulsion from the synagogue in Amsterdam. For Spinoza, God was a single substance, creation and creator, that embraced all of nature. In the third proposition of the second part of his *Ethics* (1677), Spinoza put forward the following theory: "In God there necessarily exists the idea of His essence, and of all things which necessarily follow from His essence." The divine substance contains every attribute, but only number and extension are universally present and known to man. The human mind is a part of the mind of God, and so human actions are predeter-

◄ *Edward Herbert, the leading English proponent of the philosophical approach known as deism, is portrayed in this painting attributed to Robert Peake, an artist of the late sixteenth and early seventeenth centuries.*

▲ By the eighteenth century Francis Bacon's notion that the search for truth should begin with the material and the particular was in the ascendant. Joseph Wright of Derby (1734–1797) captured the changing approach to "natural philosophy" in atmospheric paintings of scientific experiments, such as the one pictured here, An Experiment on a Bird in the Air Pump (1768).

With the desire for certainty, mathematics became the model for learning; by 1669 Isaac Newton (1642–1727) had discovered calculus. The success of Baconian science, with its reliance on the senses as the way to genuine knowledge, encouraged the attempt to understand philosophy on the basis of the model provided by physics. Yet the study of nature was on the verge of breaking free of philosophy. Called natural philosophy in the eighteenth century, by 1850 the study of nature would simply be called science.

At the beginning of the Renaissance, the Italian scholar Petrarch (1304–1374) had proposed that the medieval idea of man existing to give glory to God should give way to the idea that simple human joys should be one's principal interest this side of the grave. When the Renaissance passed into the Enlightenment around 1700, Petrarch's proposal had still not been realized, but the means to its realization had been put in place. The Baconian project developed slowly; not until two centuries after *The Advancement of Learning* did science and industry begin to provide evidence for the notion that people could indeed be at home in the world, that time, space, disease, and even discomfort could be conquered, at least among the favored classes of the technologically competent West.

mined. Humankind's ultimate aim is the contemplation of God and the forming of passions through the use of reason.

The Legacy of the Renaissance

During the Renaissance the idea of nature had changed: the living world of Aristotle, a world in which the reasons within things were bringing those things to fruition—acorns becoming trees—was transformed into the idea that the living mind presided over a world of dead matter. The idea of human nature had also changed: the optimism of the humanists and deists and the pessimism of Hobbes laid the background for the modern argument as to whether human beings are innocents needing only education or animals requiring discipline.

Philosophical interest in God continued unabated. In England the Cambridge Platonists taught that divine reason was a force that united God and humankind. For Descartes the quest for philosophical truth relied upon God's guarantee that human knowledge of the world is reliable. Spinoza developed a kind of pantheism in which God and the world, creator and creation, were identified as a single entity. This tendency to interconnect God and history would be perfected by Georg Wilhelm Friedrich Hegel (1770–1831) in his lectures on the philosophy of history. Hegel saw history as a gradual enactment of God's ultimate purpose for mankind: human freedom.

FURTHER READING

Cassirer, Ernst, ed. *The Renaissance Philosophy of Man.* Chicago, 1948.

Copenhaver, Brian P., and Charles B. Schmidt. *Renaissance Philosophy.* Oxford, 1992.

Kristeller, Paul Oskar. *Renaissance Philosophy and the Medieval Tradition.* Latrobe, PA, 1966.

———. *Renaissance Thought and Its Sources.* Edited by Michael Mooney. New York, 1979.

James A. Patrick

SEE ALSO
• Aristotle • Bacon, Francis • Calvinism
• Descartes, René • Florence, Council of
• Galilei, Galileo • Hobbes, Thomas
• Humanism and Learning • Lutheranism
• Machiavelli, Niccolò • Magic • Mathematics
• Petrarch • Pico della Mirandola, Giovanni
• Platonism • Spinoza, Baruch

Pico della Mirandola, Giovanni

GIOVANNI PICO DELLA MIRANDOLA (1463–1494) ATTEMPTED A SYNTHESIS BETWEEN CHRISTIANITY AND EVERY OTHER FORM OF THOUGHT AND RELIGION KNOWN TO HIM, AN ENDEAVOR THAT TYPIFIED THE SPIRIT OF THE RENAISSANCE.

In February 1463 Giulia, the wife of Giovanni Francesco Pico, count of Mirandola and Concordia, gave birth to the family's youngest child, Giovanni Pico. The boy had two older brothers and three older sisters. The family had lived for many years in the castle of Mirandola in the northern Italian duchy of Modena, just west of Ferrara. The county had gained its independence in the fourteenth century, and in 1414 the Holy Roman emperor Sigismund had granted to Mirandola the fief of Concordia.

▶ According to contemporary reports, Giovanni Pico della Mirandola cut a handsome figure in the scholarly circles of Renaissance Italy. This illustration, from a 1616 work by Giovanni Battista della Porta, gives an impression of a well-favored young man.

Giovanni Pico's love of learning manifested itself early on. By age fourteen he had renounced the share of the family estate that would have been due to him on his father's death and left it to his two brothers. Thus unencumbered, Pico journeyed to Bologna to study canon law in preparation for a life of service to the church.

Scholarly and Humanistic Pursuits

The imaginative and curious Pico soon wearied of studying canon law and instead became fascinated by the speculative wonders of theology and metaphysics. Over the next seven years, from 1479 through 1486, he moved from one university to another, studying philosophy, theology, Greek, Latin, Hebrew, Syriac, and Arabic. He studied at some of the most famous universities of his day, including those of Ferrara, Padua, and Paris. At Padua he absorbed himself in the works of Aristotle, which he read in Latin translation. In 1482 he began to study Greek with Emanuel Adramyttenus, who had fled from the island of Crete in the wake of its conquest by Muslims.

Attendees at the Council of Florence (1439–1445) included representatives of Byzantine Christianity, who had traveled to Italy in the hope of healing the schism that had divided the Roman church from the Christians of the East since 1054 CE, when Pope Leo IX had excommunicated the patriarch of Constantinople. Although the effort at reunion ultimately failed, the influx of delegates from the Greek-speaking Byzantine Empire and its churches stimulated a renewed interest in the ancient Greek language and in the philosophy of Plato. Foremost among the students of Greek—the language of Homer and Aristotle as well as of Plato—was Marsilio Ficino (1433–1499), the founder of the famed Florentine Academy. The academy thrived under the patronage first of Cosimo de' Medici (1389–1464) and later of his son Lorenzo the Magnificent (1449–1492). Ficino used his knowledge of Greek to translate the writings of Plato and some of Plato's later commentators and disciples into Latin. In 1484 Pico traveled to Florence, where, under Ficino's tutelage, he began to study Platonic philosophy.

The remarkable events that supposedly surrounded the birth of Pico were described in 1510 in a biography written by Pico's nephew (this translation is by the English humanist Thomas More).

A marvelous sight was there seen before his birth: there appeared a fiery garland standing over the chamber of his mother while she travailed and suddenly vanished away: which appearance was peradventure a token that he which should that hour in the company of mortal men be born in the perfection of understanding should be like the perfect figure of that round circle or garland: and that his excellent name should round about the circle of this whole world be magnified, whose mind should always as the fire aspire upward to heavenly things, and whose fiery eloquence should with an ardent heart in time to come worship and pray almighty God with all his strength: and as that flame suddenly vanished so should this fire soon from the eyes of mortal people be hid.

Giovanni Francesco Pico, *Giovanni Pico della Mirandola*

▶ *In this 1842 painting by the French artist Hippolyte Delaroche, the precocious infant Pico sits in his mother's lap as they peruse a book together.*

Until this time Pico's intellectual life had been guided by the medieval system of inquiry known as Scholasticism, whose basis was the philosophy of Aristotle. Although Pico had encountered humanist teachers at Ferrara and elsewhere, the perspective he experienced at Florence was new. Although it involved philosophical discipline, the Florentine approach departed from Scholasticism in its concern with beautiful and noble uses of language, a hallmark of the humanistic outlook pioneered by the poet Petrarch (1304–1374). Pico never fully embraced humanistic ways; his admiration for such Scholastic thinkers as Thomas Aquinas (1225–1274) and John Duns Scotus (1270–1308) was at odds with the humanists' disdain for the Scholastics' halting Latin. In a famous letter to the Venetian humanist Ermolao Barbaro (1454–1493), Pico proclaimed his preference for the inelegant Latin of the Schoolmen, since its end was to reveal the truth (Pico himself could write with eloquence and fire when it suited him). At best, Pico might be said to have attempted a synthesis of speculative Scholastic inquiry with the linguistic excellences of humanism. The substantive influence of humanism on Pico was to introduce him to Platonic thought. Like his mentor Ficino, Pico believed in and defended the essential unity of Aristotelian and Platonic philosophy.

During Pico's youth, at the time of his intellectual formation, a charlatan sold him sixty manuscripts written in Hebrew and convinced him that they were texts of the kabbalah, an esoteric system of Jewish mysticism. Pico maintained his belief in kabbalistic mysticism for years and entwined its subtleties into his philosophical research.

Controversies

After spending time at the University of Paris, Pico returned to Rome. In Paris learned disputations had long played an integral role in the university's approach to academic study. Upon arrival in Rome, Pico announced his intention to debate nine hundred theses in public with whoever cared to challenge him. He even offered to underwrite the costs incurred by anyone traveling a great distance to dispute these matters with him. The breadth of learning and tenacity of

memory required to undertake the defense of the various theses reflects the brilliance and ambitiousness of Pico's youthful mind. Written in Scholastic Latin, the language of learning at Paris, the propositions included assertions of the unity of the philosophies of Aristotle and Plato, new philosophical insights that had stemmed from Pico's study of Platonic and Aristotelian thought, and philosophical statements in the ancient Pythagorean system, which involved using numbers as the basis of investigation. Pico's theses also included speculations on the kinds and effects of magic and interpretations of the secret and mystical philosophies of the ancient world. To introduce the nine hundred theses, Pico wrote an oration entitled *On the Dignity of Man*.

Unfortunately for Pico, his proposed disputation never took place. Pope Innocent VIII (reigned 1484–1492) concluded that seven of the theses smacked of heresy, while six fell under suspicion of possible error. The pope prohibited the disputation and prevented the publication of the book containing the theses. Pico wrote a defense of his theses, but despite his best efforts, the pope condemned the ambitious young scholar. At this point Pico decided to travel. He went to France, where he was arrested by the papal authorities but released shortly afterward.

▲ *Marsilio Ficino's teaching at the Academy in Florence helped revive interest in Neoplatonic philosophy. Ficino reportedly esteemed Plato so highly that in his room he kept a light burning before a bust of the ancient Athenian philosopher. This depiction of Ficino, a woodcut by Tobias Stimmer, is from a 1577 volume devoted to the lives of illustrious men of letters.*

ON THE DIGNITY OF MAN

Pico wrote his oration *On the Dignity of Man* to provide the proper context for his heroic challenge to dispute nine hundred theses in public. The oration defines Pico's motives for setting forth the theses for debate and justifies his inclusion of so many questions by asserting the importance of each. If, he claims, he had truly wished to split hairs, the sum of subtle points and divisions of questions that he could have made would have been without number. However, the most profound passages of the oration are Pico's meditations on humanity's place in creation and on the one gift with which God endowed humankind to distinguish people from all other creatures.

In his discourse Pico evokes the traditional concept of the great chain of being, according to which humanity occupies the highest place in the hierarchy of bodily creatures but also partakes of the nature of the spiritual beings above—a place "a little lower than the angels." Yet Pico introduces a subtle but important modification that causes the links in the chain to slip somewhat. He asserts that man's dignity lies in the ability to transform his nature. According to Pico, God placed man at the center of the world he created in order to contemplate and admire it; he made man a microcosm of that world by fashioning man as a composite of all of its constituent parts. God then invested man with the distinct honor of determining his own place in the hierarchy of being through freely chosen pursuits. By choosing his thoughts and actions, man could either sink to the nature of the brutes or rise to the status of divinity. Pico maintains that people may rise to the highest levels of the spiritual hierarchy through the activity of philosophizing.

With this admixture of notions drawn from Platonic philosophy and Christian theology, Pico locates the essence of human nature in the freedom individuals enjoy to shape their own spiritual status. This emphasis on the God-given freedom to determine where one resides in the chain of being probably constitutes Pico's most distinctive contribution to the history of thought in the West. His focus on individuals' capacity to make themselves and to define their world sounds the keynote of Renaissance thinking.

▼ *Although his papacy was tainted with financial scandal, Innocent VIII showed great zeal in trying to eradicate certain heresies that plagued the church. His suspicion of Pico's nine hundred theses makes sense in view of his abiding concern with the purity of church doctrine. This profile of the pontiff comes from an unsigned copper engraving dating from the sixteenth century.*

Return to Italy

Pico's friend Marsilio Ficino asked him to return to Florence. Having taken up this invitation, Pico was given a villa in Fiesole by Lorenzo de' Medici. There he retired to continue his studies of the liberal arts and theology. During this period Pico wrote *On Being and the One,* his definitive attempt to reconcile Aristotelian and Platonic metaphysics. The subtle philosophical controversy Pico was addressing turns on the question of whether the One (a single principle from which reality emanates) has primacy over being. Neoplatonists conventionally held that in Plato's thought the One exists prior to being, while in Aristotle's thought being precedes the One. In his typically composite style, which invokes pagan, Hebrew, and Christian authorities, Pico claims that the question is one of semantics; Plato intended to express by the term *the One* what Aristotle described as *being.* Pico justifies his position by affirming that both words ultimately refer to God, who is both the ultimate unity and the sum of all being.

In his efforts to lead a life less at variance with the church, Pico became a follower of Girolamo

Savonarola (1452–1498), the fiery Dominican priest who denounced the luxury and immorality of Florence during the reign of the Medicis. Under his influence Pico's work took a decidedly more pious turn. At this time he wrote *Heptaplus,* in which he offered a commentary on the account of the world's creation found in the first chapters of the book of Genesis, and also wrote prayers and commentaries on the Psalms. He burned the poetry he had written in his early life because he now considered it profane. He turned away from secular learning and resolved to devote his mature years to defending the church against its enemies, be they Muslims, Jews, or astrologers. Pico petitioned Pope Alexander VI (reigned 1492–1503) for a full pardon from his condemnation for heresy; the pope duly granted his request.

In Pico's thirty-first year, he grew ill with a fever that resisted all treatment. On November 17, 1494—the same day that Charles VIII of France entered Florence to overthrow the Medicis at Savonarola's urging—Giovanni Pico della Mirandola died. He was laid to rest in the Church of San Marco in Florence, which was known for its association with the humanists of that city. At the requiem mass for Pico, Savonarola himself preached the sermon.

FURTHER READING

Celenza, Christopher S. *The Lost Italian Renaissance: Humanists, Historians, and Latin's Legacy.* Baltimore, 2004.

Pico, Giovanni Francesco. *Giovanni Pico della Mirandola: His Life by His Nephew Giovanni Francesco Pico.* Translated by Thomas More. Edited by J. M. Rigg. London, 1890.

Pico della Mirandola, Giovanni. *On the Dignity of Man; On Being and the One; Heptaplus.* Translated by Charles Glenn Wallis, Paul J. W. Miller, and Douglas Carmichael. Indianapolis, 1998.

Donald Carlson

SEE ALSO

- Education • Erasmus, Desiderius • Florence
- Humanism and Learning • Magic • Medicis, The
- More, Thomas • Philosophy • Platonism

Pilgrimage

A PILGRIMAGE IS A JOURNEY TO A
SACRED PLACE. PILGRIMAGES WERE
THOUGHT TO INFLUENCE ONE'S
PHYSICAL AND SPIRITUAL WELL-BEING;
THEIR VALUE DERIVED FROM THE
JOURNEY AS WELL AS THE DESTINATION.

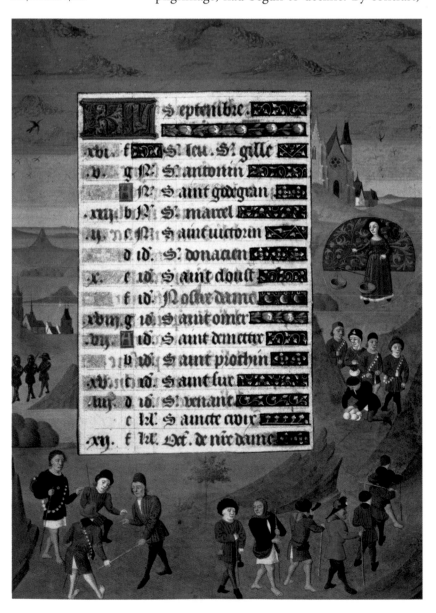

This illumination comes from the fifteenth-century Book of Hours of the Duchess of Burgundy. *It depicts pilgrims returning from their summer pilgrimage to the shrine of Saint James at Santiago de Compostela in Spain.*

Pilgrimage was a popular mode of expression of religious devotion among Christians. The fourteenth century marked the beginning of what is generally held to have been a golden age of pilgrimage. By the seventeenth century, however, Christian pilgrimage, especially long-distance pilgrimage, had begun to decline. By contrast, pilgrimage remains a central feature of Islamic theology and practice. The hajj, a pilgrimage to Mecca (in present-day Saudi Arabia), is one of the five pillars of Islam, and as such, all Muslims are required to make the journey at least once in their life unless circumstances (incapacity, for example) absolutely prevent it.

Reasons for Christian Pilgrimages

Typical destinations for Christian pilgrims included a saint's burial place or another location venerated for its connection to events in the life of a saint; the site of a relic, such as a piece of the true cross; and the site of a miracle, a vision, or the appearance of an image of the Virgin Mary. Such places were believed to have particular spiritual power that would benefit all those who visited them.

A person might want to experience the benefit of that holy power for a number of reasons. Some pilgrims were especially devoted to a particular saint; others were devout Christians who desired to see as many shrines as possible. Some made pilgrimages as a form of penance. During the Renaissance and the Reformation, Christians in western Europe learned to confess their sins to a priest, at first in public but later increasingly in private. The priest would require the repentant sinner to do penance; in some cases the sinner's penance would be to engage in a significant act, such as a pilgrimage to a major shrine in the surrounding region. Some pilgrims might set out on a mission of self-assigned penance to a shrine, whether nearby or at great distance.

Another reason to go on pilgrimage was to fulfill a vow. Many people prayed to God, the Virgin Mary, or one of the saints in a time of particular distress—when experiencing physical illness or crop failure, for example. The petitioner might vow that, if delivered from distress, he or she would make a pilgrimage to the shrine of the saint who effected the miracle to express gratitude. Some pilgrims made the journey to a shrine because they were in need of healing. In some cases the illness passed after the sufferer had merely decided to go on pilgrimage, and the pilgrimage became one of gratitude.

Each shrine was maintained and cared for, usually by priests, monks, or friars, who carefully recorded cases of healed pilgrims in large miracle books as a tangible record of the power of the holy place they tended. It was not uncommon for a person to begin a quest for healing at a local shrine and then travel farther afield to a bigger shrine if the first attempt met with failure.

By the fourteenth century indulgences and dispensations had become increasingly important in motivating people to make pilgrimages.

▲ This illustration from a fourteenth-century manuscript features Pope Boniface VIII (left), whose proclamation in 1300 of the first jubilee year encouraged pilgrims to travel to Rome.

CRITICS OF PILGRIMAGE

Pilgrimage was not a universally approved activity during the Renaissance. An examination of the negative views of pilgrimage held by some commentators of the period demonstrates the diversity of opinion among Christians. What is also clear is how those divisions grew in the fifteenth and sixteenth centuries.

Even before the Reformation, European Christians disagreed about the efficacy of pilgrimage and the supposed spiritual power of the shrines pilgrims visited. Many clergymen pointed out that false shrines had been set up simply to take money from gullible believers. Others launched more serious criticisms. There was a significant debate in the late-medieval church, for example, over whether holiness could really be concentrated in a particular location, such as a shrine. Others questioned whether pilgrimage was a wise use of money— long-distance pilgrimages, such as those made by English and French pilgrims to Rome or to Santiago de Compostela in Spain, could drain a family's resources. Moreover, many people seemed to treat the pilgrimage as a holiday rather than a devotional exercise. Theologians were also troubled that some pilgrims, misunderstanding the doctrine of indulgences, believed that a pilgrimage was an easy way to earn forgiveness for all their sins. The sight of the poor dressed in pilgrim's clothes and begging for food and money led more than a few individuals to suspect that some people were taking advantage of the particular privileges of pilgrims to enrich themselves.

By the fifteenth century criticisms of pilgrimage began to gain force in a manner that anticipated the sixteenth-century attacks of Protestant Reformers. Thomas à Kempis (c. 1379–1471), in his *Imitation of Christ*, urged the devout to look for God in the sacramental bread and wine at Mass rather than in pilgrimages that encouraged idle curiosity and sightseeing. Desiderius Erasmus (c. 1466–1536), too, questioned an ignorant devotion to the saints and imagined instead a "pilgrimage" through one's own house, during which a pilgrim would care for the members of his or her family. Reformers generally picked up on and elaborated these themes; they condemned pilgrimage, and it was gradually eliminated from the practices of the devout. Newly Protestant England, for example, outlawed pilgrimage in 1538.

A dispensation was a formal authorization to engage in an act, such as begging, that was usually frowned upon or to do something forbidden by canon law, such as divorce a spouse. Dispensations could be granted by priests at a place of pilgrimage. An indulgence was a full or partial reduction in the time a sinner would have to spend doing penance, either on earth or after death in purgatory. The power to grant indulgences in exchange for good acts was reserved for the pope and, to a lesser extent, archbishops and bishops. From the eleventh century on, a plenary indulgence (a full remission of the punishment due for sin) was the traditional reward for any Christian who made a pilgrimage to Jerusalem. In 1300 Pope Boniface VIII announced the first jubilee year, a yearlong church celebration during which all pilgrims visiting Rome would receive a plenary indulgence. Jubilee years followed in 1350, 1390, 1450, and every twenty-five years thereafter. Penitents streamed to Rome to visit the basilicas of the apostles and thereby earn the indulgence.

Although the spiritual motivations for making a pilgrimage were many and varied, there is no doubt that some pilgrims undertook such journeys as much for amusement as for spiritual benefit. The travel with companions could be quite pleasant, and there might be side trips along the way. Pilgrimage sites themselves were particularly well equipped to entertain large numbers of what were in effect tourists.

The Experience of Pilgrimage

A pilgrim might be male or female, young or old, rich or poor, and from any walk of life. However, evidence indicates that it was somewhat more common for pilgrims to be men than women. Owing to the existence of local and regional shrines, pilgrimage did not necessarily involve a long and potentially costly journey; poverty was thus not a serious impediment to pilgrimage—although the poorest of the poor did not undertake pilgrimage as frequently as better-off peasants did. Unsurprisingly, the more expensive and prestigious pilgrimages tended to attract those who could more easily afford the trip. There are indications, too, that people in their twenties and thirties were more likely to go on pilgrimage to local shrines, while those on pilgrimage to major international shrines such as Rome, Jerusalem, and Santiago de Compostela were, on average, older.

Once a person decided to go on pilgrimage, he or she needed to prepare for the journey. Such preparations did not necessarily involve acquiring a ready supply of money. Begging was part of a pilgrim's experience, and it was regarded as a way of heightening the spiritual rewards of the

This early-sixteenth-century woodcut, by Hans Grien Baldung, shows Saint James of Compostela in the garb of a pilgim and carrying a staff and pilgrim's bag. The shell badge on his hat was (and is) the symbol of his shrine.

Margery Kempe c. 1373–1438

The remarkable story of Margery Kempe demonstrates the power that religious sentiment had over many believers during the Renaissance and the ways in which pilgrimage could be part of a devotional life. Margery, who lived for most of her life in the town of King's Lynn, in eastern England, was a wife and a mother of fourteen children. Barely literate, she worked as a brewer, a common occupation for women, and late in her life was inducted into the prestigious Trinity Guild of Lynn (a religious association). Although the bare biographical details suggest nothing exceptional, Margery's life was anything but ordinary. She had frequent visions of Christ, fasted and wept out of religious devotion, meditated, and—in obedience to the messages she believed she received from Jesus—abstained from meat and sexual relations. She also traveled extensively on pilgrimage. Her journeys took her not only to shrines in England but also to Italy—Rome, Venice, and Assisi—and even to Jerusalem. In *The Book of Margery Kempe*, which she apparently dictated to her confessor toward the end of her life, she wrote at length about her experiences as a pilgrim.

▲ *This image from a fifteenth-century edition of Geoffrey Chaucer's* Canterbury Tales *depicts the Wife of Bath, one of the pilgrims who makes the journey to England's most popular pilgrimage site, Canterbury Cathedral. Though women made fewer pilgrimages than men, female pilgrims were nevertheless a familiar sight on the roads of Europe.*

trip. Pilgrims were granted special dispensation to beg publicly, and those who gave alms to pilgrims were considered blessed by this act. However, some pilgrims did receive financial support from a sponsor, who would hope to gain spiritual benefit from helping someone else to make the journey.

To receive the full spiritual value of pilgrimage, it was important to identify oneself as a pilgrim. This end was achieved by crossing oneself somehow at the outset of the journey, perhaps simply by making the sign of the cross. Some pilgrims seem to have held their hands in a certain way. Others sewed a cloth cross onto their clothes. Often travelers would wear particular clothes that marked them as pilgrims—not only a cross but also a loose gown with a hood, a staff, a hat, and a pilgrim's badge that identified where they were going and provided them with some protection on the road.

Finally, pilgrims heading for the same destination gathered together to set a departure date. Travel was timed to coordinate both with local events at the shrine and with the demands of the weather. Pilgrims would make a journey to a nearby shrine in time to celebrate a special holiday or some other event particularly connected with that shrine. At shrines dedicated to the Virgin Mary, ceremonies were held to mark one of the major feasts associated with events in Mary's life, such as the Annunciation (in March) or the Assumption (in August). The shrine of a particular saint would be visited by pilgrims on that saint's day. Travelers to the large international shrines also timed their journeys to arrive at the time of a significant festival, but for these pilgrims concerns about when they could reasonably travel the long distances involved and make the necessary land and sea voyages were also crucial factors.

▼ *The cathedral at Santiago de Compostela was one of the most important pilgrimage sites of the early modern period.*

Shrines

Shrines ranged in size from the small sites that attracted local pilgrims to large shrines that welcomed thousands of pilgrims every year from across Europe. Pilgrims could collect from all but the smallest shrines a souvenir of their visit. Indeed, most of the faithful regarded such objects not merely as souvenirs but as religious items with spiritual power. Ampullae, for instance, were small containers for holy water; the water, which could be carried home, was believed to partake of the miraculous power of the shrine itself.

Many pilgrims also took offerings to a shrine. Those who believed they had been healed through the intervention of a saint might, as a token of their gratitude, take an ex-voto, a small piece of wax in the shape of the healed body part—an eye or leg, for example. Others took crutches or some other object that symbolized the difficulty overcome. It was not unusual for released prisoners who attributed their freedom to the assistance of a saint to take their chains. The walls of the church of Our Lady of Guadalupe in Spain were covered with the chains of freed prisoners.

Settlements grew around the larger shrines, which were fed by an extensive road network that brought pilgrims from all directions. Some settlements eventually grew into tourist cities that provided numerous places to eat and sleep. Cobblers and tailors carried on a thriving trade, since long-distance travelers often needed to replace their worn-out shoes and clothes when they arrived. With a well-maintained road network and a large numbers of vistors, the site of an important shrine often became a major trade center.

Changing Attitudes in the Reformation

In the fifteenth and sixteenth centuries, attitudes toward pilgrimage began to change. Pilgrimages to the major international shrines of Jerusalem, Rome, and Santiago de Compostela had already become less popular. Local political unrest made these places more difficult to visit, and the massive depopulation and disruption that followed the Black Death, a catastrophic plague outbreak in the mid-fourteenth century, may well have made people less inclined to travel far from home. The fact that other important pilgrimage sites, such as the shrine of Thomas Becket (c. 1118–1170) in Canterbury, also declined in popularity suggests that people had become increasingly disenchanted with journeys that kept them away from home for several months. There may be a link between the fading appeal of such journeys and the fact that criticisms of pilgrimage, especially expensive long-distance pilgrimage, became more common at this time.

The change in attitudes toward long-distance pilgrimage did not signal the end of the age of pilgrimage. Rather, attention turned increasingly to local shrines. In most cases these shrines had existed long before the decline of pilgrimage in the later Middle Ages, although new local centers of devotion did continue to emerge. Some of the local shrines were dedicated to recognized saints or to the Virgin Mary, but there were many that honored "unofficial" saints—those who were venerated locally without the sanction of the church.

The Reformation dealt a severe blow to pilgrimage. Protestant Reformers were hostile both to pilgrimage itself and to the cult of saints that underlay the pilgrimage tradition. As a result, the number of pilgrims from northern Europe declined, and the status of shrines there diminished; eventually, pilgrims and shrines virtually disappeared. Catholic countries, on the other hand, encouraged both the reverence of saints and pilgrimage. In those countries local shrines especially flourished, and by the mid-seventeenth century, therefore, the most common form of pilgrimage was the relatively short trip to a local shrine.

Muslim Pilgrimage

Pilgrimage was also a major feature of the life of Muslims during the early modern period. Although some Muslims visited the graves of the prophet Muhammad, the imam Ali, and other important figures in Islamic history, such pilgrimages were less central to Islam than was the hajj, the journey to Mecca. Muslim pilgrimage was not bound up with such considerations as indulgences, vows, and healing. For Muslims the pilgrimage to the Kaaba—the shrine that Muslims believe was built by Ibrahim (the patriarch Abraham in Jewish and Christian tradition)—is important because of the spiritual power present at the site.

Muslim pilgrims traveled to Mecca from all parts of the Islamic world—from Spain (until 1492) and North Africa in the west, from central Asia and India in the east, from the Balkans and southern Russia in the north, and even from a few southerly regions of Africa. There was an annual pilgrimage season, and some pilgrim caravans raced to get to Mecca in time. The trip itself was an important part of the experience of the hajj; pilgrims were required to meditate on the power of God as they traveled. While on the road they did not cut their hair or nails, and men

◀ *Pilgrims traveled from across the Muslim world to take part in the hajj. This image, from the sixteenth-century Ottoman manuscript* Hunername (Book of Accomplishments), *by Loqman, shows Muslim pilgrims traveling to Mecca by boat.*

One of the finest eyewitness accounts of the pilgrimage to Mecca comes from the Arab Ibn Battutah (1304–1368), who spent much of the period between 1325 and 1354 traveling throughout the Muslim world. Battutah wrote about his journeys in several autobiographical volumes. In the excerpt below, he describes seeing Mecca and the Kaaba.

We entered the illustrious Holy House [Mecca], wherein "he who enters is secure," by the gate of the Banu Shaiba and saw before our eyes the illustrious Kaaba (God increase it in veneration), like a bride who is displayed upon the bridal-chair of majesty, and walks with proud step in the mantles of beauty, surrounded by the companies which had come to pay homage to the God of Mercy, and being conducted to the Garden of Eternal Bliss. We made around it the [sevenfold] circuit of arrival and kissed the Holy Stone; we performed a prayer of two bowings at the Maqam Ibrahim and clung to the curtains of the Kaaba at the Multazam between the door and the Black Stone, where prayer is answered; we drank of the water of Zamzam, which, being drunk of, possesses the qualities which are related in the Tradition handed down from the Prophet (God bless him and give him peace); then, having run between al-Safa and al-Marwa, we took up our lodging there in a house near the Gate of Ibrahim. Praise be to God, Who hath honored us by visitation to this holy House, and hath caused us to be numbered amongst those included in the prayer of al-Khalil (blessing and peace upon him), and hath rejoiced our eyes by the vision of the illustrious Kaaba and the honorable House, of the Holy Stone, of Zamzam and the Hatim.

The Travels of Ibn Battutah

did not trim their beards. It was forbidden to kill any living being or to indulge in sexual activity. Once the pilgrims reached a predetermined site close to Mecca, men and women changed into identical pilgrim's clothes. They then continued on to the mosque that held the Kaaba. (The pilgrimage was considered valid even if the pilgrims were unable to enter the mosque.) Once inside, they would circle the inner courtyard seven times, touching the cloth covering of the Kaaba in the hope that their prayers would be answered. If it was possible to move through the crowds, pilgrims would approach the black stone built into the Kaaba and kiss it. Some of them went to the well of Zamzam within the mosque, whose waters supposedly had healing and blessing powers. After leaving the Kaaba, the pilgrims went to race between the two hills of Safa and al-Marwa, an event that commemorates the flight of Hagar following Ibrahim's rejection of her and her son Ishmael.

Early on the final day of the hajj, pilgrims congregated at a plateau east of Mecca to listen to a sermon. For the hajj to be valid, the pilgrims had to be present at the site before the sermon ended. Over a set number of days, they had carried out the ritual stoning of a rock, which represented the devil. Finally, on the last day of the ceremonies, the pilgrims returned to the Kaaba to repeat the rituals that they had performed on the day of their arrival (and perhaps at other times in the interim). Then, with the men clean shaven and with everyone's nails trimmed, the pilgrims returned home.

Making the hajj involved many challenges. The greatest was financial. Few Muslims could easily afford the costs of a lengthy journey away from home, and some who did attempt the trip were impoverished en route. Others brought goods with them to trade along the way in an attempt to offset the costs of travel. Still others taught in mosques and theological schools in cities on the road, especially Baghdad. Those Muslims who did successfully complete the hajj earned special respect upon their return home. Residents of pilgrims' hometowns welcomed those returning from the hajj with celebrations and processions and thereafter gave each the honorary title hajji.

▲ In this illustration from a sixteenth-century Persian manuscript titled Haft Awrang, a Muslim pilgrim is depicted kissing the black stone built into the Kaaba, the focus of the hajj.

FURTHER READING

Chaucer, Geoffrey. *The Canterbury Tales.* Translated by Nevill Coghill. Rev. ed. New York, 2003.

Faroqhi, S. *Pilgrims and Sultans: The Hajj under the Ottomans, 1517–1683.* London, 1994.

Kempe, Margery. *The Book of Margery Kempe.* Translated and edited by Lynn Staley. New York, 2001.

Melczer, W. *The Pilgrim's Guide to Santiago de Compostela.* New York, 1993.

Webb, D. *Pilgrims and Pilgrimage in the Medieval West.* London, 2001.

Gretchen Starr-LeBeau

SEE ALSO
• Chaucer, Geoffrey • Erasmus, Desiderius
• Islam • Popular Culture • Reformation
• Religious Orders • Rome • Women

Pius II

ENEA SILVIO PICCOLOMINI (1405–1464) HAD A LONG CAREER AS A SECRETARY AND ENVOY BEFORE HE TOOK HOLY ORDERS. AS POPE PIUS II HE TRIED HARD TO ORGANIZE A CRUSADE AGAINST THE OTTOMAN EMPIRE.

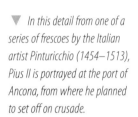

▼ In this detail from one of a series of frescoes by the Italian artist Pinturicchio (1454–1513), Pius II is portrayed at the port of Ancona, from where he planned to set off on crusade.

Enea Silvio Piccolomini was born in 1405 at Corsignano, in the territory of Siena. Both his father, Silvio Piccolomini, and his mother, Vittoria Fortiguerri, belonged to noble families that had recently become poor. Raised in poverty but conscious of his noble heritage, Enea helped his father on the land. Having been educated by the village priest, he went to the University of Siena in 1423, where he studied classical literature and civil law.

Piccolomini made his living as a secretary and envoy. His first employer, Cardinal Domenico Capranica, was out of favor with the pope, Eugenius IV (reigned 1431–1447), and in 1431 Piccolomini accompanied the cardinal to the church council at Basel, which was defying a dissolution order from the pope. He later returned to Basel with another cardinal, Niccolò Albergati, who was sent there as a papal legate in 1435. Piccolomini was committed to the aims of the council—to reform the church and assert the primacy of such councils over the papacy—and as an official in its secretariat, he produced antipapal propaganda. He also served Felix V, the antipope elected in 1440 by the council. In later years Piccolomini changed his mind about the council and the ideas it had promoted; as pope, in 1460 he issued a famous bull, *Execrabilis,* that condemned the practice of appealing the decisions of the pope to a future council.

In 1442 Piccolomini accepted an invitation to join the staff of the Holy Roman emperor Frederick III (reigned 1440–1493). By the mid-1440s he was becoming more serious minded, and religion assumed more importance for him. When he was sent to Rome on an embassy for the emperor in 1445, he asked the forgiveness of Pope Eugenius for his earlier support for the Council of Basel. In 1446 he was ordained deacon, and within a year he had taken priestly orders. He was made bishop of Trieste in 1447 and bishop of Siena in 1450. His episcopal commitments did not prevent him from continuing to serve the emperor, and in 1451 he accompanied Frederick when he went to Italy to meet his bride and to be crowned in Rome. Sent to render the obedience of the empire to the new pope, Calixtus III (reigned 1455–1458), Piccolomini stayed in Italy and was created a cardinal in December 1456. Friendly and courteous, he was popular with his colleagues in Rome, and after the death of Calixtus was elected pope. He took the title Pius II.

Efforts to Promote a Crusade

From the earliest days of his papacy, Pius was deeply preoccupied with efforts to promote a

In another scene from his frescoes of the life of Pius II, Pinturicchio here depicts Piccolomini submitting to Pope Eugenius IV and thus repudiating his former support for the Council of Basel.

crusade against the Ottomans. He decided that a major congress of the European powers was needed to discuss his proposal. He did not want mere diplomatic representatives to meet together; he wanted the rulers of Europe to attend in person. No doubt he hoped to inspire them by his eloquence, although he would have known from his experience of addressing diets (legislative assemblies) in Germany on the subject of a crusade that the practical effects of his rhetoric had so far been limited. Nevertheless, he wanted to discuss such practical measures as how many men and ships were needed, who should lead them, and where the attack should be launched.

Pius left Rome in January 1459 and after a leisurely journey reached Mantua, where the congress was to be held. The only ruler there, apart from the marquis of Mantua himself, was Bianca Maria, the wife of Francesco Sforza, duke of Milan, and she left soon afterward. Few representatives of other powers arrived, and some of those who came were of lower status than the pope wished; he refused even to recognize the English delegates, two obscure priests, as ambassadors.

Pius II's eloquence was much admired, not least by Pius himself. In his autobiographical *Commentaries*, he frequently refers to speeches he gave and the effect they had on his audiences. For example, he recounted how a speech he made at an imperial diet at Frankfurt in 1454 rekindled enthusiasm for an expedition against the Turks (although, in fact, nothing came of the proposed expedition).

But when the assembly met again and Enea spoke, then, wonderful to relate, suddenly all became taken up again by the earlier enthusiasm for the war. Enea spoke for about two hours, and was heard with such attention that no one coughed even once, and no one took their eyes off the face of the speaker, no one thought his speech too long, or welcomed its end. Numerous other speakers were heard, but they seemed boring and ridiculous. . . . Enea's oration was praised by all and many made transcriptions of it.

Commentaries, book 1, chapter 27

The most prestigious representative at the congress was the duke of Cleves, who had been sent by his uncle the duke of Burgundy, but he had left Mantua by the time Francesco Sforza, the only ruling prince to attend the congress, arrived. Pius thought of Sforza as a potential commander for the crusading army, but Sforza's principal interest was in winning Pius's support for King Ferdinand I of Naples (reigned 1458–1494), who was fighting off a challenge from a rival claimant to his throne, the French prince René of Anjou.

As usual, the secular powers were not prepared to lay aside all other disputes and projects to dedicate themselves to a crusade. In fact, Pius himself, while he declared he would put temporal affairs at risk for the sake of the crusade, in practice gave precedence to the affairs of Italy. Nor did he show much tact in handling the delegates. In addition to snubbing the English representatives, he angered King Charles VIII of France (reigned 1483–1498) by criticizing him openly and then refusing to allow the French envoys to make a public defense, and he agreed to proposals made by German representatives even though he would have known from his knowledge of German affairs that those proposals could not work. Yet Pius was very disap-

▶ Despite the splendor of the scene at Mantua depicted in this fresco by Pinturicchio, Pius II's dream of presiding over a congress of European powers was never fully realized. The event came to symbolize only the grandiosity of his ambitions for papal influence.

Given the poverty of his childhood and his awareness of how the Piccolominis had lost their former wealth and power, it would have been satisfying for Pius II to establish his nephews among the leading men of Siena. He built a spacious loggia for his family in the city near the palaces of his nephews Jacopo and Andrea and also built a palace for his sister Caterina and her daughter Antonia. This latter abode became known as the palace of the *papesse* ("popesses"). He made the bishopric of Siena, which he gave to his nephew Francesco, into an archbishopric. As the last outposts of the Byzantine Empire fell to the Ottomans, precious Christian relics were brought to Italy and given to the pope. One of these relics—the arm of Saint John the Baptist—was deposited in Siena shortly before Pius died. In 1461 he canonized a local woman, Caterina Benincasa, who had attracted great devotion even during her lifetime in the later fourteenth century. Saint Catherine of Siena became one of the most revered saints of the Catholic Church.

Pius visited Siena several times during his papacy and spent months in the Sienese countryside, enjoying its beauty and seeking relief for his gout and arthritis at the famous medicinal baths. Some Romans even feared that he might want to transfer the papacy to Siena. Nevertheless, his relations with the government of Siena were not cordial. As gentiluomini (gentlemen or nobles), the Piccolominis were excluded from most government offices in Siena; the regime in Siena was an explicitly popular government. Soon after Pius was elected pope, the Piccolominis themselves were given the right to hold any office in the Sienese government, but Pius wanted all the nobles to have this right. His idea met with great resistance from the Sienese, who said it was unnatural for nobles to be members of a popular government. Annoyed that they would not do what he wanted, Pius accused the Sienese of ingratitude. Eventually, and after much difficulty, in 1459 it was agreed to admit the gentiluomini to full political rights and a share in the government offices. Pius was aware how grudgingly this concession had been made, and while he thanked the Sienese, he warned them he would want more. When he died, all the gentiluomini except the Piccolomini were expelled from the government again. His nephews, however, became respected and influential political figures in Siena.

▼ *Pius II told the architect Bernardo Rossellino (1409–1464) that he had done well to conceal how much the Palazzo Piccolomini (pictured here) and other works in Pienza would cost, because he, Pius, would never have agreed to spend so much. Nevertheless, the pope pronounced himself delighted with the buildings.*

pointed by the meager achievements of the congress when he declared it closed in January 1460.

Pius did not abandon his hopes for a crusade against the Ottomans; he tried to rally support for it but could not gather effective pledges of men and money. An attempt to employ his own weapon of eloquence, in the form of an open letter to Sultan Mehmed II urging him to convert to Christianity, was fruitless; it is doubtful that the sultan ever saw it. Finally Pius decided he would lead by example. When the infirm and aging pope declared that he was going on crusade in person, few believed him. He left Rome in late June 1464 and after a painful journey reached Ancona, on the Adriatic coast. Galleys from Venice came to transport the few troops that rallied to accompany the pontiff, but on August 14, three days after they arrived, Pius died.

Wars in Italy

The main military effort of Pius's pontificate was not a crusade but support for King Ferdinand I in the war for the throne of Naples. The king faced rebellion from important barons, who supported the claims of René of Anjou. Papal troops joined

▼ *Sigismondo Malatesta, in a portrait by Piero della Francesca (1410/20–1492). Pius II accused Malatesta of many crimes, including murder, rape, incest, adultery, sacrilege, perjury, and treachery; he had an effigy of Malatesta burned in Rome.*

the Milanese forces sent by Francesco Sforza in the campaigns that began in early 1460. Sforza's resolution helped to maintain Pius's support for Ferdinand, despite the difficulty the pope had in keeping his troops in the field, and by October 1463 Ferdinand was sufficiently secure for the papal troops to be safely withdrawn. Pius's commitment to Ferdinand's cause was reinforced by the marriage of the pope's nephew Antonio to a natural daughter of the king in 1461.

Pius acted as the arbitrator in a complicated dispute between Ferdinand and others on one side, and on the other, Sigismondo Malatesta (1417–1468), who was lord of a number of territories in the northeastern part of the Papal States, including the city of Rimini. The pope was not impartial; he promised Ferdinand before he pronounced his decision that certain lands would be taken from Malatesta. The breakdown of the settlement that Pius declared drove Malatesta to make a bitter enemy of the pope, particularly by siding with the Angevins in Naples. Pius, who became unrelenting in his determination to destroy Malatesta, excommunicated him, accusing him of crimes against God and man. The military campaigns Pius directed against Malatesta were hindered by lack of money, but in late 1463 Malatesta finally had to ask the pope for pardon and peace. The terms of the settlement left Malatesta in control only of the city of Rimini. Among those who were given the remainder of his lands were two of the pope's nephews.

Nepotism

Pius was very fond of his two sisters, Laudomia and Caterina, and of their children. In common with other popes of the period, he used the opportunities offered by the papacy to advance the fortunes of his family, but he was comparatively restrained in his gifts. None of his relatives had undue influence over him.

Laudomia's sons were all given the surname Piccolomini by their uncle. Antonio, having become the son-in-law of Ferdinand I, was made the duke of Amalfi in the kingdom of Naples and was given Sinigaglia and Mondovì from the lands taken from Malatesta. Jacopo was given Montemarciano, another of Malatesta's territories, and Andrea was given Castiglione della Pescaia and the island of Giglio—places in Tuscany that had been taken by Ferdinand's father, Alfonso V of Aragon. Francesco, made bishop of Siena when his uncle was elected pope, was made a cardinal in March 1460. Francesco would become pope himself, as Pius III, for a few weeks in 1503. It was he who commissioned the series of frescoes by Pinturicchio depicting the life of Pius II for the Piccolomini library of Siena's cathedral.

Pius's Writings

For most of his adult life, Pius earned his living from writing and speaking, fields in which he was highly skilled. When he became pope, literary men and scholars hoped to gain his patronage, but they were disappointed; nor did Pius spend great sums on building up the papal library, as might have been expected.

Before and after he became pope, Pius wrote prolifically, for his own pleasure as well as to persuade or inform others or to advertise his skill. He generally wrote in a brand of Latin that was not always quite correct but was often lively and humorous. In addition to his many letters and orations, he was also the author of a racy play, *Chrysis,* and a story about an adulterous love affair, *Historia de Eurialo et Lucretia.* Among his other works were a geographical description of Germany, a tract on the Holy Roman Empire, a history of the Council of Basel, and treatises on the care of horses, the education of boys, and the art of rhetoric.

▲ *Pius II had the Cathedral of Pienza remodeled to resemble a church he had seen in Austria, which he recalled as being filled with light. He forbade any changes to be made to his original plan.*

The writings for which Pius is best known to modern scholars are his *Commentaries,* which record his own life and times. Writing of himself in the third person, he describes what he did and saw and includes frequent descriptions of the regions through which he traveled. He also provides potted histories of various lands. His subjects range from wars and church councils to the mishaps of his little dog, Musetta. As might be expected, this work is not an impartial account. There is much praise of himself, especially of his eloquence and wisdom, and he also relates the discomfiture of those who tried to challenge him. While this relentless self-promotion diminishes to some extent the charm of the work, it nevertheless provides an extraordinary and vivid self-portrait of a Renaissance pope.

FURTHER READING

Gabel, L. C., ed. *Memoirs of a Renaissance Pope: The Commentaries of Pius II.* Translated by F. A. Gragg. New York, 1959.

Mitchell, R. J. *The Laurels and the Tiara: Pope Pius II 1458–1464.* London, 1962.

Christine Shaw

SEE ALSO

- Byzantium • Holy Roman Empire
- Italian City-States • Italian Wars • Papacy

Platonism

THE PHILOSOPHICAL TRADITION KNOWN AS PLATONISM, INSPIRED BY THE THINKING OF THE CLASSICAL GREEK PHILOSOPHER PLATO (C. 428–348/7 BCE), WAS AN IMPORTANT INFLUENCE UPON THE WORK OF LEADING RENAISSANCE SCHOLARS.

Together with his teacher Socrates, Plato is generally regarded as the father of the Western philosophical tradition. Born to a wealthy and important Athenian family around 428 BCE, Plato initially planned a career in the civic life of Athens as a politician, but his exposure to the teachings of Socrates and the execution of Socrates by the city of Athens for impiety inclined him toward a career as a philosopher.

▼ Plato and Socrates are depicted as medieval scholars in this illumination from a fourteenth-century English manuscript by Bernardus Silvestris.

Plato's influence on the Western philosophical tradition has been so great that in 1929 the philosopher Alfred North Whitehead described philosophy as "a series of footnotes to Plato." Although Plato's works cover an exceptionally wide range—including politics, ethics, metaphysics, and epistemology (theory of knowledge)—the doctrines most relevant to an examination of Renaissance Platonism are his theory of forms and his teachings on love. The theory of forms claims, in short, that physical objects are really imperfect copies of perfect forms, which exist on a higher plane of reality. The famous speech of Diotima—recounted by the figure of Socrates in Plato's *Symposium*—provided a concept of love that would greatly influence the Platonist tradition.

Innate Ideas and Recollection

Essential to Plato's theory of forms are his doctrine of innate ideas and his theory of recollection, both of which are expounded in the *Meno*. The main characters in this dialogue are the philosophers Meno and Socrates. The *Meno* begins with a discussion of the topic of virtue and the search for an adequate definition of that concept. Socrates and his interlocutor quickly conclude that neither of them can define virtue, and both must therefore admit that they do not truly know what it is.

The conversation then moves to the very nature of knowledge: "How can one begin an inquiry when one is not even sure what one does not know?" In addressing this question, Socrates cites the lyric poet Pindar (c. 522–c. 438 BCE), who claimed that all souls had been reincarnated countless times. In consequence of this multiple reincarnation, Socrates claims, humankind has learned everything there is to know in previous lives. This notion is the crux of the Platonic doctrine of innate ideas. There is no need to search for truth outside oneself, for the truth already lies within. Unfortunately, most people do not realize that they possess so much latent knowledge, and it therefore remains untapped and unexamined.

What is required is a skillful questioner who will draw knowledge out of the seeker of truth, in much the same way that a midwife draws a child out of a pregnant woman. Indeed, Socrates, whose mother was a midwife, identifies himself metaphorically as a "midwife of ideas." In the Socratic and Platonic view, everything that a person believes he or she has learned was already present within in the form of a memory from a previous incarnation. Thus, there is no learning, only recollection. The process of studying and mastering material is at base a matter of remembering forgotten knowledge from past lives and organizing it in such a way as to make it useful.

Since knowledge is inborn, a teacher is really just a facilitator, one who helps students to realize that all of the knowledge they need is already within them. This notion is illustrated in the *Meno*, in which Socrates demonstrates both the doctrine of innate ideas and the theory of recollection by questioning Meno's servant boy. Although the servant boy lacks formal education, he responds to Socrates' expert questioning by unconsciously producing Euclidean geometric proofs. Socrates claims that this achievement proves that such fundamental knowledge is innately possessed by everyone.

▼ *The death of Socrates, who was forced to poison himself with hemlock, forms the subject of this 1787 work by Jacques Louis David.*

Socrates   c. 470–399 BCE

Relatively little historical information survives about Socrates. His philosophy (or something reasonably close to it) is presented in the dialogues of Plato, Socrates' most famous disciple. According to Plato's account, Socrates began life as a philosopher following a visit by his friend Chaerephon to the oracle at Delphi. Chaerephon's seemingly simple question, "Who is the wisest man in Athens?" received a reply that appeared more straightforward than it was: "There is no one wiser than Socrates."

Upon being told of this pronouncement from the oracle, Socrates professed bewilderment. All that Socrates claimed to know was that he knew nothing. Puzzled and seeking to disprove the oracle's surprising claim, Socrates traveled around the city of Athens and questioned those who were regarded as wise by the citizens of the city. He discovered that very few of those he questioned on such topics as truth, wisdom, and justice were able to answer him with any degree of confidence or precision.

In the process of engaging the leading lights of Athens in dialogue—and embarrassing them by exposing the ignorance of those who regarded themselves and were regarded by others as wise—Socrates earned himself various unflattering nicknames, such as "stinging gadfly" (an insect that forces indolent horses into motion) and "torpedo fish" (which stuns its prey prior to devouring it). Socrates agreed to the accuracy of the first appellation but claimed that while he stung the lazy horse (Athens), he did so out of love and a desire to see it live up to its potential for excellence rather than idle about in sunny fields. As for his being a torpedo fish, he told his accuser, Meno, that if he had the effect of inflicting intellectual torpidity on others, it was only because he himself was torpid.

In the end Socrates was accused, tried, and sentenced to death for teaching about gods other than those of the city of Athens (as well as about things below the earth and above the heavens), for making the weaker argument defeat the stronger, and for corrupting the young with his teaching. Ordered to drink hemlock, he died of the poison.

▲ *Shadows of the world beyond play on the wall of the cave in this depiction of Plato's famous allegory, which was painted by an unknown Flemish artist of the sixteenth century.*

The Theory of Forms and the Allegory of the Cave

Plato's theory of forms is closely related to his views on innate ideas and learning as recollection. Although the theory of forms appears in a number of Plato's writings, including the *Phaedo*, its most famous manifestation is in the allegory of the cave in Plato's masterwork, *The Republic*.

In the seventh book Socrates, who once again plays the role of spokesman for Plato's philosophy, tells the story of men who are chained in a cave in such a way that they can see only its rear wall. Light from outside, shining through the entrance of the cave behind them, plays against the rear wall and casts shapes upon it. These shapes are the shadows of real things that exist in the world outside the cave, but the chained men, unable to turn their heads and see this reality, can only guess at its nature from the shadowy representations it casts.

In the allegory one man breaks free of his chains. He walks to the mouth of the cave and,

after recovering from the temporary blindness caused by the direct sunlight (to which as a prisoner in the cave he is unaccustomed), sees things as they truly are. He need no longer content himself with shadows and partial truths; he has gained true sight and hence true knowledge. As such, he has become a philosopher, a lover and seeker of wisdom.

This man turns back to his comrades, frees them from their chains, and tries to lead them to the mouth of the cave. He is scorned by his fellows for forcing them to give up their illusion and face the truth head-on. He even risks being killed by those he seeks to liberate.

This allegory, says Plato, describes the human experience of reality. The world that appears to the senses is akin to the shadow of reality cast on the back wall of the cave. These shadows are cast by what Plato calls the forms of reality; the realm they reside in (corresponding to the world outside the cave) is beyond the perception of most people. The forms are divine and perfect; the world people experience via their senses is a mere copy of the forms. The task of the philosopher is to free himself from his belief in the reality of sensory objects and learn to contemplate the forms of reality. By this means he will gain knowledge of the most important forms: the True, the Good, and the Beautiful.

Plato's *Symposium:* Love

Plato's *Symposium* is a dramatic retelling of the events of a banquet, at which the attendees give speeches on the nature of love. After listening to various orations, Socrates recounts to those present his own instruction in love by a woman named Diotima. In contrast with the views presented by others, Socrates, following Diotima, claims that since love desires beauty, it cannot itself be beautiful; for one does not long for what one already has. Neither, says Socrates, can love be good in itself; the good and the beautiful are in effect one and the same, and love, desiring the beautiful, therefore also desires the good (and so does not already possess that quality). If love is not good, it cannot be a god. Yet not being a god does not necessarily make love mortal. Instead, Socrates contends, love is an intermediate spirit between gods and people. He further contends that love is the offspring of Poros (Plenty) and Penia (Poverty). As an intermediary between the immortals and the mortals, the realm of wisdom and the realm of ignorance, love shares the nature of a philosopher.

In a reprise of the theme of recollection and what might be called the notion of the midwifery of ideas, love emerges in Socrates' oration as a force that seeks immortality via procreation. In its least spiritual form, love desires sexual union, which leads to the creation of new life when a woman "gives birth to beauty." Socrates stresses, however, that a person may be be pregnant in soul as well as in body and that the creations of statesmen, lawmakers, and artists are a more beautiful (or better) form of offspring than children. People are born, live, and then die, but a man who manages to "deliver" wisdom from his pregnant soul leaves behind an eternal legacy.

In this way Socrates reveals love as being integral to the task of the philosopher. As the self-proclaimed "midwife of ideas," Socrates is instrumental in drawing forth wisdom from other "pregnant" souls and delivering them into the world. Love, the desire for the good and the beautiful, is a powerful creative force—even more so when it is experienced in the mind (in which case the result is the creation of new ideas) than when it is experienced in the body (in which case the result is the creation of children).

PLATO'S ACADEMY

Prior to his second visit to Syracuse in 367 BCE, Plato founded a school on a large enclosed plot of land in an area of Athens known as the grove of Akademos (named in honor of a legendary Athenian hero of the Trojan Wars). On Plato's death in 348 or 347, his nephew Speusippus assumed leadership of the Academy, to the apparent chagrin of the more talented Aristotle, who had been a member of the Academy for twenty years. (Aristotle founded his own school, the Lyceum, in 335 BCE.)

Plato's school became a mainstay of intellectual life not merely in Greece but in the entire Western world. It seems that pupils there were instructed in mathematics, dialectics (a method of argumentation), natural science, and statesmanship. The Academy endured until 529 CE, over eight hundred years after its founding, when it was closed at the order of the emperor Justinian.

▲ *This first-century-CE Roman mosaic, found in a villa in Pompeii, shows a gathering of ancient Greek philosophers. The figure rubbing his chin is apparently Socrates; directly in front of the trunk of the tree is Plato. The Athenian Acropolis can be seen in the background.*

Plotinus and Neoplatonism

Platonism is not so much a historical movement concerned with perpetuating the legacy and ideas of Plato as it is a philosophical position or attitude. This characteristic of Platonism is clearly manifested in the work of Plotinus (205–270 CE), an Egyptian-born Roman philosopher who updated and adapted elements of Plato's doctrines into a more systematic body of work known as Neoplatonism.

Plotinus's work was published under the title *Enneads*. He was deeply concerned—as Plato had been—with the problem of the One and the Many. The question he addressed was whether there is one thing that is fundamentally real (and if so, what is that thing?) or whether instead people exist in an essentially meaningless world of sensory objects, each of which is real in itself but none of which points to some realm that is superior to the here and now. Plato resolved this problem by assigning physical objects a lesser degree of reality and divine forms a greater one. As imperfect copies of the perfect forms, sensory objects, although they qualified as real for Plato, were in a fundamental sense less real than the forms that engendered them.

Plotinus deviated from the orthodox Platonic view by proposing a so-called divine trinity consisting of the One, the nous (which may be defined as "divine mind"), and the Soul. Plotinus's trinity, in common with the Christian Trinity (Father, Son, and Holy Ghost) is essentially a unity; three manifestations of a single essence. In Plotinus's conception the One is the source of all reality and truth. From it emanates nous, the intellectual principle that expends the power of the One in creating the Soul.

The Soul is manifested in each individual as his or her own soul. The movement of the soul of an individual back toward the One (and hence toward the source of its origin and power) is the better course to take, for in this way individual souls may recall and approach the force that brought them into existence. The wrong course is for the soul to turn away from the One. Thus, each person must choose either to return to the One or to reject it in favor of seeking the source of truth and wisdom in the material world. Plotinus rejects the senses as primary sources of knowledge—as did Plato—owing to the lack of unity among sensory objects. In stark contrast, the Soul is inherently unified, and its ability to turn toward contemplation of the One makes it a far more reliable source of knowledge. As an embodied soul turns away from the One toward the material world, it becomes less unified and hence less able to discern truth.

Plotinus explained evil by claiming that as the divine trinity—also called a divine unity—emanates out from itself in the process of creating lower physical realms of reality, its perfection and unity become increasingly fragmented, partial, and hence imperfect. Since evil is in large part the absence of perfection, it stands to reason that disunity gives rise to evil. This tendency is exacerbated by the fact that the lower, corrupted objects of sense are more readily known than the higher, perfect One. People accordingly have a natural tendency to settle for

▼ *This marble head of Plotinus, which comes from a collection in Ostia, near Rome, probably dates from the late third century CE.*

debased, immediate knowledge rather than turn back toward the One in pursuit of genuine truth.

A further complication in Plotinus's thought is his concession that the One cannot be known directly, nor can knowledge of the One be directly communicated. The One can be known only indirectly, by a kind of process of elimination wherein the seeker of knowledge comes to understand something about the nature of the One by negation. In other words, the enquirer determines what the One is by first determining what the One is not. There is a mystical quality to Plotinus's discussion of the One that reflects the attempts of earlier thinkers, such as the pre-Socratic philosopher Parmenides and his famous student Zeno, to explain the concept of unity.

Although the connection may not be immediately or intuitively obvious, Plato's teachings on love have considerable bearing on a discussion of the One. The lover desires that which he lacks; thus, the very act of loving implies both a recognition of imperfection and the desire to correct it. Since the Soul is a product of nous, which itself emanates from the One, even the Soul possesses a lesser degree of unity—and hence of perfection—than does the One. Thus, a properly ordered soul should desire the One much as the lover pursues the object of his affection. Indeed, according to this view it is literally true that love is the only source of unity in a fragmented, disjointed world of disparate objects. Only the force of love, as expressed in the Soul's movement back toward the One, can effectively counteract the natural tendency toward disunity and entropy. The Soul's desire for the beautiful draws it back toward the One and reminds it that it comes from the One. Plotinus owes this idea of the Soul's love for the beautiful and unified One to Plato; it finds its most direct and notable expression in the Athenian's dialogue *Phaedrus*.

Nicholas of Cusa

The path traveled by Platonism from the time of Plotinus was by no means a straightforward one. This fact is unsurprising considering the heterogeneous nature of the various schools of Platonic thought. One particularly significant figure in Platonism's transition from the Middle Ages to

THE ONE AND THE MANY

The problem of the One and the Many is central to Western philosophical thought. It dates back at least to pre-Socratic philosophers of the sixth century BCE and finds its most eloquent expression in the contrasting views of Parmenides and Heraclitus. Parmenides and his famous student Zeno maintained that since knowledge is only of things that are permanent and since the world is in a state of perpetual flux, people can have no true knowledge if they seek it in the material world. Rather, the only true object of knowledge is the One, which is understood as an inherently cohesive, indivisible unity whose nature cannot be captured in the merely partial, fragmented language of human beings. Parmenides and Zeno went as far as to say that such obvious elements of sense experience as movement and change are in fact illusions, a contention that Zeno aimed to prove via the famous paradoxes that bear his name.

The aristocratic Heraclitus was dubbed the weeping philosopher owing to his conviction that nothing was real in any fundamental sense. In Heraclitus's view reality was flux and flux was reality. A famous Platonic paraphrase of Heraclitus's teaching states that one cannot step into the same river twice. Although Heraclitus apparently never made that statement, if anything it understates his position—which is that everything is in such a state of continual change that one cannot even step into the same river *once*.

Plato took it as integral to his philosophical project to reconcile these two divergent views in his theory of forms, in which a permanent realm of unchanging beings creates the changeable and imperfect world of objects. The Neoplatonic view of emanation and return owes a great deal to this earlier Platonic teaching.

▲ *A symposium was a lively gathering, perhaps following a banquet, at which men would drink, listen to music, and exchange ideas. Depicted on this fifth-century-BCE krater (bowl) are two men listening to a flute.*

Platonism was used as the basis for diametrically opposed religious philosophies, a fact that appears to underscore its relative lack of consistency when taken as a whole. Plotinus's disciple Porphyry (223–309) was a vehement anti-Christian—at least in part because he saw within Christianity certain elements, such as the Incarnation, that would over time undermine or at least drastically modify his brand of Neoplatonism. Interestingly, such Christian Platonists as Clement of Alexandria (c. 150–c. 211), Origen (c. 185–c. 254), and Augustine of Hippo (354–430) used many of the same basic Platonic insights to justify a radically different position from that taken by Porphyry.

► In this work an unknown Italian artist of the fourteenth century imagined a conversation between two great philosophers: Porphyry (right), a student of Plotinus, and Ibn Rushd (1126–1198), known in the West as Averroës. The two philosophers shared an enthusiasm for Aristotle, their studies of whose work also reflect the influence of Neoplatonism.

the Renaissance was Nicholas of Cusa (1401–1464), whose doctrine of learned ignorance, as presented in his *De docta ignorantia* (published in either 1439 or 1440), was influenced greatly by the teachings of Plato and especially of Plotinus. The central tenet of Cusanist teaching is that wisdom consists in learning the limits of the mind; in other words, in coming to a full understanding of what is not known. Putting a distinctly Christian face on this ancient Socratic and Platonic position, Nicholas claimed that God exists at the limits of human knowledge and understanding and in consequence can be known only "negatively." Simply by replacing the word *God* by *the One*, the similarities between Nicholas of Cusa and Plotinus become plain.

Like Plotinus, Nicholas of Cusa maintained that from observing that the perfect being (for Cusa, God; for Plotinus, the One) does not possess certain qualities, such as limitation, imperfection, and fallibility, it follows that he must possess the opposite characteristics. The knowledge of God gained thereby is naturally limited by people's own imperfect comprehension, but it does at least give the seeker some idea of the nature of the absolutely perfect and unlimited being.

Since Nicholas's Platonism is explicitly Christian, Jesus Christ plays a significant role in his philosophy. Nicholas conceives of God as both the absolute minimum and the absolute maximum, in keeping with the view that God is the alpha and the omega—the beginning, the end, and everything in between. As the man who is fully God and the God who is fully man, Christ instantiates this divine characteristic of encompassing both the material world and the spiritual realm.

The influence of Plotinus on Nicholas is clear in the latter's notion of God as having all things "enfolded" in his nature even before they come to exist. Since these things are not actually part of God, he is no more lessened by their progressive "unfolding" than is an architect whose building progresses from plans to completion. The material world unfolds from God's plan in a manner reminiscent of Plotinus's view of the relationship between the One, nous, and the Soul. It should come as no surprise, then, that Nicholas shares Plotinus's distrust of matter (although not quite to the same extent) and extols the progressive mortification of the flesh as a means to attain holiness and purity on earth. For Nicholas, God is known via the intellect through the word of God, which he equates with the world-soul. A created being who returns to God via contemplation is "re-enfolded" within him; yet that being avoids being completely merged or losing its own identity.

The Influence of Plethon

Around 1439, at roughly the same time as Nicholas of Cusa was working out his philosophical and theological system in central and northern Europe, the Florentine ruler Cosimo de' Medici (1389–1464) resolved to establish in his city a school in imitation of Plato's Academy. Although the exact date of its founding is uncertain, the Florentine Academy's first head is generally considered to have been the Byzantine philosopher George Gemistus Plethon (c. 1355–1452). Plethon, virulently anti-Aristotelian, denigrated Aristotle's philosophy (which had been, and remained, the dominant philosophical influence on the Catholic Church's theology) in favor of that of Plato. Plethon was a powerful spokesman for Platonism, although he failed to distinguish clearly between the writings of Plato and those of later Neoplatonic thinkers, including Plotinus. His position as head of the Florentine Academy made him an especially significant figure in Renaissance Platonism.

Bessarion

Bessarion, sometimes called Johannes Bessarion (1403–1472), like Nicholas of Cusa, began his adult life as a man of letters and ended it as a cardinal of the Roman Catholic Church. A brilliant student, in 1423 he began studying philosophy under Plethon, who was at that time teaching in the Peloponnese, in Greece. Although Bessarion was impressed by Plethon's erudition and passionate advocacy of Platonic philosophy over Aristotelianism, he did not entirely share his teacher's partisan views. Leaving aside his noteworthy accomplishments as a religious leader and political figure, Bessarion was best known in scholarly circles for his attempts to reconcile Platonism and Aristotelianism. Although this project met with only limited success, it reflected Bessarion's general bent toward unity and

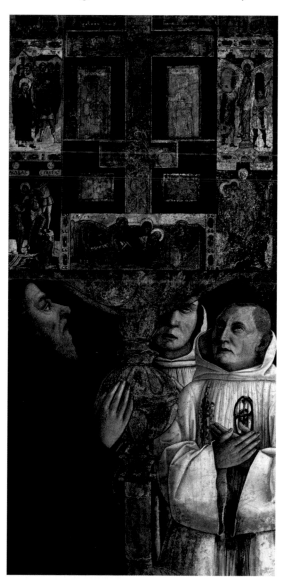

In this 1472 painting on wood by the Italian artist Gentile Bellini, Cardinal Bessarion is portrayed in front of his reliquary of the cross with two brothers from a religious order.

The Florentine Academy was established by Cosimo de' Medici as a school to imitate the model of Plato's Academy in ancient Athens. The later institution achieved remarkable success in advancing the philosophy of Platonism in a short period of time. This success was attributable to the brilliance of its members, who included George Gemistus Plethon, Marsilio Ficino, and Giovanni Pico della Mirandola (1463–1494).

Ficino is sometimes credited (questionably) as the true founder of the Florentine Academy. If he were its founder, the date of its establishment would be pushed back to 1462, the year in which Cosimo de' Medici gave Ficino a villa in Careggi, a town near Florence, as a reward for Ficino's relationship with the Academy and as an inducement to him to continue that relationship. Although it is likely that Ficino acted as the Academy's head at some point, Plethon seems by far the more plausible candidate for its first head. If Ficino is to be credited with the honor, there must have been twenty-three years between Cosimo's resolution to found the Academy and its actual establishment, a view that strains credibility. What is certain is that the Florentine Academy was an important center of scholarship during the Renaissance and that, well after their deaths, its members continued to influence other thinkers and writers by the power and cogency of their thought.

▼ *The title page of a 1525 edition of Ficino's best-known work, the* Theologia Platonica de immortalitate animae, *a treatise on the immortality of the soul.*

M.D.XXV.

harmony, as demonstrated elsewhere by his more successful efforts to counter schismatic tendencies in the church with pleas for reconciliation and understanding. Although Bessarion studied under Plethon prior to the establishment of the Florentine Academy and also spent a good deal of time in Florence, his connection to the Academy proper seems to have been quite limited, since by the time of its establishment, he was occupied with his ecclesiastical duties.

Marsilio Ficino

Marsilio Ficino (1433–1499) seems to have been introduced to Platonism via the writings of Augustine of Hippo. A skilled translator with great proficiency in both Latin and Greek, Ficino began a translation of the collected works of Plato in 1463. The resulting work represented the first complete translation from the original Greek of all of the known writings of the founder of the Western philosophical tradition. His translation was probably completed around 1469 but did not appear in print until 1484. Ficino also contributed to Platonism by writing commentaries on Plotinus as well as on Plato.

Ficino was far more than a translator and commentator. In his philosophical and theological works, he presents a complete cosmology that owes its foundation to earlier Platonists. As a Christian (and a clergyman), Ficino put God at the top of a hierarchy of perfection, with declining degrees of perfection progressively attributed to angels, ensouled beings (humans), animals,

plants, and base natural matter. Although, like Nicholas of Cusa, Ficino had a distinctly Christian point of view, his methodology is more in keeping with that of Plotinus than it is with Christian philosophy. Ficino did, however, change the Plotinian model considerably. Rather than simply the One, nous, and Soul, Ficino identified five substances: God, the angelic mind, the rational soul, quality, and body. The basic concepts of emanation and return are still present, but man (as rational soul) is placed in the middle of Ficino's schema—lower than God and the angels but higher than quality and body (understood as matter or raw material being). The central place man occupies in Ficino's hierarchy is attributable to both Ficino's humanist background and his Christian faith, both of which tend to stress the dignity of man and his centrality in the created world (whether regarded from a Christian or a non-Christian standpoint).

Ficino and Platonic Love
Although study of Ficino frequently focuses on his impressive metaphysical and cosmological

► *This atmospheric work by the French artist Antoine Caron (1520-1599), called* Dionysius the Areopagite Converting the Pagan Philosophers, *dates from the 1570s. Mystery surrounds the identity of the so-called Pseudo-Areopagite, but among the many theories is the view that he may himself have been a pagan convert.*

insights, his teachings on love were also of great significance. His main source, unsurprisingly, was Plato, whose *Symposium* formed the basis for much of Ficino's thinking on the subject. Other influences included Aristotle's *Nicomachean Ethics* and Cicero's teachings on friendship. Combining these ancient pagan sources with his own understanding of Christian theology, Ficino coined the famous term *platonic love.* In Ficino's formulation platonic love (sometimes also called Socratic love) generally refers to a deep bond of loving friendship between two people who are bound together by their shared love of God. The common modern understanding of platonic love as a term referring to a nonsexual relationship between a man and a woman has its basis in Ficino's attempt to bind various types of love— including the chivalric ideal known as courtly love, which was explored in numerous medieval romances—into a single philosophical concept.

Dionysius the Areopagite

Dionysius the Areopagite—also frequently referred to as Pseudo-Dionysius—is a profoundly enigmatic figure. It is not even possible to say with certainty when in the first millennium he was born. In the Roman Catholic tradition, he is said to have been the judge of the Areopagus (the aristocratic council) who was converted to Christianity by Saint Paul (Acts 17:34) and may have served as the bishop of Athens. Many scholars believe, however, that Pseudo-Dionysius was born around 500 CE and is therefore not the person referred to in the Acts of the Apostles.

What is certain is that numerous writings attributed to Pseudo-Dionysius, including *Celestial Hierarchy, Mystical Theology,* and *Divine Names,* influenced the development of Platonism, particularly in the Renaissance. His attempts to reconcile the perfect divine unity with the imperfect, disharmonious, created world both anticipated and amplified Platonism's concerns with the same theme.

However it was conceived, Ficino's notion of platonic love exercised significant influence well into the sixteenth century, as indeed did all his work. Ficino's most celebrated student, Giovanni Pico della Mirandola, was another major figure at the Florentine Academy whose influence continued into the late Renaissance. Pico's writings drew inspiration from Jewish kabbalistic literature and from Pseudo-Dionysius.

The work produced by the Florentine Academy exercised considerable influence on a group sometimes called the Oxford Reformers. Prominent among these men was John Colet (1466–1519). Colet and Ficino corresponded directly, and—like Pico—Colet incorporated Pseudo-Dionysius into his writings.

Other noteworthy writers and thinkers may be considered as at least auxiliaries in the Platonist camp. Thomas More (1478–1535) was both a friend of Colet and an admirer of Plato. Indeed, the communistic form of government and social order proposed in More's famous work *Utopia* (1516) was directly inspired by Plato's most influential dialogue, the *Republic*. The *Civitas solis* of Tommaso Campanella (1568–1639) also owes its inspiration to Plato's masterwork. The work of Francis Bacon (1561–1626) differed greatly from that of More and Campanella, but the influence of Plato can be seen in the title of his *New Atlantis*, which he took from Plato's dialogue *Critias*.

As the mathematical approach became increasingly important to scientific thought in the sixteenth century and even philosophical thought became more systematic, the role played by the broad metaphysical and cosmological speculations characteristic of Platonism diminished. Although Platonism flowered once again during the last half of the seventeenth century under the Cambridge Platonists and continued to have some influence in the fields of poetry and literature, it made little contribution to metaphysics or philosophy, generally following the decline of the Florentine Academy after Pico. Although Platonism survives in various forms to this day, it did not well or long endure the stricter standards of scientific method of the seventeenth and eighteenth centuries. In the present day Platonism has very little impact outside of the rather narrow confines of academic philosophy.

FURTHER READING

Barzman, Karen-Edis. *The Florentine Academy and the Early Modern State: The Discipline of Disegno.* New York, 2000.

Bremer, John. *Plato and the Founding of the Academy.* Lanham, MD, 2002.

Gerson, Lloyd P., ed. *The Cambridge Companion to Plotinus.* New York, 1996.

Raffini, Christine. *Marsilio Ficino, Pietro Bembo, Baldassare Castiglione: Philosophical, Aesthetic, and Political Approaches in Renaissance Platonism.* New York, 1998.

A contemporary of Desiderius Erasmus and Thomas More, the Oxford Reformer John Colet became dean of Saint Paul's Cathedral and founder of a school that still exists. He is pictured here on an engraving by an unknown English artist of the nineteenth century.

Daniel Horace Fernald

SEE ALSO

• Aristotle • Humanism and Learning
• More, Thomas • Philosophy
• Pico della Mirandola, Giovanni

Poland

THE PERIOD EMBRACING THE RENAISSANCE AND THE REFORMATION, WHEN POLAND WAS BRIEFLY EUROPE'S LARGEST KINGDOM, IS WIDELY SEEN AS THE COUNTRY'S GOLDEN AGE.

Poland entered the Renaissance having little more than a marginal impact on western European politics. Under the rule (sometimes nominal) of the Piast dynasty from its foundation in 966, by the late fourteenth century the divided Polish kingdom had frequently been the target of Mongol and German invasion. The last Piast king, Casimir III (reigned 1333–1370; called "the Great"), strengthened royal influence and reconquered lost territory, but his death in 1370 slowed the movement toward further national consolidation.

Casimir's designated heir was his nephew, the Angevin king Louis I of Hungary, who was willing to grant the Polish nobility political and financial privileges in return for their support. Louis may have regarded these concessions as a temporary expedient, to be withdrawn when his dynasty was firmly established. As he died unexpectedly without a male heir in 1382, however, the concessions were never withdrawn. A weak crown and strong nobility became a permanent feature of the Polish state and constitution.

► Wladyslaw Jagiello, grand duke of Lithuania, became king of Poland through his marriage to Jadwiga in 1386. This engraving by Aleksandr Lesser (1814–1884) emphasizes Jagiello's kingly status as a defender of his people and the Christian faith.

Louis's death created a succession problem, and much blood was shed by rival factions before his youngest daughter, ten-year-old Jadwiga (1374–1399), was crowned in 1384. In medieval Europe women rarely ruled in their own right. A woman in Jadwiga's position was expected to marry and defer to her husband, who would become the effective ruler. The question of her marriage was therefore a very serious political issue and the subject of renewed dispute between different factions of the nobility, each of which had its favored candidate.

Union with Lithuania

The husband eventually chosen for Jadwiga—as a minor, she had no say at all—was Jagiello (c. 1351–1434), the grand duke of Lithuania. The choice was remarkable: Lithuania was the last pagan country in Europe, and Jagiello's conversion to Roman Catholicism was a condition of the marriage. Jagiello was baptized on February 15, 1386, and took the Christian name Wladyslaw (Ladislaus). He was married to Jadwiga three days later. Before his coronation as Wladyslaw II, the new king promised that Lithuania would be integrated fully into Poland, but he never made good his promise, and both countries continued to be administered separately until the Union of Lublin in 1569.

The marriage was an advantageous one for almost everyone involved. Poland and Lithuania were both threatened by German expansion; their dynastic union created a state that was large enough to assert itself internationally. Because of its paganism, Lithuania was constantly subject to attack by the German crusading order of the Teutonic Knights. By converting to Christianity and ordering his subjects to do the same, Wladyslaw hoped to deny the order any justification for continuing its attacks. Poland gained prestige by advancing the cause of Christianity, and because the Lithuanians had often raided Polish territory, it also secured its long eastern border. The only loser by the marriage was Jadwiga herself. She seems to have been very unhappy with Wladyslaw, who was over twenty years her senior, and devoted the rest of her short

EUROPE'S LAST PAGANS

The Lithuanians held to their pagan beliefs long after other European peoples had been converted to Christianity. Attempts by German crusaders to convert the Lithuanians by force only strengthened their determination to remain pagan; Christ was called simply "the German god." Even after their ruler Jagiello converted for political reasons in 1386, pagan beliefs persisted, and many eventually passed into folklore.

The Lithuanians were polytheists who worshiped a pantheon of gods and goddesses, including Pramzimas, the overlord of the gods; the sun goddess Saule, who traveled the sky in a chariot pulled by swans; her daughter Auszrine, the morning star; the moon god Menuo; the sky god Dievas and his wife Zemnya, goddess of the earth; and Laimas, the goddess of fate. Laimas spun the thread of each person's life at birth and attached it to a star. It was believed that when a person died, the thread broke, and the star fell from the sky.

The most popular god was Perkunas, a thunder god who was seen as the protector of Lithuania. The cult statue of Perkunas was said to have held in its hand a precious stone, colored like fire, in the shape of a lightning bolt. The oak tree was held sacred to Perkunas, and a fire of oak wood was kept burning day and night in front of the statue. If the fire ever went out, it had to be rekindled with sparks struck from the stone. Anything that was struck by lightning became sacred to Perkunas, who was worshiped in sacred enclosures built around oak groves. Anyone lucky enough to survive being struck by lightning was honored as someone who was specially favored by Perkunas. The main festival of Perkunas was held at the winter solstice, when a goat was sacrificed to him. The midsummer solstice was a time for religious celebrations that involved ritual bathing and bonfires.

life to charitable work among the poor. When she died in 1399, she had had no children. A childless marriage would have been a reason to terminate the union, but no one wanted a return to succession disputes. Wladyslaw finally had a son, who later became Wladyslaw III, in 1424, by which time he was seventy-two and in his fourth marriage. He died ten years later; his dynasty, called the Jagiellonian after him, would rule Poland-Lithuania until 1572.

Wladyslaw had hoped that Lithuania's official conversion to Christianity would end the attacks by the Teutonic Knights, but instead Poland was drawn into Lithuania's quarrels. The knights claimed that it was their right—rather than that of the Polish church—to oversee the evangelization of the Lithuanians, and so their attacks continued. In 1410 Polish and Lithuanian forces won a stunning victory over the knights at the Battle of Tannenberg. After this battle the Lithuanians concentrated their efforts on eastward expansion and by the mid-fifteenth century had pushed their borders to the Black Sea. Alone, the Poles were unable to follow up their victory. The lands of the knights were protected by many strong castles, and the Poles lacked the resources for prolonged siege warfare.

Further wars followed in 1414 and 1422 and from 1431 through 1435, with little profit to either side. War came yet again in March 1454. Faced with a recruitment crisis, the knights had increased taxes on their subjects so much that rebellions broke out in the major towns. Encouraged by the knights' apparent vulnerability, Poland declared the knights' lands in Prussia annexed. The Poles hoped for a quick victory, but the war dragged on for thirteen long years.

Although one Polish noble complained that "the war had cost the king more than Prussia is worth," the knights were gradually ground down. In 1457 the order's headquarters at Marienburg Castle (Malbork) fell, and peace was finally concluded in 1466. The rich lands of western Prussia, including the important port of Danzig (now Gdańsk), were ceded to Poland. The knights retained their lands around Königsberg (Kaliningrad), but the order's grand masters became vassals of the Polish crown.

The Rise of the *Szlachta*

Poland-Lithuania in the year 1500 covered an area twice the size of France; its vast territory made it the largest kingdom in Europe. Despite its great extent, however, the kingdom was only sparsely peopled (its population of only seven million was around half that of France). The economy of Poland-Lithuania, less developed than those of most western European kingdoms, depended heavily on grain exports. Poland's largest city was the port of Danzig, which had about 35,000 inhabitants in 1500; away from the Baltic coast, towns were few in number and small. Even Poland's capital, Kraków, had only about 14,000 inhabitants.

▶ The union in 1386 of Poland and Lithuania, occasioned by the marriage of their monarchs, fused two already powerful kingdoms into a single formidable state that posed an immediate threat to the Teutonic Order.

THE BATTLE OF TANNENBERG

The victory of the Poles and Lithuanians over the Order of the Teutonic Knights at the Battle of Tannenberg is seen as one of the most important in the history of eastern Europe. The Teutonic Knights were a crusading order of warrior monks. They became involved in the Baltic in 1227 at the invitation of the Polish duke Conrad of Mazowsze (Mazovia), whose lands were threatened by the pagan Prussians. After conquering Prussia, the order began attacks on the pagan Lithuanians and also the Christian Poles. By encouraging German peasant settlement of their conquests, the order contributed greatly to the eastward movement of German cultural influence.

The Battle of Tannenberg was fought near Grünwald on July 15, 1410. At 39,000 strong the Polish-Lithuanian army outnumbered the knights by more than 10,000, but the knights were certainly not intimidated by their opponents' numerical advantage: they had brought twenty carts loaded with shackles for the prisoners they expected to take, and before the battle they sent Wladyslaw II the present of a sword, saying that he was going to need all the help he could get. The knights' confidence was misplaced. How the battle turned against them is not known, but by the end of the day, over half of the Teutonic Knights, including the grand master of the order, were dead. Although they lost no territory as a result of the defeat, the prestige of the order was severely damaged, the knights experienced increasing difficulty in recruiting new members, and German expansion in the east ground to a halt. The grand master of the order became a vassal of the Polish crown in 1466, and the order was finally dissolved in 1525, when the last grand master, Albert of Brandenburg, converted to Lutheranism.

By the nineteenth century the Battle of Tannenberg had come to be seen as an ethnic contest between German and Slav. Germans saw the defeat as a national humiliation that justified their ambitions for territorial expansion in eastern Europe. When the Germans defeated a Russian army at Tannenberg in August 1914, shortly after the outbreak of the First World War, there was national rejoicing that Germany's humiliation by the Slavs had been avenged. In the Second World War, Soviet propagandists, appropriating the first Battle of Tannenberg, presented it as a precursor to the destruction of the German army at Stalingrad in 1942 and the final Russian victory in battle in 1943.

▲ The subject of this highly romanticized painting by the Polish artist Jan Matejko (1838–1893) is the victory of the Poles and Lithuanians over the Teutonic Knights at the Battle of Tannenberg. The painter used this historical subject to express nationalist aspirations at a time when the Polish state had been dismembered by its powerful neighbors.

Under the Piast dynasty that had ruled Poland during the Middle Ages, the right to elect the monarch and sit on the king's advisory council had been confined to around ninety of the leading aristocratic families. The empowerment of the general nobility, or *szlachta*, was begun by Louis I and continued by Wladyslaw, who saw them as a counterbalance to the aristocracy. The *szlachta* provided the core of the royal army, which gave this social group a strong negotiating position. The Privilege of Nieszawa (1454) considerably advanced the *szlachta*'s power by giving the provincial assemblies of nobles *(sejmiki)* the right to raise taxes and call up troops.

Between 1493 and 1496 the Sejm, a national assembly with two chambers, was founded. The lower house was made up of the representatives of the *sejmiki*, while the upper house, or senate, was made up of royal appointees. In 1505 the Nihil Novi constitution gave the Sejm the right to approve all laws. The Union of Lublin greatly enlarged the *szlachta* by extending its privileges to the Lithuanian nobility. The newfound freedom of the nobility was paid for by the peasantry. In the Middle Ages the Polish peasantry had been free tenants, but from the late fifteenth century onward the *szlachta* took advantage of their political power to drive their tenants down into serfdom.

▲ *An unattributed portrait of Katarzyna Lubomirska on the occasion of her marriage to Janusz Ostrogski, prince of Volhynia. This accomplished work, which dates from 1597, is one of the earliest-known examples of Polish portraiture.*

By 1700 the Polish nobility stood alone in Europe in its independence from centralized government control. In 1728 the English writer Daniel Defoe, who came from a kingdom where the nobility had long been subordinate to the crown, voiced his shock at this state of affairs.

In Poland this vanity of birth is carry'd up to such a monstrous extravagance that the name of gentleman and the title of a Starost, a Palatine, or a Castellan gives the man a superiority over all the vassals or common people, infinitely greater than that of King or Emperor, reigning over them with more absolute Power, and making them more miserable than the subjects either of the Grand Sultan or the Khan of Tartary, insomuch that they trample on the poorer people as dogs and frequently murder them: and when they do are accountable to nobody.

For take the nobility and gentry of POLAND ... as they appear in history; in the first place, they are the most haughty, imperious, insulting people in the world. A very valuable historian of our times says they are proud, insolent, obstinate, passionate, furious. These are indeed the born gentlemen. ... Yet if you should ask a Polander what he is he would tell you he is a gentleman of Poland; and so much they value themselves upon the name, that they think they are above being tyed to the rules of honour which are the onely constituting laws of gentlemen.

The Compleat English Gentleman

The End of the Jagiellonian dynasty

Lithuania's conversion to Roman Catholic Christianity may have appeased the western European powers, but it created new enemies in the east. Lithuanian expansion into what are now Belarus and Ukraine brought under its control a substantial population of Orthodox Christians. Non-Catholics were barred from positions of authority in Lithuania; so for many Orthodox nobles, entering the service of Moscow was an attractive option. Since the fall of the Byzantine Empire in 1453, Moscow had seen itself as the champion of Orthodoxy and freeing Orthodox Christians from Catholic rule as a justification for territorial expansion. In 1492 Czar Ivan III (reigned 1462–1505) launched the first of four wars against Lithuania. The Russian advance was halted only with difficulty at the Battle of Orsha in 1514. With the pressure of further devastating Russian attacks in the reign of Ivan IV (usually referred to as Ivan the Terrible; reigned 1533–1584), Poles were called on more and more often to support Lithuania. The Poles in turn demanded the full incorporation of Lithuania into Poland, achieved finally by the Union of Lublin in 1569. Three years later Sigismund II (reigned 1548–1572), the last of the Jagiellonians, died without a male heir.

Renaissance Culture in Poland

Poland was little touched by the influence of the Renaissance until the late fifteenth century, when the Italian humanist scholar Filippo de Buonacorsi, also known as Callimachus, came to teach at Kraków. Italian Renaissance influences became stronger following the marriage of King Sigismund I (reigned 1506–1548) to the Milanese princess Bona Sforza in 1518. Sigismund invited Italian artists and architects to Kraków, and the medieval Wawel Castle was rebuilt in the Italian style. The royal court became a major center of Renaissance culture, and Polish aristocrats and bishops had their palaces decorated with paintings and sculptures that clearly exhibited the Italian influence. The Jagiellonian University at Kraków briefly became the most prestigious center of learning in eastern Europe and attracted scholars from Germany and Italy. With the Renaissance came the first significant Polish vernacular writers, such as the satirist Mikolaj Rej (1505–1569) and the poet Jan Kochanowski (1530–1584). Previously, Polish writers who had wanted to be taken seriously had written in Latin.

Nicolaus Copernicus (1473–1543) was undoubtedly the most important figure of the Polish Renaissance. Copernicus was the first astronomer since ancient times seriously to question the prevailing belief that the earth stood immobile at the center of the universe while the sun and the other planets orbited it. Copernicus's book *On the Revolutions of the Celestial Spheres*, which proposed a heliocentric universe, was published only shortly before his death in 1543. Access to the book was restricted by the Catholic Church in 1616, but through its earlier influence on Galileo and Johannes Kepler, it helped to give birth to modern astronomy.

▼ *Wawel Castle in Kraków was the chief residence of the Polish kings from the early fourteenth century until the capital was moved to Warsaw in 1611. The medieval castle was remodeled in an Italianate style in the early sixteenth century.*

A historic declaration signed on January 28, 1573, gave complete religious freedom to all Christian denominations.

Whereas there is a great dissidence in the affairs of the Christian Religion in our country, and to prevent any sedition for this reason among the people such as we clearly perceive in other realms—we swear to each other, on behalf of ourselves and our descendants, in perpetuity, under oath and pledging our faith, honor and consciences, that we who differ in matters of religion will keep the peace among ourselves, and neither shed blood on account of differences of Faith, or kinds of church, nor punish one another by confiscation of goods, deprivation of honor, imprisonment, or exile.

The Compact of Warsaw

▼ *The great altarpiece in Saint Mary's Cathedral, in Kraków, was carved by the German sculptor Veit Stoss. It is regarded as one of the finest works of art of the Polish Renaissance.*

Reform and Toleration

The Reformation came to Poland at almost the same time as the Renaissance did. The Polish response to the Reformation was religious toleration. The devoutly Catholic Sigismund I at first opposed the spread of Protestantism but soon came to terms with its growing influence, and neither he nor his son, Sigismund II, imposed religious conformity. Lutheranism found many followers in the cities, especially those in the north close to the coast. Calvinism spread among the nobility of Lithuania and central Poland. There was also a homegrown Protestant movement known as the Polish Brethren (or Arians and Anti-Trinitarians), which preached pacifism and social equality. The Sandomierz Agreement of 1570 between Polish Lutherans and Calvinists defended the principle of religious freedom, while the Compact of Warsaw of 1573 made religious toleration the official policy of the Polish state. Despite these Protestant successes, Roman Catholicism remained the religion of the vast majority of the Polish peasantry. Still, with lands containing large numbers of Orthodox Christians and Jews and even a small Muslim Tatar minority, sixteenth-century Polish kings may have ruled the most religiously diverse group of subjects in Europe.

Reformation Poland's population of 150,000 Jews made it home to one of the world's largest Jewish communities. Faced with persecution in Germany during the period of the Crusades, large numbers of Jews had drifted east into Poland, where they enjoyed strong royal protection from the thirteenth century onward. Because a number of the Jews brought with them financial and commercial skills that were lacking in Poland's largely agrarian economy, Jews came to fill the role of a middle class between the nobles and the peasantry. Many of them served the nobility as estate managers and tax collectors. With the cooperation of the crown, Polish Jews gained the right of communal self-government with the setting up of the Council of the Four Lands. The granting of this privilege, however, fed popular anti-Semitism, and Jews were thus required to wear distinctive clothing by which they could be identified.

Religious toleration helped to improve educational standards in Poland. Education was recognized as a way to infuse young people with particular beliefs; consequently, different religious groups set up their own schools. The Catholic Church was particularly astute in this regard. Later in the sixteenth century the Jesuits set up schools of such a high standard that even Protestants sent their children to them. Many of these children became Catholics as a result. In this way the Catholic Counter-Reformation gradually began to gain ground in Poland. The Catholic recovery was also aided by the wars with Lutheran Sweden in the seventeenth century, which encouraged many Protestant Poles to convert as a way of demonstrating their patriotism. Catholic propagandists successfully persuaded many Poles that the difficulties their country was experiencing were the result of "the abominable vice of tolerance." Catholicism had regained its dominant position by the end of the seventeenth century, and in 1718 the policy of religious toleration was abandoned; from then on, Protestants were subjected to various legal disadvantages.

The Republican Commonwealth

The end of the Jagiellonian dynasty in 1572 offered an opportunity for the *szlachta* to assume the dominant role in Polish political life. Poland became a republican commonwealth with a monarch elected directly by the Sejm, in which every noble had a vote. Each new king was presented with the Pacta conventa, which was a contract between the king and the *szlachta* that guaranteed the *szlachta* the right to freely elect the next monarch (in effect, a repudiation of hereditary monarchy), religious toleration, meet-

ings of the Sejm every two years, and the right to renounce their allegiance to the king if he broke the contract. The *szlachta,* guarding its status jealously, restricted election to the ranks of the nobility. However, if it was difficult to gain entry to the *szlachta,* it was virtually impossible to be ejected from it. The *szlachta* insisted on the absolute legal equality of all who possessed noble blood. As a result, a nobleman could fall on hard times and lose all his lands, yet he and his descendants would remain members of the *szlachta.* By 1700 thousands of landless nobles worked as tenant farmers, laborers, and even domestic servants. Known collectively as the *holota* ("rabble"), they remained proud members of the *szlachta,* carried wooden swords if they could not afford the real thing, and displayed their family coat of arms over their cottage door.

▲ This illuminated page is from a Jewish prayer book made in Poland in the sixteenth or seventeenth century. Poland was home to Europe's largest Jewish community during the Renaissance.

KRAKÓW

Kraków was the capital of Poland from 1320 to 1611. The city originated as the stronghold of the Wislanie (Vistulans), one of the Slav tribes united by the Piast dynasty in the tenth century to form the kingdom of Poland. The city became an important commercial and ecclesiastical center in the twelfth century, but in 1241 it was destroyed by the Mongols. Kraków was quickly rebuilt, and in 1257 it became a self-governing municipality. King Wladyslaw I, known as "the Short" (reigned 1305–1333), who reunited Poland after a period of division, chose Kraków as his capital. Thereafter the city's Wawel Castle became the main residence and coronation site for the kings of Poland, while Wawel Cathedral became the royal burial place. The city became Poland's main cultural center after Casimir III founded an academy there in 1364; this institution became a prestigious university under the Jagiellonian kings.

Kraków went into decline after the capital was moved to Warsaw in 1611 but revived after it came under Austrian control in 1795. The city was returned to Poland in 1918. Kraków was one of the very few Polish cities to escape the Second World War without suffering mass destruction, and so much of its medieval and Renaissance architecture survive. Among the most significant Renaissance buildings are Saint Mary's Church (1397), which contains a magnificent altar (created 1477–1489) by Veit Stoss; the royal palace on the Wawel Hill, which dates from the early sixteenth century; and the Cloth Hall (1555) built by the Italian architect Giovanni il Mosca. Kraków was designated a World Heritage Site by the United Nations in 1978.

▼ Pictured below are two of the most important Renaissance structures in Kraków. Both the town hall tower and the Cloth Hall, the center of the city's commerce, were built at the end of the fourteenth century but were extensively remodeled in an Italianate style in 1555 by an Italian architect, Giovanni il Mosca.

The first king of Poland to be directly elected was Henry of Anjou (reigned 1573–1575). Used as he was to the centralist traditions of the French monarchy, Henry could not come to terms with the power of the *szlachta,* and he returned to France the following year. Henry was deposed for abandoning his kingdom, and in his place was elected Stephen Báthory (reigned 1575–1584), an ambitious Hungarian who dreamed of creating a vast eastern European empire by uniting Russia and Hungary with Poland. A condition of Stephen's election was that he marry the daughter of Sigismund II, Anna Jagiellonka, and so preserve a symbolic link with the Jagiellonian dynasty. Stephen, an able soldier, reformed and modernized the Polish army. In 1579 he went to war against Ivan the Terrible and forced Russia to cede Polotsk and Livonia to Poland at the truce of Yam Zapolsky in 1582. Stephen was planning campaigns against the Crimean Tatars and the Ottoman Empire when he died unexpectedly in 1584.

Stephen's successor was Sigismund III Vasa (reigned 1587–1632), grandson of the Swedish king Gustav I Vasa. The Poles hoped that Sigismund's election would lead to a union with Sweden and thus make Poland a major northern European power. Sigismund was a Catholic, however, and therefore barred from succession to the throne in Lutheran Sweden. The religious bar notwithstanding, Sigismund refused to sur-

render his claim, and his efforts to make it good dragged Poland into an inconclusive series of wars with Sweden. Poland also became embroiled in wars against Russia, which was then in the middle of a period of political instability and civil war known as the Time of Troubles. In 1610 a Polish army occupied Moscow. The Muscovite nobility was prepared to accept Sigismund's son Wladyslaw as czar, but the king vetoed the proposal, and so the military success brought no political benefits. Sigismund kept Poland out of the Thirty Years War, but he nonetheless gave diplomatic support to the Catholic Hapsburgs. This support provoked a war with the Ottoman Empire, the Hapsburgs' great rival in the Balkans, that lasted from 1620 to 1621. Poland won the war after initial setbacks.

A major contribution to the Polish success against the Ottomans was made by the Ukrainian Cossacks. The Cossacks felt that their support for the Poles entitled them to be admitted to the *szlachta,* and they became increasingly rebellious when their demand was refused. Sigismund's son and successor, Wladyslaw IV Vasa (reigned 1632–1648), attempted to address Cossack discontent, but the Sejm opposed any concessions, as it feared that the king might use an alliance with the Cossacks to strengthen his authority. In 1648 a major Cossack rebellion broke out under Bohdan Khmelnytsky, and the Poles were driven out of Ukraine. Wladyslaw's death, which occurred shortly after the rebellion broke out, did not help the Poles. Khmelnytsky wanted to create an independent Ukrainian kingdom, but defeat by the Poles in 1651 forced him to submit to Czar Alexis of Russia (reigned 1645–1676). By 1655 Ukraine had been irrevocably lost to Russia.

The Cossack rebellion had a particularly serious impact on Polish Jews. As so many of

This 1688 account of the siege of Jasna Góra, which emphasizes the intervention of the Virgin Mary in the defense of the monastery, demonstrates the extent to which Poles came to equate Catholicism with patriotism during the wars with Sweden.

Jasna Góra was not saved by men. The holy place was preserved by God, and more by miracles than by the sword. A thick mist screened the monastery from attack. Müller [the Swedish commander] himself saw a Lady in a shining robe on the walls, priming the cannon and tossing shells back in the direction from which they came. There were Swedes who froze stiff whenever they put their eye to the sights of their musket, and others whose cheeks stuck to the gun barrel till the surgeon could cut them free.... In the monastery a grenade which landed and exploded in a baby's cradle did not hurt him, whilst in the Swedish camp six gunners were blinded in a single explosion.

Of course no heretic [that is, no Protestant] will believe that cannon-balls were repulsed from the walls of Jasna Góra by supernatural means. But all that I have described is true ...

Wespazjan Kochowski, *Annals of Poland*

▲ *This engraving by Gabriel Bodenehr (1673–1766) depicts the monastery of Jasna Góra under siege by Swedish forces in 1655. The heroic resistance of the garrison against overwhelming odds inspired Polish national resistance to the Swedish invasion.*

them worked for the hated Polish landowners, the Jews were a major target for the rebels. Large numbers of Jews were forced to convert to Christianity, thousands of others were massacred, and still others were sold into slavery among the Tatars. Subsequent outbreaks of anti-Semitic violence became an all-too-common phenomenon in Poland.

While Poland was still reeling from this defeat, another war broke out with Sweden. Concerned by the growth of Russian power, King Charles X Gustav (reigned 1654–1660) used the refusal of Wladyslaw's successor, John II

Casimir Vasa (reigned 1648–1668), to surrender his claim to the Swedish throne as a pretext to invade Poland in 1655. Charles's real aim was to seize control of the commonwealth for himself. The Swedes quickly overran and occupied Poland. Polish opposition to the occupation was limited, but the seemingly miraculous defense of a fortified monastery at Jasna Góra against a superior Swedish force inspired a national resistance movement. In 1660 the exhausted Swedes withdrew.

Poland recovered some prestige after King John III Sobieski (reigned 1674–1696) relieved Vienna from a siege by the Ottomans in 1683, but afterward the country was in constant decline, its territory fought over by neighboring powers. In 1795 Poland's remaining territory was partitioned among Russia, Prussia, and Austria, and the country disappeared from the map of Europe until 1918.

FURTHER READING

Davies, N. *God's Playground: A History of Poland.* Oxford, 1981.

Lukowski, J., and H. Zawadzki. *A Concise History of Poland.* Cambridge, UK, 2001.

John Haywood

SEE ALSO
• Copernicus, Nicolaus • Ivan IV Vasilyevich
• Judaism • Lutheranism • Sweden

Popular Culture

A REGION OR NATION'S POPULAR CULTURE IS THE CULTURE OF THE COMMON FOLK—ORDINARY PEOPLE— AS OPPOSED TO THAT OF THE ARISTOCRACY OR THE WELL-EDUCATED.

When applied to medieval and early modern Europe, *popular culture*—literally, the culture of the populace—refers to the culture of the great majority of the population, who were neither aristocrats nor gentry nor wealthy townsfolk but who were instead mostly rural, uneducated, and comparatively poor people. Yet the term can be misleading because there was no single monolithic culture: the culture of Basque fishermen, for instance, was different from that of Scottish farmers; the culture of women was different from that of men; and the culture of the old was different from that of the young. Perhaps it is best, then, to think of *popular culture* as a sort of shorthand term for a network of overlapping, interactive cultures that varied according to region, occupation, age, and gender.

▶ *Peasants sometimes attributed the attacks of particularly cunning, savage wolves to werewolves, as illustrated by this woodcut,* The Werewolf *(c. 1512), by Lucas Cranach the Elder. Despite the werewolf's sinister reputation, a few people actually believed that they were werewolves and claimed to do good work. In the seventeenth century an old "werewolf" from Livonia (present-day Latvia and Estonia) testified that he and his fellows spent their time thwarting the evil deeds of witches.*

The Culture of the Common Folk

Despite their diversity, premodern popular cultures shared several important characteristics. First and perhaps most important, popular cultures were preliterate, and so the people handed down their traditions, attitudes, and beliefs through spoken words. Consequently, popular cultures lacked the uniformity imposed by written records; instead, local, regional, and geographical variations were the norm. Very different terms of existence separated the lower classes from the rich and powerful and imposed other basic differences between popular and elite cultures. Most members of the aristocracy lived relatively safe from the dangers of starvation and violence; theirs was a culture of comfort and security. For the common folk, on the other hand, life was typically short and hard; theirs was a culture of pervasive anxiety.

All peasants were intimately familiar with real hunger, since frosts, floods, droughts, and blights brought scarcity and hardship and, at least once or twice each generation, devastating famines. Malnutrition left people susceptible to diseases of all kinds, from which the young especially suffered an appalling mortality. Wolves were yet another common threat, particularly during hard winters. So reliable did wolf attacks become that in a notorious incident around 1420, a French noble known as the Bastard of Vaurus ordered a young pregnant girl suspected of some crime to be tied to a tree outside the town walls of Meaux; when she gave birth, the wolves came, and she and her child were eaten. Foxes might have presented an even greater danger than wolves, since they carried rabies—a horrible disease for which there was no cure; for this reason, it was the unhappy duty of relatives to smother to death infected victims before they could become a danger to others. Add to these the dangers of robbers, rampaging armies, childbirth, and the countless possible accidents to which the common folk were prone, and it is easy to understand that the dread of danger—both real and imagined—was simply a part of daily life. Popular cultures reflect this insecurity in a variety of ways.

While the celebrations and revelry that accompanied a wedding provided a kind of communal sanction for a marriage, the charivari in France (whence the English word *shivaree*) and the skimmington in England were obvious expressions of collective disapproval. Often when an old man married a young girl, or an older woman a young man, or a girl married a man from outside her community, a band of young, unmarried men, perhaps wearing masks or costumes, met the couple on their way to church and demanded money in exchange for passage. If the money was not forthcoming (and sometimes even if it was), the youths harassed the couple with shouts of ridicule, loud noises ("rough music"), a barrage of garbage, and much jostling and petty vandalism.

Village youths handed out similar treatment to those whose behavior violated accepted social norms or disturbed the general peace. Men who drank to excess or were suspected of homosexual inclinations and wives who dominated their husbands or were suspected of adultery were forced to wear silly costumes and ride a donkey backward through the streets, to the accompaniment of jeers, rude noises, loud music, and man-handling. In May, "women's month," when wife beating was supposedly prohibited, men who broke the rule might also be subject to this ritual shaming.

Although humiliating for the victims, charivaris made the social expectations of the community quite clear: people knew and cared about what others did and were prepared to take steps to ensure that behavior did not transgress acceptable bounds. The charivari also provided peasants with a custom that could be adapted to express protests of other kinds. Thus, in France the charivari eventually became primarily a form of political protest inflicted upon unpopular politicians and government officials. Similarly, in Naples in 1585, a despised local official was ridden through the streets backward and hatless prior to his lynching.

▲ In this scene from the comic poem Hudibras, illustrated by William Hogarth (1697–1764), the hero encounters a raucous skimmington: a henpecked man is seated behind his wife on a horse, facing backwards, and is enduring much loud mockery and abuse.

Communities and Neighborhoods

In most places the common folk lived in simple nuclear households, usually consisting of a man and wife, their children, and perhaps a few other relatives besides, in a small house with few rooms. They had no privacy to speak of. A cluster of households, a parish church, a mill, and a few other structures made up the village, a tightly integrated community bound together with a dense web of social ties, the bonds of kinship, marriage, godparentage, friendship, neighborliness, and economic cooperation among them. The common folk lived their whole lives in close contact with a small circle of neighbors, friends, and kin, among whom they were born, worked, played, courted, married, and died. It is almost impossible to overstate the importance of these social relations. In a world fraught with dangers, people depended upon their neighbors and relatives for the only security

that they could find; hence the corresponding importance of social solidarity and harmony.

Public performances (rites of passage) and their accompanying sacraments—baptism, matrimony, and extreme unction—marked the stages of a peasant's life. Birth was the first performance; by long-established custom men were not present at birth, but the women congregated around the fellow villager in childbirth, the most knowledgeable among them acting as midwives. Birth was extremely dangerous for mother and child, and midwives employed a whole battery of charms and prayers to safeguard them both. Baptism was a second important public performance, during which an infant received exorcism, a blessing, a name, godparents, and recognition as a new member of the community.

Childhood ended with marriage, but not too soon—married couples had to be an economically viable social unit, and thus, peasants usually did not marry until their late teens. The decision to marry was most often collective, the result of negotiations involving the couple, their families,

their neighbors, and the local church. The wedding ceremonies revealed the communal nature of this process: the engagement, the announcements, the ceremony itself outside the local church, and the subsequent celebratory feast all involved the community, and to leave someone out was a serious insult.

Death was the last performance, and it was as public and communal as birth and marriage. Dying in the modern world is usually private and enclosed within a hospital or a special facility, but in the Middle Ages and Renaissance the dying were constantly attended by family and friends. A priest administered the last sacrament, and then bells at last announced the moment of death to the whole community. Before the corpse was buried, the village held a wake, a memorial party with the deceased as the guest of honor to remind everyone that in life he or she had been a welcome, valued member of the community. Burial in the churchyard followed, but the dead remained very much a part of the community, regularly remembered and honored.

▲ *Peasant weddings were important communal celebrations marked by eating, drinking, and revelry, although perhaps not generally to the extent pictured in this portrayal of rustic fun, The Kermesse, by Peter Paul Rubens (1577–1640).*

► *Agricultural scenes were popular illustrations for late medieval and Renaissance devotional texts. Sheep shearing, which took place in May or June, is depicted in the* Book of Hours of the Blessed Virgin, *produced in France in 1475 by an unknown artist.*

The Seasons of the Year

Peasant life was naturally cyclical, attuned to the rhythms of the agricultural year and the regular sequence of plowing, sowing, and harvesting. Broadly speaking, the year was divided into two, with an agricultural and secular half running from May through November and a sacred half from December through April. Festivals, both sacred and secular, punctuated the changing seasons of the year.

By December most of the year's agricultural tasks were done, and with Advent people began to prepare for both the celebration of Jesus's birth and the onset of cold weather. For most European peasants, there was comparatively little to do during this time of year, and so on winter evenings women gathered by the fire in a large home to spin, sew, and socialize. Young men with an eye on the younger women might attend as well, as occasionally did older men. During these parties, called *veillées* in France and *Spinnstuben* in Germany, people told stories— folktales, legends, histories, and personal anecdotes—and passed on the whole oral lore of the village to the next generation.

In northern Europe peasants celebrated the darkest days of midwinter and the gradual return of longer days with fire festivals on the feast days of Saint Nicholas (December 6) or Saint Lucy (December 13). The rest of Europe waited to celebrate until Christmas, a time of joy, eating, drinking, singing, and games that lasted for the canonical twelve days until the feast of the Epiphany. In February carnival was another time of riotous play and celebration that ended abruptly with the penances and austerities of Lent. These came to an end in turn with the triumphant celebration of Christ's resurrection at Easter, the spiritual high point of the year.

Popular secular festivities began in May with May Day, a festival usually associated with fertility and courtship. The young people of many communities elected a May queen to supervise the celebrations. In France young men planted trees or bushes *(mais)* in front of houses containing eligible girls—the kind of plant provided a clue to the girl's desirability. Elsewhere, from England to Russia, young people danced around that venerable symbol of fertility, the maypole (there is, however, no evidence that people actually thought of these flower-garlanded poles as phallic symbols; more probably, they represented simply the return of flowers and spring). Reform-minded aristocrats viewed this open celebration of human sexuality with distaste and alarm: the Elizabethan Protestant Philip Stubbes, for example, remarked, quite wrongly, that if a hundred maidens set out to May, "scarcely the third part of them returned home undefiled" (*Anatomie of Abuses*, 1583).

The secular festivities reached their culmination on Saint John's Night (June 24), the festival of midsummer, with bonfires, masking, dancing, and games. For the remainder of the summer, most peasants had work to do, at least until harvest festivals began in the fall. In Catholic countries All Souls' Day (November 2) was an important celebration, a time when the dead were remembered with prayers and acts of charity. In many communities but especially in parts of Britain, children and the village poor went door to door and offered their prayers for the departed in return for small presents of food and drink (the custom was called "souling" and is the likely origin of trick-or-treating on modern Halloween).

CARNIVAL AND LENT

Lent, the forty days preceding Easter, was a period of spiritual preparation and renewal. All Christians were supposed to confess their sins, attend sermons, abstain from sex, avoid sin, and eat no meat, milk, or eggs. Immediately before Lent, people celebrated carnival, or Shrovetide as it was known in England. This festival involved food, drink, sex, and violence—everything that Lent prohibited. During carnival people ate and drank to enormous excess, danced, played games, donned costumes and masks, and generally behaved in ways completely contrary to the dictates of prudence and religion.

The lord of the carnival, a jovial fat man or his effigy, presided over this madness, assisted by his elected officers, kings and abbots of misrule. Carnival was a time of inversion, when children taught school, altar boys presided at Mass, and fools became kings; meanwhile, priests dressed up in women's clothes, played cards, and ate sausages. Entertainments included ball games, races, fights and mock combats, obscene processions, and songs. In France unmarried girls had to pull a plow through town. Fights and insults were also very common: an English visitor to Venice in the sixteenth century recorded that during carnival, seventeen were killed and many more wounded besides. In London young men's vandalism and violence were said to be as common as pancakes (a very popular carnival food). Carnival culminated with Fat Tuesday (Mardi Gras, or Shrove Tuesday), often with a ritual battle between the lord of carnival and Lent, a tall, skinny, unattractive woman. Ultimately, carnival was defeated, and either his effigy or a fat pig in its place was roasted on the bonfire.

Some see carnival as a sort of lingering pagan festivity, and certainly there was little obviously Christian about it. More important, though, than any archaic pagan connotations was the opportunity carnival afforded to do the forbidden, to flout convention and social controls, and to turn the rigid social hierarchy on its head. Breaking rules and transgressing social boundaries also served to remind people exactly where the boundaries were and why there were rules in the first place. The common people were delighted to imagine the world turned upside down, with the inversion of everyday rules and norms. These inversions provided opportunities for social protest, for "blowing off steam," and for dealing with the anxieties of daily life. For these reasons, even in northern Europe, where carnival never achieved the same popularity as in the south, similar sorts of inversions, excesses, and social transgressions marked other popular holidays, most notably Christmas and the Feast of Fools, which was celebrated on January 1.

▲ *Pieter Bruegel the Elder (c. 1525–1569) captures the riotous excess of Shrove Tuesday in the sixteenth-century Netherlands in* The Struggle between Carnival and Lent, *1559. The captains in the foreground are attended by their respective followers—fools, drunkards, and gluttons on the side of carnival and the virtuous and censorious on the side of Lent.*

Popular Religion

The peasants and common folk of late medieval and early modern Europe were overwhelmingly orthodox, practicing Christians. They went to confession and took communion at least once each year, they went to church and heard Mass on most Sundays, and they were expected to know the Creed, the Ten Commandments, and the Lord's Prayer, which they were sometimes tested on during confession. Yet theirs was a more inclusive, less systematic, more "magical" religion than that officially prescribed by the church. Even manuals of instruction drawn up by the clergy for the benefit of lay folk emphasized not what a Christian ought to believe but what he or she ought to do. This policy was a pragmatic one because for most peasants the bases of Christianity lay in seasonal ritual performances and not in theologically determined sets of beliefs. Indeed, peasants could sometimes be disturbingly vague about what constituted acceptable Christian belief. One northern Italian miller, for example, ran afoul of the Inquisition when he argued that the world had emerged out of a gob of fermenting cheese. In the French bishopric of Lyon, people spontaneously began to venerate the memory of a heroic dog, now presumed to be at God's right hand, and prayed to him to heal infants. The cult of Saint Guinefort, the Holy Greyhound, appealed so tenaciously to popular imagination that, despite the efforts of the Inquisition, his miracles and cult were still remembered in the nineteenth century. Peasants needed all the help they could get, and as Guinefort's cult illustrates, they would turn to any plausible, reliable source of divine power regardless of official sanction. Local parish priests in particular had to walk an uncomfortably narrow line between the demands of their superiors for orthodoxy and local expectations that priests deploy their spiritual power in practical, utilitarian ways. Most tried to keep all important aspects of devotion under official control while at the same time agreeing to bless the fields and the animals; bless salt, water, and wax for domestic use; ring church bells to divert storms; and send the troublesome walking dead to their rest.

▶ *Childbirth in the Middle Ages and Renaissance was an entirely feminine domain to which men were not admitted, an essential fact neatly captured in* Le nouveau-né (The Newborn), *by Georges de La Tour (1593–1652). The absence of masculine control over so important an event caused considerable anxiety to early modern authorities, who tried with limited success to force midwives to act as their agents.*

Medieval and early modern ghosts usually walked abroad only when they required something of the living. Ghosts might have "unfinished business," such as an unpaid debt, that prevented them from finding rest, or they might require prayers or acts of charity to help them leave the torments of purgatory and find bliss in heaven. Still another possibility is illustrated in the story of Richard Roundtree, as recorded by a Yorkshire monk around the year 1400. One night, while keeping watch, Richard saw a strange procession coming down the road: a company of the dead was riding by, some mounted on horses, others on cows or sheep. Bringing up the rear was a small boy rolling along the ground in a shoe. When Richard asked who the child was, the infant replied that he was none other than Richard's own son, "stillborn without baptism and buried without a name." Understandably upset, Richard wrapped the child in his own shirt and named him, whereupon the infant happily walked off to rejoin the procession, leaving Richard to seek further explanations from his wife.

Denied baptism, buried in secret, not even acknowledged by his own family as a complete human being, Richard's son had never had a place among the normal community of the living and was similarly excluded from the dead. He was lucky, however, because when his father retroactively accepted him into the community through gifts of clothing and a name, the dead accepted him as well, and his spirit could continue its journey into the next world. The story provides an unusual example of the power of ritual to define boundaries and place in peasant communities, but it is not the only one. In Italy in 1681, the Inquisition investigated a number of women who claimed to be able to bring dead babies back to life just long enough to receive baptism. There is also evidence that not all ghost babies were as sweet tempered as Richard's son: in several medieval books of penance, the clergy condemn "wicked women" who secretly buried dead infants with a stake through their little heart to prevent them from rising from the grave.

The Reformation and the Peasants

The people of traditional early modern agricultural communities were pious Christians; their religion played a vital role in their lives and served their most important needs well. Owing to their strong beliefs and their instinctive conservatism, peasants generally resisted the innovations of the Reformation. Yet they were certainly not uniformly satisfied with the status quo: they objected to ignorant, absent, or immoral priests; chafed under the burdens of tithes; and resented the intrusions (and punishments) of ecclesiastical courts. Peasants also tended to look to God and the church to end social injustice. Variations of the rhyme "When Adam delved and Eve span, who was then a nobleman?" were found in most European languages, and many of the common folk assumed that Christ would abolish the evil of social distinctions before the end of days. This conflict between innate conservatism and a deep desire for social change (although always conceived in peasant minds as a return to the "good old days") helps to explain why the so-called popular Reformation fared differently throughout Europe. Usually, however, the religious preferences of the peasants really mattered very little, since most decisions affecting official religion would be made by their lords. For this reason, the Reformation was most successful in communities under the jurisdiction of rulers who were themselves Protestant.

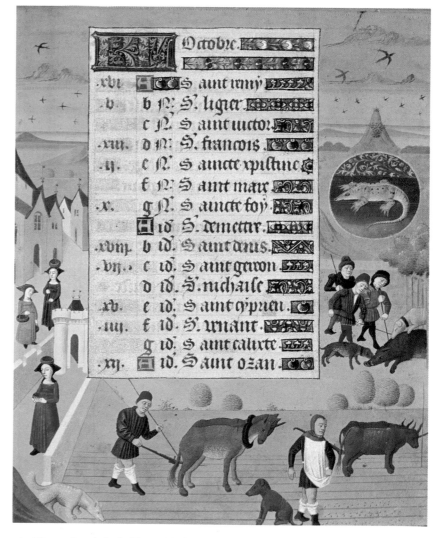

▲ This scene from the Book of Hours of Duchess Mary of Burgundy (1477) depicts peasants plowing the fields in October in preparation for the planting of winter grain while their more aristocratic neighbors hunt wild boar.

In most such places, the rural peasantry eventually embraced Protestantism, as Protestant ministers replaced parish priests and official support for most Catholic ritual practices ceased. Because of the peasantry's habitual conservatism, however, thorough conversion often took place only after several generations and required a degree of compromise from local ministers.

In other places, particularly where pastoral care was perceived as inadequate, peasants sometimes acted on their own. Peasants were not, however, usually too concerned with theological controversy or the details of salvation theory; they had more practical concerns. In 1523 the German village of Wendelstein wearied of a series of negligent, incompetent, and litigious parish priests and hired their own "Christian preacher," a Lutheran, to care for their needs. Despite this first step toward Reformed Christianity, however, the village later accepted a new Catholic priest, provided that he "live the gospel in [his] deeds" and live within his means. Like most villagers, the people of Wendelstein wanted religion that was good and cheap; other things were secondary.

Regardless of their religious preferences, the common folk used the traditional idioms available to them to express their opinions. For example, in the German town of Buchholz in 1524, Protestants subjected an image of the pope to a kind of charivari by placing it on a dung carrier and parading about town before throwing the image into a fountain. Elsewhere, effigies of the pope and priests replaced the figures of

▲ *Peasants lived for holidays. The amusements depicted in this work by the Flemish painter Pieter Balten (c. 1525–1598) were otherwise altogether foreign to peasants' daily life.*

FOOTBALL

Peasants regularly made time for entertainments and pastimes, and by the late Middle Ages football was especially popular. On holidays rival teams met in the open fields between their villages to play. Rules varied widely from place to place, but there were seldom set limits on the size of the playing field or the number of people on the teams (every able-bodied young man was expected to play), and the games usually lasted until dark. For a ball the men used a pig's bladder filled with dried peas. The object of the game was to move the ball across the opponent's goal line by some combination of throwing, kicking, and running. There were few fouls. In some parts of England, rules distinguished between civil play—in which wrestling and kicking were allowed—and rough play, in which competitors could also use their fists.

Unsurprisingly, these games were violent and dangerous in the extreme, and this casual acceptance of violence is a notable aspect of early modern popular culture. In Dorset, in southwestern England, players each year contributed to an accident fund to pay for the funerals of those unluckily killed during play. Parents and spectators also sometimes joined in the melee: in 1598 a brawl broke out among the players in an English village football game, whereupon the father of one of the players, a respectable man in his fifties, waded in and beat two boys to death with the pommel of his dagger (though he was subsequently acquitted of murder). The thuggish violence of football so offended aristocratic sensibilities that in his 1531 work *The Book Named the Governor*, Thomas Elyot condemned the sport as "nothing but beastly fury and extreme violence" and in consequence entirely unsuitable for "all noble men." Nonetheless, the games served useful functions beyond simple entertainment. In village football games young men bonded, gained prestige and a sense of identity, learned the rewards of teamwork, and acquired the inevitable badges of honor—bruises, scars, and broken bones. Indeed, football served social functions in the peasant community that were very similar to battle and tournaments among young aristocrats.

Death or Judas during Lenten processions. On the other hand, when England's Henry VIII (reigned 1509–1547) defied the church of Rome and divorced his Spanish Catholic queen, Catherine of Aragon, a Spanish town replaced the whore of Babylon in its carnival parade with an image of the king's new queen, Anne Boleyn.

Transformations of Popular Culture

Although popular culture refers to the culture of the common people, the common and the privileged members of society did regularly interact. Nobles visited taverns, bishops inquired into the beliefs of rural parishioners, and wealthy merchants danced in the streets at carnival. At the same time, the common people observed aristocratic dress and manners, listened to occasional learned sermons, and went to courts for discipline and instruction. Most modern scholars argue that the interaction between social classes was most frequent and intense during the Middle Ages; as nobles embraced education, civility, and manners as status markers, they retreated from popular culture and restricted social exchange between themselves and the common people. For the educated the world gradually became a less magical place, in which the understandable and impersonal forces of nature replaced the direct actions of God, demons, and other sentient beings. This process was famously described by the sociologist and historian Max Weber (1864–1920) as the *Entzauberung der Welt* ("disenchantment of the world").

Both Catholic and Protestant clerics waged a full-scale war on what they regarded as popular superstition and tried to force traditional communities to conform to their own standards of religious devotion. Secular authorities cracked down upon the anarchy they saw rampant in peasant culture: they reined in the excesses of carnival, the violence of peasant games, and the (alleged) promiscuity of May Day. The precise targets of this assault on popular culture differed from place to place, as did the degree of its success. Almost everywhere, though, popular cultures gradually evolved in response to social interactions: literacy became more widespread, religious beliefs evolved, and the influence of the magical universe was slowly constricted.

◄ *Early modern aristocrats relentlessly mocked what they considered to be the credulity and superstition of the peasants. Here, in the 1799 etching* What a Tailor Can Do! *Francisco Goya (1746–1828) shows a mob of peasants on bended knee offering penance to a mendicant's robe left hanging carelessly on a tree.*

FURTHER READING

Burke, Peter. *Popular Culture in Early Modern Europe.* New York, 1978.

Harris, Tim, ed. *Popular Culture in England, c. 1500–1850.* New York, 1995.

Hutton, Ronald. *Stations of the Sun.* Oxford, 1997.

Muchembled, Robert. *Popular Culture and Elite Culture in France, 1400–1750.* Translated by Lydia Cochran. Baton Rouge, LA, 1985.

Muir, Edward. *Ritual in Early Modern Europe.* 2nd ed. New York, 2005.

Scribner, Robert. *Popular Culture and Popular Movements in Reformation Germany.* London, 1987.

Hans Peter Broedel

SEE ALSO
• Astrology • Bruegel, Pieter • German Towns
• Henry VIII • Heresy • Households • Magic
• Peasants' Revolts • Printing • Reformation
• Women

Population

AFTER CATASTROPHIC DECLINES IN THE 1300s, THE POPULATION OF EUROPE STABILIZED IN THE 1400s AND GREW AFTER 1500. IT FINALLY REGAINED ITS PRE-1300s LEVELS BY THE OPENING OF THE 1600s.

The arrival of the Black Death in Europe during the late 1340s transformed the demographic history of Europe and shaped both the Renaissance and the Reformation. When the Black Death first appeared in 1347, it devastated a population that had been expanding for over three centuries. Since the year 1000 the growing population had transformed the European landscape from a series of relatively isolated settlements in a vast expanse of forest and wasteland into a dense network of settlements tied together by market towns and cities. Indeed, the best estimates indicate that between the years 1000 and 1300 the population of Europe nearly doubled, to between 75 and 80 million people. This long-term expansion started to put serious strains on

European society, as agricultural production could not keep up with the needs of the population especially in years when the harvest was poor. In many places this imbalance led to chronic food shortages. For instance, the region surrounding Paris experienced a series of food crises: from 1315 to 1322, in 1328 and 1334, and in 1341 and 1342.

The Black Death dramatically halted the growth in population. It consisted of two related diseases, the bubonic and pneumonic plagues, both of which are caused by the same bacterium, *Yersinia pestis,* an organism found mainly in rodent populations. The primary means of contracting the bubonic plague was through the bite of a flea. Thus, under normal conditions the plague only rarely made the leap from rodents to humans, as it required a flea to bite both an infected rat and then a human. However, if an infected flea did bite a human, the plague bacteria could quickly multiply in the human body. Once the infection reached the lungs, it became possible to transmit the bacteria directly to other people. The pneumonic plague is distinguished

▶ Life in the Countryside, *an oil by the Flemish painter Jan Brueghel the Elder (1568–1625). This bustling village scene includes depictions of the varied tasks that made up daily life for the rural population of northern Europe.*

The following extract is drawn from a popular medical treatise written by a practicing doctor. The writer seeks first to explain in quasi-astrological terms how the plague originated and spread and then to give practical instructions on how to avoid contracting it. His advice is typical of the approach to medicine in the fourteenth and fifteenth centuries.

Everything below the moon, the elements and the things compounded of the elements, is ruled by the things above, and the highest bodies are believed to give being, nature, substance, growth and death to everything below their spheres. It was, therefore, by the influence of heavenly bodies that the air was recently corrupted and made pestilential.... The result was a widespread epidemic, traces of which still remain in several places. Many people have been killed, especially those stuffed full of evil humours, for the cause of the mortality is not only the corruption of the air, but the abundance of corrupt humours within those who die of the disease.... As a result, cleansed bodies, where the purgation of evil humours has not been neglected, remain healthy. Likewise those whose complexion is contrary to the immutable complexion of air remain healthy. For otherwise everybody would fall ill and die whenever the air is corrupted.

You should avoid over-indulgence in food and drink, and also avoid baths and everything which might rarefy the body and open the pores, for the pores are the doorways through which poisonous air can enter, piercing the heart and corrupting the life force. Above all sexual intercourse should be avoided. You should eat little or no fruit, unless it is sour, and should consume easily digested food and spiced wine diluted with water. Avoid mead and everything else made with honey and season food with strong vinegar. In cold or rainy weather you should light fires in your chamber and in foggy or windy weather you should inhale aromatics every morning before leaving home: ambergris, musk, rosemary and similar things if you are rich; zedoarcy, cloves, nutmeg, mace and similar things if you are poor.

John of Burgundy

from the bubonic plague by this direct transmission of the plague bacteria. In pneumonic plague the lungs were the initial point of infection, and the victim usually came into contact with the bacteria by inhaling it in water vapor from an already infected person's cough. The victim of pneumonic plague was infectious to others almost from the moment he or she contracted the disease.

Medieval medicine could offer no protection from either form of the disease. Doctors were able to identify diseases through their symptoms—the appearance of swellings, or buboes, being a key early symptom of the bubonic plague—but did not understand their underlying causes and could therefore devise little in the way of effective treatment. Medical thought focused on the idea that the body was made up of four substances, or humors, that needed to be kept in balance to maintain health; disease occurred when a person had too much or too little of one of the humors.

While both pneumonic and bubonic plague were potentially deadly, the pneumonic plague was probably more responsible for the very high death toll during the fourteenth century because

it spread more easily among the population and killed a higher percentage of its victims. By 1351 between a quarter and a third of the population of Europe had perished, and in more heavily populated areas, such as parts of England and northern Italy, closer to half the population died. The initial devastation wrought by the Black Death was followed by further deadly outbreaks, which continued into the seventeenth century.

▲ *In stark contrast to the thriving scene on the facing page, Jan's father, Pieter Bruegel the Elder, offers a grim vision of country life in* The Triumph of Death *(c. 1560). Sudden, early death from disease, famine, and war remained a constant threat in early modern Europe.*

The Stagnant Fifteenth Century

Europe's population experienced little immediate recovery following the initial outbreak of the Black Death. Half a century later, in 1400, the population of Europe stood at around 52 million people, far smaller than the estimated 75 to 80 million people prior to the Black Death. The collapse in population had a profound impact on the landscape, as whole villages were abandoned, towns shrank in size, and the amount of land farmed declined. For instance, in France perhaps a fifth of the land cultivated in the opening half of the fourteenth century was abandoned in the decades following the Black Death.

For a century following the outbreak of the Black Death, Europe experienced an unstable fluctuation in the population without any meaningful long-term growth. Continued high mortality rates from disease played a role in this ongoing stagnation. Moreover, while survivors enjoyed less competition for land and rising wages owing to the scarcity of labor, these advantages were often outweighed by the economic disruption caused by the death of so many people. Thus, while land was available for survivors, the markets for their products had often disappeared or shrunk.

The Sixteenth-Century Recovery

Only after 1450 did the population of Europe achieve sustained growth again, ultimately regaining and then surpassing levels reached in the opening half of the fourteenth century. During this period lands abandoned in the aftermath of the Black Death were reoccupied, and in low-lying areas, such as Holland, marshes were drained for the first time for farming. Cities, which had in many cases sustained their populations through inward migration despite the Black Death, grew even more rapidly than the overall population. By the opening of the sixteenth century, many had surpassed the size they had been in the early 1300s. The needs of these cities had an effect on the surrounding countryside as farmers increasingly specialized in producing food for the cities instead of merely seeking to grow enough food for their families.

By the opening quarter of the seventeenth century, Europe was reaching population levels that strained the capacity of the agricultural system to sustain them. Although population growth began to stagnate in some regions, by the second half of the seventeenth century, Europe once again faced food crises associated with overpopulation.

POPULATION GROWTH DURING THE SIXTEENTH CENTURY

After a century of decline, the overall population of Europe began to expand during the late fifteenth century and continued to expand into the opening half of the seventeenth century. Between 1500 and 1650 Europe's population rose from around 61 million to nearly 75 million and thus regained levels last seen before the arrival of the Black Death in the 1340s. However, as this table indicates, the population growth did not occur evenly. While the population of northern and western Europe nearly doubled and that of central and eastern Europe experienced moderate growth, the region along the Mediterranean Sea experienced only a very small rise in its population. One reason for this disparity may have been the already high concentrations of people living in the Mediterranean region compared with the number of people in northern Europe. Moreover, the overall numbers mask structural changes in the population, especially the rising proportion of the population living in urban rather than rural environments in the 1500s and 1600s.

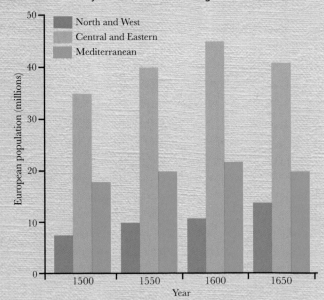

The Malthusian Cycle in Europe

Scholars studying the demographic history of Europe have drawn heavily on the theories of the English economist Thomas Robert Malthus (1766–1834) to explain why Europe's population collapsed in the fourteenth century, only to recover by the seventeenth century. Malthus argued that the supply of food effectively limited the size of premodern populations, something no longer true in modern Europe, where technology, transportation, and medicine have practically eliminated the risk of death from a shortage of food. According to Malthus, populations in the premodern world naturally grew until they overstretched their food supplies. Then, usually after a poor harvest, the population collapsed under the combined pressures of famine and outbreaks of disease that took an unusually heavy toll on the malnourished. After such a collapse Malthus predicted that a population would recover again as food became more plentiful for the survivors. While Europeans were able in part to alleviate the worst effects of this Malthusian cycle, it was an accurate predictor of population patterns in Europe until the nineteenth century.

European population history during the Renaissance and Reformation was defined by two periods of sustained growth, from 1000 to 1300 and from 1450 to 1600, each of which was followed by population decline and stagnation. Studies reveal that as Europe's population reached the limits of its ability to produce food, a series of unexpectedly poor harvests, often brought on by bad weather, created food shortages that drove prices up either in specific regions or across much of the continent. The poorest members of communities could no longer afford enough food and became malnourished. The death rate increased not only through starvation but also—and perhaps even more noteworthy—because people were left vulnerable in the face of disease. The very young and the old in these communities tended to suffer the most, since they were particularly susceptible.

▲ *Victims of famine lie unburied in open countryside in this illumination from* Les chroniques d'Angleterre, *produced in the late fifteenth century by Jean de Wavrin.*

The overall population of Europe during these crises was put under further pressure because of declining birthrates. Three reasons lay behind the decline in births. First, malnourished mothers were less likely to have successful pregnancies. Second, the loss of spouses reduced the pool of families producing children. Third, unmarried members of the community were more likely to postpone marriage during times of famine and disease. Collectively, the lack of food, the spread of disease, and the reduced number of births led to a collapse in the population. This collapse might also be accompanied by warfare or other forms of disorder that resulted from the stresses of famine and epidemic. While one can identify certain periods, such as the 1340s, when these trends occurred across much of the conti-

nent, individual regions that either were overpopulated or that experienced prolonged weather problems could also undergo a collapse in population even if the rest of the continent did not suffer to the same extent.

However, as Malthus predicted, evidence indicates that populations ultimately recovered in Europe. Those who survived famine and the subsequent spread of diseases found less pressure on resources and enhanced opportunities for financial and material self-improvement, a situation that led to better survival rates. It also led to increased marriage at younger ages and thus a higher birthrate as couples produced more children. Over the long run high birthrates made up for the loss of population until the population reached the limits of its resources once again.

Malthus's mechanism for population correction takes on a human dimension in light of such an account as the following, wherein an unidentified eyewitness provides a description of the great famine of 1315.

The people were in such great need that it cannot be expressed. For the cries that were heard from the poor would move a stone, as they lay in the streets with woe and great complaint, swollen with hunger and remaining dead of poverty, so that many were thrown by set numbers, sixty and even more, into a pit.

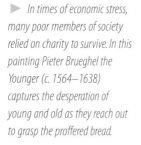

► In times of economic stress, many poor members of society relied on charity to survive. In this painting Pieter Brueghel the Younger (c. 1564–1638) captures the desperation of young and old as they reach out to grasp the proffered bread.

Human Actions and Malthus's Cycle

Population levels are driven by three factors: mortality rates (the number of deaths in a community), fertility rates (the number of births in a community), and migration. While most scholars agree that Malthus's cycle played a critical role in defining the population levels of Renaissance and Reformation Europe, some modern historians have also noted that human intervention in the form of governmental action, social customs, and economic forces also shaped population levels and even moderated the full effects of Malthus's cycle.

In terms of mortality rates, modern scholars have confirmed that famine and disease had profound effects on population levels, as Malthus predicted. However, these studies have also shown that the scarcity of food on its own did not decide how devastating a toll a famine took on the population. Two other factors must be taken into account. First, the types of epidemic diseases that spread in afflicted regions had a key impact on the mortality rates. Thus, the arrival of the Black Death during a period of overpopulation and famine had a devastating effect on overall population in the 1340s and 1350s, while in other periods famine took a smaller toll because less-deadly epidemic diseases spread among the malnourished and weakened population. This natural variable in mortality rates fits within Malthus's theory, but a second variable identified by modern historians shows that people could intervene to moderate the effects of famine as well. As a result, Europeans were not completely at the mercy of natural forces in the way Malthus's theory implied they would be. In some cases well-organized governments were able to alleviate the worst effects of a crisis by, for instance, organizing the purchase and transportation of food for a city or quarantining infected households to limit the spread of a disease. These human interventions had a noticeable impact on the death rates during famines.

Modern historians have also found that Europeans during the Renaissance and the Reformation were able to alter birthrates through social customs concerning marriage. Two factors had a profound effect on the number of children born in a premodern society. The first is the per-

The age at which couples married had a significant effect on the size of families and thus upon the rate of population growth. The wedding of a wealthy couple is depicted in this detail from Rogier van der Weyden's Redemption Triptych, created in the mid-fifteenth century.

centage of people who married, since unmarried couples were less likely to reproduce. The second is the age at which two people married, as, particularly for a woman, the older she is at the time of marriage, the fewer children she is likely to have.

In much of the world in the premodern period, some 90 percent of women married and did so at young ages, and as a result birthrates were high. In Europe, by contrast, marriage customs had the effect of encouraging a higher birthrate during periods of underpopulation and a low birthrate during periods of overpopulation. Key to this pattern was the expectation that a man and woman would marry only when they had the resources to sustain a household. During periods of economic opportunity, couples could raise these resources and achieve financial security relatively early in life. Thus, they married younger and had, on average, more children. During periods of economic stress, both women and men would have fewer opportunities and therefore would be less likely to marry young or to marry at all and by implication would have less time to produce a large family.

▶ Naples is depicted in this detail from the renowned Tavola Strozzi, the earliest known representation of the city. One of the largest cities in early modern Europe, Naples, like other European cities, relied on immigration from the countryside to maintain its population.

In rural communities young men and women often had to wait for the death of their parents before sufficient family resources would be freed for them to set up their own household. In cities men often worked as artisans, laborers, or servants as they sought to earn enough money to settle down. Women worked, too, as domestic servants or in the textile industry. This unusual marriage pattern provided a check on the population of a region and thus had the effect of moderating the natural cycle.

Finally, migration also played a role in reducing the impact of the Malthusian cycle on European population levels. Established regional patterns of migration developed, as rural people migrated first to a local city and then on to a larger regional city. Other populations migrated regularly between rural homelands and cities, seeking seasonal work in both locations. Collectively, the growth of cities in western Europe helped to alleviate overpopulation in the countryside and address local crop failures. However, migration across large geographical distances or across cultural borders, which would prove so important to European population growth in the eighteenth and nineteenth cen-

turies, was only a small factor outside of Spain and Portugal before 1650. Migration dealt primarily with local and regional population issues during and after the Renaissance.

Urban Populations

General trends in population over the centuries can obscure the significant variations in life experiences among different parts of the population. Perhaps the most dramatic divide separated those living in urban from those living in rural environments. By 1300 a network of thousands of towns and cities had developed around western Europe. Although small by modern Western standards, with only a few inhabited by more than 100,000 people, cities played a key role in European society because they served as centers of commerce, manufacturing, and administration. Perhaps 7 or 8 percent of the total population lived in these urban centers by 1300. Cities existed throughout Europe, but the Mediterranean region possessed the densest networks of urban settlements in comparison with the north and east of the continent.

The Black Death had a particularly devastating effect on cities, where the number of people living in close proximity to one another, together with primitive sanitation systems, contributed to higher death rates. The largest cities, such as Florence, where nearly half the population is believed to have perished, suffered most from the plague. However, despite the higher death toll in the cities, it was the urban areas, rather than rural communities, that recovered more quickly. Although both urban and rural populations suffered economic and social disruption, the fact that urban centers offered better opportunities to make a living after the initial epidemic provided an incentive for rural workers to migrate to cities.

By 1500 around 10 percent of the total population of Europe lived in urban areas. Indeed, many cities were reaching and surpassing the population levels they had experienced before the Black Death, with Paris and Naples reaching around 200,000 inhabitants. This trend was set to continue, particularly in the most urbanized areas of Europe, such as northern Italy, where by 1600 around 17 percent of the population lived in cities of at least 5,000 inhabitants.

Constraints on Urban Population

The growth in the urban population during the fifteenth and sixteenth centuries is all the more striking when one takes into account the mortality rates in the cities of Renaissance and Reformation Europe. The mortality rate in urban areas was generally higher than in less populated rural areas. Diseases spread more efficiently in densely populated cities, and despite the efforts of local authorities, sanitation and public health measures in most cities remained

primitive. Moreover, as large quantities of food were needed to feed urban populations, city authorities had to struggle constantly to secure adequate provisions. The threat of famine was an ever-present concern for urban dwellers across Europe. Florence, for instance, was wracked by famines in 1276, 1282, 1286, 1291, 1299, 1302/1303, and 1305. A resident of Florence could thus expect to experience food shortages regularly over the course of his or her life.

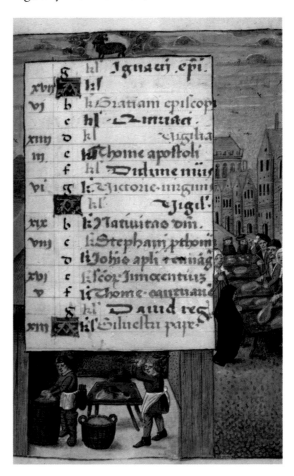

◀ Securing a regular supply of food was one of the chief responsibilities of town officials. In this illumination from a late-fifteenth-century Flemish book of hours, meat is being sold from the market stalls, while, in the foreground, butchers are at work preparing fresh supplies.

All large cities in western Europe had higher mortality rates than birthrates and relied on a continuous flow of migration from rural areas both to maintain their populations and to grow. Documenting migration has proven difficult. Nevertheless, evidence suggests that in the largest cities of Europe, such as Naples and Paris, a majority of the residents at any given time were probably born elsewhere. Many of these residents were temporary migrants serving as apprentices, servants, or common laborers before returning to their villages. Prominent among such migrants were young women; European cities typically housed more women than men.

City authorities faced difficulties in maintaining urban populations. One key challenge lay in the provisioning of cities, a need that was in part met by the rural lands surrounding the urban centers. It was in these regions, which enjoyed steady demand for their products, that farmers started to specialize in producing surplus food for urban markets. Indeed, in some regions,

such as northern Italy and the region around Paris, new landholding patterns and farming techniques were pioneered to provision cities. In other regions—Holland, for example—investors drained marshy lands specifically to produce foods for city markets. Still, cities the size of Paris or Florence could not rely solely on farms in their immediate vicinity to feed their populations, and so elaborate supply networks were created to meet the demand. Grain for Paris, for instance, was purchased from as far away as the shores of the Baltic Sea and, in the case of Florence, from the island of Sicily.

City officials faced a further problem, maintaining public sanitation systems. In their early stages cities developed without planning and were made up of narrow, dark mazes of streets. Owing to a lack of organized sewage systems and garbage removal programs, private latrines often overflowed into unpaved streets, where human waste mixed with detritus of all sorts in the muddy lanes. Moreover, as authorities sought to make

► This sixteenth-century map of Marseilles by an unknown French artist gives an impression of how densely populated the cities of southern Europe were during the Renaissance.

MARSEILLE.

The following extracts reveal the variety of activities that city authorities—in this case, those of Bologna, in Italy—attempted to regulate in an effort to improve public health during the early Renaissance. Taken together, they also produce a vivid impression of what life in the city must have been like.

We order that no one throw or cause to be thrown into the piazza of the commune of Bologna or in the crossroads at the Porta Ravennate any stinking or dead animals or rotten fish or shellfish or any filthy or stinking thing or food scraps, sweepings, dung or prison filth. Item, that no butcher or anyone else, is to slaughter … any animal within four houses of the piazza, nor to pour onto it the blood or intestines of any animal….

Item, that all water of dye-works or anything else pertaining to dying that contains filth … or tanners' waste … is not to be disposed of in the city or suburbs except into the Aposa or Savena [two rivers] when it flows, and then only at night….

We order that no person is to throw grape-skins or dung or horses, asses, dead meat or other filth along the walls or into the city ditches…. The same penalty is to be incurred by anyone who takes a horse, mule, ass, dog, cat or other animal for skinning on the bridge of the Aposa or in the Aposa.

Item, we say that where several houses have latrines over an alley they are to have it cleaned and washed by the Savena once a year….

We order that everyone must remove from the street in front of his house mud, earth, grape-skins …and all other dirt….

We order that each district of the city and suburbs that has a neighbourhood well is to have it cleaned twice a year and is to keep by the well a water-container of stone or wood, a basin or cask.

From the city statutes of Bologna, 1288

cities more hygienic, they also had to contend with a tradition in some towns, including Paris, of keeping livestock, especially pigs, in the city.

Efforts by the authorities to address the worst threats to public health through regulation began in the Renaissance towns of northern Italy and gradually spread to urban centers in northern Europe. City authorities required that wider roads be built and often ordered the purchase and destruction of dwellings to allow for road widening. They also paved roads with brick, cobbles or flagstones so that they could be more effectively cleaned. They required households to build covered drains into which sewage could flow and organized garbage collection.

Perhaps their most important efforts were directed toward securing a clean water supply. Waterborne diseases were particularly dangerous in these densely populated towns. Poor sewage systems contaminated the water supply, as did two important industrial processes that took place in many cities: the dying of textiles and the tanning of animal hides to make leather. Dying and tanning both required the use of poisonous chemicals that could potentially contaminate water supplies. Town authorities were also concerned about the risks to health presented by the slaughter of animals, as is reflected in the many town regulations that dealt with the disposal of animal by-products.

▲ *Like country folk, town dwellers killed pigs in December and salted the meat for food through the winter. The practice is depicted in this anonymous illustration from a fifteenth-century French book of hours.*

▲ European farmers became more productive after 1000, in part because of the increased use of horses and heavy plows such as those depicted here. The illumination was produced in the workshop of Simon Bening between 1520 and 1530.

closely tied to agricultural production. Weather and crop disease played a major role in deciding the fate of villagers because, until the arrival of the railroads in the nineteenth century made possible the long-distance transportation of bulky foodstuffs, regional crop failures regularly resulted in local famines.

In 1300 Europe was reaching the end of a long agrarian cycle that had begun around 1000. A series of technological advances, including the development of heavier plows, the rotation of crops to maintain key nutrients in the soil, and the greater use of horses in place of oxen, had allowed for more productive agriculture, which had sustained the growing population of Europe. However, by the 1320s Europe was reaching the limits of its agricultural potential; new technological breakthroughs would be required if yields were to increase further. To support the growing population, it became necessary to place even land with poor fertility under the plow; meanwhile the overworking of better-quality land ultimately reduced its fertility.

In the opening half of the fourteenth century, a series of bad harvests led to widespread famines, and as a result, the increasingly malnourished residents of the overpopulated countryside became particularly susceptible to epidemic diseases, including the Black Death. These pressures resulted in the collapse of rural populations and in some places a sustained crisis of falling population, falling prices for grain, high wages for agricultural labor, and declining land values. These problems were especially pronounced in regions with poor soils, although recent research has shown that migration to towns may have played as important a role in depopulating less productive agricultural regions as the Black Death itself.

When the recovery began to take root in the early fifteenth century, certain regions of Europe revived more quickly than others. Within the collapse in population were the seeds of recovery. Overpopulation problems disappeared, and marginal lands were abandoned. Survivors were thus able to increase agricultural productivity. However, the fifteenth and sixteenth centuries saw little in the shape of technological advances in food production. By the second half of the six-

Rural Populations

While urban areas grew in importance during the Renaissance and the Reformation, throughout both periods and in all regions of Europe, the vast majority of the population lived in rural areas and farmed. Rural regions provided both the food and the labor that fueled the growth of Europe's cities. The fate of rural populations was

Unlike students of modern demographics, historians researching the Renaissance and the Reformation have few censuses or other surveys of the rural population to work from. Instead, they have to draw conclusions concerning the population of rural areas, the types of agriculture practiced in specific regions, and the relative wealth of communities from a range of indirect evidence.

Sometimes researchers have access to documents such as tax rolls (in Italian, *catasti*) and records from local courts. Such documents often contain census data that, however inadvertently, aid in the construction of a more or less accurate working image of all or part of a community. Tax rolls, such as the famous *catasto* of the territories of Florence in 1427, have proven particularly useful, as they often include the name of the property holder, the size and makeup of his household, and an estimation of his relative wealth. However, even the *catasto* does not offer a full picture of the population, since tax officials, whose primary purpose was to raise revenue for the state, might easily have failed to record individuals who did not own property.

Historians have also used developments in technology to facilitate the study of rural populations. One particularly fruitful approach has been to map from the air the settlement patterns of the past. From the air historians are able to identify features in the landscape such as mounds and ridges created by human activity, long-abandoned field systems, and unusual patterns of grass and other vegetation growing over buried foundations and walls. Through careful study of aerial photographs, historians have been able to map the changing distribution of land through the splitting up or bringing together of fields. They are also able to discover and map settlements abandoned during times of population declines spurred by disease or famine. Once these sites have been identified from the air, it is also possible to conduct archaeological digs to secure even more information about these lost settlements.

▼ *Carrying wooden rakes, three young women head for the fields to help bring in the harvest in this 1565 painting by an unknown artist. The cycles of planting and harvest defined the year for rural workers.*

teenth century, some regions of Europe had reached population levels that once again strained agricultural resources, and by the second quarter of the seventeenth century, much of rural Europe was once again experiencing the social and economic strains that resulted from overpopulation.

New Solutions to Old Problems

Although European populations continued to suffer from periodic epidemics and famines into the nineteenth century, the demographic conditions that defined the centuries of the Renaissance and the Reformation slowly changed. The growth of European overseas empires, especially in the Americas, helped to lessen the impact of overpopulation by providing new territories to settle and cultivate. From the early seventeenth century the number of emigrants began to rise, a pattern that continued into the twentieth century.

In addition, the increased trade sparked by European overseas expansion triggered the growth of manufacturing in Europe. New industries developed, both to process raw materials from the empires and to produce manufactured goods for the empires. The greatest impact was in

WARFARE AND POPULATION

Like disease, warfare could have a devastating effect on local populations. The period between 1300 and 1650 witnessed a rapid expansion in the size of armies, as princes for the first time formed professional standing armies and supplemented them with poorly paid mercenaries. Not only did the size of armies change during this period, but so did their tactics. From the thirteenth century on, armies increasingly sought to devastate enemy territory, so as they passed through, they burned villages and destroyed crops. These raids, while limited in scope, had the same effect as crop failure on the population. The arrival of enemy troops also created large numbers of refugees who sought protection within walled cities in a region and thus placed further pressure on a city's limited resources.

While warfare affected all of the population, it had its greatest impact on rural peasants who lacked the means of protecting their property. If wars continued for long periods of time, areas of frequent conflict were often deserted. For instance during the Hundred Years War in France, villagers abandoned their farms in regions where French and English forces regularly clashed. Two centuries later, during the opening half of the seventeenth century, regions of the Holy Roman Empire were similarly abandoned by their inhabitants as the Thirty Years War raged.

▼ *The pillaging of a city by soldiers is depicted in this fifteenth-century illumination by an unknown French artist.*

cities, where manufacturing and trade were concentrated. Indeed, by the late seventeenth century, cities such as Bordeaux, in France, Bristol and Liverpool, in England, and Amsterdam, in the Netherlands, were becoming major centers of trade, and by the eighteenth century they dwarfed in size many cities that during the previous three centuries had been among the foremost urban centers of Europe. These new towns and their growing populations altered the demographic makeup of European society and the very presumptions of demography itself.

FURTHER READING

Brady, Thomas, Heiko Oberman, and James Tracy, eds. *Handbook of European History, 1400–1600: Late Middle Ages, Renaissance and Reformation.* Vol. 1, *Structures and Assertions.* Grand Rapids, MI, 1994.

Huppert, George. *After the Black Death: A Social History of Early Modern Europe.* 2nd ed. Bloomington, IN, 1998.

Rowlands, Alison. "The Conditions of Life for the Masses." In *Early Modern Europe,* edited by Euan Cameron. Oxford, 1999.

Eric Nelson

SEE ALSO

• Agriculture • Dams and Drainage • Disease
• Manufacturing • Medicine • Peasants' Revolts
• Science and Technology • Trade • Warfare
• Women

Portugal

A POOR COUNTRY FOR MOST OF THE
MIDDLE AGES, PORTUGAL ENJOYED A
BRIEF PERIOD AS A MAJOR POWER IN
THE SIXTEENTH CENTURY AFTER ITS
SEAFARERS PIONEERED NEW TRADE
ROUTES TO ASIA.

Portugal gets its name from Portus Cale, the ancient name for the city of Porto. The country had its beginnings in 1095, when Henry of Burgundy was appointed count of Porto by Alfonso VI (reigned 1065–1109) of the Spanish kingdom of Castile and León. Henry's son, Afonso (reigned 1128–1185), asserted his independence from Castile and León and was recognized by Pope Alexander III (reigned 1159–1181) as king of Portugal in 1179. The Burgundian dynasty came to an end two centuries later, on the death of King Ferdinand in 1383.

Ferdinand's illegitimate half brother, John of Aviz (reigned 1385–1433), then claimed the Portuguese throne. King John I of Castile and León, who also had a claim through his marriage to Ferdinand's daughter, disputed John's right to succeed. By this time, however, the people of Portugal, who had developed a sense of national identity, supported John of Aviz. He also enjoyed the support of England. When John I invaded in 1385, he was defeated by a Portuguese and English army under Nuno Álvares Pereira at the Battle of Aljubarrota. In 1386 Portugal and England concluded a formal alliance under the Treaty of Windsor—one of the oldest international treaties still in force. In the following year John of Aviz sealed the alliance by marrying Philippa of Lancaster, a princess of the English royal family. Castile finally recognized Portuguese independence in 1411.

The House of Aviz

The victory at Aljubarrota secured John of Aviz's claim to the Portuguese throne; his descendants would rule Portugal until 1580. John strengthened the powers of the monarchy and promoted the interests of artisans, merchants, and the lower nobility at the expense of the aristocracy, many of whom had favored the Castilian succession. During its early years Portugal had frequently been at war with the Muslim Moors who occupied the southern part of the Iberian Peninsula. These wars had ceased in 1249, when Portugal achieved roughly its modern borders. John decided to revive the wars against the Muslims, and in 1415 he captured the port of Ceuta in Morocco, which became the first European colony in Africa. John hoped to use Ceuta as a base to win control of the caravan routes across the Sahara Desert. Before the discovery of the Americas by Europeans, most of the gold in circulation came from sub-Saharan Africa, and so winning control of these routes from the Muslims would have had important political and economic consequences. However, John's attempts to break out of Ceuta failed, and the city became a heavily fortified enclave under constant threat from the Moors.

More fruitful in the long term than John's military expeditions were the voyages of exploration along the coast of Africa sponsored by one of his younger sons, Prince Henry the Navigator, the initiator of the great age of European explo-

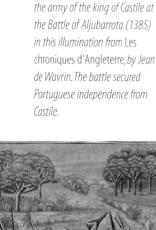

▼ English archers are seen helping the Portuguese defeat the army of the king of Castile at the Battle of Aljubarrota (1385) in this illumination from Les chroniques d'Angleterre, by Jean de Wavrin. The battle secured Portuguese independence from Castile.

THE CARAVEL

As the first European ship capable of making long ocean voyages, the Portuguese caravel, more than any other technological innovation, made the Age of Discovery possible. The caravel was developed from a type of fast, single-masted, open sailing boat used for fishing and short coastal trading voyages by the Moors of Spain and North Africa. The transformation of the caravel into an oceangoing ship took place under the patronage of Prince Henry the Navigator, and from 1440 onward caravels were used for all the major Portuguese voyages of discovery. The caravels of discovery were relatively small, full-decked ships, around 75 feet (23 m) long and with three or four masts. Early caravels used triangular lateen sails, but by the end of the fifteenth century, these had been replaced on the forward masts by square sails, which were better suited to oceanic voyaging. Caravels were also widely used by the Spanish; two of the three ships Columbus took on his first voyage to the New World, the *Pinta* and the *Niña*, were caravels. Despite their good sailing characteristics, caravels gradually went out of use in the sixteenth century. The narrow hulls, which gave them their speed, also limited them: they could not carry large cargoes in merchant service or heavy armament if being used as warships, and so they were supplanted by the larger galleon.

▼ *Prince Henry the Navigator (1394–1460), the initiator of the great age of European exploration, is portrayed in this detail from the altarpiece of Saint Vincent. The artist, Nuno Gonçalves (active 1450–1472), was the finest Portuguese painter of the Renaissance.*

ration and colonization. Despite his nickname, which was given to him by the English, Henry never went on voyages of exploration in person: his role was confined to providing financial and political support.

Henry began to sponsor voyages of exploration in 1418. He was appointed head of the crusading Order of Christ in 1420 and from then on used the order's wealth to subsidize exploration. Henry's interest in exploration was only partly the result of a thirst for geographical knowledge. A devout Catholic, Henry's dream was to find a new trade route to India, convert pagan peoples to Christianity, and find allies against the Muslim powers. Henry founded a school of navigation at Sagres that improved mapmaking techniques and navigational instruments. He also oversaw advances in shipbuilding that led to the development of the caravel, the first European ship capable of making oceanic voyages. Explorers sponsored by Henry discovered the Azores and the Cape Verde Islands; by the time of Henry's death, they had reached as far south as present-day Sierra Leone.

The Age of Prosperity

John II (reigned 1481–1495) earned the nickname "the Perfect" for his success in bringing the aristocracy under firm royal control and maintaining friendly peaceful relations with the Spanish kingdoms. John moved away from the policy of trying to conquer territory in Morocco and instead put more resources into maritime exploration. Under his direction an expedition led by Bartolomeu Dias (c. 1450–1500) set out in 1487, rounded the Cape of Good Hope, and entered the Indian Ocean in the following year. In 1485 John had turned down a proposal from Christopher Columbus (1451–1506) that John equip an expedition to reach China by sailing west across the Atlantic Ocean—a decision that the king must later have regretted.

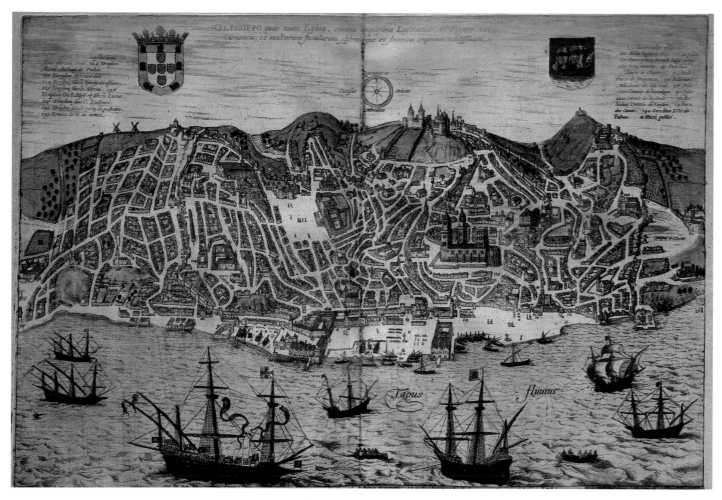

John was a humane ruler, and he gave refuge to thousands of Jews who were expelled from Spain in 1492, although, under pressure from Spain, most of these refugees were later expelled or forced to convert to Christianity by John's successor and cousin, Manuel I (reigned 1495–1521). In 1506 rioters in Lisbon killed many of the Jews who were still living in Portugal, but Manuel did at least punish those responsible and protect the survivors.

Manuel I reaped the benefits of the maritime exploration begun by Henry the Navigator. In 1498 Vasco da Gama (c. 1460–1524) pioneered a new sea route to India around the Cape of Good Hope, and within a few years the Portuguese had won control of the lucrative trade in spices from the East Indies (modern Indonesia). Up to this time Portugal's position in the far west of Europe had been a disadvantage—the main trade routes passed through the Mediterranean and then overland to the Rhine River and the north—and its only important trading partner was England, to which it

exported wine. Thanks to the new Atlantic trade routes, Portugal now became a wealthy country, and Lisbon Europe's main port of trade with Asia. The royal court became a center of Renaissance art and culture, and Portugal's first printing press opened in Lisbon in 1489.

Lisbon continued to grow under Manuel's extravagant, high-spending son John III (reigned 1521–1557). To preserve good relations with Spain, John married Catherine, the sister of the Spanish king and Holy Roman emperor Charles V (reigned 1516–1556), while Charles married John's sister, Isabella.

John, a Catholic, responded to the onset of the Reformation by setting up an inquisition. Like its Spanish equivalent, the Portuguese Inquisition sometimes used severe methods, including torture, against dissenters. During this time most of Portugal's remaining Jews left for the Netherlands, which profited from the financial expertise they brought with them. University education in Portugal came under the control of the Society of Jesus (the Jesuits).

▲ *The panoramic map of Lisbon pictured here depicts the city as it looked before the great earthquake of 1755. The map comes from Braun and Hogenberg's* Civitates orbis terrarum *(Cities of the World), which was published in the German city of Cologne in the late sixteenth century.*

▲ This bronze statue of a West African king comes from Benin. Firearms and chain mail (which this figure is wearing), introduced by the Portuguese in the fifteenth century, began a revolution in the conduct of warfare in West Africa.

Disaster and Conquest

The downfall of the Aviz dynasty was brought about by John's grandson, Sebastian (reigned 1557–1578). Sebastian was only three years old when he succeeded to the throne, and Portugal was ruled by a regency until he began his personal rule in 1568. Educated by Jesuit tutors, Sebastian grew up with the dream of leading a crusade against the Muslims. After years of military preparation, he invaded Morocco in 1578, only to meet with a crushing defeat by a superior Muslim army at the Battle of Ksar al-Kebir (Alcázarquivir). Sebastian and most of his army were killed. The shock of the defeat was so great

that many Portuguese simply refused to believe that their king was really dead. Indeed, a short-lived messianic cult developed, a central belief of which was that Sebastian would one day return and reclaim his kingdom. Between 1584 and 1598 four impostors, all of them claiming to be Sebastian reincarnate, made unsuccessful attempts to seize Portugal's throne.

As Sebastian had no heir, the throne passed to his elderly great-uncle, Cardinal Henry. As a celibate churchman, Henry (reigned 1578–1580) also had no heirs, and everyone realized that because of his age Henry's reign was not likely to be a long one. The next in line to the throne was John III's nephew, Philip II of Spain (reigned 1556–1598), but few Portuguese wanted a union with Spain. The Spanish king made his plans accordingly, and when Henry died in 1580, Philip immediately launched an invasion of Portugal to make good his claim. Portuguese resistance, led by António of Crato (an illegitimate son of John III's brother Luís), was crushed, and Philip II of Spain became Philip I of Portugal (reigned 1580–1598).

The Portuguese Colonial Empire

The maritime exploration initiated by Henry the Navigator in 1418 made Portugal the pioneer of European overseas expansion. Although Portugal was a relatively poor country, religion was almost as important a motive for exploration as the desire to find wealth and new trade routes. Many medieval Europeans believed in the existence of a Christian kingdom in sub-Saharan Africa ruled by a king named Prester John. If this kingdom could be found, it would surely make a great ally against the Muslim powers who threatened Christian Europe. The Portuguese also hoped to strengthen Christendom by finding and converting pagan peoples to Christianity.

The first important Portuguese discoveries, Madeira (1419) and the Azores (1427), were quickly settled; the islands' subtropical climate made them ideal for producing sugar, at that time an expensive luxury in Europe. In 1434 Gil Eanes sailed south of Cape Bojador (in what is now Western Sahara), which for more than two thousand years had been regarded as the southern limit of navigation. Superstition held that a ship that sailed beyond the cape would be swept away by unfavorable currents. With this psychological barrier passed, Portuguese exploration of the coast of West Africa proceeded steadily. In 1456 the Cape Verde Islands were discovered and colonized. The Atlantic slave trade began soon after, when the Portuguese reached present-day Sierra Leone and started to buy African slaves to work on new sugar plantations in the Cape Verde Islands.

LISBON

Lying on a fine natural harbor at the mouth of the Tagus River, Lisbon has been a port city since ancient times, when it was known as Olisipo. In the eighth century the Moors captured Lisbon, built a castle, and fortified the city with defensive walls. The Portuguese, aided by English and Flemish crusaders, drove out the Moors in 1147, but it was not until 1256 that Lisbon became the capital of Portugal.

Lisbon was always a port of call on the long sea route between the Mediterranean and northern Europe, but it did not really come into its own until the fifteenth century, when Portuguese mariners began to explore the Atlantic coast of Africa. Thanks to its position at the far western point of Europe, Lisbon became a boomtown in the early sixteenth century as new trade routes opened up to Asia and the Americas. Valuable spices and other exotic products were unloaded at Lisbon's docks before being re-exported at great profit to other European countries. King Manuel I spent much of the wealth that flooded into Lisbon on impressive new buildings. Among the most important were the monastery of the Hieronymites, founded in 1502 to celebrate the new maritime discoveries, the Tower of Belém (an ornate five-story fortress by the Tagus), a new palace, and a city square called the Rossio.

Lisbon's prosperity did not last, partly owing to the activities of the Inquisition. By forcing the emigration of Lisbon's Jews, who were heavily involved in banking, the Inquisition undermined the city's financial base. Worse still was the period of Spanish rule, when the Dutch seized control of the spice trade with Asia and so deprived Lisbon of much of its income and importance. In 1755 a massive earthquake devastated the city and killed over 30,000 people. Lisbon was elegantly rebuilt under the direction of the marquess of Pombal but on a new street plan, which obliterated much of the medieval and Renaissance city.

▲ The cloister of the monastery of the Hieronymites in Lisbon, built between 1502 and 1551, is the finest example of Portugal's Manueline style, which combined Gothic form with Renaissance ornament.

West Africa was an extremely unhealthy place for Europeans, and it was not until 1482 that the Portuguese founded a permanent settlement on the mainland—Elmina ("the mine"), on the coast of Ghana, a fortress to protect their traders from Spanish interference. The establishment of direct trade between tropical Africa and Europe not only enriched Portugal but also led to a decline in the caravan routes across the Sahara and thus lessened the influence of the Muslim kingdoms that controlled them. Another breakthrough came during 1487 and 1488, when Bartolomeu Dias's voyage around the southern tip of Africa and into the Indian Ocean proved that it was possible to sail directly from Europe to India.

After Columbus reached the New World in 1492, Spain and Portugal concluded the Treaty of Tordesillas (1494) to avoid conflict over the astonishing new discoveries. The terms of the treaty divided the world along a line drawn 370 leagues (1,185 miles, or 1,900 km) west of the Cape Verde Islands: the Spanish were to keep to the west of the line, the Portuguese to the east. This agreement gave Portugal a free hand in the East and also allowed it to claim Brazil after its discovery in 1500.

After Vasco da Gama made the first direct voyage from Portugal to India (1497–1499),

Portuguese influence in the East increased rapidly. Francisco de Almeida (c. 1450–1510) eliminated Muslim sea power in the Indian Ocean at the Battle of Diu in 1509. In 1510 Goa, in India, was captured, and in the following year the strategic port of Malacca was also seized. Malacca lay on the straits between Malaya and Sumatra, and its capture gave Portugal control of the important spice route from the Molucca Islands. Before refrigeration, spices were essential to disguise the flavor of rotting meat, and Europeans were prepared to pay handsomely for these exotic tropical products.

In 1520 Portuguese merchants reached Guangzhou, in China. Their habit of raiding Chinese ports and smuggling when they could not get favorable trade terms made for difficult relations at first, but in 1557 the Portuguese were allowed to found a trading colony at Macao. The first European enclave in China, Macao remained under Portuguese control until 1999. By 1542 the Portuguese had also opened trade links with Japan. Their attempts to convert the Japanese to Christianity were later suppressed, but their introduction of firearms transformed warfare in Japan and led to the forcible unification of the country under the Tokugawa shoguns.

The success of the Portuguese was due partly to the superiority of their ships and cannon, but even more important was the lack of unified resistance in Asia. Although the Portuguese were few in number, they were able to deal with their enemies one at a time. By the 1570s they had lost these advantages. Muslim ships began to carry cannon, and as the Mogul Empire expanded to include most of India, Portuguese expansion began to slow.

Unfortunately for Portugal, the impact of colonialism was not entirely positive. The great wealth that flowed into what had been a poor country benefited mainly the crown, the aristocracy, and the merchant class; very little found its way down to the lower classes. Nor was the wealth invested wisely. Much of it was spent on extravagant buildings and luxuries rather than on agricultural improvements or on the development of crafts and industries that would have benefited the whole nation. Colonialism also

The commander of the Portuguese forces wrote the following description of the capture of Malacca in 1511.

The sultan of Malacca and his son, who were mounted upon their elephants, seeing they were pursued by our men, turned back again with 2,000 men.... The Portuguese captains awaited their coming at the head of a street, and with great effort and brave determination fell upon the elephants with their lances, as they were coming on in the vanguard.... And whereas elephants will not bear being wounded, they turned tail and charged the Moors behind them and put them to rout. The elephant on which the sultan was riding, maddened by the mortal wound it had received, seized with its trunk the black man who was leading it; and roaring loudly dashed him to pieces, and the sultan, being already wounded in the hand, sprang out of the castle on its back, but escaped because he was not recognized.

Afonso de Albuquerque

◄ *This image of a Portuguese galleon was painted on silk by an unknown Japanese artist of the early seventeenth century. In 1542 the Portuguese became the first Europeans to open trade links with Japan. Their attempts to convert the Japanese to Christianity led to their expulsion from the country in the seventeenth century, when the Tokugawa shogunate closed Japan to virtually all European people and commerce.*

resulted in a serious loss of manpower; most of the men who traveled to the tropics hoping to make their fortune died there of diseases to which they had little or no resistance.

The Renaissance in Portugal

The influence of Italian Renaissance culture began to be felt in Portugal in the early fifteenth century. The Portuguese court developed close contacts with Florentine scholars and booksellers through bureaucrats and churchmen who had visited or studied in Italy. One of them was Vasco Fernández de Lucena (c. 1410–1495). Lucena was sent to the University of Bologna to study law, but while there he became so fascinated by the works of the great Italian poet Petrarch that he pawned his law books to devote himself to studying poetry. When he returned home, Lucena worked at the royal court, where he translated classical Greek and Roman literature into Portuguese and wrote the official chronicle of events.

Lucena also wrote regularly to scholars in Florence and Rome to tell them about the discoveries of Portuguese explorers. In the prosperous years of the early sixteenth century, Manuel I and John III were able to attract scholars from across Europe to teach in Portugal. In 1537 John III founded a university at Coimbra that was dedicated to the study of the arts and staffed mainly by French scholars.

The prosperity of Manuel I's reign led to the development of a new Portuguese style of architecture, named Manueline after the king. Manueline architecture was influenced by late Gothic and Moorish styles, but its most important characteristic was its rich ornamentation, which was inspired by the Portuguese voyages of discovery. Realistic carvings of ropes, heraldic shields, navigational instruments, anchors, and sea creatures were all used to decorate architectural features. The Manueline style lasted only a few decades and then gave way to classical styles of architecture introduced from Italy and Spain. Baroque architecture became popular in the seventeenth century.

In the fifteenth century Portuguese painters were greatly influenced by Flemish styles and techniques. Probably the most important Renaissance Portuguese painter was Nuno Gonçalves, who became court painter to Afonso V (reigned 1438–1481). His greatest work is a large altarpiece painted on six wooden panels and dedicated to Saint Vincent. The panels include portraits of most of the leading statesmen of the time, including Henry the Navigator, as well as ordinary people, such as fishermen, and even a Jew and a Muslim—a sign of the tolerance of Afonso's court. In the sixteenth century Spanish and French styles came to dominate Portuguese painting and sculpture, and in the seventeenth century the baroque style predominated.

The greatest achievement of the Portuguese Renaissance was a work of literature, the epic poem *The Lusiads,* published in 1572, by Luíz Vaz de Camões (1524/5–1580). The poem, which gets its name from Lusitania, the ancient Roman name for Portugal, is an imitation of the *Aeneid,* the epic poem on the origins of the Roman people by Virgil (70–19 BCE). The ostensible subject of *The Lusiads,* Vasco da Gama's voyage to India, is interwoven with the whole story of the Portuguese people. Like Virgil, Camões used his poem to glorify his nation, but it is also a remarkable imaginative response to the great geographical discoveries of the age. So great was the popularity of Camões's epic that its influence is still apparent in the intense pride of present-day Portuguese in their sailors' achievements. Another important literary figure was the

◀ The main entrance of Coimbra University, pictured here, is popularly known as the Iron Gate, after the gates that were closed at night to try to prevent students from visiting inns and brothels. The statue above the gate represents King John III, who founded the university in 1537.

The introduction to Luíz Vaz de Camões's epic poem sets the tone for the rest of the work, which celebrates Portugal and its people:

Arms and the heroes, who from Lisbon's shores,
Through seas where sail was never spread before,
Beyond where Ceylon lifts her spicy breast,
And waves her woods above the watery waste,
With prowess more than human forced their way
To the fair kingdoms of the abundant day:
What wars they waged, what seas, what dangers past,
What glorious empire crowned their toils at last....
Illustrious names, with deathless laurels crowned,
While time rolls on in every clime renowned.

The Lusiads

▲ *The Tower of Belém is an ornate fortress built in the Manueline style between 1515 and 1520 to control the entrance to Lisbon harbor. When it was built, the tower was over four hundred yards (366 m) out to sea: it is now much closer to the shore because the land was raised in the earthquake of 1755.*

playwright Gil Vicente (c. 1465–c. 1536), who wrote religious plays called *autos* and comedies that satirized immoral behavior.

Spanish Rule

On his accession as King Philip I of Portugal, Philip II of Spain had promised to respect Portugal's autonomy and appoint only Portuguese to positions of government. Philip kept his word, and so when the English tried to seize Lisbon in 1589, start an anti-Spanish rebellion, and place António of Crato on the throne, they found little support. Philip's successors ignored his promises,

however, and Portuguese resentment against Spanish rule increased rapidly. There were unsuccessful rebellions in 1634 and 1637.

The union with Spain was a disaster for Portugal, which was forced to participate in Spain's ruinously expensive wars. For example, Portugal provided a large contingent of ships for the Spanish armada that sailed to attack England in 1588. Participation in Spain's wars made Portugal's colonies and shipping legitimate prey for Spain's enemies, especially the Dutch, who seized Portuguese colonies in the East Indies and ended Portugal's monopoly on the spice trade. The Dutch also temporarily occupied part of Brazil. The Spanish government saw Portugal mainly as a source of taxes and had little interest in the welfare of the country.

The critical moment came in 1640. Spain was faced with a serious internal rebellion in Catalonia, and its government demanded that Portugal send troops to help suppress the revolt. The Portuguese seized the opportunity offered by Spain's temporary weakness to begin a national uprising and expel the Spanish garrisons and administrators. The duke of Bragança was recognized as having the strongest claim to the throne by virtue of his descent from both Manuel I and—through an illegitimate line—John I and was duly declared King John IV (reigned 1640–1656). Years of intermittent warfare followed before Spain finally recognized Portuguese independence in 1668. Under the Bragança dynasty Portugal repossessed its territories in Brazil and recovered a measure of prosperity, but it was never able to regain its former commercial preeminence.

FURTHER READING

Birmingham, D. *A Concise History of Portugal.* Cambridge, 2003.

Boxer, C. R. *The Portuguese Seaborne Empire, 1415–1825.* London, 1970.

Camões, Luíz Vaz de. *The Lusiads.* Translated by Landeg White. Oxford, 1992.

John Haywood

SEE ALSO

• Armada, Spanish • Exploration • Petrarch
• Philip II • Spain

Index

Page numbers in **boldface** type refer to entire articles.
Page numbers in *italic* type refer to illustrations.

Illustration Credits

akg-images: 881 (Sotheby's), 882 (Orsi Battaglini), 916, 918, 920, 933, 934, 936, 943, 952, 954, 956 (John Hios), 957 (British Library, London), 958, 961 (Sotheby's), 970, 985 (Erich Lessing), 1002, 1019 (Hervé Champollion), 1031, 1034 (CDA Guillemot), 1040 (Joseph Martin), 1050, 1051 & 1055 (Erich Lessing), 1067, 1075, 1076, 1077 (Rabatti-Domingie), 1078, 1093, 1099, 1107, 1110–1112 (Erich Lessing), 1115, 1119 (Erich Lessing), 1136.
Art Archive: 871 & 872 (Galleria dell'Accademia, Florence/Dagli Orti), 874 (Dagli Orti), 876 (Chiesa di San Lorenzo, Florence/Dagli Orti [A]), 877 (Joseph Martin), 885 (Tate Gallery, London/Eileen Tweedy), 888 (Musée des Beaux-Arts, Dijon, France/Dagli Orti), 889, 890 (Museo de Guadalupe, Mexico/Dagli Orti), 891 (Biblioteca Nazionale Marciana, Venice/Dagli Orti), 893 (Private Collection/Dagli Orti), 894 (National Palace, Mexico City/Dagli Orti), 895 (Kobe Municipal Museum, Japan/Laurie Platt Winfrey), 896 (Kodaiji Temple, Kyoto/Laurie Platt Winfrey), 899 (Musée Carnavalet, Paris/Dagli Orti), 900 (Bibliothèque des Arts Décoratifs, Paris/Dagli Orti), 902 (Bibliothèque des Arts Décoratifs, Paris/Dagli Orti), 903 (Bibliothèque Nationale, Paris/Harper Collins), 906 (Musée du Louvre, Paris/Dagli Orti [A]), 907 (Museo del Prado, Madrid/Dagli Orti [A]), 908 (Musée du Château de Versailles, France/Dagli Orti [A]), 911 (Dagli Orti), 913 (British Library, London), 914 (Musée du Château de Versailles/Dagli Orti), 915 (Doges' Palace, Venice/Dagli Orti [A]), 924 (Galleria degli Uffizi, Florence/Dagli Orti [A]), 926 (Musée Calvet, Avignon, France/Dagli Orti), 927 (Victoria and Albert Museum, London/Sally Chappell), 928 (Museo Capitolino, Rome/Dagli Orti), 929, 932 (Château de Blois, France/Dagli Orti), 938 & 939 & 941 (Russian Historical Museum, Moscow/Dagli Orti [A]), 944, 945 (Musée Royale des Beaux-Arts, Antwerp, Belgium), 949 (Musée du Louvre, Paris/Dagli Orti), 950 (Galleria Sabauda, Turin, Italy/Dagli Orti), 960 (Museo del Prado, Madrid/Dagli Orti), 965, 967 (Sienese State Archives/Dagli Orti [A]), 968 (Archives Nationales, Paris/Marc Charmet), 969 (University Library, Prague/Dagli Orti), 971 (Galleria Nazionale dell'Umbria, Perugia, Italy/Dagli Orti [A]), 972 (Musée des Beaux-Arts, Orléans, France/Dagli Orti [A]), 973 (British Library, London), 974 (Doges' Palace, Venice/Dagli Orti), 975 (Museo del Prado, Madrid/Dagli Orti), 976 (Musée du Louvre, Paris/Dagli Orti), 977 (University Library, Heidelberg, Germany/Dagli Orti), 978 (Palazzo Pubblico, Siena, Italy/Dagli Orti), 979 (Galleria Sabauda, Turin, Italy/Dagli Orti), 980 (Galleria degli Uffizi, Florence/Dagli Orti [A]), 982 (Saint Peter's Church, Louvain, Belgium), 983l (Duomo, Florence/Dagli Orti [A]), 983r (Dagli Orti [A]), 984 (Museo del Bargello, Florence/Dagli Orti), 987 (Museo Civico, Sansepolcro, Italy/Dagli Orti [A]), 988 (Chiesa di Santa Maria dei Frari, Venice/Dagli Orti [A]), 989 (Accademia, Venice/Dagli Orti [A]), 990 (Galleria degli Uffizi, Florence/Dagli Orti [A]), 991 (Palazzo del Tè, Mantua, Italy/Dagli Orti [A]), 992 (Accademia, Venice/Dagli Orti [A]), 994 (Joseph Martin), 1000 (Doges' Palace, Venice/Dagli Orti), 1003–1007 (Dagli Orti), 1009 (Palazzo Farnese, Rome/Dagli Orti), 1010 (University Library, Prague/Dagli Orti), 1011 (Museo Storico del Castello di Miramare, Trieste, Italy/Dagli Orti [A]), 1012 (Palazzo Pitti, Florence/Dagli Orti [A]), 1013 (Nationalmuseet, Copenhagen/Dagli Orti [A]), 1015, 1016 (Museo Diocesano, Trento, Italy/Dagli Orti [A]), 1017 (Chiesa del Gesù, Rome/Dagli Orti [A]), 1018 (Museu Nacional de Arte Antiga, Lisbon/Dagli Orti), 1021 (Private Collection/Dagli Orti [A]), 1025 (Palazzo Farnese, Caprarola, Italy/Dagli Orti), 1027 (Dagli Orti), 1029 (Musée Carnavalet, Paris), 1032 (Musée du Château de Versailles, France/Dagli Orti), 1033 (Musée des Beaux-Arts, Lausanne, France/Dagli Orti [A]), 1035 (Musée Carnavalet, Paris/Dagli Orti), 1036 (Museo Storico Aloisiano, Castiglione delle Stiviere, Italy/Dagli Orti), 1037 (Galleria Borghese, Rome/Dagli Orti), 1041 & 1042 & 1046 (British Library, London), 1049 (Bibliothèque Universitaire de Médecine, Montpellier, France/Dagli Orti), 1056 (Museo del Prado, Madrid/Joseph Martin), 1058 (Monasterio de el Escorial Spain/Joseph Martin), 1059 (Museo del Prado, Madrid/Joseph Martin), 1061 (Dagli Orti), 1062 (Duomo, Padua, Italy/Dagli Orti), 1066 (National Museum of Prague/Dagli Orti), 1070 (Institut de France, Paris/Dagli Orti), 1079 (Biblioteca Bertoliana, Vicenza, Italy), 1080, 1081 (Victoria and Albert Museum, London/Eileen Tweedy), 1084 (Topkapi Museum, Istanbul [Elliott 149 folio 29v]/Dagli Orti), 1085 (Bodleian Library, Oxford), 1086 & 1087 (Piccolomini Library, Siena/Dagli Orti [A]), 1089 (Dagli Orti), 1090 (Musée du Louvre, Paris/Dagli Orti), 1092 (Bodleian Library, Oxford [Digby 46 folio 41v]), 1095 (Archaeological Museum, Naples/Dagli Orti [A]), 1096 (Archaeological Museum, Ostia, Italy/Dagli Orti), 1101 (Biblioteca Nazionale, Turin, Italy/Dagli Orti), 1113 (Maritime Museum, Stockholm/Dagli Orti [A]), 1117 (Musée du Louvre, Paris/Dagli Orti [A]), 1118 (British Library, London), 1120 (Musée des Beaux-Arts, Rennes, France/Dagli Orti), 1121 (Musée Condé, Chantilly, France/Dagli Orti [A]), 1122 (Museo Civico, Cremona, Italy/Dagli Orti), 1124 (Museo del Prado, Madrid/Dagli Orti), 1125 (Museo del Prado, Madrid), 1128 (Museu Nacional de Arte Antiga, Lisbon/Dagli Orti), 1129 (Museo del Prado, Madrid/Dagli Orti), 1130 (Museo di Capodimonte, Naples/Dagli Orti [A]), 1131 (British Library, London), 1133 (Victoria and Albert Museum, London/Graham Brandon), 1137 (British Library, London), 1138 (Museu Nacional de Arte Antiga, Lisbon/Dagli Orti), 1139 (Biblioteca Nazionale Marciana, Venice/Dagli Orti [A]), 1140 (Antenna Gallery, Dakar, Senegal/Dagli Orti), 1142 (Marine Museum, Lisbon/Dagli Orti), 1143 (Suntory Museum of Art, Tokyo/Laurie Platt Winfrey).
Bridgeman Art Library: 870 (Alinari), 873 (British Museum, London), 875 (Vatican Museums and Galleries), 878 (Private Collection/Christie's Images), 884 (Birmingham Museums and Art Gallery, UK), 892 (Massachusetts Historical Society, Boston), 897 (Comédie Française, Paris/Archives Charmet), 898 (Bibliothèque Nationale, Paris/Lauros/Giraudon), 904 (Kunsthistorisches Museum, Vienna), 905 (National Library of Scotland, Edinburgh), 909 (Philip Mould Historical Portraits Ltd., London), 910 (Bibliothèque Nationale, Paris), 912 (British Library, London), 917 (Palazzo Ducale, Mantua), 919 (Musée du Louvre, Paris/Peter Willi), 921 (Galleria Borghese, Rome), 922 (Galleria Barberini, Rome), 925 (Philip Mould Historical Portraits Ltd., London), 940 (Tretyakov Gallery, Moscow/Estonian), 942 (Saint Bavo Cathedral, Ghent, Belgium/Giraudon), 946 (Bibliothèque Nationale, Paris), 947 (Private Collection), 948 (Musée du Louvre, Paris), 951 (Fogg Art Museum, Harvard University Art Museums), 953 (Private Collection), 955 (Museo del Prado, Madrid), 959 (Hermitage Museum, Saint Petersburg), 962 (Private Collection), 963 (Museo Civico, Bologna, Italy/Giraudon), 964 (Kunstmuseum, Basel), 966 (Palazzo Vecchio [Palazzo della Signoria], Florence), 981 (Chartreuse de Champmol, Dijon, France/Peter Willi), 986 (Vatican Museums and Galleries), 993 (Casino dell'Aurora Ludovisi, Rome), 995 (Walker Art Gallery, Liverpool/National Museums, Liverpool), 996 (National Gallery, London), 997 (Musée des Beaux-Arts André Malraux, Le Havre, France/Giraudon), 998 (Metropolitan Museum of Art, New York/Giraudon), 999 (Mauritshuis, The Hague, Netherlands/Giraudon), 1001 (Musée du Louvre, Paris/Peter Willi), 1023 (Vatican Museums and Galleries), 1024 (Private Collection), 1028 (Musée Carnavalet, Paris/Dagli Orti), 1030 (Victoria and Albert Museum, London), 1039 (Fuji Art Museum, Tokyo), 1043 (Westminster Abbey, London), 1044 & 1045 & 1047 (British Library, London), 1053 (Museo Correr, Venice), 1054 (Bibliothèque de la Faculté de Médecine, Paris/Archives Charmet), 1057 (The Berger Collection at the Denver Art Museum), 1060 (Musée du Louvre, Paris/Lauros/Giraudon), 1063 (Biblioteca Medicea Laurenziana, Florence [Plut 82.6 C.1]), 1065 (Lambeth Palace Library, London), 1068 (Private Collection), 1069 (Biblioteca Nazionale Centrale, Florence), 1071 (Powis Castles, Wales), 1072 (National Gallery, London), 1073 (The Stapleton Collection), 1074 (Musée des Beaux-Arts, Nantes, France/Giraudon), 1083 (Museum of London), 1088 (Piccolomini Library, Siena), 1094 (Musée de la Chartreuse, Douai, France/Giraudon), 1097 (Bonhams, London), 1098 (Bibliothèque Nationale, Paris/Giraudon), 1102 (J. Paul Getty Museum, Los Angeles), 1103 (Ken Welsh), 1104 (Bibliothèque Polonaise, Paris/Bonora), 1105 (Electa), 1108 (Muzeum Narodowe, Warsaw), 1114 (Private Collection), 1123 (Index), 1127 (British Library, London), 1132 (Musée du Vieux-Marseille, France/Lauros/Giraudon), 1134 (British Library, London), 1135 (Lobkowicz Collections, Nelahozeves Castle, Czech Republic).
British Library, London: 883.
Corbis: 886 (Bettmann), 935 (Andrea Jemolo), 1022 (Massimo Listri), 1091 (Dennis Marsico), 1109 (Chris Lisle).
John Haywood: 1141, 1144, 1145.
Mary Evans Picture Library: 930, 1116.
National Portrait Gallery, London: 880.
Redferns: 923 (Ron Scherl).
Topfoto: 879, 887, 901 (Collection Roger-Viollet), 931, 1008 (Michael Hockney), 1014 (Art Media/National Gallery, London), 1020, 1038 & 1048 (Woodmansterne), 1064 (Roger-Viollet), 1100 (Fotomas).